OLDER
PEOPLE
AND THEIR
SOCIAL
WORLD

OLDER
PEOPLE
AND THEIR
SOCIAL
WORLD

The Sub-culture of the Aging

Editors:

ARNOLD M. ROSE, Ph.D.
Professor of Sociology
University of Minnesota

and

WARREN A. PETERSON, Ph.D.
Director, Department of Social Problems and Education
Community Studies, Inc.
Kansas City, Missouri

F. A. DAVIS COMPANY
PHILADELPHIA, PA.

© 1965 by F. A. DAVIS COMPANY

Printed in the United States of America

Library of Congress Catalog Card Number 65-22238

Preface

A wide range of subject matter in social gerontology is covered in this book, and a variety of techniques of social research are utilized. The first set of researches deal with general aspects of the social integration of older people. The thesis concerning the vanguard of those older people who now have pride in being elderly and have a sense of group identification with other older people is tested by the "known-group technique" in the chapter on "Group Consciousness among the Aging." Videbeck and Knox report on a systematic survey of a representative sample of the Nebraska population with regard to social participation to indicate the various patterns of participation among the elderly. Pihlblad and McNamara also use the sample survey, but to ascertain the forms and extent of social adjustment of older people in small towns.

A set of separate researches by Miller, Christ, Moberg, and Taves deals with the specific participation and integration of older people in leisure-time pursuits and in religious activities. Here case studies are added to statistical data abstracted from cross-sectional surveys.

A survey by Smith of the literature on family interaction patterns of the aging opens the section on the family. Papers by Pihlblad and Habenstein and by Hawkinson then delve into specific aspects of the orientation and interaction among the three generations within the family.

The health of older people is considered in both its physical and mental aspects. The causes of mental disturbances among the aging and the relation of physical health to mental outlook are analyzed in papers by Rose. Coe and Barnhill report on research relating social participation to health. Coe and Anderson independently study the impact of institutionalization on self-conception among the elderly, and Wessen considers "Some Sociological Characteristics of Long Term Care."

v

The focus of most of the studies in this volume is the Midwest. Cowgill presents the demographic characteristics of older people in this region from the Census, and a group of sociologists report on their social characteristics and attitudes, based on surveys of representative samples. Cleland undertakes a study of mobility among the elderly, and Marshall demonstrates how outward migration of younger people from a rural county leaves that county dominated by older people and their problems.

An analysis of theory in social gerontology by Rose, and an interpretation by Taber of how research findings in the field can be applied to questions of social policy, close the book.

Thus an interplay of research, theory, and interpretation characterizes the book, and the varying aspects of social gerontology are covered.

ARNOLD M. ROSE
WARREN A. PETERSON

Contributors

NANCY NEWMAN ANDERSON is a graduate student at the University of Minnesota. She has a Master's degree in sociology from that institution.

FRANCIS G. CARO is Assistant Professor of Sociology at Marquette University. He holds a Ph.D. degree from the University of Minnesota. He was formerly Research Associate at Community Studies, Inc. of Kansas City, and has lectured at the University of Kansas.

EDWIN A. CHRIST is Associate Professor of Sociology at the University of South Dakota. He received his Ph.D. degree at the University of Missouri in 1957. His major published works include: (with Robert W. Habenstein) Professionalizer, Traditionalizer, and Utilizer (University of Missouri, 1955, second edition, 1963); Nurses at Work (University of Missouri, Institute for Research in the Social Sciences, 1956); and Missouri's Nurses (The Missouri State Nurses' Association, 1957).

COURTNEY B. CLELAND is Associate Professor of Sociology at the University of Arizona. At the time of the research reported here he was located at North Dakota State University in Fargo. He received his Ph.D. degree at the University of Minnesota. His publications include: (co-author) The Senior Years, North Dakotans Tell Their Story (Bismarck, 1960), and Shifting population in North Dakota and its relation to the aged, and Process is our most important product, in Action for the Aging (University of North Dakota Press, 1962).

RODNEY M. COE is Assistant Professor of Sociology at Washington University and Executive Director of the Medical Care Research Center at Washington University and Jewish Hospital. He received his Ph.D. degree at Washington University in 1962.

DONALD OLEN COWGILL is Chairman of the Department of Sociology and Anthropology at Wichita State University. He received his Ph.D. degree at the University of Pennsylvania in 1940. He has held the following positions related to aging: Delegate, White House Conference on Aging (1961); President, Kansas Citizens' Council on Aging (1961-62), and Chairman, Midwest Council for Social Research on Aging (1962-64). His publications include: Our Senior Citizens (Wichita, 1960), and The use of leisure time by older people, The Gerontologist, 2 (March, 1962).

ROBERT W. HABENSTEIN is Professor of Sociology at the University of Missouri. He holds the Ph.D. degree in Sociology from the University of Chicago. He has conducted the leading researches in the sociology of bereavement and funeral practices.

GARY D. HANSEN is director of the Institute of Gerontology at Mt. Angel (Oregon) College. He holds the M.A. degree in Sociology from the University of Minnesota. He was formerly director of the Michigan State Commission on Aging.

WILLIAM P. HAWKINSON was Associate Professor of Sociology and Chairman, Department of Child Development and Family Relations, North Dakota State University. He holds the Ph.D. degree from the Ohio State University (1959). He is the author of The family in our culture, published in Nursing Diagnosis (U.S. Department of Health, Education and Welfare, 1963).

ALAN B. KNOX is Associate Professor in the Departments of Educational Psychology and Educational Administration, and head of the office of Adult Education Research at the University of Nebraska. He received his Ph.D. degree at Syracuse University. His publications include: The Audience for Liberal Adult Education (Chicago: Center for the Study of Liberal Education for Adults, 1962); and (with Richard E. Videbeck) Adult education and adult life cycle, Adult Education, 13 (Winter, 1962-63).

DOUGLAS G. MARSHALL is Chairman of the Department of Rural Sociology at the University of Wisconsin. He received his Ph.D. degree at the University of Wisconsin in 1943. His publications include: Wisconsin's Population—Changes and Prospects 1900-1903, (University of Wisconsin, 1963).

ROBERT L. MCNAMARA is Chairman of the Department of Sociology and Anthropology and Rural Sociology at the University of Missouri. He received his Ph.D. degree at Ohio State University in 1944. He was a member of the Research Committee on Aging in Missouri's preparations for the White House Conference on Aging.

STEPHEN J. MILLER is Faculty Associate and Research Project Director at the Florence Heller School for Advanced Studies in Social Welfare, Brandeis University, Waltham, Massachusetts. He received his Ph.D. in 1963 at St. Louis University. His major research interest is in medical sociology.

DAVID O. MOBERG is Professor of Sociology and Chairman of the Department of Social Sciences, Bethel College, St. Paul, Minnesota. He received his Ph.D. degree from the University of Minnesota in 1952. He is co-author (with Robert M. Gray) of The Church and the Older Person (Eerdman, 1962) and the author of The Church as a Social Institution (Prentice-Hall, 1962) and of numerous articles pertinent to social gerontology and other areas of sociology.

WARREN A. PETERSON is Director, Department of Social Problems and Education, Community Studies, Inc., Kansas City, Missouri, and Co-ordinator of the Midwest Council for Social Research on Aging. He has his Ph.D. degree from the University of Chicago, and has taught at the University of Missouri, Park College, University of Chicago, University of Kansas City, and Syracuse University.

C. TERENCE PIHLBLAD is Professor of Sociology at the University of Missouri. He also received his Ph.D. degree from the University of Missouri in 1925. He was chairman of the Research Committee on Aging of the University of Missouri Committee of the White House Conference on Aging, 1961.

ARNOLD M. ROSE, Professor of Sociology at the University of Minnesota, received his Ph.D. degree at the University of Chicago in 1946. He headed the Minnesota delegation to the White House Conference on Aging, and chaired the Minnesota Planning Committee for that Conference. He served for four years as a member of the Minnesota Citizens' Council on Aging. He is the editor of Aging in Minnesota (University of Minnesota Press, 1963), and author of several research articles in social gerontology.

HAROLD E. SMITH is Associate Professor of Sociology at Northern Illinois University. He received his Ph.D. degree at Cornell University in 1947. His publications include: Health Practices of Indiana Families (Purdue University, 1955).

MERLIN A. TABER was Associate Professor of Social Work at the State University of Iowa, and currently holds a like position at the University of Illinois. He received the Ph.D. degree from the State University of Iowa in 1962. He is the author of Community services for older citizens: problems, preferences and policy, Bulletin of the Institute of Gerontology, 8 (October, 1961).

MARVIN J. TAVES is Assistant Director, Office of Aging, U.S. Department of Health, Education and Welfare. He received his Ph.D. degree at the University of Minnesota in 1954. He was a delegate to the White House Conference on Aging. He contributed a chapter to Aging in Minnesota (Minneapolis, 1963), and has published other research articles in social gerontology.

RICHARD VIDEBECK is Professor of Sociology at Syracuse University. He received the Ph.D. degree from the University of Nebraska in 1953. He is working on a study of Adult Education and Adult Life Cycle.

SAMUEL YOSHIOKA is a predoctoral fellow in Medical Sociology at the University of Colorado. He has done graduate work at the University of Missouri and the University of South Dakota.

ALBERT F. WESSEN is chairman of the department of Sociology and Anthropology at Washington University, and also a co-chairman of the Medical Care Research Center in St. Louis. He holds the Ph.D. Degree from Yale University (1951). He has conducted many studies in medical sociology.

Table of Contents

                                                                       Page

Introduction xiii

I. A THEORETICAL SUGGESTION

Chapter

1. The Subculture of the Aging: A Framework for Research in
   Social Gerontology 3
   by Arnold M. Rose

II. GENERAL PATTERNS OF ADJUSTMENT AND PARTICIPATION IN THE COMMUNITY

2. Group Consciousness among the Aging 19
   by Arnold M. Rose

3. Alternative Participatory Responses to Aging 37
   by Richard Videbeck and Alan B. Knox

4. Social Adjustment of Elderly People in Three Small Towns 49
   by C. Terence Pihlblad and Robert L. McNamara

III. ADJUSTMENT AND PARTICIPATION IN SPECIFIC ACTIVITIES

5. The Social Dilemma of the Aging Leisure Participant 77
   by Stephen J. Miller

6. The "Retired" Stamp Collector: Economic and Other Functions
   of Systematized Leisure Activity 93
   by Edwin A. Christ

XI

Chapter Page

7. Church Participation and Adjustment in Old Age 113
    by David O. Moberg and Marvin J. Taves
8. The Integration of Older Members in the Church Congregation . . 125
    by David O. Moberg

IV. INTERACTION IN THE FAMILY

9. Family Interaction Patterns of the Aged: A Review 143
    by Harold E. Smith
10. Social Factors in Grandparent Orientation of High School Youth . 163
    by C. Terence Pihlblad and Robert W. Habenstein
11. Wish, Expectancy, and Practice in the Interaction of Generations 181
    by William P. Hawkinson

V. THE HEALTH OF THE AGING

12. Mental Health of Normal Older Persons 193
    by Arnold M. Rose
13. Physical Health and Mental Outlook among the Aging 201
    by Arnold M. Rose
14. Social Participation and Health of the Aged 211
    by Rodney M. Coe and Elizabeth Barnhill
15. Self-Conception and Institutionalization 225
    by Rodney M. Coe
16. Institutionalization, Interaction, and Self-Conception in Aging . . 245
    by Nancy Newman Anderson
17. Some Sociological Characteristics of Long-Term Care 259
    by Albert F. Wessen

VI. POPULATION CHARACTERISTICS AND COMMUNITY SETTING

18. The Demography of Aging in the Midwest 275
    by Donald O. Cowgill
19. Older People in the Midwest: Conditions and Attitudes 311
    by Gary D. Hansen, Samuel Yoshioka, Marvin J. Taves, and
    Francis Caro
20. Mobility of Older People 323
    by Courtney B. Cleland
21. Migration and Older People in a Rural Community: The Story
    of Price County, Wisconsin 341
    by Douglas G. Marshall

VII. IMPLICATIONS OF RESEARCH ON THE AGING

22. A Current Theoretical Issue in Social Gerontology 359
    by Arnold M. Rose
23. Application of Research Findings to the Issues of Social Policy . . 367
    by Merlin Taber
Index 381

Introduction

This book is the product of the Midwest Council for Social Research on Aging, which is supported by a grant to Community Studies, Inc., by the Kansas City Association of Trusts and Foundations and by the Hill Family Foundation of St. Paul, Minnesota. Some of the authors of the separate chapters have received additional aid for their researches from sources reported in introductory footnotes to the chapters.

The Midwest Council for Social Research on Aging (MCSRA) has had a crescive growth. In January 1959, the state of Minnesota started its preparations for the White House Conference on Aging,[1] scheduled to be held in Washington in January 1961, and included among them a survey of the conditions, needs, and use of facilities among the aging. The other Midwestern states started their programs later that year, and some of them found it convenient to utilize the schedules and other research procedures developed in Minnesota. This was true of Iowa, Missouri, North Dakota and South Dakota, and the common procedures used by these geographically contiguous states made it possible for them to compare their results.

The possibility of comparing results sparked a series of meetings of the sociologists who had conducted the five-state studies as well as other sociologists interested in aging research in the Midwest. The third meeting,[2] held at the time of the White House Conference in Washington, D.C., formulated the initial plans for the MCSRA. In addition to publishing a summary comparison of the characteristics and conditions of the elderly in the five states, the group looked forward to an expanded program of basic research on aging. During the winter and spring of 1961, a search was made for funds for MCSRA. Community Studies, Inc., provided an initial small grant for organizing purposes, and a short time later the Kansas City Association of Trusts and Foundations and the Hill Family Foundation provided equal

---

[1]Chairman of the Minnesota Planning Committee was Arnold M. Rose of the University of Minnesota; he appointed Marvin J. Taves of the same University as director of the research section of the Minnesota program.

[2]Preliminary discussions had occurred in April and August of 1960.

sums for the research program for two years.[3] MCSRA was formally organized at a special session of the meetings of the Midwest Sociological Society at Omaha in April, 1961, and nearly all of the Midwestern sociologists interested in research on aging (outside of Chicago)[4] were included in the membership. An executive Committee was elected, and its first task was to organize a "seminar" that was to initiate and carry out the research. The first seminar was held in St. Paul in June, 1961, and subsequent meetings were held in August 1961, April 1962, June 1962, April 1963, and September 1963.[5] At these meetings, attended by the authors of the various chapters of this book, specific research proposals were formulated, criticized and revised; there was discussion of theoretical and methodological problems in research; plans were laid for the promotion of research and teaching in social gerontology in the Midwest; first drafts of manuscripts were criticized and revised; and there was a certain amount of "social life." Each member of the seminar had his own research project, but each benefited from the stimulation and criticism of the others, so that this book may be considered a truly collaborative effort. In some instances, even the research problem or the interpretation of data used by a member came out of the group discussions. MCSRA has been an experiment in regional cooperation and a means of developing the interest and talents of social scientists in the field of aging. With the first phase of its research program completed and reported in this book, it now looks forward to a second phase with somewhat different research interests and personnel.

The basic objective of the MCSRA program is to expand research on aging systematically in a region which includes unusually heavy concentrations of older people in a variety of community settings. To accomplish this becomes a problem of recruiting social scientists to the field, of developing their potentials, and of providing favorable conditions for conducting research, and for educational and consulting functions. Further, the MCSRA has sought to establish the means by which work undertaken could be integrated with, and related to, that being done by others, and to provide the instrumentalities for intercommunication to maintain participants' awareness of agreed-upon goals, progress made toward these goals, and the means to effect collaborative effort when it appears that such is desirable. The full benefits of the MCSRA program cannot be judged from this book—especially its educational and consulting achievements—but the book does provide a measure of the initial research achievement. To facilitate the collaborative research in this book (1) Small grants were

[3]Amelia Wahl of the midwest regional office of the U.S. Department of Health, Education, and Welfare did much of the organizing work, under the guidance of Marvin J. Taves, of the University of Minnesota, and of Warren A. Peterson of Community Studies. Taves became the first president of MCSRA, Wahl the secretary, and Peterson the coordinator.

[4]The Chicago social gerontologists are almost as numerous as those in all the rest of the Midwest and they already had established research institutes. At an early phase of MCSRA, Wisconsin and Illinois were added to the initial group of Iowa, Kansas, Missouri, Minnesota, Nebraska, North Dakota and South Dakota. The region is thus defined by the limits of the Midwest Sociological Society.

[5]Some of these meetings were held at the same time as the annual meetings of the Midwest Sociological Society and were very brief. In 1962 Donald O. Cowgill became the second president of MCSRA, to be succeeded by Robert L. McNamara in 1964 and by Rodney M. Coe in 1965.

given to assist the research operations. (2) Each contributor was given a modest summer fellowship to enable him to devote at least a month to analysis and writing. (3) Seminars were held at the mentioned times to facilitate collaboration among the contributors.

The book reveals both the individual independence in responsibility for the research and the mutual stimulation at every stage of carrying it out. The specific subject matter of each chapter is seldom related to that of the other chapters, except that they all belong to the field of social gerontology and the research was conducted in the Midwest. The methods of research are equally varied—ranging from systematic interviewing of large samples, through intensive interviewing of small selected samples, to selective observation and library research. On the other hand, the theme of "subculture of the aging" crops out in most of the chapters, there are frequent references to the other chapters throughout the book, and the two concluding chapters interpretive of the field of social gerontology have been influenced by all the preceding research chapters. Thus, there is both diversity and unity in this book. The authors are responsible for their respective chapters, but each is greatly indebted to the others. We thus offer this book as a body of research, theory, and methodological discussion in social gerontology and as a joint product of Midwestern sociologists.

ARNOLD M. ROSE, University of Minnesota

WARREN A. PETERSON, Community Studies, Inc.

I

A Theoretical Suggestion

CHAPTER 1

The Subculture of the Aging: A Framework for Research in Social Gerontology*

ARNOLD M. ROSE

This paper presents a theoretical framework for research in social gerontology which would parallel, but not necessarily be in opposition to, researches which are centered around the concepts of loss of social roles, social adjustment and maladjustment, and disengagement.

The Developing American Subculture of the Aging

A subculture may be expected to develop within any category of the population of a society when its members interact with each other significantly more than they interact with persons in other categories. This occurs under two possible sets of circumstances: (1) The members have a positive affinity for each other on some basis (e.g., gains to be had from each other, long-standing friendships, common background and interests, common problems and concerns). (2) The members are excluded from interaction with other groups in the population to some significant extent. In American society, both sets of circumstances occur for a large and perhaps growing proportion of older people, although for some (who thereby become isolates) only the second develops with age, and these individuals never come to express an affinity with other older people. In other words, the aging subculture is developing and is, at the present moment, far from comprehensive in content or in coverage of older people.

The positive affinity which many older people feel for each other is based in some measure on their physical limitations, and hence common interests in a physically easy and calm existence, partly on their common

---

*An abbreviated early draft of this paper was published in The Gerontologist, 2: 123-27, 1962.

role changes, and partly on having had common generational experiences in a rapidly changing society. The rejection by younger age groups is based to some extent on the same factors, but also on the low value given to inefficacy in our general culture. Retired people—who can no longer earn a living, whose physical abilities to "get around" and engage in sports are limited, and whose prospects for new achievements and success in competition are slim—experience a sharply diminished status. This is abetted by the absence of special marks of prestige attached to aging which are found in other societies—such as the attribution of special wisdom, the automatic accession to a higher political position, or the use of titles of respect (such as the title "U" in Burma, applied to all persons over 40 years of age). Thus for both sets of reasons, the elderly tend to interact with each other increasingly as they grow older, and with younger persons decreasingly, and hence develop a subculture. The greater the separation of older people from other age categories, both as individuals and as a social group, the greater the extent and depth of subcultural development. In other words, older Americans are now historically in the process of changing from a category into a group, although the extent of this change varies from individual to individual. Every group has a subculture—a set of meanings and values which is distinctive to that group—although not every group is necessarily conscious of its distinctiveness or of the fact that it is a group. This chapter will consider some of the respects in which older people in the United States are developing a subculture, and will pose the question as to whether or not they are becoming conscious of themselves as a distinctive group.

There are certain trends occurring in our society which are tending to create some of the conditions necessary for the development of a subculture. These trends are of three types—demographic, ecological, and social organizational—and will merely be listed here with a minimum of discussion. First, there is the growing number and proportion of persons who live beyond the age of sixty-five, from 4.1 per cent in 1900 to over 9 per cent in 1960. This is relevant only in that there are more people eligible for creating an aging subculture, that is, there is more opportunity now than formerly for older people to interact with each other. Second, because of the advances in preventive medicine and in acute, communicable disease control, and because of general progress in sanitation and increased use of birth control (reducing the age at which most women stop bearing children), there has been a tendency for a much larger proportion of the population to reach the age of sixty-five in physical vigor and health, and hence capable of creating a subculture. Third, the same causes have resulted in a larger proportion of older people attaining an advanced age when they are likely to develop chronic illnesses[1] which cost a great deal more to treat than acute illnesses because of the long period of treatment.

---

[1]Whereas in 1901 only 46.0 per cent of deaths were caused by chronic illnesses, the proportion had risen to 81.4 per cent by 1955. Source: Metropolitan Life Insurance Company, Statistical Bulletin, 39 (August, 1958), p. 9.

This is a new major common grievance to older people. It was a major source of the political battle in the Congress, beginning in 1957, over the Forand Bill and its successors in dealing with medical care for the aging which has given many older people a sense of common lot and common interest.

Fourth, there have been some self-segregating trends among older people. "Retirement communities" in Florida and in other areas of good climate *to* which older people migrate are well known examples of this self-segregation. Now there are studies showing that older people often do not follow general patterns of migration *out* of a rural county and so are left behind to form the dominant element in the population of the area.[2] This trend also seems to be operating *within* a metropolitan area: apparently it is the young adults, mainly, who move to the suburbs and the outlying sections of the city, leaving the older people concentrated in the inner section of the city.[3] Further, older suburbanites now show some tendency to move back to the central city. This ecological accessibility of older people to each other helps to create the conditions necessary for the development of a subculture.

Fifth, there has been an increase in compulsory and voluntary retirement, and a corresponding decline in self-employed occupations (at which a healthy older person could work as long as he wished past the age of sixty-five). The decline in employment of older people, independent of its other effects and values, has meant a loss of integration into the general society because an occupation necessarily obliges one to interact with others of various ages. Sixth, because of the long-run improvement in the standard of living and in educational level, an increasing proportion of people reach the age of sixty-five with the means (in terms of funds, knowledge, and leisure) to do something they consider constructive, and what they do often becomes part of their subculture. Seventh, the development of social welfare services for the elderly (particularly group work activities that bring older people together) serves to enhance their opportunities for identifying with each other and for developing a subculture. The increasing number of retirement homes, nursing homes, housing projects, specialized recreational facilities and meeting places for the elderly—sponsored by churches, fraternal associations, and other private associations as well as by government—tend to separate older people from the rest of the society. Eighth, for various reasons associated with increasing migration and apartment-dwelling, there has been less of a tendency for adult children to live in the homes of their parents who retain their positions as heads of the household, and more of a tendency for older people to live by themselves, or for intergenerational dwelling-together

---

[2] Jon A. Doerflinger and D. G. Marshall, The story of Price County, Wisconsin, Agricultural Experiment Station, University of Wisconsin, Research Bulletin 220, 1960.

[3] This does not apply to certain minority groups who are prevented from moving freely to the suburbs.

to take the form of the elderly parents living as dependents in the homes of their adult offspring.[4] This separation of vigorous older people from constant[5] contact with their adult offspring helps to create the conditions for the development of a subculture.

Not all of the distinctive behavior of the elderly can be attributed to the aging subculture; the following may also be involved: (1) biological changes and personal idiosyncrasies associated with physical aging; (2) general cultural norms for the behavior of the elderly held by all in the society (for example, conservative styles of clothing which are favored for the elderly by all age levels); (3) generational changes which cause older people to act out a "general culture" appropriate for an earlier period but which has become "old-fashioned" for contemporaries. This last-mentioned point brings out the fact that American society, like most others, is to some extent age-graded throughout. People tend to associate to a large extent with those of their own age level at every age. However, we shall be asserting throughout this paper that there are certain cultural trends which are making the elderly more segregated from other age categories than is true for the rest of the society.[6]

Since a person only gradually becomes old, and must continue to play some role in the general society, the elderly retain a good deal of the general culture and some even carry on roles typical of younger age groups. The extent of isolation from the larger society—for example, through congregate living or through differential migration—varies from one older person to the next. Thus, different old people have different degrees of involvement in the aging subculture. An age-graded subculture must necessarily be limited as compared to a subculture which has members who live most or all of their lives in it (e.g., that of an ethnic group, a class, a region). In an age-graded subculture, the time it takes to be socialized into it and out of it and the limited period for which it is expected to be followed by an individual are factors which prevent the subculture from becoming highly elaborate or enveloping most of its followers completely. This is true of the teen-age subculture and of the young marrieds' subculture, as it is of the subculture of the past-sixty-five.

---

[4]This is here suggested to be a long-run trend, not necessarily as yet a dominant factor nor always a short-run trend. A study by Shanas suggests that most intergenerational dwelling together still takes the form of adult children living in the homes of their aging parents. See Ethel Shanas, Family Relationships of Older People, New York: Health Information Foundation, 1961, especially p. 12.

[5]Many recent studies, by Marvin Sussman, Eugene Litwak, and others, show that there is a great deal of intergenerational visiting. As we have suggested elsewhere (Reactions to the mass society. The Sociological Quarterly, 3: 316-30, 1962) this is probably on the increase after a period (roughly 1880-1940) in which intergenerational visiting reached a low point.

[6]Obviously the degree of age-group separation is a function of such mechanical factors as the number of age groups and the number of persons in each age group, as well as of cultural and demographic factors. In this paper, only the latter are considered.

There may even be categorical differences in involvement of older people in the aging subculture. For example, the possible tendency for the wealthy and educated elderly to retain more contact with the larger society than do the poorer and ill-educated, and hence to acquire less of a distinctive aging subculture. Perhaps one of the most important bases of differentiation among older people in regard to the extent to which they participate in an aging subculture is the type of community they live in. Those in retirement communities, in rural communities from which younger people are rapidly emigrating, and in the central parts of big cities are most age-separated and hence are most likely to develop a subculture. Those, on the other hand, who live in typical small cities, villages and rural areas, and in suburbs and the outlying parts of large cities are probably least age-separated. In the former settings, the elderly may so dominate the community that the culture of the entire community may be characterized by what we are calling the aging subculture: the commercial establishments, the recreational facilities, the newspapers, and many other local institutions may be marked by the domination of the elderly. This is more likely to be apparent in a small town than in a large city, even when the proportion of older people happens to be equally great in the latter. When there is a large proportion of the elderly in a large city, and the latter have developed a subculture, it is more likely to be segregated from the rest of the city. In a small town, the aging subculture could more readily become dominant. If this differential does in fact exist, it could be a function of the class composition of the elderly as well as a function of the size of the community. In the large city, it seems likely that the segregated elderly would include more lower class persons, while in the small town, they would include more middle class persons who could more readily dominate the town.

The aging subculture is a general one that cuts across other subcultures —those based on occupation, religion, sex, and possibly even ethnic identification—which are characteristic of the middle-aged population.[7] Insofar as older people are somewhat more likely to unite on the basis of age than on the basis of these other divisions, relatively speaking, they are likely to weaken the other subcultures as they substitute a new one for them. On the other hand, for some of the elderly, perhaps for those who have been socially mobile, there may be regression to earlier ethnic and class characteristics of their childhood which had been temporarily superseded in middle age.

Influences which keep the elderly in contact with the larger society, and thus tend to minimize the development of an aging subculture, include: (1) The contacts with the family, which are not reduced by the parents getting older and in some respects may increase as the adult children settle down after marriage and as the older man after retirement has more time for association with his family. Declining health may also force closer

[7]For case evidence of this, see Gordon J. Aldridge, Informal social relationships in a retirement community, Marriage and Family Living, 21: 70-73, 1959.

dependence on, and hence more frequent contact with, adult children. (2) The mass media, which seem to play an increasing role in contemporary society and which have a tendency to cut across all subcultural variations. (3) Continued employment, even on a part-time basis, which keeps the older person in contact with a work group, an occupational association, and the economic standards of the general society. (4) The increasing number of contacts with social welfare agencies, both public and private, which "do" things for the elderly. The social workers themselves are generally not elderly, although they often put the older people into closer contact with each other and tend to separate them from the rest of the society. (5) An attitude of active resistance toward aging and toward participation in the aging subculture. This might result from unusually good physical and mental health so that the person is biologically younger than his chronological years would indicate, from an opportunity to have a special identification with some younger group in the society, or from a rejection of the aging and the aging subculture. The latter alone, if not associated with some opportunity to have contacts with the general society beyond those afforded to most older people, will often result in isolation and group self-hatred.[8]

Characteristics of the Subculture of the Aging

Let us turn from a consideration of the general factors creating and influencing an aging subculture in our society to a consideration of some of the specific contents of that subculture. The areas of life chosen for analysis represent some of the variation in the facets of the aging subculture; they do not present a comprehensive picture. In one respect, a subculture may be said to mold the entire lives of those who participate in it, so that in singling out a few aspects of a subculture we are selecting only its more salient and distinctive ones. On the other hand, a subculture exists within a general culture, and the elderly whose subculture we are examining must also be understood to be Americans whose lives are dominated by a general American culture.

Just as the reasons for the formation of the aging subculture are both positive and negative, so the content of the subculture is both positive and negative. The positive things are those which older people enjoy doing together, or which the whole society encourages them to do together, or which they interpret as being a special opportunity for those with their status. The negative things are those which the elderly do together because they find themselves rejected or otherwise in opposition to the rest of the society. While it may not always be possible to specify that a given behavior pattern or way of thinking of older people is positive or negative, it should be recognized that to some extent the

---

[8]By "group self-hatred" I mean a strongly negative attitude toward the self because one has a negative attitude toward the group or category which nature and society combine to place one in. The concept grew up in dealing with certain social and psychological phenomena in minority groups. See, for example, Arnold M. Rose, The Negro's Morale, Minneapolis: University of Minnesota Press, 1949, pp. 85-95.

aging subculture is a contraculture—in opposition to the rest of the society. In some ways the contraculture of the aging is similar to that of other discriminated-against groups in the society, certain ethnic minorities, for example. But the aging are not distinguished from the rest of the society solely by discrimination and segregation, so that their subculture has a positive aspect even though distinctive from the general culture.

First, the status system of the elderly is only partially a carryover of that of the general society.[9] Two kinds of status must be recognized for the retired elderly—one accorded them by the general society (which is generally markedly lower than that for a younger person of like wealth, education, achievement, and so forth), and one developed out of the distinctive values of the aging subculture. Certainly wealth carries over from the general culture as an important factor in status, with some significant exceptions: (1) With income from occupation gone, the variation in incomes from investments, pensions, and Social Security tend to be significantly less for most persons than were previous incomes from occupations, and the reduced variation probably tends to diminish the use of wealth for invidious distinctions of status. (2) Some of the attitudes toward wealth must develop of the type "you can't take it with you," and yet expenditures for night life, travel, and other expensive amusements must be curtailed for reasons of health, so that wealth must have somewhat less importance than it did at any earlier age. Possibly occupational prestige also carries over into old age, but its effect is probably less when the occupation is no longer practiced by the individual and the occupation itself is changing. The same is true of the prestige arising from the former holding of power. As previous holding of power and earlier achievement fade into the past, they are of diminishing influence in conferring prestige. General education probably carries over more since it is of current utility to the aging, but it, too, must have something of a dated quality. In preceding generations, youngsters were much less likely to be kept in school to the levels they are now likely to be, and the education they received is, in some respects at least, regarded as old-fashioned today.

These sources of status which carry over from the earlier years are probably of maximum influence for the elderly when they continue to live in the same community. If they have changed communities, occupational prestige after retirement must go down markedly, and the other factors be of reduced importance. If the aged individual is socially isolated, as sometimes happens, these factors in former status carry current prestige only as a sort of legend.

Two related factors may be hypothesized as having special value in conferring status within the subculture of the elderly. One is physical and mental health. This is not a highly significant value for most younger people (except for the relatively small percentage who do not have it, and they react as individuals, not as members of a group with a sub-

---

[9] For case evidence of this, see Aldridge, op. cit., and G. C. Hoyt, The life of the retired in a trailer park, American Journal of Sociology, 59: 361-70, 1954.

culture).[10] But good health is sufficiently rare, and becomes rarer with advancing age, so that old people make much of it and exhibit a special admiration for those who remain healthy. A sickly old man who cannot take care of himself has little status among the elderly (or among any others in the society, except perhaps his family) even if he is wealthy, whereas a vigorous old man with keen senses will be accorded high status among his compeers even though he lives exclusively on a modest pension.

The second distinctive factor in the status system of the aging is social activity. This is, of course, partly based on physical and mental health, but it includes much more. Especially in recent years, many of the aging accord high status to those of their number who are willing and able to assume leadership in various associations of a social influence or expressive character composed primarily of the aging. We shall give more extended consideration to this in our later discussion of aging group consciousness. Here it may simply be noted that, because social activity among some of the elderly is based partly on physical and mental health, some of those who rise to prominence among the aging are persons of little previous eminence or skill and experience in group leadership.

There may be other distinctive factors in the status system in the aging subculture which deeper observation would reveal. One approach would be through an examination of the social participations and communications of the elderly. Little is known about this among social gerontologists, but there must be quantities of data in the commercial studies of audiences for the mass media and in other types of public opinion polls. A content analysis of the many magazines for the elderly, which have appeared during the last decade or so, should reveal much about the specific values of the aging subculture and suggest some of the processes through which that subculture is emerging.

Another important social value toward which the attitudes of the aging must differ markedly from those of the rest of the population is sex. While recent studies[11] suggest that older people are more capable of having sex relations and actually do have them than was formerly supposed, it seems likely that interest in sex declines with the years. Many older people in the United States today were raised in an era of sexual puritanism and the "double-standard," in which it was assumed to be natural that men had strong sex drives until they grew impotent in old age, while women naturally did not have significant sexual drives and they lost what they did have when they became older. This generational factor helps to keep interest in sex

---

[10]Cultural values have at least one characteristic in common with economic values: to have high value they must be relatively scarce. Thus, younger people do not gain much status merely by being healthy (because most of them are) unless they are prize specimens of good health.

[11]Mainly the Kinsey studies: A. C. Kinsey, W. B. Pomeroy, and C. E. Martin, Sexual Behavior in the Human Male, Philadelphia: W. B. Saunders, 1948; A. C. Kinsey, W. B. Pomeroy, C. E. Martin, and P. H. Gebhard, Sexual Behavior in the Human Female, Philadelphia: W. B. Saunders, 1953.

low. There are, of course, a few sexual radicals among older people, who keep up a high level of sexual interest and activity.

It was estimated for 1959 that about 2.4 per cent of all marriages taking place in the United States were those involving a bride or groom, or both, over the age of sixty-five. Of these marriages, about one-third joined brides and grooms who were both over sixty-five. Of the approximately 16,000,000 older people in the United States, about one-third of one per cent got married during the typical recent year of 1959. Of course, the majority of older people were already married, and hence not currently eligible for marriage. About 93 per cent of the older brides and grooms had been married at least once before.[12]

After retirement, when men spend as much time around the house as do housewives, and there is much less of a clear-cut difference in economic roles, the social and sexual distinctions between men and women are diminished. Many older men and women, particularly in the lower income groups, seem to seek sex differentiation by means of their social life. The unbalanced sex ratio among older people (121 women past sixty-five for every 100 men) must have some effect on their attitudes toward sex and sex differentiation. Perhaps it is simply that men are pampered and fussed over by their female associates; perhaps it is a woman-dominated social relationship in which men's wishes and interests are ignored because they are so greatly outnumbered.

There are many other areas of the aging subculture that could be analyzed and speculated about. Their self-conceptions, their attitudes toward death, marriage,[13] their interpersonal relationships and leisure activities,[14] their argot, their distinctive rituals,[15] their hobbies,[16] and scores of other important factors in their behavior and outlook must be significantly affected by the particular social settings in which they interact. There is perhaps less basis for speculation about these topics, in the almost complete absence of empirical data, than about the topics we have already considered. There is one topic, however, for which there is some empirical evidence available, one which is of growing significance for the aging. This is what I call "aging group consciousness," and to define it effectively I must first talk about the "aging self-conception." These concepts, as aspects of the aging subculture, will take up the remainder of this paper.

---

[12]These statistics are derived from Cupid comes to older people, Aging, No. 93 (July, 1962), pp. 8-9.

[13]Robert W. Kleemeier, Moosehaven: Congregate living in a community of the retired, American Journal of Sociology, 59: 347-51, 1954.

[14]Hoyt, op. cit.; L. C. Michelen, The new leisure class, American Journal of Sociology, 59: 371-78, 1954; R. W. Kleemeier, ed., Aging and Leisure, New York: Oxford University Press, 1961.

[15]Wayne Wheeler is undertaking a study of rituals among the aging.

[16]Edwin Christ's study of hobbies among the aging is partially reported in Chapter 6 of this book.

The Aging Self-Conception

The age of sixty-five has more or less come to be considered as the age of entering "old age" in American society. It seems likely that the Social Security Act of 1935 did more to define this limit than any other single event. Most private pension schemes adopted or proposed since that date have taken the age of sixty-five as the date of retirement. Compulsory retirement requirements have become much more frequent since 1935, and they have often adopted sixty-five years as the age of effectuation. The double exemption on the income tax for those past the age of sixty-five did not become highly significant until the great increase of tax rates during the Second World War, but then it served to accentuate the importance of turning sixty-five. Thus a legal definition helped to differentiate more sharply a social category. But even today not all persons past the age of sixty-five are considered elderly. The exceptions among men are mainly those who are not retired, which is mainly among the self-employed, and generally in the upper status occupations. Among non-gainfully employed women, for whom there is no definite age of retirement or who have in effect retired much earlier when their youngest child left home, entrance into the social category of "the elderly" is not so clear-cut.

Regardless of precisely at what age they begin to think of themselves as elderly, for most Americans there tends to be a marked change in self-conception. This includes a shift in thinking of oneself: as progressively physically and mentally handicapped, from independent to dependent, and from aspiring to declining.[17] Because most of the changes associated with the assumption of the role and self-conception of being elderly are negatively evaluated in American culture, and because there is no compensatory attribution of prestige, as in other societies, the first reaction of many older people is some kind of disengagement and depression. The disengagement is by no means completely voluntary. The older person is *pushed* out of his occupations, out of the formal and informal associations connected with occupation, and even out of leadership roles in many kinds of non-occupational associations. It is a matter mainly of social fact, not so much of natural inevitability, that many Americans reaching the age of sixty-five shift into a social role of disengagement.[18] The actual physical and

---

[17]These changes in social role and self-conception have been discussed more fully in my paper, The mental health of normal older persons, Geriatrics, 16: 459-64, 1961. Also see Irving Rosow, Retirement housing and social integration, The Gerontologist, I, 85-91, 1961.

[18]Compare Elaine Cumming and others, Disengagement: A tentative theory of aging, Sociometry, 23: p. 23-35, 1960; Elaine Cumming and William E. Henry, Growing Old, New York: Basic Books, 1961. Cumming's theory of disengagement applies to those elderly persons who are in good physical and mental health. Those in poor health are necessarily disengaged, of course, and thus their disengagement is not a matter of sociological theory but of biological fact. Cumming's theory also excludes family contacts from the definition of disengagement. With these qualifications, Cumming hypothesizes disengagement of the elderly to be a matter of "natural inevitability"—which places her theory in opposition to that presented in this paper.

mental decline is not generally very great under today's conditions of advanced medical science and social welfare, and in any case usually develops gradually rather than suddenly. But the culture defines the past-sixty-five person as elderly, and this definition is applied in a variety of ways. Some, of course, resist the shift to the new role and the negative self-conception; they try, whether successful or not, to hold onto the pre-sixty-five role and self-conception. When senility, feebleness, chronic illness, or mental illness sets in, of course disengagement from the society is the only possible condition for all but the most unusual older persons.

Aging Group Consciousness

During the past decade in the United States, we have been witnessing the growth of a new phenomenon which is greatly expanding the scope of the aging subculture. This is what may be called "aging group consciousness" or "aging group identification." Some older people have begun to think of themselves as members of an aging group. In their eyes the elderly are being transformed from a category into a group. Probably only a minority of the elderly have so far taken this social psychological step, but their number is growing. One of the early manifestations of this attitude is for them to join some kind of recreational or other expressive association in which they can interact almost exclusively with persons of similar age. Then they begin to take some pride in the association, as evidenced, for example, by the titles of such organizations—"Golden Age Club," "Senior Citizens Club," or "Live Long and Like It" club. A social worker may have helped to get the club started, but the elderly sometimes take it over and the social psychological transformation toward group pride is theirs. This group-identification of the elderly may take place within organizations that are not age-graded—that is, the elderly members simply interact more with each other than with the other members because of their physical limitations or their common attitudes and interests. But they are more likely to develop group-identification in organizations that are set up exclusively for the elderly. There their distinctive characteristics and interests are clearly made evident to them and they can develop their distinctiveness unhindered by obligations to a non-age-graded group.

The next phase occurs when they begin to talk over their common problems in a constructive way. Probably elderly people have been complaining for some time about their reduced income, their inadequate housing, the difficulty of paying for medical care if they should be struck with a chronic illness, their reduced prestige and general social neglect. But recently some have come to talk about such problems not only with reference to themselves as individuals, but with an awareness that these things occur to them as a social group. Furthermore, they have begun to talk in terms of taking social action, not merely individual action, to correct the situation. Thus far, this advanced minority has supported certain government actions, both legislative and executive. Their current support of Congressional bills for financing health care is to be seen in this context. It is all the more significant that they are radical supporters of this legislation for the benefit of the elderly when the majority of them are political conservatives on most other issues.[19] The elderly seem to be on their way to becoming a voting bloc with a leadership that acts as a political pressure group. Even the elderly who are organized into recreational groups sometimes shift naturally into political pressure groups. For example, in San Francisco and Los Angeles social clubs for the elderly formed a pressure group to get reduced bus fares for those past sixty-five, ostensibly so that their low income members could afford to get to the meetings. It remains to be seen whether the future political activities of the aging become integrated into the existing political parties, or whether they become segregated as in the McLain movement in California.[20]

The trends listed on an earlier page as contributing to the development of an aging subculture are also specifically contributory to an aging group self-consciousness. All of these trends have combined to create new problems for the older population at the same time as it has given them a new, distinctive position in the society, set apart more from those under the age of sixty-five. These are the conditions which enhance the likelihood that the elderly will develop a sense of group consciousness.

For the growing minority that has reacted against the negative self-conception characteristic of the aging in our society and has seen the problems of aging in a group context, there are all the signs of group identification. There is a desire to associate with fellow-agers, especially in formal associations, and to exclude younger adults from these associations. There are expressions of group pride and corollary expressions of dismay concerning the evidence of "moral deterioration" in the out-group, the younger generations. With this group pride has come self-acceptance as a member of an esteemed group, and the showing off of prowess as an elderly person (for example, in "life begins at eighty" types of activities). There are manifestations of a feeling of resentment at "the way elderly people are being mistreated," and indications of their taking social action to remove the sources of their resentment. These are the signs of group-identification that previous sociological studies have found in ethnic minority groups.[21] I do not mean to exaggerate this parallel, or

[19]Angus Campbell, Psychological and social determinants of voting behavior, paper presented at Fourteenth Annual Conference on Aging, University of Michigan, Ann Arbor, June 19, 1961.

[20]F. A. Pinner, P. Jacobs and P. Selznick, Old Age and Political Behavior, Berkeley: University of California Press, 1959.

[21]Probably the first to note the minority group aspects of the aging was Milton L. Barron in Minority group characteristics of the aged in American society, Journal of Gerontology, 8: 477-82, 1953. See also: Milton L. Barron, Attacking prejudices against the aged, in Growing With the Years, New York State Legislative Committee on Problems of Aging, Legislative Document No. 32, pp. 56-58, 1954; Leonard Z. Breen, The aging individual, in Clark Tibbitts, ed, Handbook of Social Gerontology, Chicago: University of Chicago Press, 1960, especially p. 157; Samuel M. Strong, Types of adjustment to aging, Proceedings of the Minnesota Academy of Science, 35-36, 398-405, 1957-58, especially p. 399; James H. Woods, Helping Older People Enjoy Life, New York: Harper, 1953, pp. 1-2.

to state that most older people today show most of these signs. But the evidence of the growing group-identification among older people in the United States today is available to even the casual observer.

Future Research on the Subculture of the Aging

Sociologists now need to go beyond casual observation and engage in systematic studies of this formation of group identification, of this transformation of a social category into a social group. The whole area of the subculture of the aging needs objective investigation, in the same manner in which sociologists have already studied ethnic, regional, and occupational subcultures. The opportunity to study these things in birth and in development should not be missed. One reason they have been neglected by sociological researchers thus far is that the aging have been a low prestige segment of the population, and only those interested in social reform have been willing to study them. But the objective trends seem to point to a higher status for the aging in the future, so we can anticipate that even the sociologists will find it respectable to conduct research in this field.

In conducting this research, it is to be recalled that by no means all persons past the age of sixty-five participate in the subculture. There are those who retain the identifications and the cultural behavior patterns of middle-aged persons. It may be that, as the social movement of aging group consciousness gains more prestige for the elderly, the number of the past-sixty-five who are not forcibly disengaged from the general society but are allowed to continue their prestige roles in that society will increase. If this happens, the self-segregating aspects of the aging group consciousness movement will decline and ultimately disappear, and the movement itself thus become automatically self-liquidating. Secondly, there are those elderly persons who "disengage" and become relatively isolated from all cultural patterns and all associations except those of the family, either by their own volition or as a consequence of rejection by the larger society, or because of physical and mental decline which forces disengagement. Thirdly, there are some who combine both of these sets of characteristics because they *never* were "engaged" in most of the institutional and associational structures of the society, and remain so after they reach the age of sixty-five. Those elderly persons who develop and participate in an aging subculture, such as we have described in these pages, are different from the individuals in these other three categories. We need to know something about the *characteristics* of these people and the *conditions* under which they form or participate in the subculture. We should also remember that individuals participate in the subculture to different degrees, and the factors associated with this *extent* and *form* of participation can be studied at the same time. Insofar as we approach the study of the aging subculture with these questions, the observations of this paper may be considered as hypotheses for testing in order to develop nomothetic generalizations, rather than as statements of empirical fact which contribute to a historical description of a single society at a given time.

The extent of participation in an aging subculture varies with types of communities—e.g., declining rural areas, central cities, retirement towns—and a delineation of characteristics of their residents and conditions under which they participate in an aging subculture will further add to our knowledge. We have hypothesized, too, that several significant trends now affecting American society will favor the conditions under which elderly people engage in a subculture. These trends need to be studied for their effect and for their relationship to the aforementioned conditions under which the aging are found currently to engage in subcultural behavior.

II

General Patterns
of
Adjustment and Participation
in the Community

CHAPTER 2

Group Consciousness
among the Aging*

ARNOLD M. ROSE

Definitions: Formal and Operational

In an earlier paper, "The Subculture of the Aging," I described the social conditions increasingly producing a new category of persons in the United States—which I called the "aging group conscious."[1] The purpose of the present chapter is to find out more about these people. Conceptually, they are defined as elderly persons who become aware, not merely that they are old, but that they are subject to certain deprivations because they are old, and they react to these deprivations with resentment and with some positive effort to overcome the deprivations. Further, they are aware that most, or all, older persons are subject to these deprivations, and they feel a positive sense of identification with other elderly persons for this reason. For them, the elderly are a group, and not merely a category.

/As people become old in American society, some are able to maintain most of their roles as typical adults without any deprivations. A much larger number lose their adult roles, and resign themselves to this without seeking substitute roles./ Neither of these categories of the elderly become aging group conscious. But if the aging react to the loss of their accustomed adult roles by seeking to develop new ones, their lives can take one of two courses: Either they succeed in creating new independent roles, or they create new roles for themselves in an aging subsociety which is different from

*The assistance of the following persons in collecting the samples of aging group conscious persons for this study is acknowledged and appreciated: Bea Kersten, Mary Stolze and Opal Tews. The aid of the Graduate School of the University of Minnesota is also gratefully acknowledged.

[1]See Chapter 1 of this book.

the general American one. The last named are those who become "aging group conscious." In referring to them as "conscious" we do not mean that they are aware of all that is happening to them sociologically. We simply mean that they become conscious of a subsociety of the aging and develop some identification with it. There are obviously degrees of being aging group conscious.

So much for a formal definition; a more complete delineation will emerge from our empirical research. To do this initial research, we must also adopt an operational definition—that is, one that will allow us convenient access to a number of persons whom we can study. Like most operational definitions, ours will be a crude and imperfect one in relation to the formal definition. Our operational definition of aging group conscious persons will simply be those who join formal organizations whose memberships consist only of elderly people. Not all such persons have a positive identification with the aging subsociety—that is, not all are aging group conscious, but probably most are. Those who do not join such organizations (operationally defined as the non-aging group conscious) may actually in some instances really be aging group conscious. They might not join such organizations because they are home-bound, because they are fearful to join any kind of formal organization, or because they are not aware that such organizations are available for their affiliation. Even though they do not affiliate with formal organizations, they may still associate mostly with elderly people and feel identified with them. Thus, our operational categories are not "pure." Further, as we have already suggested, the non-aging group conscious are not homogeneous. They include the ones who are still functioning as though they were younger adults, those who are disengaged or becoming disengaged from all social relationships except perhaps those of their family, and those who have succeeded in creating new roles for themselves as isolated individuals. Since there are at least these three types in our non-aging group conscious sample, to compare our aging group conscious sample with them will probably result in some lack of sharp contrast. Ideally, we should be able to compare homogeneous groups. Such will be the major defects in our initial study, which attempts merely to delineate the social characteristics of the aging group conscious.

Sample and Procedure

The research design for this study calls for a comparison of a sample of persons who are aging group conscious and a sample of those who are not. All cases in both samples are sixty-five years of age or over. None is over eighty-five years old, as the chances of being physically or mentally deteriorated greatly increase after that age.[2] All persons in our samples live in the Twin Cities of Minneapolis and St. Paul.

There are a variety of types of groups organized by and for the elderly, and we have used three of them to provide our sample of aging group

---

[2]The few over eighty-five who appeared in either sample were discarded in the tabulations.

conscious persons. Perhaps the most numerous is that organized by a social worker to meet the special needs for sociability and recreation among the aging. This type probably encourages only a low degree of aging group consciousness since it is organized originally by a non-elderly and professional person. But the more active members soon take over its direction, and all those who join must feel some need to associate with their "own kind." An organized group of this type in St. Paul, a very active group, provided 38 cases for our sample.

A second type is that organized from among the elderly members of a non-age-graded association with a social action purpose. Since these persons pull out of the general association, and are encouraged or forced to do so by the others who are not elderly, the elderly members must have a significant degree of aging group consciousness. Yet they carry over some of the social action purpose of the general association and retain a loose affiliation with it. An "Old-Timers' Club" consisting of retired persons formerly actively associated with a certain trade union in Minneapolis provided 30 cases for our sample.

The third group in our sample of the aging group conscious consists of the members of an organization in Minneapolis known as "Legislative Goals for Senior Citizens' Study Club." This organization has members representing—either by appointment or by election—the 37 senior citizens clubs in Minneapolis. While the parent associations are engaged largely in social and recreational activities, our group was formed for the purpose of informing themselves about proposed legislation affecting the elderly, taking an explicit policy position toward such bills, and bringing information about them back to their parent groups. All members of this group must be highly conscious of themselves as an aging group with distinctive political goals. This association provided 40 cases for our sample.

All three of the sub-samples were self-selected from among the total membership of their associations (with the union Old-Timers Club having the greatest proportion of drop-outs). Reasons for a member not being included in our sample include: non-attendance at the meeting of their association at which we requested them to fill out our questionnaire; unwillingness to cooperate in our study (which was explained to them in terms of getting more information about the problems of older people), or misplacement of the questionnaire or of the self-addressed, stamped envelope which we provided them. Since our purpose was to get a range of aging group conscious persons rather than a representative sample of them, we do not consider this attrition of cases important; it is quite possible that the attrition gave us a "purer" sample, since those who would be least concerned with "the problems of older people" would be likely to be the ones to drop out.

The sample of those considered lacking in aging group consciousness was drawn from a study conducted three years earlier in the Twin Cities for the purpose of getting facts about the composition, characteristics, and attitudes of the elderly. The original sample had been drawn from a random selection of census tracts and a probability selection of city blocks within those tracts. Each house and apartment in those blocks had been visited, and if there were any persons in them over sixty-five years of age they were asked for an interview. From the completed interviews, we selected those cases of persons who had indicated they were not affiliated with any kind of organization that was age-graded for the elderly. These persons were then contacted by telephone, if still alive and living in the same residence, and asked if they would be willing to be interviewed again. Those willing were interviewed in their own homes by a student trained and experienced in interview techniques. All cases were interviewed with the same schedule, which was identical with the questionnaire self-filled-out by the aging group conscious sample. Fifty cases from St. Paul and 44 from Minneapolis were included in this sample of non-group conscious persons.

The answers to open-ended questions on the completed questionnaires and schedules were coded, using empirically developed classifications of answers. The answers were then tabulated for each group separately. Comparison of the answers, in percentage distributions, will be made here between the 108 cases in the sample of the aging group conscious and the 94 cases in the sample of the non-aging group conscious. Differences between groups were tested for significance by the usual chi-square or t-test and are reported here as significant differences only if they fell within the limits set for the 5 per cent level of statistical significance. It is understood that differences in responses to our questions which do not meet this test might do so if our samples were larger. On the other hand, since the many differences predicted by our theory do in fact appear between our two samples, we feel justified also in calling attention to the questions and characteristics for which no differences appear between the two samples.

For example, there are no statistically significant differences in certain background characteristics between the two samples, and we believe that such findings indicate that these characteristics are not important for aging group consciousness. For all such background traits, census data for Minneapolis and St. Paul also show practically no difference.[3] For example, women constitute 62 per cent of our aging group conscious, 63 per cent of our non-aging conscious, and 60 per cent of the total aging population of the Twin Cities. From this evidence we draw the tentative conclusion—until larger and "purer" samples are studied—that sex is not a factor in determining whether an older person becomes aging group conscious or not.

Findings

Just as sex cannot be said to differentiate our two samples, the same is true for education: 51 per cent and 50 per cent, respectively, have a grade school education only; 31 per cent and 28 per cent, respectively, have at least some high school training but no more. This finding is perhaps sur-

---

[3]The census data are not absolutely comparable, as they include those past eighty-five years and those dwelling in nursing homes and other institutions which our samples do not include.

prising, and it is very important for our understanding of aging group consciousness. It might be thought that those who participated in organizations for the elderly would be more educated, but education does not seem to differentiate the aging group conscious. This is all the more surprising when we find (Table 1) that the aging group conscious are much more participant in non-age graded organizations (with the possible exception of the church). From this table it may be calculated that the aging conscious average 1.58 participations apiece, while the non-aging conscious aver-

Table 1. Non-age Graded Participations*

Type of Organization	Aging Group Conscious	Non-Aging Group Conscious
Church and church affiliated	87	68
Community, welfare, and civic	13	7
Political	4	0
Social and fraternal (non-age graded)	22	13
Occupational	12	7
College alumni	2	0
Hobby groups	3	2
Other recreational	6	4
Cooperatives	2	0
Veterans'	4	4
Educational	3	0
Sum of percentages of participation†	158	105
Percentage indicating no participation	2	28

*Percentages who are members of indicated types of organizations.

†Percentages add to more than 100 per cent since an individual may have more than one participation.

age only 1.05. (These figures are for non-age-graded participations only, and hence exclude the participation by which the aging group conscious were identified.) Many previous studies have shown the close linkage of education and social participation for the general population; either this does not apply to the same degree among the elderly, or it applies only to non-age-graded participation among those who are not elderly.[4]

Table 2. Subjective Social Class Identifications*

Class	Aging Group Conscious	Non-Aging Group Conscious
Upper upper	—	—
Lower upper	3	2
Upper middle	29	32
Lower middle	27	32
Upper lower	25	20
Lower lower	2	—
Don't know and no answer	14	14
	100	100

*Percentages saying they are now in the indicated class.

---

[4]Both of these possibilities are probably true.

The absence of educational differences between those who are aging group conscious and those who are not would lead us to expect that there are also no differences in class identifications. Table 2 shows this to be the case; if anything the aging group conscious persons have a lower class identification than do the others, on the average. *Thus, we verify our initial assumption that aging group consciousness is not the same kind of participation as most others* which have been shown for the general population to be correlated with education and other indices of class.[5]

There is an age differential between our two samples, which would help to explain some of the differences in participation. Whereas 50 per cent of the aging group conscious sample is between sixty-five and seventy-one years of age, only 28 per cent of the non-aging group conscious sample is in this "younger" age category. The latter sample is not, however, bunched at the upper extreme of the age range we studied. The proportions of those aged eighty-one to eighty-five years are 3 and 5 per cent respectively. Thus, there is a statistically significant age difference between the two groups, although it is not great: The median ages are 71.5 and 76 years, respectively. This age difference is to some extent reflected in current marital status: Whereas 41 per cent of the aging group conscious are married and living with their spouses, this is true of 37 per cent of the non-aging group conscious. An additional 7 per cent of the former group are divorced or separated from living spouses, but this is true of only 2 per cent of the latter group. The largest difference in marital status is in the category of "single, never married": Whereas only 4 per cent of the aging group conscious are single, there are 20 per cent among the non-aging group conscious. There is an even greater discrepancy in the number of living children these elderly people have, because of the difference in the proportions of those who never married: Whereas 15 per cent of the aging group conscious have no living children, this is true of 37 per cent of the others.

There is no significant difference in the proportion currently employed between our two samples: Only one person in both of our samples is fully employed (he is in the non-aging conscious sample), and only 7 per cent of the aging group conscious and 13 per cent of the non-aging group conscious are employed part-time. Further, only 2 persons, one in each sample, has a spouse who is fully employed. There is thus not much support for a hypothesis we orginally held that those pushed out of employment would more likely become aging group conscious. Most older people are pushed out of employment. However, our data show that more of the aging group conscious give this as a reason for retirement: 60 per cent of the aging group conscious, compared to only 28 per cent of the other sample, mention being forced to retire when asked reasons for retirement. Thus, it may be that forced retirement is a factor creating aging group consciousness, but the data presented here are insufficient to prove it.

---

[5]Subjective class identification reported here is not the same as objective class, but it may be considered to be an index of class.

Table 3 indicates both how the two samples are now spending their time and how this compares to their pre-retirement distribution of time as the subjects remember it. Despite the large proportions of "no answers," certain patterns show up clearly in this table. The aging group conscious show an increase in most retirement or leisure-time activities which is clearly greater than that of the non-aging group conscious. This is even true for such a

Table 3. Comparison of Present Activities with Pre-retirement Activities, in Percentages*

Aging Group Conscious

Do you spend more time, about as much time, or less time *than before retiring*:	*More Time*	*Same Time*	*Less Time*	*NA*
1. Staying around the house with your wife or husband	41	9	6	44
2. Working around the house	65	19	10	6
3. Listening to the radio or watching television	63	21	6	10
4. Following your hobbies	55	16	4	25
5. Doing things you want to do	66	13	5	16
6. Just sitting and thinking	16	10	27	47
7. Participating in church or religious activities	41	30	7	22
8. Participating in social activities other than church	62	18	6	14
9. Taking part in the leadership of social or community organizations	25	13	10	52

Non-aging Group Conscious

Do you spend more time, about as much time, or less time *than before retiring*:				
1. Staying around the house with your wife or husband	31	6	2	61
2. Working around the house	28	33	35	4
3. Listening to the radio or watching television	54	39	7	0
4. Following your hobbies	48	17	17	18
5. Doing things you want to do	43	33	22	2
6. Just sitting and thinking	35	57	6	2
7. Participating in church or religious activities	15	46	28	11
8. Participating in social activities other than church	8	37	33	22
9. Taking part in the leadership of social or community organizations	4	13	18	65

*Percentages add across to 100 per cent for each item.

passive "activity" as listening to the radio and watching television. The only item showing a large proportion checking "more time" among the non-aging group conscious is the purely passive one of "just sitting and thinking." In such activities as working around the house, participating in church or other religious activities, and participating in other social and community activities, the proportion of non-aging group conscious indicating they spend less time currently than before retirement is greater than the proportion indicating they spend more time—which might indicate that the former are becoming disengaged.[6] The things these non-aging group conscious persons do definitely more of are: staying around the house, listening to the radio or watching television, following their hobbies, doing things they want to, and just sitting and thinking. All but "following hobbies" might be interpreted as disengagement. It is understood that these statements are based on high proportions, not on the total sample of the non-aging group conscious. Some individuals who are not aging group conscious indicate a higher participation in retirement activities, and hence a higher "engagement" in retirement roles, but they are not preponderant.

For the aging group conscious, on the other hand, the greater "engagement" in all active retirement roles is preponderant. Table 3 shows that more of them even say that they have *less* time for "just sitting and thinking" since they retired than say they have more time for this. Over two-thirds of them spend more time currently in work around the house and in social activities other than church than before retirement. A full fourth of these aging group conscious persons are even spending more time in community and organizational leadership. Clearly, these aging group conscious persons have not become disengaged from social roles as a result of aging or retirement. Rather, for most of them aging and retirement have opened up new roles, because of the increase of leisure time *and* because of their aging group consciousness. *Thus, our data contradict the Cumming and Henry thesis that older people inevitably disengage.* There is nothing in our study, however, which indicates the relative proportions in the population at large of the aging group conscious and the non-aging group conscious, and external data[7] indicate that the former are a small proportion of the total population of the elderly. But our data do not indicate that all, or even a majority, of the non-aging group conscious disengage, although this pattern is evident among a significant minority of them. *Disengagement, then, is not inevitable, and one reason why it does not happen to some older people is that they become aging group conscious.* Aging group conscious people become *increasingly* engaged as they pass retirement age. It would not be proper to say that they are "re-engaged," since probably many of them were never disengaged, and since their new engagements are not identical with their earlier ones; rather, there has been a reorganization and a stepping up of their engagements.

Further support for these interpretations comes from Table 4, which asks the older subjects whether they would *like* to spend more, less, or the same amount of time, compared to what they currently do, in various retirement activities. While the very large number of "no answers" throws considerable doubt on any interpretation, we shall hazard a few observations about those who do answer. Among the aging group conscious, the

---

[6]Elaine Cumming and William E. Henry, Growing Old, New York: Basic Books, 1961.

[7]That is, it is known that only a small proportion of older people belong to organizations primarily for the elderly.

Table 4. Comparison of Preferred Activities with Present Ones, in Percentages*

Aging Group Conscious Considering your present health, would you *like* to spend more time, about as much time, or less time than you now spend:	More Time	Same Time	Less Time	NA
1. Staying around the house with your wife or husband	15	27	6	52
2. Working around the house	31	37	6	26
3. Participating in church or religious activities	38	28	5	29
4. Participating in social activities other than church	37	29	6	28
5. Taking part in the leadership of social or community organizations	18	28	10	44
6. Listening to the radio or watching television	16	33	12	39
7. Following your hobbies	32	28	5	35
8. Just sitting and thinking	6	12	32	50
Non-aging Group Conscious Considering your present health, would you *like* to spend more time, about as much time, or less time than you now spend:				
1. Staying around the house with your wife or husband	2	32	3	63
2. Working around the house	20	70	8	2
3. Participating in church or religious activities	18	67	0	15
4. Participating in social activities other than church	13	67	0	20
5. Taking part in the leadership of social or community organizations	3	30	0	67
6. Listening to the radio or watching television	6	83	9	2
7. Following your hobbies	24	59	0	17
8. Just sitting and thinking	0	82	16	2

*Percentages add across to 100 per cent for each item.

pattern of Table 4 is similar to that of Table 3. That is, the tendency among a significant number in this sample is to engage in still more active retirement roles, and to avoid the passive "just sitting and thinking"—which is the same pattern of responses they claim for their actual behaviors when comparing post- and pre-retirement. Among the non-aging group conscious, on the other hand, there are significant discrepancies between Tables 3 and 4. While the preponderant response to all items is to indicate that they are satisfied with how they spend their time, a minority would like to participate in the more active retirement roles. *None* wishes to spend more time "just sitting and thinking," and *none* would reduce the time he spends in church, social, community, and hobby activities. In other words, none of the non-aging group conscious says he would like to become more disengaged, although a great many are satisfied with their present degree of disengagement. *Thus, disengagement is not necessarily something the older person looks forward to*: Among both our samples, significant minorities of the cases would prefer to spend more time in the active retirement roles, and practically none would prefer to spend less time in these or in the passive retirement roles.

Table 5. Percentages Participating in Earlier and Current Hobbies

	Earlier (Pre-Retirement)		Current (Post-Retirement)	
	Aging-Group Conscious	Non-Aging Group Conscious	Aging-Group Conscious	Non-Aging Group Conscious
Active Hobbies:				
Active performance of arts	7	9	6	4
Active performance of sports and games	28	20	31	7
Dancing and singing	7	6	9	0
Organizational participation	9	13	13	6
"Do-it-yourself" activities around home	10	15	12	4
Hand crafts	38	35	50	46
Social welfare (helping others in general)	7	4	6	2
Traveling	6	13	3	11
"My work"	9	9	2	2
Taking care of family	15	13	15	6
Gardening	16	0	16	20
Passive Hobbies:				
Observing arts	0	7	3	4
Observing sports and games	2	11	2	9
Conversation on local and world affairs	0	0	2	0
Reading	10	15	10	20
Talking, gossiping	2	0	2	2
Listening to radio, TV	2	4	6	3
Never had hobbies	13	13	2	0
No hobbies now	0	0	7	24
No answer	10	0	7	2

There are a few sharp differences between the aging group conscious and the non-aging group conscious in regard to the hobbies they engaged in before they retired (Table 5). The former were somewhat more likely to engage in sports and games actively rather than merely to observe them. The former also were more likely to engage in gardening. But at the present time, in their retirement years, there are some definite patterns of difference between the two samples. First, the non-aging group conscious includes a significantly large proportion who say they engage in no hobbies at all. Second, there is some tendency for the aging group conscious to participate in what we have arbitrarily called the "active" hobbies to a greater extent than do the non-aging group conscious (except for traveling and gardening). This shows up most clearly in the active participation in sports and games. But in what we have arbitrarily labelled the "passive" hobbies, the non-aging group conscious are at least as participant as the aging group conscious: They continue to be passive observers of sports and games more frequently, and they are more likely to engage in reading.

The non-aging group conscious include a large proportion of persons who never participated in organized group activities, in contrast to the aging group conscious who have always been participant but are more so now in their old age than earlier.[8] In answer to a question about activity in clubs and organizations now and when they were fifty, the aging group conscious include only 4 per cent who say they were never active and 56 per cent who say they are more active now. In contrast, the non-aging group conscious include 43 per cent who say they were never active and only 9 per cent who say they are more active now. The same pattern, although not so extreme, shows up in regard to church attendance. Whereas only 3 per cent of the aging group conscious say they have never gone to church and 15 per cent said they went to church more frequently when they were fifty years old than they do now, among the non-aging group conscious the corresponding figures are 11 per cent and 28 per cent. The organizations the aging group conscious most frequently have left are those associated with their occupation (by 25 per cent) and the general category of "fraternal and social" (by 13 per cent). Among the non-aging group conscious the corresponding figures are 22 and 19 per cent, but in addition they have dropped out of civic organizations to a significant extent (20 per cent). In giving reasons for dropping out of organizations, poor health was *not* given as a reason by a significant number in either sample (5.9 per cent of the aging group conscious and 5.6 per cent of the other). *The single most frequent reason for dropping out of an organization was that the respondent was forced out*, that is, he or she reached the mandatory age of disaffiliation, usually for an occupational association (for 12 per cent of the aging group conscious and 13 per cent of the others). A significant small proportion (9 per cent) of the non-aging group conscious say they are still formally affiliated with some organization but are no longer active. The only other significant reason for disaffiliation was "moving away"—given by 11 per cent of the non-aging group conscious and 7 per cent of the group conscious.

---

[8]This verifies a hypothesis we have had about the aging group conscious, but it does not mean that all those who are participant in earlier life will become acting group conscious. The earlier participants might remain active in non-age graded activities, or they might disengage.

The question might be raised as to *why* the non-aging group conscious do not belong to an organization primarily for the elderly. We approached this problem in two ways. The first was to ask them whether there exist "any clubs or organizations for older people that you *could* belong to?" Forty-four per cent said there was none, and an additional 33 per cent answered "yes, one or two." (The corresponding figures among the aging group conscious—who by definition belong to such an organization—were 10 per cent and 32 per cent respectively.)[9] It must be understood that all members of both samples reside in the Twin Cities where there are a number of organizations for the elderly available to any of them who are not home-bound (the home-bound constitute 5.6 per cent among the non-aging group conscious only). Our second approach was to ask all respondents why they did not belong to more clubs or organizations for older people. The most frequent answers given by the non-aging group conscious were "no interest" (by 57 per cent) and the meaningless cliché "I have no time" (by 26 per cent). Smaller proportions answered "poor health" (13 per cent) and, "I

Table 6. Health and Incapacity

	Per Cent of Aging Group Conscious	Per Cent of Non-aging Group Conscious
In general, how is your health?		
Very good	13	24
Pretty good	37	37
About average for my age	44	26
Not very good	6	11
Very poor	0	2
Are you able to get out by yourself without much difficulty?		
Yes, can get out	93	82
With some difficulty	7	13
No, cannot get out by myself	0	5

don't like clubs for older people" (7 per cent).[10] All these answers are to be expected from non-aging group conscious persons.

We have seen that poor health is seldom the reason for dropping out of an activity, which is contrary to the common impression about older people. As a matter of fact, the great majority of the subjects in both samples say their health is not bad (Table 6). Only 5.6 per cent of the non-aging group conscious cannot get out by themselves, and this is true of none

---

[9]These figures demonstrate what was said earlier about the operational definition of the aging group conscious in this study being inadequate: Many in this sample are not aware of their affiliation with an organization primarily for the elderly. Thus, even though they are in fact members of such an organization, they are not aging group conscious.

[10]Other answers, such as "have to care for my wife," "no money," "too old," "not old enough," "I don't like to go out alone," and "I belong to enough already," were given by one person each.

of the aging group conscious. The difference in these proportions—indicating relatively poorer health among the non-aging group conscious—can be readily explained by their somewhat greater age. Certainly, *poor health cannot be considered a significant reason for non-participation*, including non-participation in age-graded associations which identifies our sample of the aging group conscious.

Nor is there a significant difference between the two samples in life satisfaction. In response to a question about their way of life *today*, 96 per cent of the aging group conscious, and 94 per cent of the non-aging group conscious, said they are very satisfied or fairly satisfied. In response to another question about satisfaction with their *whole* life, similar overwhelming percentages of both samples said they were satisfied. Thus, general life satisfaction cannot be considered as associated with aging group consciousness. Nevertheless, there is a difference between the two samples in the outcome of their expectations for their lives as old persons. The relevant question reads, "As you get older, would you say things are getting better or worse than you thought they would be?" Among the aging group conscious, over 54 per cent answered "better" and only 31 per cent said "same," whereas among the non-aging group conscious only 28 per cent said "better" and 65 per cent said "same." Fifty-three per cent of the aging group conscious said they feel younger than their years, as compared to only 37 per cent of the other sample (very few of either group said they feel older than their years, the others say "the same"). Thus *growing old can be considered a more satisfying experience (or a less dissatisfying experience) to the aging group conscious*. They are also more likely to wish they had a different kind of earlier life. When asked, "If you had a chance

Table 7. Frequency of Association with Relatives, Friends, Neighbors

	Per Cent of Aging Group Conscious	Per Cent of Non-aging Group Conscious
See some relatives other than children:		
At least once a week	19	26
Once or twice a month	31	9
Once or a few times a year	41	28
Almost never	6	35
No answer	3	2
Get together with "friends you're closest to":		
At least once a week	50	44
Once or twice a month	38	24
A few times a year	9	21
Almost never	0	11
No answer	3	0
Get together with neighbors:		
At least once a week	46	72
Once or twice a month	17	2
A few times a year	9	0
Almost never	18	26
No answer	10	0

to live your life over again, would you do the same things or would you do it differently?" about a third of the aging group conscious sample would have liked a different job and a different family life, and would have been more religious, as compared to only about a sixth of the non-aging group conscious sample who wanted these things. Smaller proportions of both groups would have preferred different kinds of friends and social activities.

There are different informal associational patterns for the two samples, as shown by Table 7. The aging group conscious tend to see their close friends more frequently than do the other group. In two other respects, the aging group conscious are more homogeneous than the non-aging group conscious: They tend to see some of their relatives both not so frequently and not so infrequently as the non-aging group conscious. They tend to get together with their neighbors both not so frequently and not so infrequently as the non-aging group conscious. The non-aging group conscious sample includes a sizeable minority that almost never sees relatives or neighbors. These different associational patterns of the two samples reflect a change in their present behavior as aged persons compared to what it was when they were younger. Whereas only 25 per cent of the aging group conscious say they saw more of their relatives (other than children) when they were fifty years of age than now, a full 74 per cent of the non-aging group conscious gave this answer. Similarly, whereas only 19 per cent of the aging group conscious say they had some close friends whom they saw regularly when they were fifty, a full 63 per cent of the non-aging group conscious give this answer.

As far as relations with members of their immediate families are concerned, there is little difference between the two samples. Practically no one admits not getting along with his or her spouse, if there is one. There are practically no complaints about lack of respect from children. Only about 10 per cent in both samples complain that their children don't help them as much as they ought to, and these are perhaps balanced by the same proportions who think their children help them *more* than they ought to. While the aging group conscious are more likely to have children, there are no significant differences between the two samples in the proportion living with their adult children or in the distances they live from the home of their nearest adult child.[11]

There are also few differences between the two samples in the problems they experience. Large medical expenses is the most frequently mentioned problem in both samples, and it is cited by almost a third of both samples. The second most frequently mentioned problem—"not enough income to live on"—is cited by a larger proportion of the aging group conscious (31 per cent) than by the non-aging group conscious (20 per cent). "Poor health" is more likely to be cited by the non-aging group conscious (20 per cent) than by the other sample (12 per cent). Problems mentioned by even smaller proportions of the two samples, without significant dif-

---

[11]These findings go against a hypothesis we originally held, that aging group conscious persons became so because they were distant from, or estranged from, their adult children, and so felt rejected.

ferences between them, are: not knowing what to do with free time, not having anything worthwhile to do, and inadequate housing. None in either sample mentioned as a problem not getting along with children, not getting along with other close relatives, or being pushed out of organizations they used to be active in, nor did they mention other problems not listed in the questionnaire.

Relationships with other persons in their own age group are part of the definition of aging group consciousness, and—as we predicted—there are large differences between the two samples in answers to questions on this topic (Table 8). *The aging group conscious have found, as they have grown older, that they tend to associate more with their own age group more than do the non-aging group conscious.* They also are somewhat more likely to say they have always associated mostly with their own age group. Further, many more of them say they have more in common with their

Table 8. Relationships with Own Age Groups

	Per Cent of Aging Group Conscious	*Per Cent of Non-aging Group Conscious*
Since you have grown older, do you associate more with people of your own age group, or associate less?		
Associate more with own age group	54	41
Associate less with own age group	4	28
About the same; have always associated mostly with own age group	35	29
About the same; have never associated with own age group	3	2
No answer	4	0
Since you have grown older, do you feel you have more in common, or less in common with people of your own age group?		
More in common	62	39
Less in common	4	30
About the same	34	31
Do you like to associate with people of your own age group, or do you like to associate with younger people?		
Prefer my own age group	15	43
Prefer younger people	4	9
Makes no difference; like to associate with everyone	78	43
Makes no difference; don't care to associate with anyone	3	5

own age group. This tendency, however, does not reflect a preference: The aging group conscious are less likely to say they *prefer* association with their own age group. This does not mean that they prefer the company of younger persons; it is rather that the age of their associates is less likely to make any difference to them.

The conversation of the aging group conscious when they are with people of their own age also differs from that of the non-aging group conscious in the expected directions. They talk more about health and medical care (25 per cent compared to 2 per cent) and about the other problems of old age (16 per cent compared to 5 per cent). They also talk more about their own family (31 per cent compared to 17 per cent). They talk *less* frequently than do the non-aging group conscious about newspaper items (32 per cent compared to 63 per cent), about friends and gossip (15 per cent compared to 26 per cent), and about past events, personal or general (13 per cent compared to 28 per cent). There is no significant difference in the proportions of the two groups talking about the other topics they listed: hobbies, art, sports and games, food, general social problems, the mass media, traveling, work, religion, the weather, or organizations.

We now come to a series of questions which might be included in a definition of aging group consciousness. They are not included in our operational definition because we found it expedient to use membership in an organized group of older people as an operational definition. Besides, we believe that aging group consciousness is only in a nascent stage in American society, and group demands, resentments, and pride have not built up as much as in, say, an ethnic minority group. Still, we expect to find more of this in the sample of the aging group conscious than in the sample of the non-aging group conscious. Table 9 presents data which show that these expectations are borne out in fact. They reveal that *the aging group conscious have more demands, resentments, and pride associated with aging, despite the fact that their personal situation is, if anything, better than that of the non-aging group conscious, and growing old has not burdened them with any more hardships.*

We learn from Table 9 that *there are many more of the aging group conscious, as compared to the non-aging group conscious, who think there ought to be more organizations for the elderly, that older people ought to organize to demand their rights, that older people ought to be more active in politics, and that they themselves are more likely to vote.*[12] They are also somewhat more likely to believe that older people are treated badly by younger people (although they are no more likely to report such an experience with their own children), that younger people do not show enough respect for older people, and that they are prevented from using their full capacities by younger people. The difference in the proportion proud of having attained their present age is not statistically significant.[13]

---

[12]All of the aging group conscious say they generally vote, and 91 per cent said they voted in the most recent election. This is not unusual for the Twin Cities, where over 90 per cent of the total eligible population actually does vote in a general election.

[13]This question may be inadequate for our purpose since it refers to pride in age rather than pride in belonging to an aged group.

Table 9. Identifications with the Elderly as a Group

	Per Cent of Aging Group Conscious	Per Cent of Non-aging Group Conscious
Do you think there ought to be more clubs and organizations for older people?		
Yes	68	33
No	22	61
No answer	10	6
Do you believe that older people ought to organize to demand their rights?		
Yes	68	39
No	19	50
No answer	13	11
Do you think older people ought to be more active in politics?		
Yes	74	48
No	18	45
No answer	8	7
Do you usually vote in elections? When was the last time you voted?		
Yes	100	74
No	0	26
1962 Election (most recent election)	91	67
Earlier election	6	17
Never voted	0	4
No answer	3	12
Do you believe that older people as a group are treated badly by younger people?		
Yes	19	13
No	37	61
They are treated just like everyone else	34	26
No answer	10	0
Do you feel that younger people show enough respect for older people?		
Yes	53	80
No	37	20
No answer	10	0
Do you believe that older people who are in good health are prevented from doing things they are able to do because younger people run everything?		
Yes	31	18
No	60	78
No answer	9	4
Are you proud to have reached your present age?		
Yes	88	83
No	10	17
No answer	2	0

—the aging group conscious. They are not distinguished by their sex, education, or social class identification, or even significantly by their health. They are distinguished by their participations in organizations, by their relationships with others, and by many attitudes. While there may be personality and social background characteristics which influence many of them to become aging group conscious when they reach old age, there is nothing in this study which indicates that only one kind of personality or social type become aging group conscious. If the analysis of the social conditions creating the aging group conscious (presented in my earlier paper, The subculture of the aging) is correct, which predicts that they are likely to increase in number and proportion, they deserve further study.

Conclusion

This paper might be considered a definitional study of a category of older people believed to be relatively new but growing in American society

CHAPTER 3

Alternative Participatory Responses to Aging[*]

RICHARD VIDEBECK and ALAN B. KNOX

Introduction

In a period of rapid social change, adults are again and again confronted with situations that call for major revisions in the pattern of their daily lives. Increasing residential mobility, the growing trend toward mandatory age for retirement, and the expansion of leisure time and leisure opportunities, are but a few of the conditions underlying the alterations to be observed today. Although passage through the adult life cycle has customarily been accompanied by the task of assuming some age-graded responsibilities and prerogatives, the pace of contemporary innovation has increased the number and magnified the consequences of the adaptive problems facing adults. These adaptive problems are often occasioned by major change-producing events. Some of the critical events that occur in the lives of most adults, such as birth of the first child, have been faced by antecedent generations. Other critical events, such as mandatory retirement, are of a more recent origin. All such events necessitate major alterations in social relations, in activities, and in ecological settings. Whether the changed circumstances occur suddenly or emerge slowly, the individual is compelled to make substitutions in his pattern of social participation. Social participation is herein defined as any recurring activity which, at a general level of analysis, involves either interaction with other people, or solitary activities with major social significance (e.g., newspaper reading). Social participation might occur in any domain of life (family, political, voluntary asso-

*The research reported in this paper was supported by funds granted to the Nebraska Continuing Education Center, University of Nebraska, and was conducted under the direction of Alan Knox.

ciations, informal activities, recreation, church, etc.). In some cases, the individual must find a replacement for an important complex of persons, places and activities that has been removed. The death of a spouse, or the youngest child leaving home, creates a void in an important sector of one's life. A person's day is still twenty-four hours long and either existing patterns of participation and activity must expand to fill the void, or new activities and acquaintances must be found. In other cases, he must find a way of incorporating new social relationships and obligations into his established network of participation.

The purpose of this paper is to examine the effects of aging on various participatory domains and to examine the relationship between the level of participation of older adults and their participation earlier.

It is frequently assumed that chronological age itself is a major determinant of behavior, implying both that physiological changes associated with aging markedly affect behavioral potentials, and that age-related role expectations are uniform for all persons of a given age. However, we shall proceed upon two assumptions that diverge from this more common assumption. First we assume, barring disabilities and senility, that age serves mainly to limit engagement in those activities requiring maximum physical performance. Second, we assume that the kinds of social participation with which we deal are learned and modifiable. Given these notions, we propose that the amount and style of an aged person's participation are an extension of an emerging pattern begun in childhood, and shaped in earlier adulthood. Thus age is less important in predicting participation patterns than are the "routes" one has taken through life. Where correlation between age and participation is observed it can be accounted for primarily by variables such as age-related role expectations, by generational differences in standards of social behavior, by different age composition for various size communities, and by variations in financial resources. Therefore, we assume that correlation between age and participation is the spurious product of their joint relationship to those major adult statuses which define one's life conditions. While age sets outside limits upon participation, expansions and contractions of opportunities to participate are a function of one's life statuses such as sex, socio-economic status, marital status, employment status, and family status. These statuses are viewed as identifying situational conditions or forces that propel one into participation at the one extreme, and prohibit participation at the other. Because these statuses are alterable, shifts in them would be expected to influence participation.

An examination of alternative responses to aging, regarding participation, provides a specific opportunity to examine the degree to which chronological age, itself, has a substantial influence on participation. However, before examining some of our data regarding age and participation, it might be well to review the conceptual framework within which we will be examining it.

The notion of adjustment to old age is a normative concept, predicated upon some standard of desirability or normality. In the absence of consensus about standards of either normality or of desirability, the usefulness of adjustment concepts is severely restricted. At all times, the use of adjustment concepts requires constant referral back to the implied standards. Taking the leap into normative assumption is neither necessary, nor, in the light of diversity of opinion, desirable. The behavior and performance of persons at any stage of the life cycle can be understood without it. We have attempted to replace the adjustment concept with a taxonomy of mutually exclusive and exhaustive alternative responses to aging. It is not necessary to claim that any of the determinable responses are normal and/or desirable. The alternatives are merely plausible and probable.

The taxonomy proposed here is a comparative one. It requires knowledge of both present and past participation patterns. However, because of the lack of longitudinal data, we shall compare age-classified cross sections of a population for some analysis. Self-report data on shift in participation during the previous five years is also analyzed. In order to explore possible responses to later maturity in an orderly fashion, we propose the paradigm in Figure 1.

Fig. 1. Paradigm—alternative participatory responses to aging.

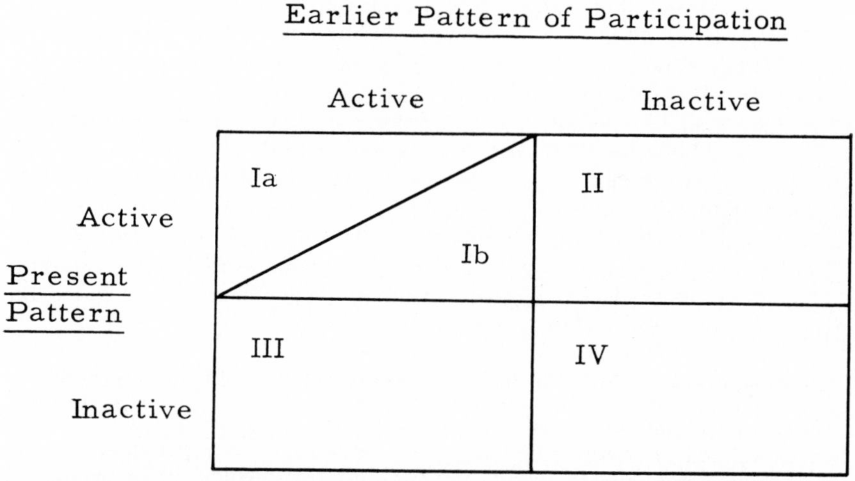

Earlier Pattern of Participation

Ia. Continuance of earlier type and relatively great amount of participation
Ib. Maintenance of relative amount of participation but change in type (emergence of an aging subculture)
II. "Late Blooming" participation where present level is higher than earlier pattern
III. "Disengagement" where present level of participation is lower than earlier pattern
IV. Continuance of earlier tendency toward inactivity.

For all of the five types of response to aging described in Figure 1, some life history data are necessary. The interpretation of reactions Ia and IV would seem to require examination of enduring personality traits, on the one hand, and unchanging situational factors on the other; either of which might be seen as inhibiting or facilitating participation. An interpretation of response type II would probably include analysis of change in circumstances affecting participation by removal of deterrents or opening of opportunities for participation. Response type Ib is similar to type Ia except that change in circumstances results in change in type of participation rather than in an increase in amount. Response type III is the reverse of type II, in that there is a decrease in opportunities and/or an increase in restrictions.

Source of Data

The data that we are reporting here is cross-sectional from the first round of interviews in a longitudinal study. The comparisons, therefore, are between different people at different ages rather than the same people at different ages. However, self-report data covering the previous five years are available and are reported.

In order to examine the degree to which age is associated with changes in social participation during later maturity, we analyzed relevant data from the Baseline Study of Adult Participation in Nebraska. The data were collected in 1961-1962 from 1500 adults, a representative sample of the adult population of Nebraska, age twenty-one through sixty-nine. Data were collected in one and a half hour interviews at the respondents' homes.

As part of the preliminary analysis of this cross-sectional data, fifty participation variables were examined regarding fluctuations in degree of participation between five-year age categories. Variations with age were very different for the fifty variables. Some increased from twenty-one to sixty-nine, some decreased, and some did not change. For some types of participation, amount increased from young adulthood until middle age and then declined until later maturity, while other variables declined in middle adulthood and then increased in old age. Some few fluctuated several times during the adult life cycle. The findings from this analysis underscore the importance of clearly specifying what participation variables are being employed in any analysis. The subsequent findings are based on data from respondents aged fifty through sixty-nine.

Participation in Relation to Socio-Economic Status and Community Size

Social participation of older adults is undoubtedly influenced by many factors related to both personality and situation. Both personal predisposition and major changes in life circumstances would be expected to influence participation. However, both personal predisposition and change in life circumsances occur within the larger context of circle of friends and community. Before proceeding to examine how specific changes in life circumstances influence social participation, it would seem well to identify gross participatory differences between subpopulations based on socio-economic status and community size, which variables have been identified in previous studies as being related to degree of participation.

Both variables reflect, among other things, the participatory opportunity system available to the older adult. A composite measure of socio-economic status provides an indication of the style of life of the individual, with its facilitators and barriers regarding various types of social participation. Communities of various sizes differ in the number and variety of activities available to an interested adult. However, the participatory opportunity system may serve to limit participation for specific individuals only when the number of available activities drops below a minimum level.

Seven participation variables were employed in the following analysis, so as to represent various domains and types of non-sustenance participation. Brief descriptions of each of these participation variables are listed below:

1. *Church Activity.* The low category consisted of non-church members, the middle category of church members who participated in no church related activity other than attending church services, and the high category of persons who were active in one or more church related activities.

2. *Number of Voluntary Associations.* The low category was no voluntary association memberships, and the remaining categories consisted of increasing numbers of active memberships.

3. *Time Spent in Voluntary Associations.* The categories were based on relative number of hours typically spent in voluntary association activities during an average month.

4. *Number of Public Meetings Attended.* The categories were based on the relative number of public meetings attended during the prior year. The low category was none; remaining categories consisted of increasing numbers of public meetings not directly connected with association memberships.

5. *Time Spent Reading Magazines.* The categories were based on relative number of hours spent in a typical week reading magazines. The low category was no magazine reading, and the remaining categories consisted of increasing numbers of hours.

6. *Number of Books Read in Prior Year.* The low category consisted of persons who had read no books in the previous year, the middle category consisted of persons who had read one through five books, and the high category was persons who had read six or more.

7. *Political Participation.* The categories were based on the scores on the Roper-Woodward Political Participation Scale.

Socio-economic status categories were differentiated within the frame work described by Warner in *Social Class in America*, using three variables: level of occupation, level of education, and rating of dwelling. The overall rating was trichotomized. Community size was classified in five population categories: farm, towns under 2,500, towns 2,500-9,999, cities 10,000-50,000, and cities 50,000-300,000.

In order to identify how participation varies with both socio-economic status and community size, each was compared with participation while controlling for the other. When controlling for community size, most of the participation variables were positively correlated with socio-economic status. The one exception was church activity, for which there was no significant difference between the distribution of persons in the three broad socio-economic categories. There was a significant decline with socio-economic status for the populations in communities of every size in the number of voluntary associations, the amount of time spent in voluntary associations, the number of public meetings attended and the amount of time spent reading magazines. The number of books read in the previous year was positively correlated with socio-economic status for all communities except farm dwellers, where book reading was not significantly related to socio-economic status. Political participation was positively correlated with socio-economic status for all communities, except the non-farm small towns under 2,500 population. For the subpopulation residing in these small communities the mean political participation scores were somewhat lower than for either farm dwellers or for persons in larger communities, and there were no significant differences in political participation related to socio-economic status.

When controlling for socio-economic status, there were comparatively few positive correlations between community size and the seven participation variables. Church participation was not related to community size, nor was number of public meetings attended. For four of the participation variables—number of voluntary associations, time spent in voluntary associations, time spent reading magazines, and political participation—there was no significant relationship with community size with one exception. The one exception was for the high socio-economic status group, where the small town subpopulation scored significantly lower on the four participation variables than did the other community subpopulations. Controlling within more limited categories for age reduced part of the difference for high status, small-town residents, but the remaining difference suggests a difference between the small town and either the farm (with the variety of farm-related organizations) or the larger communities, in opportunities to participate. A second significant difference is related to political participation. The political participation of the low status subpopulation in middle-sized communities was significantly higher than for the low status persons residing on the farm or in the big city. The one significant relationship between participation and community size occurred for the high and middle status subpopulations in which the number of books read during the previous year increased significantly with community size. There was no significant relationship between community size and book reading for the low status subpopulation.

In general, for adults aged fifty through sixty-nine, degree of social participation is positively correlated with socio-economic status and is not significantly correlated with community size, except in very small towns where high status persons participate less than high status persons in other-sized communities.

Changes in Participation with Age

It now remains to examine data dealing directly with alternative responses to aging. In an earlier section of this chapter we suggested that age is a less important variable in predicting participation patterns than are the life statuses which characterize a person's stage in the life cycle. In this section we shall present two sets of data which bear upon the issue of how much of the participation variance is accounted for by age itself. The first set of findings indicates that the characteristics which identify the high participators among the aging group are the same as those which identify high participators in our sample as a whole including all age levels from twenty-one to sixty-nine. The high participators live in urban places, have high educational levels, a higher occupational category, and a higher socio-economic status than the low participators. In addition, the high participators tend to evaluate political activity as being efficacious and tend to hold higher ideals for themselves and have higher aspirations. In sum, these findings are similar to those presented by Scott, Foskett, and others.[1] Furthermore, our first set of findings strongly suggests that age alone is insufficient to predict an individual's level of activity.

The second set of findings which bear upon the relationship of participation and age utilizes the respondents' (age fifty to sixty-nine) own estimations of how active they were at the time of the interview as compared with five years earlier. For a large number of different activities, each respondent was asked whether the activity had increased, decreased, or remained about the same during the past five years. A composite index of "change in participation" was constructed, based upon their responses to these questions. A general index of the respondents' present level of participation was constructed from their answers to questions about the number of activities they engaged in in a wide range of settings and the relative amount of time they spent in these activities. Using the composite "change in participation" score and the general index of participation scores, individuals were cross-classified into the four quadrants illustrated in Figure 1.

Respondents whose general index of participation scores were in the upper quartile and whose change in participation score indicated stability or increase were placed in Quadrant I. Those respondents who were also in the upper quartile in the general index of participation but whose change in participation score indicated a decrease were placed in Quadrant II. Respondents with participation scores in the lower quartile but whose "change" scores indicated increase in the level of activities over the past five years, were placed in Quadrant III, and those whose participation scores were in the lower quartile but whose change in participation scores indicated stability or decrease were placed in Quadrant IV.

Nine out of ten of those *presently active,* i. e., in the upper quartile of the general index of participation, were located in Quadrant I. Similarly, nine out of ten of those *presently inactive,* i.e., in the lower quartile of the participation index, were located in Quadrant IV. Thus, using self reports of present participation levels compared with their participation of five years ago, our sample of fifty- to sixty-nine-year-olds revealed they had changed

[1]John C. Scott, Jr., Membership and participation in voluntary organizations, American Sociological Review, 22: 315-26, 1957; John M. Foskett, Social structure and social participation, American Sociological Review, 20: 431-38, 1955.

relatively little in their activity. Age, again seems to be of little consequence in predicting a person's level of participation; in fact, it is rather clear that *the best estimate of how active an older person is at any particular age is how active he was at an earlier date.* A similar analysis of responses from those in other age categories in our sample leads to the same conclusions for all age groups.

Age Change in Life Circumstances and Participation

Utilizing the responses of persons fifty to sixty-nine years of age in our total sample, we examined the relationship between age, change in life circumstances, and selected types of participation. By "change in life circumstances" we refer to any major alteration that has occurred in the person's environment or in his social relationships. Four such changes were used for comparisons:

(1) *Mover versus non-mover.* Those who had moved to the present community within the past five years compared with those who had not made such a move.

(2) *Widowed versus married.* Those who had been married but had lost their spouse compared with those persons who were still living with their spouse.

(3) *Retired versus non-retired males.*

(4) *Job change versus no job change.* Males who had changed jobs within the past five years as opposed to those who had not made such a change.

Seven measures of participation were used in this analysis:

(1) The relative amount of time spent in a typical month on a large number of non-sustenance activities. These included primary group, formal association, and solitary and audience type activities.

(2) The total number of non-sustenance activities a person engaged in.

(3) The total number of active memberships in voluntary associations.

(4) Political participation as measured by the Roper-Woodward Political Participation Scale.

(5) The level of activity in church and church-related groups.

(6) The relative amount of time spent in activities with the immediate family, based upon Key's Family Participation Scale.

(7) The relative amount of time spent in a typical month on activities such as reading, collecting, watching T.V., that an individual engages in primarily alone, but may have social significance.

For the purpose of our analysis we have classified our respondents into four age categories as follows:

(I)   50–54 years
(II) 55–59 years
(III) 60–64 years
(IV) 65–69 years

The statistical reliability of all comparisons in this section were evaluated by the Mann-Whitney U Test. This test allows conclusions regarding differences between nonparametric measures which are similar to conclusions drawn on the basis of the "t" test for metric data.

The only statistically significant participation differences between age levels which we found to be related to age indicate that respondents in the 50–54 age category tended to participate in more activities and in more voluntary associations than did the 55–59-year group. For all other measures of participation there were no differences between any of the four age categories. The only statistically reliable differences between those who had and those who had not experienced a change in life status was for familial participation. Here we found that the widowed respondents participated less than the non-widowed and the retired less than the non-retired in a variety of family settings. Again, no other statiscally reliable differences in participation were found for any of the other change–no change comparisons. In sum, neither age alone nor change in life circumstances alone predict much of the variability in the seven participation measures used.

Analysis of the interactional effects of status change and age upon the participation brings forth a number of interesting differences. These are summarized in Table 1.

Table 1.

Line	A Sub sample	B Type of Participation	C Difference	D Level of Significance
1	60–64 yrs.	Immediate family	married..widowed	.001
2	60–64 yrs.	Solitary	non-retired..retired	.01
3	60–64 yrs.	Church	mover..non-mover	.05
4	60–64 yrs.	Church	job change..no job change	.01
5	65–69 yrs.	Amount of time in non-sustenance activities.	mover..non-mover	.05
6	Non-mover	Number of different non-sustenance activities.	50–54..55–59	.001
7	Non-mover	Number of voluntary association memberships.	50–54..55–59	.001
8	Married	Number of different non-sustenance activities.	50–54..55–59	.001
9	Married	Number of voluntary association memberships.	50–54..55–59	.001
10	Married	Solitary	60–64..65–69	.05
11	Non-retired	Number of different non-sustenance activities.	50–54..55–59	.001
12	Non-retired	Number of voluntary association memberships.	50–54..55–59	.001
13	Non-retired	Political participation	50–54..55–59	.05
14	Retired	Family participation	65–69..60–64	.01
15	No job change	Solitary	60–64..65–69	.05
16	Job-change	Number of different non-sustenance activities.	50–54..55–59	.05

The first two columns (A and B) in this table identify the subsample and the activity for which a significant difference has been found. The third column (C) indicates the two categories which have been found to be significantly different at the level indicated in the fourth column (D).

Some observed differences are not very startling. For persons in the 60–64 age category, widowed persons participate less in immediate family activities than do married respondents (line 1). Other differences can be given an interpretation only by straining at the theoretical bit. Why employed 60- to 64-year-old men engage more in solitary activities than retired men of the same age makes little sense (line 2). Still other differences raise interesting but unresolvable questions. For example, 60- to 64-year-old persons who move, as compared with those who have not experienced such a change, attend church more frequently and are more involved in church activities (line 3). Is one of the functions of churches in American society to introduce recent arrivals to the community and to satisfy affiliation needs of newcomers, at least until they reestablish themselves in a network of associations? Of course this leaves unanswered the question of why this should occur in this particular age range, and not at other points in a person's life history.

Aside from the theoretical significance that might be attached to each of the observed differences, a marked pattern in the findings deserves extended examination and a search for meaning. For those persons whose life circumstances are stable (i.e., have not experienced a change in familial, residential, or employment status), some socially important forms of participation decline significantly during the fifties. Specifically, the total number of different non-sustenance activities (lines 6, 8, 11, 16), the number of voluntary association memberships (lines 7, 9, 12), and the level of political participation (line 13) decline. There are two points of special interest. First, the decline is not continuous with age, but rather occurs within the 50–54 and 55–59 age categories, Second, although the observed contraction in participation is a general one, as suggested by the decline in the total number of non-sustenance activities, two of the types of activities are formal and tend to reflect special interests and/or socially visible participation in community affairs.

Decline or deterioration of health and physical strength hardly accounts for these findings. Why should physiological decline affect only these types of activities and why at this particular point in the life history? It is more plausible to view the participatory contractions as directly related to the stability of life circumstances. The observed patterns of differences in participation reflect a life cycle phenomenon.

Casting our cross-sectional data within a developmental framework, we see a tapering off in the formal activities of married persons sometime between 50 and 60 years of age. Glick's analysis of the characteristics of American families reveals a number of changes in family structure that are likely to occur at this point in the life cycle span.[2] The number of children

---

[2]Paul C. Glick, American Families, New York: Wiley, 1956.

under 18 in households which have a head who is between 55 and 64 is strikingly less than in those in which the head is between 45 and 54 (18.6 per cent vs. 51.5 per cent). Similarly, the size of immediate families declines with the age of the head of the household. The medium size of families whose head is between 45 and 54 is 3.25 persons and for heads of households aged 55-64 is 2.46 persons. In family life cycle terms, the "nest" typically empties when the head of the family is in his fifties. This marks a crucial change for parents. For the majority of them it brings the conclusion of pressing concern with the education of their children. For example, their concern about the adequacy of school program facilities tends to become depersonalized. The promotion and support of community services for youth become academic problems, if not threats to the conservation of community resources. A major impetus to participation in community affairs is removed with the departure of the children.

Based upon the foregoing interpretation the decline of participation is attributable to a change in family composition and not to age. Modally, the youngest child leaves home when his father is in his mid-fifties. Logically, however, we would also expect a decline to occur following the change in family composition regardless of the age of the father.

Further information from Glick's analysis of family structure bears upon this problem. For women with no young children, there is a marked decline between the ages of 45 and 65 in the proportion who are in the labor force. Other studies indicate that a high level of participation in non-sustenance activities is highly and positively associated with being employed.[3] The fact that the median income ($3,290), of families the age of whose head is between 55 and 64, is not much different from that of families whose head is between 45 and 54 ($3,601), rules out income as a central variable. Employment provides the person with a wider range of contacts outside the home and is attended by a greater awareness of participatory opportunities in the community. Furthermore, the firm contractual relations and obligations associated with employment orient a person toward a formal and instrumental type of participation. The financial rewards of employment merely foster the salience of this orientation. Insofar as careers both for females and males are modally associated with age, age will also be associated with trends in participation.

A residential move imposes upon an individual changes in life circumstances which are different in character from changes in familial or employment status. These latter can be viewed as associated with the progression of stages in the life cycle. They result in the removal of several spheres of activities without, in our society, any prescription for their replacement. While moving to a new neighborhood wipes out a large portion of the established network of primary and formal relationships in the old

[3]M. Axelrod, Urban structure and social participation, American Sociological Review, 21: 13-18, 1956; Frederick A. Bushee, Social organizations in a small city, American Journal of Sociology, 51: 217-26, 1945; Ronald Freedman and Morris Axelrod, Who belongs to what in a great metropolis, Adult Leadership, 1: 6-9, 1952.

one, counterparts of them can be found in the new community. In a study of social participation of housewives, Videbeck found that recently mobile (within the past year) housewives will spend more time seeking informal social interaction and belong to more organizations than residentially established housewives.[4] Furthermore, the level of participation varies directly with how active the housewives were prior to the move. Residential moves seem to arouse a search for replacements for the participatory opportunities lost in the move.

The evidence from the present study does not justify the conclusion that a person intensifies his search for participatory opportunities after his move, but rather that if the person's life circumstances are characterized by residential stability, then the person's participation will decline at around the age of fifty-five. A composite of our evidence and that of previous research would suggest that residential mobility intrudes upon the association of the life cycle progression, on the one hand, with trends in participation, on the other. The disruption may or may not lead to relatively permanent divergences from the modal life cycle pattern. This will depend upon idosyncratic, subjective factors such as personal needs and also upon whether the recent move is a unique or common event in the person's life.

Summary and Conclusion

The social activity characteristics of older persons (fifty to sixty-nine years) are identical with the characteristics of active persons in younger age categories. Although it is generally concluded that participation declines with age, our findings suggest that this is not the case. How active or inactive one is depends upon individual, subjective factors as well as upon statuses within the life cycle. Persons whose early life history has been characterised by much social participation are not likely to show a decline in the relative level of activity as they grow older. Activeness is an individual factor which in part derives from subjective needs and habits. However, it is modifiable by alterations in life statuses. For persons whose life circumstances are characterized by residential and employment stability, shifts in life statuses that are not elected by the individual but result from family maturation lead to less activity.

There is little doubt that life cycle statuses are correlated with age. One must be cautious, however, in attempting to relate age to behavior variations. As we suggested earlier, the correlation between age and participation is a spurious product of their joint relationship to those major adult statuses which defines one's life condition. Whether for research or policy issues, to treat the aging population as a homogeneous class of persons does violence to the facts of the matter. The aging population is not homogeneous in either history of participation, or the routes taken through the life cycle, or in the present conditions of life. These are factors which predict participation in any population.

[4]Richard Videbeck, unpublished report on social participation in Scottsbluff, Nebraska.

CHAPTER 4

Social Adjustment of Elderly People in Three Small Towns

C. Terence Pihlblad and Robert L. McNamara

Introduction

The great increase in the number of aging and in the proportion of elderly in the general population are matters of general public recognition and concern. Since the turn of the century, the population of the United States 65 years of age and older has increased from about three million to nearly 17 million, an increase of nearly 500 per cent while the general population during the same period has increased only about 135 per cent. It is perhaps not so well known that the proportionate size of the aging population is uneven among the states, with the highest proportions in the New England and West North Central states and lower proportions in the South, West, and eastern industrial areas. Three states (Iowa, Missouri and Nebraska) rank above all others in the proportion of the elderly in their populations.

A distinctive residential characteristic of the aging in the North Central states is the relative concentration of older people in the smaller centers. When population materials are arranged as in Table 1 to show the urban, rural-nonfarm, and rural-farm components by regions and selected states, it is clear that only in the North Central region does rural-nonfarm residence account for the largest relative proportion of the aging. In fact, in other regions of the nation the small towns and villages tend to have smaller proportions of aging in their population than do either the urban or rural-farm categories. Clearly, the selected states shown in Table 1 have a relative concentration of the aging in the smaller centers and it therefore appears most appropriate to undertake research in the small centers in this section of the nation. Missouri, for example, has about 800 of these

Table 1.Percentage of Population 65 Years of Age and Older
in Regions and Selected States, by Residence 1960*

	Total	Urban	Rural Nonfarm	Rural Farm
United States	9.2	9.1	8.9	9.3
Northeast	10.1	10.0	9.0	10.7
North Central	9.8	9.3	10.7	9.4
South	8.3	8.0	8.1	9.3
West	8.6	8.6	7.6	8.0
Minnesota	10.4	10.0	12.6	7.3
Iowa	11.9	11.8	15.5	7.2
Missouri	11.7	10.8	13.2	11.5
North Dakota	9.3	8.7	12.3	5.5
South Dakota	10.5	9.9	13.9	6.7
Nebraska	11.6	10.7	16.7	7.3
Kansas	11.0	9.7	13.3	10.8

*Source: U. S. Bureau of the Census 1960 (PC-B).

smaller places with a population under 2500, and although they account for only about 8 per cent of the population of the state, about 15 per cent of the aging reside in these small places.

Very little research has been done on the aging in small towns and the present experimental work is planned as a beginning of substantial and sustained study. A review of the literature was conducted during the planning stage for this study, but diligent search revealed very little work on aging in small towns or in rural areas generally. As an example of the paucity of information on old age and retirement problems in rural areas, the bibliography compiled by the U. S. Health, Education, and Welfare Special Staff on Aging for the 1961 White House Conference contains more than 700 entries, but only three mentioned rural in either the title or notation, and these were concerned with medical care. Other standard sources were checked with only slightly more rewarding results.

There is no particular claim in this report for the applications of the findings to places other than reported here, and the lines of questioning are more limited than would be followed in a full-scale investigation. However, the queries used appear to be reasonable ones and revealed what appear to be strengths and weaknesss in this research effort. This pilot study represents preparation for a projected larger field study which would include an adequate sample, involving a typology of local places and giving attention to the strikingly different areas of the state.

The specific research interest here has been centered on the social adjustment of the aging. The purpose, then, in this report is to discuss the responses of older people in three local settings to questions on health, means of livelihood, education, living arrangements, involvement or participation in community affairs and in social institutions, and how these are associated with social adjustment. The adjustment scale used was a modification of one designed by Havighurst and Cavan for earlier work. The scale has been used in substantially the same form in five midwest states

in the preparation of materials for the White House Conference on Aging.[1]
Briefly, the scale consists of statements denoting attitudes of satisfaction or

Social Adjustment Scale*

	Agree	Disagree	Undecided
1. I never felt better in my life.	+2	—2	0
2. If I can't feel better soon, I would just as soon die.	—2	+2	0
3. My health is just beginning to be a burden to me.	—1	+1	0
4. I feel just miserable most of the time.	—2	+2	0
5. I have more friends now than I ever had before.	+2	—2	0
6. I have no one to talk to about personal things.	—1	+1	0
7. I have so few friends that I am lonely much of the time.	—2	+2	0
8. My many friends make my life happy and cheerful.	+2	—2	0
9. I am happy only when I have definite work to do.	—1	+1	0
10. I am satisfied with the work I now do.	+2	—2	0
11. I have no work to look forward to.	+1	—1	0
12. I have more free time than I know how to use.	—2	+2	0
13. Religion is a great comfort to me.	+2	—2	0
14. Religion doesn't mean much to me.	—2	+2	0
15. Religion is the most important thing in my life.	+1	—1	0
16. My life is still busy and useful.	+1	—1	0
17. This is the most useful period of my life.	+1	—1	0
18. I am just as happy as when I was younger.	+2	—2	0
19. My life is full of worry.	—2	+2	0
20. These are the best years of my life.	+2	—2	0
21. My family is always trying to boss me.	—2	+2	0
22. I wish my family would pay more attention to me.	—1	+1	0
23. I am perfectly satisfied with the way my family treats me.	+1	—1	0

*The questions were scored according to this sample. Total scores ranged from a high of +34 to a low of —19. The median score for the whole group is 14, median for town A is 17, for town B is 13, for town C is 14.

[1]Marvin J. Taves and Gary Hansen, As Senior Citizens See Themselves: A Survey of Aging in the Midwest, Midwest Council for Research in Aging, June, 1961.

dissatisfaction with the conditions of living of older people. Respondents were asked to agree or disagree with each statement; on the basis of the responses, values were assigned and a composite score was prepared for each schedule taken. A copy of the scale is included here. For the analysis of health, income, housing, and other concerns of this study, adjustment scores were grouped in quartiles, the respective proportions compared and whenever possible tests of statistical significance were computed. Persons scoring in the first quartile are termed the "low adjustment" group and those in the fourth quartile the "high adjustment" group.

Theoretical Orientation

Among the views commonly held concerning aging in small towns is the one that, because of relatively meager resources and limited institutional facilities, the smaller places are less prepared than urban centers to cope with the needs and wants of their older citizens. Also in smaller places children may have moved away and may be disinclined or unable to make provisions for parents. Another view holds that the process of growing old in the rural community may present fewer problems than under urban conditions. Role changes accompanying retirement and advancing years may take place less suddenly and be less traumatic than in the city. The network of friendship and kin groups may provide the support for persons in their advancing years which sometimes seems to be lacking in the city.

Still another view, of a somewhat different nature, is that as the aging segment increases in the population—particularly in small towns and villages where one-fourth to one-third of the population may be elderly— a group-consciousness based on advanced years may develop. Thus, identification, leadership, and the satisfactions accruing from various associations may tend to be concentrated within the older segment of the population. Social adjustment, therefore, may be less dependent on social interaction with others in the community. This point is discussed at greater length later in this report. The hypotheses implicit in these views are the central concern of this research, although at this stage of the study only partial evidence can be brought to bear to support or refute them.

Method of Study

A schedule was constructed for use in interviewing older persons. The schedule covers such areas as health and medical care, work and retirement, living quarters, leisure-time activities, education, relationships with children and family, friendship and visiting patterns, civic participation, church and religious activities. A local informant placed on plat maps the location and the name of the head of every household in which an older person lived. An experienced graduate student was employed to do the interviewing. It was learned that a most essential step was the preparation of the older people for the introduction of the study in the community. Prior to visiting the homes, newspapers were provided with copy; announcements were made in the local churches; a pre-interview letter inviting co-operation was sent to each prospective respondent; and selected local leaders otherwise helped to prepare the communities.

Three study sites were chosen: two small villages of about 500 population each, and a larger town of about 7,000 population. The three places are located in central Missouri in a generally rural setting. The two smaller villages are near larger centers upon which there is considerable economic dependence, including much commuting to jobs. The two villages have relatively high proportions of older people in their populations but there are virtually no social agencies other than churches active in meeting the needs of the aging. These small places serve as minor trade centers for the farm people living close by, but major purchases are made in larger centers. The older residents of these villages are predominantly white and Protestant, have rural backgrounds, and have lived most of their lives in the immediate locality. In these respects the two villages are similar to other villages in Missouri and other Midwestern states. In these two villages, an attempt was made to obtain an interview with an elderly person from each household containing a person sixty-five years of age or older. A total of 108 interviews was completed.

The third town, being a larger place, was sampled to provide 43 schedules with a proper representation of race and income groups. This place is an "old river town," a county seat, and is a locally important trade center. It is also the location of a military academy and a state training school. There is some institutional employment of a rather stable nature and some commuting to employment in a larger center nearby. The town has remained at the 6000-7000 population range since 1930. Additional descriptions of the study sites are included in the sections on analysis of data in the body of the report.

Sex and Age and Adjustment

The subjects were almost equally divided between males and females, 76 men and 75 women. It should be explained that the relatively equal

Table 2. Subjects Classified by Age and Sex

Age	Male		Female		Total	
	No.	Per Cent	No.	Per Cent	No.	Per Cent
65–69	18	24	16	21	34	23
70–74	21	28	26	35	47	30
75–79	22	28	18	24	40	27
80 and over	15	20	15	20	30	20
Total	76	100	75	100	151	100

number in the two sexes in no way reflects the sex ratio at these ages in the communities studied. The respondents were chosen to represent households in which there resided at least one person sixty-five years old or older.

In some households the man was interviewed, in others the woman. An attempt was made to obtain about the same number of interviews from persons of each sex. The youngest were sixty-five while a a few were over ninety years of age. Approximately one-fourth were aged 65–69, a third 70–74, one-fourth 75–79 and one-fifth were over eighty.

The distribution of adjustment scores by sex is shown in Table 3. Differences between the men and women in our sample were not great. It appears that men tended to be distributed toward the extremes of the adjustment continuum while the scores for women clustered closer to a central measure.

Table 3. Social Adjustment Scores of Males and Females

		Per Cent			
	Total Number	1st Quartile	2nd Quartile	3rd Quartile	4th Quartile
Male	76	30	17	24	29
Female	75	20	36	23	21

$X^2 = 8.60; P < .05$

It might be expected that age would show a close relationship with adjustment. One would expect that advancing years would be accompanied by changes not conducive to feelings of contentment or social adjustment. This does appear to be the case, especially for the males, although the small number of cases in the sample precludes the establishment of statistical significance between age categories. Table 4 shows the distribution of adjustment scores for the two sexes classified by age.

Table 4. Adjustment Scores Classified by Age and Sex

Males:		Per Cent			
Age	Total Number	1st Quartile	2nd Quartile	3rd Quartile	4th Quartile
65–69	18	28	—	22	50
70–74	21	29	14	24	33
75–79	22	23	32	27	18
80 and over	15	47	20	20	13
Total	76	30	17	24	29

$X^2 = 13.09; P < .20$

Females:					
65–69	16	19	37	25	19
70–74	26	15	39	19	27
75–79	18	17	33	22	28
80 and over	15	33	33	27	7
Total	75	20	36	23	21

$X^2 = 4.41; P < .90$

For men the proportion of subjects in the high adjustment group declines steadily with age, from one-half among those aged 65–69, to a little more than one-tenth among those 80 or over. At the other extreme, for those with the lowest adjustment scores, there is no marked change with age until age eighty is reached. In this group the proportion in the low adjustment class is twice as large as in any of the younger age categories. Among female subjects it is hard to detect any relation between age and adjustment except the sharp decline in the proportion of the high adjustment group, and increase in the low adjustment categories at ages over eighty. In neither sex group, however, are the differences sufficiently great to reach a five per cent level of significance.

Self-Conception of Age and Adjustment

Roles assigned to older persons, or the roles which they themselves seek to play, are not only a matter of chronological age. In our society however, with the magic age of sixty-five as a criterion of eligibility for Social Security benefits, and with formal retirement often coming at this age, there appears to be a tendency to establish this as a cut-off point for aging. Nevertheless there is some truth to the aphorism that "you are as old as you feel." Self-conception of age is undoubtedly influenced by a great number of factors: health, marital status, retirement, social participation, former occupation, education, and many other influences. In large measure self-conception of one's own age should reflect one's own sense of well-being and contentment and should correlate with self-evaluation as reflected in the score on our adjustment scale. To obtain a measure of such self-conception the subjects were asked whether they considered themselves as "middle aged," "elderly" or "old." Some validation that the scale is measuring something which might be called moral self-satisfaction, and contentment with self is reflected in the following table which classifies the subjects by score on the scale and self-definition of age.

Table 5. Adjustment Score and Self-Conceptions of Age

| Self-Conceptions | Total Number | Per Cent | | | |
		1st Quartile	2nd Quartile	3rd Quartile	4th Quartile
Middle-aged	13	8	23	8	61
Elderly	27	22	15	30	33
Old	97	29	33	22	15

$X^2 = 2.39$; $P < .01$

It is clear that self-conception of age and adjustment score are related. Over three-fifths of those defining themselves as middle-aged and one-third of those calling themselves elderly scored in the highest quartile. This compared with less than one-fifth defining themselves as old. At the other extreme, in the lowest adjustment class, were about one-tenth of the "middle aged," one-fifth of the "elderly" and a third of the "old."

Adjustment and Community

The three communities under study differed quite widely in their characteristics. Towns A and B were both small villages. Town A gives the appearance of decay and dilapidation, particularly in its business section. A number of new homes, occupied largely by younger people, employed in nearby larger towns, relieves this picture somewhat. Town B on the other hand appears more prosperous, the streets in its business section are crowded with parked automobiles, homes look well kept and a considerable number of new dwellings house a younger population that is employed in three nearby larger centers. On the basis of the field notes of the interviewer, Town B also seems to be a town in which community leadership is concentrated largely in the hands of older people.

The third town (C) is a much larger community with approximately 7,000 population. Our sample here was drawn at random from a list of names provided by the City Assessor as well as by the County Welfare Office. The proportion of respondents who were recipients of old-age assistance was the same as in the county's population as a whole.

Table 6. Adjustment Score by Community

		Per Cent			
Town	Total Number	1st Quartile	2nd Quartile	3rd Quartile	4th Quartile
A	37	22	19	24	35
B	71	27	31	25	17
C	43	26	25	19	30

$X^2 = 5.9; P < .50$

No striking difference in the distribution of adjustment scores appears in the three towns. Subjects from Town B appear to make the poorest showing with only about half as large a percentage in the high adjustment quartile as were found in the two other communities. The differences, however, are not significant at the five per cent level.

While results relative to differences among the three communities are most inconclusive, this may well be a point which would bear further investigation. On the basis of the field notes of the interviewer, one gets the impression that differences in community leadership and the local power structure may have some relevance to this problem. In Town B there were comments by some of our older respondents, as well as by other persons interviewed, expressing dissatisfaction with the local leadership, with the domination of the community by a few older and well-entrenched personalities who exercised disproportionate influence in the determination of policy. The following excerpts from field notes illustrate this point:

This informant was the pastor of a local church and was a younger fellow . . . First he vehemently attacked X . . . and the City Fathers. He said that X . . . profited from every civic improvement that had ever befallen Town B. He indicated that X made tremendous sums from the control of credit in the community . . . Many of the older people could not afford the sewer system, they could not afford the water system and many of the other improvements. But since X . . . and other community leaders had pushed so hard many of the people were forced to follow along. He [the minister] was quite angry at the fact that the town was run by these older citizens.

In an expansion of this study to other communities, extensive attention should be devoted to the possible influence of the type of community leadership and the local power structure on the social adjustment of older persons.

Health and Adjustment

Probably no problem is of greater concern to the older person than is health. With advancing years, illness and infirmity tend to become more frequent and more severe. Health status will influence almost every aspect of the older person's life: his income and outgo, the degree to which he can remain independent or must rely on the help of others, his type of residence, his degree of mobility, the extent of his participation in the life of the community, and association with other people. Morale, a sense of well-being and social adjustment are all likely, in large part, to be functions of health. In the light of these facts an attempt has been made in this study to relate self-conceptions of health to the score on the social adjustment scale.

A considerable number of queries with respect to health and related matters were directed to the respondents. They were asked to name any major health condition from which they suffered. They were also asked to estimate the general level of their health as good, fair or poor. An additional query asked them to state the degree to which their mobility was limited by their health.

As is the case with many surveys of health conditions, the reliability of the information may be questioned on the grounds that it rests on subjective evaluations rather than on objective information obtained through more reliable means, such as a physical examination. It may be that the amount of illness or disability was exaggerated in the minds of some crotchety old people. On the other hand, it is also probable that medical examinations would show conditions unsuspected by some who reported themselves in good health or free from any known health condition. About 60 per cent reported one or more major health problems. This was slightly larger than the percentage found in the population studied for the Missouri report on aging for the White House Conference (about 50 per cent). It might be mentioned in connection with the latter study that several individuals who reported themselves in good or excellent health in replying to the direct question on this matter in answer to later questions referred to medical conditions not previously mentioned.[2] Grant Youmans found in his study of a rural county in Kentucky that 68 per cent of persons sixty years and older reported that they suffered with some major physical ailment.[3] The consistency of the results in all these studies suggests that they probably

---

[2]Aging in Missouri: Report of the Missouri Committee for the 1961 White House Conference, Appendix I, Aging in Missouri, (by Peter New), 1960, Chap. 4, pp. 174-76. See also Taves and Hansen, *op. cit.*

[3]E. Grant Youmans, Aging Patterns in a Rural and Urban Area in Kentucky, University of Kentucky. Agriculture Experiment Station, Bulletin 681, March, 1963, p. 26.

present a fair picture of the health conditions found in these three small towns among the older people. It may also be pointed out that although there may not be a perfect correlation between perception of health and actual health, the former may be more significant than the latter in determining how the individual functions in the community and how he perceives himself in terms of contentment and adjustment. It was not surprising, therefore, to find that those who reported themselves as free from any major ailment took a more optimistic view of life and scored higher on the scale than did those who reported such disabilities. The relation between adjustment score and presence or absence of major health problems is shown in Table 7.

Table 7. Adjustment Score and Major Health Condition

Health Condition	Total Number	Per Cent			
		1st Quartile	2nd Quartile	3rd Quartile	4th Quartile
Present	103	43	30	16	11
Absent	61	8	15	31	46

$X^2 = 43.8$; $P < .01$

Nearly half of those who reported no health conditions scored in the "high" group in adjustment as compared with only about one-tenth of those who were so afflicted. In the low group the proportions were almost exactly reversed.

When the people in the sample were asked to rate their health as good, fair, or poor, the same relationship between health and adjustment is apparent (Table 8.).

Table 8. Adjustment Score and Self-rating of Health

Health Rating	Total Number	Per Cent			
		1st Quartile	2nd Quartile	3rd Quartile	4th Quartile
Good	69	7	17	32	44
Fair	51	22	42	26	10
Poor	31	71	19	—	10

$X^2 = 69.4$; $P < .00$

Since the degree of physical mobility is closely related to health it has seemed pertinent to include data on the relation of this factor and social adjustment. This is shown in Table 9.

Table 9. Adjustment Score and Mobility

Mobility Status:	Total Number	Per Cent			
		1st Quartile	2nd Quartile	3rd Quartile	4th Quartile
Unlimited	100	11	22	31	36
Limited or confined	50	54	34	8	4

$X^2 = 69.4$; $P < .001$

More than one-third of those with unlimited mobility scored in the highest quartile while less than five per cent of those limited or confined made scores at this level. At the other extreme, in the lowest quartile were over half of those with mobility limitations and only about one-tenth of the unlimited. Whether or not the limitations on mobility in themselves tend to lower the sense of well-being as reflected in the scale, or whether the physical disabilities and poor health which produce the limited mobility are the major factors, is difficult to determine. Probably both contribute to a lowered sense of well-being. Perhaps a more extensive and probing interview would help to throw some light on this question. Later in this report we shall consider the relationship between social participation and adjustment. It should be kept in mind that health conditions, and the amount of mobility permitted by health status, is a vital factor in such participation. Perhaps health is the overriding variable which influences all the other factors which, in turn, may be related to social adjustment. With a larger sample and more refined data, it should be possible, by holding the health factor constant, to throw some light on these problems. With the limited resources available for this study this kind of analysis has not been possible.

Marital Status and Household Arrangements

Approximately one-tenth of those studied were single (never married), a little less than half were married and living with spouse, while about two-fifths were widowed or divorced. The proportion widowed was approximately twice as great for women as for men, 30 per cent among men as compared with 57 per cent for women. While the differences in adjustment scores between the married and the widowed or single do not quite attain a 5 per cent level of significance, it does appear that the married are somewhat better adjusted than are the single or widowed. The differences, however, appear only among the men, which suggests that widowhood may have a different meaning for men than for women (the same difference between widows and widowers was noted in the summary of the five state studies of aging in the midwest).[4] About two-fifths of the married men scored in the high adjustment group as compared with one-fifth of the widowed and divorced. Among women, however, the proportion in the high group was the same for the married and widowed or divorced. It may be that since the duration of widowhood had been much greater for women than for men (50 of the women compared with only 14 of the men had been widowed five years or more) that the former were more adjusted to widowhood than were the latter. While the total number of cases in the sample is too small to justify confidence in the differences in adjustment scores between the marital groups, nevertheless this problem would appear to be worth investigating in a more extensive study.

That the relation between widowhood and adjustment for men and women may be different is also suggested by the answers to the question

---

[4]Taves and Hansen, *op. cit.,* p. 24.

Table 10. Adjustment Scores and Marital Status

Marital Status	Total Number	1st Quartile	Per Cent 2nd Quartile	3rd Quartile	4th Quartile
Single:	15	25	44	13	19
Male	7	43	43	14	—
Female	8	12	38	12	38
Married:	71	24	17	26	33
Male	47	26	13	24	37
Female	24	21	29	29	21
Widowed and divorced:	65	26	32	23	19
Male	22	37	18	27	18
Female	43	21	39	21	19

Males: $X^2 = 9.03$; $P < .20$
Females: $X^2 = 2.71$; $P < .90$

relative to household arrangements. The subjects were asked to specify whether they lived alone, with spouse, with children, or with others. Again, men living with their wives appeared to be better adjusted than did those living alone or in some other arrangement. Nearly 40 per cent of the men living with wives attained the high adjustment quartile while about the same proportion of those living alone fell in the low adjustment class. For women, differences in living arrangements were not related to adjustment score. For both sexes, those residing with "others" had the lowest proportions in the high category and the largest proportion in the lowest adjustment quartile. Distribution of adjustment scores classified by household arrangements is shown in Table 11.

Table 11. Adjustment Score and Household Arrangements

Household Arrangements	Total Number	1st Quartile	Per Cent 2nd Quartile	3rd Quartile	4th Quartile
Alone:	58	24	29	23	24
Male	21	38	19	29	14
Female	37	16	35	19	30
With spouse:	70	24	29	23	24
Male	46	26	13	24	37
Female	24	21	29	29	21
Other arrangement:	26	31	39	15	15
Male	11	37	27	9	27
Female	15	27	46	20	7

Total: $X^2 = 10.0$; $P < .20$
Males: $X^2 = 5.73$; $P < .50$
Females: $X^2 = 4.71$; $P < .70$

Income and Social Adjustment

The median income of the study group falls in the interval between $1,000 and $1,500. The exact median could not be determined since respondents were asked only to indicate the class interval in which their income would fall. The income range was from nothing in the case of a few individuals who were solely dependent on and resided with children or relatives, to more than $5,000 in the case of a few retired farmers or business men. It should be kept in mind that the data represent the income of both single and married couples. It will be recalled from the discussion above (see Table 11) that about 40 per cent of the subjects were residing alone, nearly one-half with husband or wife, and only about one-sixth in other arrangements. About half of the women were widows and residing alone.

Compared with the income distribution of heads of households aged sixty-five and over for the United States as a whole in 1960, a large proportion in this study would fall in the income level described as "destitute" by the Bureau of the Census. Slightly less than one-third (30 per cent) received incomes less than $1,000 compared with 9 per cent of families for the United States[5] (Consumer Incomes, U. S. Bureau of Census Series, P-60, No. 37, p. 27). About three-fifths had incomes ranging between $1,000 and $3,000 and 13 per cent received more than $3,000. Corresponding figures for the United States as a whole were 43 per cent and 48 per cent. Certainly we do not have here a picture of a particularly prosperous group of individuals. On the other hand, the distribution of incomes

Table 12. Income Distribution for Older Persons for Missouri Small Towns; Missouri Survey; Casey County, Kentucky, and the United States, in Percentages

Income	Missouri Small Towns 1962 Households	Missouri* Survey 1959 Households	Casey Co.,** Kentucky, 1959 Males 60 yrs. and Over	United States,*** 1960 Families
	(N = 142)	(N = 1533)	(N = 312)	(N = 3,653,000)
Under $1,000	30	38	60	9
$1,000—2,999	57	46	23	43
$3,000 and over	13	16	7	48

*Aging in Missouri, Report to the White House Conference, 1959.
**E. Grant Youmans, *Aging Patterns in a Rural and Urban Area in Kentucky*, University of Kentucky Agricultural Experimental Station Bulletin.
***Consumer Income, U. S. Bureau of Census, Series P60, No. 37, p. 27.

in this village sample did not differ greatly from the distribution found among 1700 respondents studied for the Missouri report to the White House Committee on Aging.[6] The income status of both Missouri samples

---

[5]Consumer Incomes, United States Bureau of the Census, Series 60 P. No. 27, p. 27.
[6]Aging in Missouri, p. 176.

was also considerably higher than reported by Youmans for a rural county in Kentucky.[7] For purposes of comparison we are including a table which shows the distribution of incomes for this study as compared with others referred to above (Table 12).

As might be expected there is a fairly close relation between income and adjustment score (Table 13). Since 70 per cent of these older people received incomes less than $1,500 we have divided them into three categories: under $1,000, $1,000 to $1,500, and over $1,500. It will be noted that there is no difference in adjustment scores for those with incomes less than $1,000 and those between $1,000 and $1,500. Between the highest group and the two lower income levels, however, the difference is clear. At the lowest income level only 14 per cent scored in the highest quartile, while close to one-third ranked in the low adjustment category. For those with incomes at $1,500 or more the situation was reversed, with 14 per cent in the low adjustment group and nearly one-half in the high class.

Table 13. Social Adjustment Score and Income

| | | Per Cent | | | |
Income	Total Number	1st Quartile	2nd Quartile	3rd Quartile	4th Quartile
Less than $1,000	42	29	38	19	14
$1,000—$1,499	57	30	28	26	16
$1,500 or more	43	14	16	23	47

$X^2 = 20.2; P < .05$

The subjects were also asked to report both their sources of income and their major source of income. Income was received from a great variety of sources as reported by 147 persons. These can roughly be classified into five major categories: private income such as earnings and savings, investments etc.; income from children or relatives; old age assistance; Social Security; and other sources. Since many persons reported more than one source of income the totals in Table 14 are greater than the number of respondents.

Table 14. Adjustment Score and Source of Income

| | | Per Cent | | | |
Source of Income	Total Number	1st Quartile	2nd Quartile	3rd Quartile	4th Quartile
Wages, earnings, savings	62	16	18	23	43
Children or relatives	14	29	36	21	14
Old age assistance	47	32	36	23	9
Social security	78	26	23	26	25
Other	64	25	20	22	33

$X^2 = 20.24; P < .01$

[7] E. Grant Youmans, op. cit., p. 11.

About 40 per cent reported income from private resources, more than half received benefits under Social Security, approximately one-third were old age assistance recipients and one-fifth had their incomes supplemented by contributions from children or relatives. About two-fifths also had other sources of income.

The individuals with private sources of income were clearly better adjusted than those in other classes, with 44 per cent scoring in the "high" adjustment group and only 16 per cent in the "low" category. Recipients of old age assistance show up most poorly in terms of their self-satisfaction, with less than one-tenth in the "high" group and nearly a third in the "low." Older persons who received income from children and relatives also seemed less contented and satisfied than other income classes. Differences are significant beyond the one per cent level.

In spite of the relatively low level of incomes, most felt they "had enough to get along on" while only about one-fifth reported that they "couldn't make ends meet." A few said they had "more than enough" to meet their needs. Satisfaction with economic resources was also related to adjustment score as shown in Table 15. Those who said they could not

Table 15. Adjustment Score and Income Adequacy

Adequacy Of Income	Total Number	Per Cent			
		1st Quartile	2nd Quartile	3rd Quartile	4th Quartile
Can't make ends meet	27	42	22	11	15
Enough to get along	108	20	29	26	25
More than I need	13	15	8	23	54

$X^2 = 19.27; P < .01$

"make ends meet" showed significantly lower proportions in the well-adjusted group and higher proportions in the "low" adjustment class than did either of the other two classes. Over half of those who had no economic worries were in the highest adjustment quartile.

Education and Adjustment

About one-tenth of the older people had completed less than five grades. About half of them had finished the eighth grade and almost exactly one-third had attended high school, with about half of these completing a high school education. Eleven persons (7 per cent) claimed to have attended college. This was an unexpectedly large proportion considering that even the younger persons in the sample must have received their education forty-five to fifty years ago, when a high school education and college attendance were much more rare than at present. If the above distribution of educational attainment is compared with the nonfarm population of Missouri, the study group appears to be the better educated. While four-fifths of the nonfarm population of Missouri aged 65 and over did not go beyond the eighth grade; in these three small towns, less than 60 per cent had completed eight grades or less. For the nonfarm population in general 20 per cent had some high school education, in this group 40 per cent. A slightly higher proportion had attended college among the subjects in this study than among the older people of the state's nonfarm population.[8]

The relationship between formal education and social adjustment was not statistically significant, although there was a tendency for the better educated to show up a little better than the less well educated.

Social Participation and Adjustment

Arnold Rose has suggested that some persons in their later years, rather than being alienated from others and disengaged, as hypothesized by Cummings and Henry,[9] tend to develop an "aging group consciousness" and an "aging subculture" which provide a network of interrelationships and serve as a social and cultural milieu for the older person. Such a group self-consciousness and participation system tends to develop as older persons come to share common interests based on common past experience, and as a consequence of withdrawal or exclusion from other interrelationships.[10] If this is true, we would expect that self-satisfaction and contentment, as reflected in the adjustment score on our scale, would be related to degree of identification with such a subculture or to "aging group consciousness." Unfortunately, the design for this study was prepared before Rose's ideas were available, so that the study is not specifically oriented to support or refute the hypothesis. Nevertheless, while the data cannot show that social participation is primarily with age mates, nor that it revolves dominantly around themes of concern to older persons, it would be expected that some relationship would show up between participation and the measure of self-satisfaction and contentment which we have referred to as the "adjustment score."

One further point needs comment before proceeding with the discussion of the details of social participation and adjustment. It might be contended that the scale is itself a measure of participation and, therefore, that a high correspondence between participation and score is inevitable, since responses to questions on participation and responses to the scale items measure the same thing. This argument may have some merit. Items 4, 5, 6, 7, and 8 of the scale are concerned directly with participation. They are, however, expressions of attitudes toward participation rather than descriptions of participation behavior. In fact, all the items on the scale are designed to probe the "feeling" of the subject about himself rather than to ask him to describe how he behaves. The problem then becomes: To what degree is there a correspondence between what the

---

[8]Bureau of the Census, Census of Population, Series PC-1, 27D, Table 103, (Missouri).

[9]Elaine Cummings and W. E. Henry, Growing Old, New York: Basic Books, 1961.

[10]Arnold Rose, The Subculture of the Aging (Chapter 1, this volume).

individual says he does and how he feels about himself, and his behavior?

Children and Family. The subjects were parents of relatively small families. Of the 135 individuals who had been married, 27 or exactly one-fifth, had no living children. About one-fourth had two, one-eighth had three, one-tenth four and 12 per cent had five or more. The average number of living children per married individual was just over two, while the average number per individual who had any children was 2.6. The proportion who had living children was slightly less than reported by Youmans in his Kentucky study.[11] Of those who had living children, 10 per cent lived in the same household with children, considerably less than was the case among the rural sample in Kentucky. Nearly 40 per cent had children residing in the local community or elsewhere in the County, while three-fifths lived elsewhere.

Contacts with children appeared to be frequent, nearly 90 per cent of them reporting that they saw one or more of their children at least once a week while about 40 per cent had daily contacts. This does not support the stereotyped picture of older people abandoned by children who have migrated from the rural area. There seems to be little relationship, however, between either residence of children or contact with them and adjustment score. Only when asked whether or not their children were interested in the parents' welfare was there a tendency for those reporting lack of interest to score lower on the adjustment scale. The difference, however, did not rise to the 5 per cent level of significance. Over 90 per cent of all subjects did report their children as being interested in their parents' welfare.

While 85 per cent had living brothers or sisters, less than 10 per cent of them resided in the local neighborhood. On the other hand, nearly one-fourth of those with siblings had at least monthly contacts with them. Of those who had monthly contacts with siblings a higher proportion (one-third) scored in the upper quartile than those who saw them less frequently (one-seventh). The differences were significant at the five per cent level.

Friendship Patterns. Informal visiting with friends and neighbors seemed to play a more important role in influencing feelings of satisfaction and contentment than did contacts with children or siblings. The subjects were asked if they had friends in this neighborhood, if their friends visited with them in their own homes, if they visited in the homes of friends, and if they would like to make new friends. Only three persons replied that they had no friends in the community, and only eight said they had no friends who paid them visits in their own homes. Almost one-half reported that their friends visited in their own homes daily or frequently, while a little more than two-fifths received visits from friends occasionally. Although the frequencies in some of the categories are so small that differences do not rise to the 5 per cent level of statistical significance there is a consistent tendency for those with more frequent visits from friends to score high

[11]Grant Youmans, *op. cit.,* p. 42.

on the scale. For those who receive no visits, those who are visited occasionally, and those who are visited frequently, the percentages scoring in the high quartile were 13, 21, and 31, respectively, while in the low quartile they were 38, 26, and 22.

Active visiting in the homes of friends and neighbors was considerably less frequent than receiving friends, but was more closely related to the adjustment index. About one-fifth said they did not visit in the homes of friends, two-fifths reported daily or frequent visiting and two-fifths visited occasionally. The adjustment score was consistently related to the amount of socializing in the homes of friends. In the high adjustment class were only 3 per cent of those who did not visit friends in their homes, one-fourth of those who visited occasionally and two-fifths of those who visited frequently. At the other extreme, in the lowest adjustment class, the corresponding proportions were 55 per cent, 16 per cent and 18 per cent. Statistically, the differences were highly significant. To what extent these differences are the direct result of differences in the degree of social contacts with friends or to what extent they are a function of health and degree of mobility is difficult to determine. As discussed earlier, persons in good health and with no mobility handicaps scored much higher on the scale than did those in poor health or handicapped as to mobility. With a larger number of cases it would be possible to hold the health factor constant and separate its influence on social adjustment from that of social participation. Table 16 shows the relationship between visiting in the homes of friends and adjustment score.

Table 16. Adjustment Score and Visiting in the Homes of Friends and Neighbors

		Per Cent			
Visiting Patterns	Total Number	1st Quartile	2nd Quartile	3rd Quartile	4th Quartile
No visiting	31	55	26	16	3
Occasionally	58	16	34	26	24
Daily or frequently	56	18	21	21	40

$X^2 = 19.8; P< .01$

The major proportion (nearly 60 per cent) were quite satisfied with their friends and neighbors and felt no need to make new friends. It is interesting, however, to note that those who said they wanted to make new friends made up twice as high a proportion of the persons in the "well" adjusted group as did those who were indifferent to new friends (35 per cent as compared to 18 per cent). In the "low" adjustment class were 18 per cent of the former as compared with 29 per cent of the latter. The differences were significant at the 5 per cent level. To save space the table illustrating this point will be omitted.

Church and Religion. As is the case in most small rural communities, the church is dominantly the formal organization in which most persons participate. Over 90 per cent of the sample belonged to some church. In the five midwest state studies for the White House Conference, correspondingly high proportions of church membership were noted, ranging from 70 to 95 per cent.[12] In the Missouri study about 80 per cent belonged to a church, but it will be recalled that this study included a substantial sample of urban dwellers where church membership appeared to be less common.[13] A somewhat smaller proportion in the present study, however, participated in church activity. About three-fourths were active participants, slightly less than found by Youmans in Casey County, Kentucky.[14] Of the 137 church members, 115 belonged to three denominations: Baptist, Methodist, and Christian.

Both church membership and participation appeared to be related to adjustment score, although the relationship between membership and adjustment was not quite statistically significant. The latter is shown in

Table 17. Adjustment Score and Church Membership

Church Membership	Total Number	Per Cent 1st Quartile	2nd Quartile	3rd Quartile	4th Quartile
Members	137	23	26	24	27
Non-members	14	50	29	14	7

$X^2 = 6.32; P < .10$

Table 17. With larger numbers it seems probable that membership in a religious organization would be more clearly related to adjustment score, as has been shown in a number of studies.[15] The number of non-church members was too small to make a convincing comparison.

Table 18. Participation in Church Activity*

Church Participation	Total Number	Per Cent 1st Quartile	2nd Quartile	3rd Quartile	4th Quartile
None	43	56	28	14	2
**One or more	121	7	26	27	40

$X^2 = 54.25; P < .001$

*Includes Sunday morning service.
**Some persons participated in more than one activity.

Most older persons (about 60 per cent) confined their church partici-pation to attendance at Sunday worship services. Less than 10 per cent

[12]Taves and Hansen, As Senior Citizens See Themselves, p. 20.

[13]Aging in Missouri, op. cit., p. 171.

[14]Youmans, op cit., p. 45.

[15]See especially Robert M. Gray and David O. Moberg, The Church and the Older Person, Grand Rapids, Michigan: Wm. B. Eardmans Pub. Co., 1962.

attended weekly prayer services and about one-fourth of the women took part in church clubs, circles and the like. Participation in religious organizations was closely related to adjustment score as is shown in Table 18. Only 2 per cent of those who reported no participation scored in the high quartile while more than half fell in the lowest group. Among the participants the corresponding percentages were 41 per cent and 7 per cent. These results are quite consistent with Moberg's analysis of the relation between church membership and participation and adjustment among the respondents interviewed in connection with the five state studies of aging for the White House conference of 1961.[16] To what extent poor health and physical infirmities, which also are closely related to low morale, account for the low participation in religious activity, is again difficult to determine. Certainly the health factor plays an important role in influencing all forms of participation.

Civic and Social Participation. Opportunities for participation in formal groups, other than the church, tend to be limited in very small communities. Less than two-fifths participated in civic, social or professional groups. Relatively few, however, saw any need for additional organizations or expressed any interest in joining such groups if they were to be organized. Proposals for "golden age" clubs, "senior citizens" organizations or other

Table 19. Participation in Civic, Social and Professional Organizations

| | | Per Cent | | | |
Participation	Total Number*	1st Quartile	2nd Quartile	3rd Quartile	4th Quartile
Participants	78	14	17	30	39
Non-participants	95	31	30	21	18

$X^2 = 14.94$; $P < .01$

*Total of 56 participants in three types of organizations.

such groups seemed to have little appeal. This was also consistent with Moberg's results.[17] Membership in all social, civic and professional organizations combined was only half that of membership in the communities' churches.

Table 20. Adjustment Score and Voting in the Last Election

| | | Per Cent | | | |
Voting Behavior	Total Number	1st Quartile	2nd Quartile	3rd Quartile	4th Quartile
Voters	121	20	27	23	30
Non-voters	28	51	21	21	7

$X^2 = 12.99$; $P < .01$

[16]Ibid.
[17]Ibid.

In spite of limited participation in secular organizations, participants ranked considerably higher on the social adjustment scale than did non-participants. This is shown in Table 19.

Two-fifths of the participants scored in the high quartile as compared with less than one-sixth in the lowest group. Corresponding proportions for the non-participants were one-fifth in the high class and nearly one-third in the low group.

As an additional index of participation, voting in the last election was used. Four-fifths of the 149 respondents who had answered this question participated in the last election. This is far higher than the proportion of eligible voters participating in the last election in these counties. Voters scored definitely higher on the social adjustment scale than did non-voters. Table 20 shows this relationship. Significantly higher proportions of the voters scored at the upper end of the adjustment continuum and lower proportions at the lower end than was true for non-voters. We recognize again that poor health and lack of mobility may have been a factor in both non-voting and low adjustment score.

As a final measure of the relationship between social participation and adjustment score a measure of participation was constructed. This was done by assigning weights to membership and participation in both religious and secular organizations and computing for each individual an index which might serve as a measure of general participation. Subjects were then classified into four participation quartiles of low to high participation. The relation between adjustment score and participation index is shown in Table 21. Since all measures of participation have shown a significant relationship with adjustment score, it is not surprising that a combination of all measures should show an even higher correlation. Note that there is a steady and consistent increase in the proportion of subjects in the "high" adjustment group, with an increase in the value of the participation score, as well as a decrease in those in the lowest participation quartile. At the other extreme, those with the lowest level of participation are overwhelmingly concentrated at the lowest level of adjustment.

Table 21. Adjustment Score and Index of Participation

		Per Cent			
Participation Index by Quartile	Total Number	1st Quartile	2nd Quartile	3rd Quartile	4th Quartile
Lowest	21	61	24	10	5
Second	60	32	31	27	10
Third	46	11	31	26	32
Fourth	24	4	13	17	66

$X^2 = 51.88; P < .001$

Attitudes Toward the Community. On the assumption that attitude toward self and feelings of satisfaction and well-being should show some relationship to attitude toward and feelings about the community, a few questions were asked, designed to bring out community attitudes. Among other queries the people were asked to rate their town as a good, fair, or poor place to live. Almost nine out of ten were quite satisfied with their community and rated it as good. When those giving the community a good rating were compared with those rating it as fair or bad on the adjustment scale it is apparent that the relatively dissatisfied also were those with the low rating on the scale. One-half of the latter scored in the low quartile as compared with one-fifth of those who thought their town was "good." Differences between the two groups were significant at the 5 per cent level.

Table 22. Adjustment Score and Community Rating

| | | Adjustment Score Per Cent | | | |
Rating	Total Number	1st Quartile	2nd Quartile	3rd Quartile	4th Quartile
Good	131	21	28	25	26
Fair or bad	18	50	17	11	22

$X^2 = 7.86; P < .05$

The people were also asked how they felt about public expenditures for school bond issues and other public improvements. Half of them approved such expenditures and half either were opposed, doubtful, or had no opinion. Classifying these two categories on the adjustment score gave the results in Table 23.

Table 23. Adjustment Score and Attitudes Toward School Bond Issues and Other Public Expenditures

| | | Per Cent | | | |
Attitude Toward Public Expenditure	Total Number	1st Quartile	2nd Quartile	3rd Quartile	4th Quartile
Favor	76	16	26	22	36
Opposed or indifferent	73	36	26	24	14

$X^2 = 12.96; P < .01$

It is clear that those who tend to be more optimistic about themselves have a much stronger tendency to view the community in a favorable light and to favor its improvement than do those whose adjustment score suggests that they are discontented, unhappy, or more poorly adjusted. Differences are significant beyond the .01 level.

Table 24. Adjustment Score and Appreciation of the Needs of Older People

| | | Per Cent | | | |
Attitude	Total Number	1st Quartile	2nd Quartile	3rd Quartile	4th Quartile
Favorable	82	17	22	27	34
Negative or indifferent	67	33	33	19	15

$X^2 = 11.62; P < .01$

Finally, the respondents stated their opinions about the general perception which the community had of its older people and what role they thought older persons might occupy in the community. The specific questions asked were: Do you feel that people here appreciate the needs of older persons, and do you feel that older people still have something to contribute to the community? The distribution of scores on the adjustment scale of those who replied are shown in tables 24 and 25.

Table 25. Adjustment Score and Contribution of Older People to the Community

| | | Per Cent | | | |
Attitude	Total Number	1st Quartile	2nd Quartile	3rd Quartile	4th Quartile
Favorable	81	16	21	25	38
Negative or indifferent	67	33	33	23	11

$X^2 = 18.12; P < .001$

Elaboration of the results is unnecessary. Those who feel that there is public appreciation of the needs of older people, and those who take a positive stand with respect to the role which older persons still have to play in the community, score much higher on the scale than those who are negative or uncertain about these questions.

Summary

In final summary, we may recapitulate the characteristics of those persons who appeared to be most contented with themselves and whom we have described as well-adjusted. Those with the higher scores tended to have a youthful self-conception, good health and higher income than did those with lower scores. The well-adjusted were more frequently married than widowed or single, although this was primarily true for men rather than for women. The better-adjusted had a higher degree of social participation, both in informal contacts with friends and neighbors as well as in formal associations such as religious organizations, social and civic groups. Contacts with children or siblings showed no close relationship to adjustment score and seemed to be less important than those with friends and neighbors. Those lacking contacts with their families, however, were so few that comparisons were not very conclusive. Finally, those who took a favorable view of the community and their place in it tended to be definitely better adjusted than those who were more negative in their outlook.

Certainly it is difficult to say that the data have either supported or refuted Rose's hypothesis of an "aging group consciousness" or an "aging subculture."[18] We have demonstrated that in these three little towns most

[18]Chapter 1.

older people are enmeshed in a network of close and intimate personal relations and, contrary to the argument of some writers, do not feel themselves isolated or alienated from the community in most cases. We have also shown that those persons having the greatest degree of participation and holding more favorable attitudes toward the community tend also to have higher adjustment scores.

This study, from the beginning, has been conceived as a pilot study. It is hoped that it may be extended to include an adequate sampling of small communities in the state and also to penetrate more deeply not only into the quantity of participation of older people, but also into its quality, nature, and characteristics. If this can be done, more light could be thrown on the hypothesis of Rose and others who are interested in the sociology of aging.

SELECTED BIBLIOGRAPHY

Aging in Missouri: Report of the Missouri Committee for the White House Conference. Appendix I, Aging in Missouri. (Peter New), Joseph Stokes, ed., Jefferson City, 1960.

ALLEGER, DANIEL E.: The role of agriculture in retirement adjustment: A study of five Florida counties, Rural Sociology, 20: 124-31, 1956.

BRITTON, J. H.: Residence, Parent Role Complex in the Later Years, Pennsylvania Agricultural Experimental Station, 8: 11, 1960.

BRITTON, J. H., and W. G. MATHER: Personal and social adjustment of rural older persons, Journal of Gerontology, 12: 436, 1957.

BRITTON, J. H., W. G. MATHER and A. K. LANSING: Expectations for older person in a rural community: living arrangements and family relationships, Journal of Gerontology, 16: 156-62, 1961.

COWLES, MARY L.: Housing and associated problems of the rural farm aged population in two Wisconsin counties, Rural Sociology, 21: 239-48, 1956.

GALLOWAY, ROBERT E.: Farmers Plans for Economic Security in Old Age, Kentucky Agricultural Experimental Station Bulletin, 626, 1955.

GINZBERG, R., W. C. BRINEGAR, F. K. DUNN and WILMA OLSVARY: Improvisations in rural Iowa, in Wilma Donahue, ed., Housing the Aged, Ann Arbor: University Michigan Press, 91-103, 1954.

KAPLAN, J. and P. TAIETZ: The rural aged, Geriatrics, 13: 752-57, 1958.

KLUG, D. G., and H. M. SAUER: Study of Elderly Persons: Adjustment in the Later Years, South Dakota Agricultural Experimental Station Farm and Home Research, 12: 7, 1961.

MAYO, S. C.: The Young, the Old and the Mature, North Carolina Agricultural Experimental Station Bulletin, 365, 1949.

———Social participation among the older population in rural areas of Wake County, N. C., Social Forces, 30: 53-59, 1951.

MORRISON, DENTON E. and G. ALBERT KRISTJANSON: Personal Adjustment among Older Persons, Technical Bulletin 21, Agricultural Experimental Station, Brookings, S. D., 1958.

MCCRARY, J. S.: The Role, Status and Participation of the Aged in a Small Community, Washington University, unpublished manuscript. (Abstract in Dissertation Abstracts, 17: 914, 1957.

McKAIN, W. C. and E. D. BALDWIN: Old Age and Retirement in Rural Connecticut: East Haddam a Summer Resort Community, Agricultural Experimental Station Bulletin 278, Storrs, Conn., 1951.

MULHOLLAND, H. B.: Rural aspects of the problem of aging, National Conference on Rural Health, 12: 66-69, 1957.

ROSE, ARNOLD: The subculture of the aging: a topic for sociological research,
The Gerontologist, 2: 123-27, 1962.

SEWELL, W. H., C. E. RAMSEY and L. J. DUCOFF: Farmers Conceptions and
Plans for Economic Security in Old Age, Wisconsin Agricultural Experimental Station Bulletin No. 182, 1953.

SKRABANEK, R. L., B. LLOYD and LEWIS J. DUCOFF: Texas Farmers and Old
Age and Survivors Insurance, Texas Agricultural Experimental Station
Bulletin 886, 1958.

SMITH, T. LYNN: The aged in rural society, in The Aged and Society, Cham-
paign, Ill.: Industrial Relations Research Association, 1950.

STONE, CAROL L., and W. L. SLOCUM: Thurston Counties Older People, Washington Agricultural Experimental Station Bulletin 573, 1957.

TAIETZ, PHILIP, GORDON STREIB and MILTON BARRON: Adjustment of Retirement in New York State, Cornell University Experimental Station Bulletin
919, Feb., 1956.

OLAF LARSON: Social participation and old age, Rural Sociology, 21: 229-38,
19??.

TAVEL MARVIN and GARY HANSEN: As Senior Citizens See Themselves: A
Survey of Aging in the Midwest, Midwest Council for Research in Aging,
June, 1961.

WARREN, R. L.: Old age in a rural township, in New York State Joint Legislative Committee on Problems of the Aging, Legal Document 35, Albany,
N. Y., 1952.

YOUMANS, E. GRANT: Aging Patterns in Rural and Urban Areas in Kentucky,
Kentucky Agricultural Experimental Station Bull. 683, 1963.

III

Adjustment and Participation in Specific Activities

The Social Dilemma of the Aging Leisure Participant*

STEPHEN J. MILLER

Introduction

The contemporary concern with aging as a social problem emphasizes the material implications of growing old—for example, the economic circumstances, housing arrangements and health needs of the aged. However, a material concern with the problem, based on the assumption that the problems of aging are basically economic, neglects the social-psychological implications of growing old. In recent years, an increasing number of students of social phenomena have approached the subject of aging in terms of its more subtle aspects, that is, the effects of growing old on the social-psychological life and future of the person.[1] The object of the latter approach is to place the role of the aging in Western culture in its appropriate historical and cultural context and to explore the implications of the contemporary social scheme for the older person.

*The writer is indebted to Community Studies, Inc., for the assistance which allowed him to explore the social situation of the aging leisure participant and write this paper. He is grateful to Edwin A. Christ, Howard S. Becker, Francis G. Caro, Arnold M. Rose, Warren A. Peterson, and Gregory P. Stone, for their conversations, comments, and criticism.

[1] A statement of the social-psychological problems, in terms of interactionist concepts, is presented by Ruth Shonle Cavan, Self and role in adjustment during old age, in Human Behavior and Social Processes, Arnold M. Rose, ed., Boston: Houghton Mifflin Co., 1962, pp. 526-35. Clifford Kirkpatrick also offers a brief but adequate example of a social-psychological approach to the problems of aging, Sociological implications of retirement, Geriatrics 10: 312-17, 1959. Cf., for example, the writings of Ernest W. Burgess, Irwin Deutscher, Robert J. Havighurst, and Arnold M. Rose.

The aspect of aging which readily lends itself to social-psychological considerations is that of occupational retirement, possibly the most crucial life change requiring a major adjustment on the part of the older person. The urban-industrial society of today has developed a policy for old age which provides pensions, housing, and medical care when the worker, due to his advanced years, is no longer required to trade the major part of his time spent in labor for the necessities of subsistence. The implication of such a policy is that the worker, by his lengthy labor, has earned the right to rewards which will make his remaining years comfortable. However, it is tacitly understood, the worker is allowed to retire and receive the accompanying benefits in order to facilitate his removal from a role which he is arbitrarily considered no longer capable of playing.[2] In these terms, retirement is not so much a system of rewards as it is the instrumentality by which the removal of those persons perceived as useless is accomplished. The older persons who are so removed suffer a debilitating social loss—the loss of occupational identity and a functional role in society.

Though the occupational identity and role of each person, as well as the succession of other conventional roles, are taken very much for granted and are a matter of little conscious concern, they are the crucial elements which facilitated the varying social role performances demanded of each person. Work not only provides the individual with a meaningful group and a social situation in which to develop a culturally approved and personally acceptable self-concept, it also provides an identity with an accompanying rationale for his performance in other social situations as well. The occupational identity of the individual establishes his position in the social system at large, allowing others to evaluate his status and role and providing a context within which his social activity can be interpreted. For example, the occupational identity of a male places him in appropriate relationship to other members of his family and supports his roles in that social system. Before retirement, the role of "husband" as mediated by his occupational identity results in high prestige and supports the various roles that the person is expected to assume in the family system. It would be extremely difficult to maintain the role as "head of the family" if an occupational identity were lacking. The occupational identity is that which provides the social substance by which other identities are maintained, various roles are coordinated, and the appropriateness of social activity is substantiated. In other words, the retired person finds himself without a functional role which would justify his social future, and without an identity which would provide a concept of self which is tolerable to him and acceptable to others.[3]

---

[2] A number of socially based factors—for example, the impact of continued employment of the aged on a labor force becoming increasingly more concerned with unemployment—operate to maintain a retirement policy, though the original reasons for doing so, such as failing health, are fast disappearing.

[3] Ernest W. Burgess, in Aging in Western Societies, Ernest W. Burgess, ed., Chicago: University of Chicago Press, 1960, pp. 20-21, refers to the loss of occupational identity and a functional role as a state of being "imprisoned in a roleless role."

In anticipation of the day when the worker retires, the day he will lose his occupational identity and functional role, he is encouraged by his family, friends, and even employer, to adjust by spending his leisure time in some activity which holds meaning for him. It is assumed that the problem of retirement adjustment will be solved if the individual will engage in some sort of activity which will fill his leisure time. Such an attitude to the value of leisure for adjustment during old age takes little note of the associational aspects and social needs of life. For example, solitary leisure will not provide a person with the opportunity for interpersonal contacts and might well only increase withdrawal from social participation.[4] Even those activities which provide interpersonal contacts may not provide a social group which will replace former co-workers. A recreational group may facilitate the development of an identity, but, as Cavan notes, the identity may well be limited and may not be expressible in any group except the recreational group itself.[5]

If leisure activities are to provide a new role, the retired person must engage in some meaningful activity, appropriate in terms of cultural values, which will afford him a rationale for a social identity and a concept of self. In the case of the retired person participating in leisure activity, this poses a dilemma—that is, he must justify an identity in terms of his leisure activity which is by definition "superfluous in character, extraordinary . . . and stands apart from work."[6] "While [leisure] has a definite value," writes Cavan, "to make a career of recreation, hobbies, and the like, goes against deeply instilled values."[7]

The present chapter outlines the dimensions of such a dilemma and the manner in which it is dealt with, as observed by the writer and expressed by elderly participants in systematized leisure groups. The focus will be on the following points: (1) the nature of leisure in contemporary culture; (2) the rationale for leisure, i.e., the manner in which the older person may justify his career of recreation; (3) the portent of embarrassment, the effects of age on actual participation in the systematized leisure group.

Data for this study were gathered from a number of sources: (1) interviews and correspondence with involuntarily retired leisure participants; (2) local and national newspapers, specific interest publications, etc., which were searched for information regarding the participation of elderly persons in systematized leisure groups; and (3) the literature concerned with aging, work and leisure. In addition, the writer entered the social worlds of leisure

---

[4]Kutner, and others, in a study of older people, found morale and personal satisfaction related to participation in activities which provided achievement, status and recognition, in addition to simply filling leisure time. Cf. Five Hundred Over Sixty, New York: Russell Sage Foundation, 1956. Christ, in Chapter 6, makes the same point.

[5]Cavan, op. cit., pp. 529-30.

[6]Gregory P. Stone and Marvin J. Taves, Camping in the wilderness, in Mass Leisure, Eric Larrabee and Rolf Meyersohn, eds., Glencoe, Ill.: Free Press, p. 296, 1960.

[7]Cavan, op. cit., p. 529.

participants, posing as, and being accepted as, a young man interested in learning the intricacies of various activities. The fact that the writer was conducting field work was disclosed to only a few people. The field observation differed from systematic observation in that it was neither constant nor total—that is, field work was restricted to a level of activity which approximated the normal career of a novice participant.

The Tradition of Leisure and the Aging

Work and leisure are complementary components of human activity. The style and pattern of both are reflections of the culture of the time and subject to the societal ideology, development, and organization which are characteristic of that culture. "The problems faced in studying leisure," writes Gross, "are both consequence and cause of the problems faced in studying work, for one is usually defined as the absence of or preparation for the other."[8] In the light of the complementary nature of work and leisure, a consideration of the leisure activity of the aging must also be concerned with the social developments which affect work and the cultural values which dominate the social circumstances. Historically, three work-leisure traditions are discernible: (1) pre-industrial: traditional work alleviated by related customs, practices, and rites; (2) industrial: the polar opposition of work and leisure, and (3) post-industrial, or contemporary: the integration of work and leisure.[9]

The pre-industrial culture, based on an agricultural economy and rural in character, lacked (with few exceptions) any commercial recreation or organized leisure which would draw the person away from his work and family. Clement Greenberg notes that most work during this period was "work on the land . . . adulterated more or less by irrational practices—customs, rites, observances—that, conceived of originally as means of helping work . . . actually furnished occasions *inside* work for relief from the strain of its purposefulness."[10] The cultural tradition did not separate work and leisure, nor did the demands of labor segment the life of the person into a world of work and another of the family.[11] The place of work was the home and the economic and social roles of the person were functional, useful, and significant in terms of the family. The problem of finding some activity which would amuse or occupy the old was non-existent, for the old remained functional until failing health forced withdrawal from most, if not all, activity.

---

[8]Edward Gross, A functional approach to leisure analysis, Social Problems, 9 (Summer 1961), p. 2.

[9]Cf. Mass Leisure, pp. 38-43, 54-64, 86-95, and 253-63; also, David Riesman, The Lonely Crowd: A Study of the Changing American Character, New Haven: Yale University Press, 1950.

[10]Clement Greenberg, Work and leisure under industrialism, Commentary, 16 (July 1953), p. 58.

[11]Foster Rhea Dulles presents a picture of rural life in Chapter 26 of America Learns to Play, New York: Appleton-Century Co., 1950.

The rise of industrialization and the accompanying urbanization not only affected the economy of Western culture but had a decided impact, one still felt on the social life of the person. Work, which required organization and structure to assure efficiency and production, became the central life interest, regulating economic, social, and family life. Unlike the pre-industrial period, the place of work was no longer the home but a place removed from home and family. The extended family was becoming a thing of the past and its social life, which the aged had previously enjoyed, was rapidly curtailed.[12] "To the exact end of greater productivity," writes Greenberg, "capitalism, Protestantism, and industrialism have brought about a separation of work from all that is not work which is infinitely sharper and more exclusive than ever in the past."[13] The time not occupied by work, that is, leisure, became diametrically opposed to productive labor, and the Puritanical tradition emphasizing work as the major cultural value was established. In this period, a man's work as the basis of his social identity has its roots, and his functional role, in terms of cultural values, emerges. In accordance with the structured nature of work, labels were attached to various types of work placing men in categories and locating them in the patterned activities of society. The functional role and occupational identity of the person were readily available for evaluation by his social audience. A man's conception of himself, developed and reinforced by his recurrent social relationships, was directly influenced by his work.[14]

A society which emphasizes efficiency and production will define the value of the person in terms of his ability to play a functional role in the industrial system. When, as in the case of growing old, an individual is subject to limitations which presumably reduce his ability to play such a role, he must be removed and replaced—hence, the development of an industrial policy toward old age requiring occupational retirement at some point in the life cycle. The industrial changes not only established the occupational role as the basis for social identity but also developed the manner

---

[12]A number of studies indicate that the decline of the extended family may have been exaggerated. See for example: E. Litwak, The use of extended family groups in the achievement of social goals, Social Problems, 7:179, 1959-60; Scott Greer, Urbanism reconsidered, American Sociological Review, 21:22, 1956; Marvin B. Sussman, The help pattern in the middle class family, American Sociological Review, 18:27, 1953. The writer favors the opinion expressed by Rose in Reactions against the mass society, Sociological Quarterly, 3, October, 1962, p. 323: "The authors of all this research implicitly assume that their findings prove that extended family relationships have not declined as much as earlier sociologists thought. However, in the absence of earlier or longitudinal studies, the alternative hypothesis can reasonably be entertained that the extended family did deteriorate badly in Western cities toward the end of the nineteenth century and has been reviving somewhat within the last few decades."

[13]Greenberg, op. cit.

[14]Cf. Everett C. Hughes, for a discussion of the influence of work on the conception of the self, in Social Psychology at the Crossroads, New York: Harper & Bros., 1951, pp. 313-23.

in which that identity could be subverted.[15] The constituent elements of work—a work group and a work situation—are the basis of a culturally approved and personally acceptable self-concept. These are lost to the older person when he is retired from the vocational world to which he has belonged. In place of work, the retired worker is offered leisure which is the opposite of work and of doubtful, if not negative, cultural value. In such cultural circumstances, leisure participation cannot reduce the problem of finding a new identity and role. The lack of an occupational identity is culturally characteristic of the old, and leisure activity only supports the position of the old as non-meaningful, non-functional or, at best, superannuated.

In post-industrial society, or, for the purposes of this study, in the "American" pattern of work and leisure, work remains as the basis of social identity. However, the nature of work has changed. The boredom of routine and the performance of repetitive tasks has been noted and acknowledged—in fact, work no longer requires the degree of routine and structuralization that was necessary during the early phases of industrialization. The nature of contemporary work has led to attempts to make work meaningful and reduce fatigue and boredom, though, as Riesman notes, "by and large [they] succeeded only in making it more time-consuming and gregarious but not more challenging."[16] Whatever the reasons, though apparently they are functional, a characteristic of the twentieth century is the re-introduction of leisure into work. Gross explains the situation in terms of the concept of adaptation as follows: "Work results, inevitably, in fatigue and often in boredom, and one of the forms of leisure—recreation—is essential here insofar as it restores, though, it is recognized, it may not always do so."[17] The nature of work has come a full cycle and is marked by related customs, practices, and rites, furnishing occasions of leisure inside work to alleviate fatigue and boredom.[18] Outside work, Rose indicates that "the opportunity to engage in something creative, even if only in a hobby association, provides a compensation for the deadening effect of working on a simple repetitive task . . ."[19]

In addition to the reduction of opposition between work and leisure, a cultural value which affects the American pattern of life is the contemporary emphasis on action. In much the same manner as work and leisure were earlier opposed, activity of any sort is valued over non-activity. "People who are not active," writes Buhler, "are made to feel useless, indeed, even

[15]Cf. Chapter 15 in this volume, where such identity subversion is referred to by Coe as "devaluation" or "depersonalization."

[16]David Riesman, Leisure and work in post-industrial society, in Mass Leisure, p. 367.

[17]Gross, op. cit., p. 5.

[18]The image of the congenial group at the office water-cooler, the coffee break, and even the office Christmas party, which is fast disappearing, are examples. Of course, all such customs and practices are not occasions of leisure but may as well be worker rebellion, "goofing off," etc. Cf. Riesman, op. cit., p. 372.

[19]Arnold M. Rose, Sociology, New York: Knopf, 1956, p. 330.

worthless."[20] Hence, in terms of the contemporary scheme of work and leisure, in which leisure has become a value, the older person showing an interest in some activity, no matter what, is less subject to social labelling as "non-functional," "ineffectual," and so on, than one who disengages himself from activity. It would appear, therefore, that leisure has the potentiality to reduce the social loss to which the aged are subject and facilitate adjustment. (It is not the contention of the writer that participation in leisure activities is the only way in which the aging may establish a new identity and achieve social adjustment. The cultural trend which sets the old apart from the young may well result in the formation of a social group of the aging which will provide them with a meaningful social audience, a frame of reference, and a range of participation which will help them to develop a new identity, role, and self-concept [see Chapters 1 and 2 by Rose].) This new social situation of the aging is a way open to those of the aging who wish to remain socially active but resist "the cultural trends which are making the elderly more segregated from other age categories. They may employ their leisure as an opportunity to establish an identification with other groups in society. That is, they may reduce their social loss by participating in activities which are respected in general by others as well as by those of their own social category or group.

The Rationale for Leisure

The problem of social adjustment faced by the leisure participant is apparently rooted in the lack of social substance (meaning) or cultural value of the majority of ways in which he might occupy his leisure time. In the light of the values which are characteristic of the American pattern of life, the person who is now free of work should be socially able to overcome the problem by spending his leisure in some activity which holds meaning for him and is generally respected by others. If this were the sole dimension of the problem (as is the contention of this writer and that of Christ [see Chapter 6]), then participation in systematized leisure groups would not only fulfill the social needs of the older person, but facilitate the development of a new social identity as well. However, the work which the person is ultimately free of is exactly that which has allowed him to justify leisure or, as Mead has put it, work is not only necessary to obtain the means but the right to leisure.[21]

An employed person, prior to his retirement with its loss of occupational identity, is free to use his leisure time any way he chooses. No matter how far removed from work, so long as the leisure activity is not otherwise culturally defined as deviant, a rationale is readily available to justify its legitimacy. The interrelationship of work and leisure as a necessary condition for adjustment to and performance of work plus the value placed on

[20]Charlotte Buhler, Meaningful living in mature years, in Aging and Leisure, Robert W. Kleemeier, ed., New York: Oxford University Press, 1961, p. 35.

[21]Cf. Margaret Mead, The pattern of leisure in contemporary culture, Annals of the American Academy of Political and Social Science, 313: 11-15, 1957.

activity are the constituent elements of that rationale. Those who are engaged in work are not required to justify their leisure since socially supportive factors, occupational identity, and the halo effects of labor operate on the social circumstances to do just that. On the other hand, the older person operates without such support. For example, the employed person occupied in leisure activity of some sort will, more often than not, be perceived by others as engaged in "recreation" whereas the retired person engaged in the same activity will be perceived as occupying his "free" time. In other words, the numerous activities in which the older person may participate, thereby reducing the degree of his social loss, may have no further cultural value than that they are "activity."

A career of leisure (play) is characteristic of the socially immature (children) or the socially superannuated. For the aging individual, it can only serve to add to his social loss, negating any social benefits that might be derived from remaining active by serving to reinforce a definition of him as superannuated. There are other leisure interests—for example, genealogy, the writing of an ethnic cook book, family history or autobiography, to mention a few encountered by the writer—which are often considered to be interests peculiar to people nearing the end of life, the assumption being that such interests are reflections of a concern with perpetuating life in some manner or with death itself. It is also likely that participation in groups created for, and composed of, older people only which offer an old age identity—for example, the Golden Age Club or Senior Citizens—only aggravate the social situation of the aged by reinforcing the stereotype of the older person as one set apart from those who are not old. This is one of the factors in the development of an aging subculture. The older person, in order to establish a new identity and acceptable self-concept on the basis of leisure must first establish a rationale for the activity on which he bases that new or altered identity. He must legitimatize it in some manner other than in those terms which sanction leisure for the very young and the old. The leisure activity of the retired and elderly must, therefore, be in some way appropriate in terms of traditional and contemporary values which do not apply specifically to the aging but to the population in general.

The retired leisure participant is in the unique position not only of having to find an activity in which to participate but, once having found such an activity, if he wishes to reduce his social loss, also of establishing a meaningful rationale for participating in that activity at all.[22] The current compatibility of work and leisure offers the older person an opportunity to change his social situation—that is, to establish the cultural value of his leisure which will act as the basis for a social identity. He may do so by introducing, in much the same fashion as leisure has been introduced into

---

[22]The writer has excluded from the analysis those who have voluntarily retired, those who are subject to failing health, and the social isolate, a number of whom were met and interviewed during field work but wanted nothing more than "to be left alone."

work, aspects of work into his leisure.[23] The person may choose among the alternative avocations available to him those which offer the possibility of establishing a rationale, in keeping with the cultural and social circumstances, which will serve to legitimitize a social future. The problems posed by aging and retirement have been well documented, but the manner in which the aging introduce aspects of work into leisure and establish an appropriate rationale for this has, to the writer's knowledge, been explored only incidentally.

The attitude regarding meaningful leisure participation and the elements of a rationale are expressed in the following comments of the wife of an aging leisure participant: "Hobbies are eccentric when you never make anything [useful] out of them or get anything [monetary] out of them." It is not simply participation in *some activity* which is desirable but participation in activity with culturally acceptable manifest goals, or at least with latent implications of being useful and/or gainful in some way.

A notable example of the way in which such a rationale for useful and gainful activity may be established is the case of the aging American collector of coins, stamps, books, antiques, and what have you. (See Christ, Chapter 6.) The gainful rationale for a leisure activity is similar to the major perspective of these modern collectors which parallels and reflects the current and growing interest of the general population in the stock market, investment programs, etc., and is focused on the monetary and investment aspects of collecting. The following comments by a collector with some thirty years experience bring this out:

It [leisure] can be commercial. When I started [collecting] people took the time and trouble of assembling a collection. The real interest was research and the arrangement of your collection . . . the originality of showing, too. Only a little attention, if any, was paid the expense of collecting. Now, thousands and thousands of people, because of the publicity that has been given to the value of coins and stamps, have gone into collecting. They [collectors] go to banks and to the mints and buy coins and put them away for the future or sell them. In other words, they are *investors* and *speculators.*

A search of the literature pertaining specifically to numismatic, philatelic and similar leisure activities offers further evidence of this contemporary view of such activity. The literature is heavily laden with advertisements urging the hobbyist to invest in coins, to invest profitably in stamps, or to "cash in on your hobby," as well as others which offer investment lists of money-making items, investment bulletins, market reports, and labor guides —all of which purport to be *necessary* for the leisure participant. There also exist the usual people and organizations that one expects when dealing in a marketable commodity. For example, besides the dealers who buy and trade in the commodity, there are others who will accept the collected objects or products of leisure as security for money-lending transactions.

---

[23]For the writer, the fact that many retired individuals remain partly active in the world of work, or embark on a new work career, strengthens the argument for the need of a rationale by the aging. What could be a more appropriate work-oriented rationale for activity with which to support an identity and role than work itself?

In addition to the collector who may also be an investor and speculator, there are, for example: (1) persons who buy, restore or otherwise improve, and sell antiques, household goods, appliances, etc.; (2) the handicraftsman, who may find a market, or at least a demand, for what he makes; and (3) the do-it-yourself person who manages to supplement the neighborhood or community demand for the skilled labor which is becoming increasingly expensive and difficult to find. These examples certainly do not exhaust the variety of activities which lend themselves to a gainful rationale; they are illustrative of the way in which personally meaningful activity can be infused with the aspects of work which are culturally understood and accepted. It is interesting that many of the retired individuals who are so engaged deny that their activity is work in the traditional sense. The activity is enjoyable, interesting, or challenging, only incidentally profitable, and rarely, if ever, demanding. If what is labelled leisure were to be defined as work, the person would be expending himself entirely in work without leisure and operating in a manner contrary to the American pattern of work and leisure.

Other types of activity, though in no way economically productive, are contributory to the general good and may be exploited by the person as a basis for a new social identity. Those who offer their leisure service to others—the retired cabinet-maker who supplements the efforts of the high school manual arts teacher, or the older woman who becomes an integral part of the community hospital as a volunteer—enjoy high public esteem by acting in a subordinate auxiliary role to more essential work roles. These activities and the roles which the aged may assume in them are part of larger work systems which lend them vicarious status, authority, and other meaningful satisfactions which operate to the social advantage of the participants, allowing them to establish a useful rationale for their leisure. Though slightly more difficult for the participant to legitimitize, activity which is educational or develops a skill or talent also provides a social future since there exists the potentiality for its future productive application.

The economic perspective on leisure reflects a contemporary cultural value, an economic ethic, so to speak, while the supplemental nature of other useful activities meets certain societal needs. Activity in these spheres will be defined as acceptable if presented in the appropriate terms. It will not be perceived as far removed from work since, like work, it offers a reward for labor or is contributory to work in some way, factors which can be employed in evaluating the worth of the individual. Any activity presented in these terms has recognizable goals which lend it meaning and, therefore, is considered as an understandable activity in which to engage. Though the writer is concerned with the social life of the aging the analysis is relevant for other types of persons in the social system as well. As a case in point, the person who engages in avocational pursuits without thought of work or profit is considered at best a dilettante. It is probable that the person who manages to develop an avocational interest into a profitable business represents more of the American dream than is imagined. In the latter instance, the individual, by introducing aspects of work into his avocation, has established a rationale which enables him to meet the societal expectations that he be productive and his role meaningful. It is when this rationale is absent that the activity of the individual is defined as superfluous and lacking in meaning, and when the individual is subject to the stigma and embarrassment of being considered an idler which makes the support of an acceptable identity difficult, if not impossible.

Though the gainful and useful rationales are discussed as if they were distinct activity themes, they are not mutually exclusive, but rather variations of the same mechanism. For example, any collecting activity which is characterized by a gainful rationale also requires the classification, description and, in some cases, the authentication of that which is collected, procedures providing an opportunity to employ a useful rationale for such activity. The rationale for leisure is similar to the mechanism which Becker and Carper refer to as the *acquisition of ideology* in their discussion of the development of identification with an occupation.[24] In much the same manner as the person preparing for an occupation attempts to determine the worth of the activity on which his identity will be based, the aging retired person establishes the worth of his avocational activity to legitimitize a base for a new social identity—that is, to justify a career of leisure.

The Portent of Embarrassment

The rationale for leisure, once established, provides a background for the social participation of the involuntarily retired person which allows the projection of a meaningful and acceptable social future on which may be based a new identity. However, the person is not entirely free of the social implications of his retirement and advanced age. He has not left his occupational role in a way which reflects favorably upon his ability to perform a work role, in particular, and other social roles, in general— that is, he is still, though somewhat less, vulnerable to the stigma attached to retirement.[25] In addition, he must continue to operate in an age-graded social system which defines the aging as people who are most likely to fail. Once the person has selected a leisure activity which offers him a social future and identity, that social future remains subject, within the leisure group, to the implications of retirement and aging.

If a rationale is to be maintained and an identity developed, the person, once he participates in some activity, must be capable of supporting a role in the group throughout the social interactions and performances required of a participant. Identity, writes Gross and Stone, "must be continually

24Howard S. Becker and James W. Carper, The development of identification with an occupation, American Journal of Sociology, 4 (January, 1956), p. 297.

25Cf., for a discussion of social loss, Erving Goffman, On cooling the mark out: some aspects of adaptation to failure, Psychiatry, 15: 451-63, 1952; also, Goffman, On face-work, Psychiatry, 18: 213-31, 1955.

reaffirmed, must be maintained, and provision made for repair in case of breakdown."[26] The result of identity breakdown—a social occurrence which belies what the person has announced he is, and what he is capable of, by assuming the role of participant—is embarrassment. In turn, embarrassment makes continued role performance difficult and undermines the foundation of the new identity.

The results of embarrassment are most often treated in terms of their implications for the continued social participation of the person. That is, once an embarrassing encounter or performance has taken place the question is, what are the social implications for the person.[27] The implications of embarrassment may also be considered in a related though somewhat extended manner: A person who is aware of some socially restrictive factors to which he is subject may anticipate the embarrassing encounter and subsequent identity breakdown, and choose either to curtail or end participation entirely. That is to say, embarrassment not only has implications for continued but also for initial social participation as well. In any analysis of the leisure careers of the aging the factor of social embarrassment, including both actual and anticipated embarrassing encounters, is particularly important. The implications of actual embarrassment for social performance have been treated elsewhere by others and apply equally to the situation of the aging leisure participant; the writer will concern himself with anticipatory embarrassment, that is, the portent of embarrassment, as a correlate of social participation and its implications for social performance.

The obvious implication of the portent of embarrassment is that it may result in the aging person excluding himself from social interaction with others not of his social category. The frequency of possibly embarrassing encounters would be higher for the person participating in the social system at large than for the person limiting his participation to groups which are composed of members who share his circumstances, problems, and concerns —that is, a group of older people. The portent of embarrassment operates, in addition to the circumstances noted by Rose (Chapter 1), to facilitate the development of a subculture of the aging. It is sufficient for the purposes of this essay, since Rose discusses the subculture of the aging at length, to note that the positive affinity many other people have for each other may well be the result of negative expectations of social participation with persons not of their social category or group. A similar argument may be offered in explanation of the apparent decline in social participation of people as they grow older—that is, they become increasingly aware of the possibility of social embarrassment and make preparations accordingly.

In the work conducted by the writer, those of the aged who were only

---

[26]Edward Gross and Gregory P. Stone, Embarrassment and the analysis of role requirements, a paper read at the meetings of the Midwest Sociology Society, Milwaukee, Wisconsin.

[27]Cf. Gross and Stone, op. cit., pp. 2-4; Goffman, op. cit., and Embarrassment and social organization, American Journal of Sociology, 62: 264-71, 1956.

somewhat active offered the obvious reasons, such as, health, expense, transportation, as explanations of their limited participation. These recurrent themes, however, seemed to be but reflections of a more socially based reason for non-participation. In general, non-participation or limited participation was a matter of choice resulting from a feeling of inability to meet the demands of participating. The person who embarks on a leisure career is announcing who he is and what he is capable of; he is committing himself to a role which requires he meet the expectations of others. If he feels or finds that he is unable to meet these expectations, or expects to encounter difficulty which would subvert his identity, role, and self-concept, he is likely to choose not to make such a commitment or limit his participation to those aspects of an activity which reduce the possibility of identity subversion and embarrassment.[28]

As observed by, or told to, the writer, the instances of embarrassment which caused the aging leisure participant particular concern, and were usually accompanied by decreased commitment or participation, were one or more of the following types: (1) an inability to reciprocate due to family, economic, or health circumstances which could be attributed to aging; (2) requests for the performance of a task which the person was assumed prepared for, or capable of, because of his age and experience but for which he was not—that is, the peculiar position of the older person as a novice and subordinate to other younger participants; and (3) faux pas which announced to other participants that the person and his knowledge were superannuated ("How would you like some young wise-guy to tell you things aren't done that way anymore?")[29] The portent of embarrassment, anticipation of the occurrence of such social incidents, has, for a least a minority of the aging, a decided effect on the pattern of their participation. It influences a number of variables usually employed to measure social participation—for example, number and type of voluntary associations, frequency of attendance at meetings, number of contacts with others engaged in the activity, and the social category of those who are contacted.

It is possible that the portent of embarrassment may assume such proportions that it inhibits entirely participation in any specific activity. If a person, under these circumstances, withdraws from the activity but replaces it with another which reduces the portent of embarrassment (assuming a rationale to which he may subscribe is available), he continues to minimize his

---

[28]The writer, in an analysis of the client-practitioner relationship as a social transaction, has hypothesized that a person will increase or decrease his commitment and participation in terms of the degree to which the activity offers a favorable social-psychological outcome. Cf. Stephen J. Miller, The new car salesman and the sales transaction, a paper presented at the meetings of the Midwest Sociological Society, Milwaukee, Wisconsin, 1963.

[29]A general type of embarrassment, which applies equally to persons of the social categories as well as the aging, occurs when the motive for participation becomes obvious as peculiar to the aging, e.g., "having something to do," and contrary to the generally accepted motivation for participating. Cf., for a discussion of such embarrassment, Goffman, Embarrassment and social organizations.

social loss and retains a base for an identity.[30] On the other hand, the person who withdraws and has no suitable replacement places himself in a situation in which he is subject to the additional stigma of non-activity. The attempt to erase the stigma of non-participation usually results in solitary activity of some sort, for example, reading. A number of aging leisure participants who were interviewed had done this and employed health, expense, and transportation, as an understandable rationale for non-participation in systematized or group leisure.

The aging are not operating alone to avoid embarrassing encounters and reduce the portent of embarrassment. The aging participant is perceived as the person most likely to fail and "becomes defined as someone who must not fail, while at the same time arrangements are made to decrease the chances of his failing."[31] The arrangements made by other participants to assure that embarrassment will not occur is not the result of an altruistic or patronizing concern with the problems faced by the aging. Embarrassment not only incapacitates the embarrassed person but others with whom he is interacting as well. When the identity of the aged participant is subverted, it is difficult for others to continue interacting and inhibits the social performances of all participants. "Embarrassment," writes Gross and Stone, "exaggerates the core dimensions of social transactions, bringing them to the eye of the observer in an almost naked state, for embarrassment occurs whenever some central prop in the transaction has unexpectedly given way so that the whole encounter collapses."[32] The occurrence of embarrassment incapacitates *all* the performers for the continued and possibly future performances of their roles by disrupting identity and destroying the assumptions the performers have made about each other—assumptions on which they operate socially.

In the specific social system in which the older person is active, the portent of embarrassment may, and often does, result in his being excluded from interaction with other participants not of his social category. The result is increased interaction between the aging who share a common situation and the development of a group identification of the aging within the system. However, in systems which are not specifically for one social category, it is necessary for purposes of structure and cohesion that the roles played by the various participants be integrated into the role-scheme of the system. The need for such integration does not prohibit the development of a group of the aging who share a common social life *outside* the system and identity with each other within the system. In fact, such a group of the aging would reduce further the portent of embarrassment by permitting social life outside the system to be conducted on the basis of common interests, concerns, and shared problems. This is a situation which, since those involved are subject to similar embarrassments, reduces the chance of failure outside the system disrupting performance and subverting identity within the system.

---

[30]The portent of embarrassment offers an interesting scheme for the analysis of the acceptance of some and the rejection of other activities by the aging.

[31]Goffman, On cooling the mark out, p. 499.

[32]Gross and Stone, *op. cit.*, p. 2.

The anticipation of social difficulty for and with the aging by other participants encourages them to make available to the older person a role which he is capable of assuming, or at least less likely to fail at playing. The problem of embarrassment and its ramifications are avoided by providing the aging participant with a social role within the system which he can maintain—that is, an identity system of interactions and performances of which he is capable. The older person is induced to assume this role identity by others who ascribe the necessary attributes to him and interact with him as if he did possess these attributes. There is only a subtle difference between such action and the exclusion of the aging from social roles which would form in a public identity that might be discredited or subverted.

There are numerous cases which illustrate the action taken to avoid embarrassment for and with the aging. The family in need of home improvements, which the aging handy-man who services the neighborhood is not capable of carrying out, may call him in for consultation before hiring an outside firm or tradesman to do the work. If the handy-man had not been involved in some manner, by implication his identity would have been subverted and future interaction with him impossible. On the other hand, if he had been expected or allowed to do the work, the anticipated unfavorable outcome would have been equally embarrassing and ended the relationship. The solution was the ascription of certain qualifications as an expert to the handy-man, attributes inducing him to assume a role which he was capable of performing and allowing him to maintain his identity.

To be a member of a subordinate auxiliary group is also defined in a way which allows for a supportable identity for the older person. The main organization which the auxiliary group serves has a staff with occupational and professional roles which operate to delimit the activity of the older person. For example, the hospital volunteer is prohibited by their operational codes to assume the role of doctor, nurse, or of any other ancillary hospital personnel—only those activities which may be and are delegated to the volunteer are undertaken. The tasks delegated—for example, personal contact with the patient or with the family of the patient—comprise a role, status, or relationship, and are never such as to make great demands on the person.[33] In more formal recreation, i.e., systematized leisure, possibly the most important roles the older person may play are that of "recruiter" and "socializer." By recruiting and socializing new members the aging participant not only facilitates the entrance of the novice into the activity group, but also contributes to group structure and the efforts of the group to perpetuate itself. Other roles for which the aging are considered suited and likely not to fail at are "learned elder," "keeper of the tradition," and, for those who have specialized and are recognized as proficient, "expert" or "resource person."

Though participants in social and leisure groups attempt to induce the aging participant to assume roles which lessen the portent of embarrass-

---

[33]The observation of the aging volunteer was the result of a number of research projects the writer has conducted in general hospitals.

ment, as noted earlier, the reasons are not patronizing. In addition to the services mentioned, such roles for the aging act to reduce the demands made on the time and energy of other participants. The roles have intrinsic value and are not artificially created to meet the needs of the aging. In these terms, the "most challenging problem of solving the present roleless role of the aging" is not so much *inventing* new leisure patterns and functional roles for the aging—which will only become culturally defined as "for the old"—as determining what roles presently exist in the social system, related to a specific sub-system and offering vicarious satisfactions, that can reduce the socially debilitating loss accompanying occupational retirement.[34]

---

[34]Burgess, *op. cit.*, p. 21, has stated that the most challenging problem calls for a solution to the "roleless role of the aging" by *inventing* new leisure activities and functional roles for the aged. The writer takes little issue with Burgess but does object to what, by implication, appears to be the attempts to establish a social system for the aging apart from the rest of society—it is his contention that social adjustment for the aging can only be achieved when they are integrated into the social system at large and that there are processes and mechanisms by which many of the aging do just that.

CHAPTER 6

The "Retired" Stamp Collector: Economic and Other Functions of a Systematized Leisure Activity*

Edwin A. Christ

Introduction

In 1961, the Midwest Council for Social Research on Aging included within its program as pertinent for investigational efforts, the following questions, among others:

1. What are some satisfying roles for older people? How does one help to create and maintain such roles?

2. Can knowledge about the habits and attitudes of better adjusted older people be used to help the ones who are less well adjusted?[1]

Focusing on the broad problem-area concerning personal and social adjustment of the retired aged, it may be assumed that role deterioration most visibly and perhaps most dramatically occurs in familial and economic spheres of activity. The "empty nest" so vividly described by Deutscher,[2] is more than a nominal situation, and involuntary retirement from gainful employment is the rule. For the male, emotionally equipped only for work, economic role emasculation contributes to what has been called "the depressive retirement syndrome."[3]

---

*A less detailed and documented version of this paper was read at the annual meeting of the Midwest Sociological Society, Milwaukee, Wisconsin, 1963.

[1] A Program of Research on Aging in the Midwest (Kansas City, Missouri: Community Studies, Inc., 1961), p. 23.

[2] Irwin Deutscher, Married life in the middle years: a study of the middle class urban postparental couple (unpublished doctoral dissertation, University of Missouri, 1958.) passim.

[3] Don E. Johnson, Geriatrics, Vol. 13, May, 1958. Lancet Publications, Inc. pp. 314-19.

Loneliness, friendlessness, unhappiness, general anxiety and frustration, a sense of uselessness and pointlessness in life are characteristic of severe role impairments, especially where status losses are irrevocable and irreversible, and where the usual modes of behavior expected in the society are difficult or impossible to maintain.

The nature of contemporary urban familial and economic structures, specifically nuclear family orientations and forced occupational retirement on the basis of chronological age, may be seen as exerting pressures upon the aged to relinquish highly meaningful and essentially satisfying roles.[4] The trauma resulting from these role divestments presumably varies directly with the intensity or degree of physical and psychic, as well as economic and temporal, investments in such roles. Thus, it would seem that the trauma associated with role-divestment is especially severe and unrelieved when individuals have no truly significant other reference positions with equivalently significant role functions, in which they might find room for meaningful expansion and maintenance of a satisfactory self-conception.

It is suggested that one satisfying area for expansion in significant role interrelationships may be found in those forms of leisure which have become organized around an interest in some kind of activity in which the participants can find comfortable and meaningful roles. Such forms of leisure as those which involve the collecting of something systematically— for example, stamps, coins, antiques, mineral specimens, fossils, first editions, memorabilia[5]—have evolved complex associational structures. In addition to local, regional, national, and international "clubs,"[6] literally hundreds of these activities have established channels of communication to keep devotees "in touch," not only with each other, but with developments in their respective fields of interest. The media of communication include societal organs, newspapers and magazines independent of societal sponsorship, syndicated columns in metropolitan newspapers, and the like.[7] Additionally, and importantly, these interest groups have a market. The extrinsic value of objects is expressed in dollars and cents; catalogs listing prices are available and are brought up-to-date frequently to reflect supply and demand.[8] In short, these leisure activities simulate a complete social system, including associational and communal norms, statuses and roles, prestige and esteem, authority and leadership, together with all other attributes of

---

[4]The writer is indebted here to R. W. Habenstein, Professor of Sociology, University of Missouri, for ideas pertaining to the nuclear family in contemporary American society, and especially for the consequences of retirement in familial roles.

[5]The writer has compiled an index of nearly 800 kinds of leisure activities involving "collecting" various systematically classified objects.

[6]Some of the larger associations in the United States claim upwards of 20,000 dues-paying members.

[7]One newspaper, a weekly catering exclusively to stamp collectors, has a circulation of over 60,000. A weekly magazine for coin collectors has a circulation of 175,000.

[8]In the United States, the Standard Postage Stamp Catalog, now in its 97th year of publication, lists and prices over 200,000 varieties of the world's postage stamps.

both formal and informal organizations. Participants may, and actually do, become involved in such activities to such an extent that for them these activities constitute their primary world of reality.[9]

The Philatelic Complex

It has become apparent to the author since his earlier exploratory study[10] that the philatelic complex—its associations, communications system, economic structure—has fruitful implications for the sociology of work, the sociology of leisure, and social gerontology.

The subculture, or microcosm of systematized leisure, may have deeper and broader meaning for the aged, as Donahue has suggested in summarizing the characteristics of well-adjusted older persons:

Their life patterns have been found to include plenty of work and a liking for it; strong and varied interests; economic independence and security; good health, many social contacts; hobbies and recreations; living in the present rather than in retrospect; a desire to live life over again; and a predominance of spiritual and mental factors.[11]

Systematized *philatelic* activity includes an economic component of immense proportions.[12] Significantly, the bulk of the dollar-volume of philatelic business conducted by the gainfully employed, non-retired is transacted without face-to-face contact between buyer and seller. Among the retired, however, transactions involve principally face-to-face relationships.

The Sample

Since 1950 the writer has been able to maintain continuous contacts with 53 stamp collectors who are retired, and who began their philatelic activities upwards of ten years prior to retirement (Md. = 26.6 years). Some of these 53 persons were initially contacted long prior to retirement. Fifty-one of them are male. Fourteen had residentially relocated after retirement.

---

[9]The Adult Stamp Collector, unpublished doctoral dissertation, University of Missouri, 1957. See especially pp. 205-49 for behavior patterns and themes of participation in stamp collecting.

[10]Christ, *op. cit.* Systematized stamp collecting is one of a large number of similar avocations, the chief institutional structures of which are associations, commerce, and communications. Essentially sedentary, philately is an overwhelmingly urban phenomenon (72.45 per cent city dwellers, 19.40 per cent suburbanites), principally involving males (86.3 per cent), and has tenacious durability (52.0 per cent of the males had collected stamps twenty years or longer). Participational patterns specifying positional interdependencies in group situations were found more often than otherwise to have primary group characteristics.

[11]Wilma Donahue, Changes in psychological processes with aging, in Clark Tibbitts, ed., Living Through the Older Years, Ann Arbor: University of Michigan Press, 1949, p. 84.

[12]Christ, *op. cit.*, p. 2: "The philatelic trade includes professionals who operate retail stores and/or mail order businesses, conduct auctions, liquidate philatelic estates by private treaty, or who are in the export-import and/or wholesale business. These enterprises are conventionally structured." Recent estimates place the dollar-volume of trade annually at well over two hundred million dollars.

Twenty-three had become involved in philately economically. All those with whom contacts have been maintained are personal friends, the initial friendship bond having been a mutual interest in philatelic endeavors of one sort or another.

All 53 persons have been extensively interviewed. Initially, the interviews were nondirective. Later, some re-interviews were conducted and tape-recorded. The primary purpose of the interviews was: (1) to discover why since retirement these people systematically or unsystematically had for economic reasons entered the philatelic market, and (2) to discover in what ways the economic advantages were conceived.

A majority of the initial interviews were conducted in the informal atmosphere of a stamp collectors' convention or meeting, with the informant drawn into "conversation" in the way so often employed by David Riesman.[13] Not more than three or four of those interviewed were at that time cognizant of any motive on the part of the researcher beyond the awareness that they were conversing with a fellow stamp collector. The only criteria for selecting informants were: (1) they were retired; (2) they had collected, but had not purchased or sold stamps for monetary gain prior to retirement. At the time of the initial interviews, 21 were engaged openly in cash transactions above and beyond what was considered to be "normal" in exclusively stamp *collecting* activities. Two others, both voluntarily retired, were also involved economically, but not in such a way that they could be identified as "stamp dealers." Several general guidelines were employed by the researcher in the "conversations" with the 21 who were dealing in stamps: (1) the interviewee had rented bourse space, and/or (2) the interviewee was engaged in transactions in philatelic materials known to be outside his own collecting interest area, and/or (3) the interviewee was selling only.

Reconstruction of interviews which were not tape-recorded was done as soon as possible after the conclusion of these "conversational sessions." The rationale for this was that the exploratory nature of this study would necessarily require flexibility to permit the subject to define the interviewing situation in such a way that unguarded ventilation of personal and social beliefs would be facilitated.

To preserve some homogeneity, the two females who were interviewed, and who were economically involved in philately, were not included in this report. Hence, this study concerns 51 retired males, aged sixty-five or older. Particular attention was given to those who had *involuntarily* retired and who had continued stamp collecting activities after retirement.

---

[13]Apropos of this, Professor Riesman, in conversations and in correspondence with the writer during the period 1952-55 suggested, among other things, that stamp collecting was a "paper mining" activity, similar in economic function to the "imaginary" horse-race betting or stock market investing he had noted among rail commuters. It is true that many stamp collectors assiduously make periodic accountings of the increase in "catalog value" of their collections, and for those who do this the activity resembles some of the goals of games which have become miniature economic systems, the most familiar and long-lived of which is *Monopoly. Vide* Christ, *op. cit.*, p. 233 *et seq.*

Retirement, Relocation and Economic Activity

During the data-collecting process, two factors appeared particularly relevant to the manner in which engagement in stamp collecting as a systematized form of leisure activity functions for the retired aged. These factors were the dichotomies expressed as: (1) whether the individual had retired voluntarily or involuntarily, and (2) whether the individual had, following retirement, made a significant residential relocation. Table 1 shows the distribution according to these variables.

Table 1. Distribution of Fifty-One Retired Stamp Collectors by
Mode of Retirement and Residential Location vs. Economic
Engagement in Philatelic Activity

Economic Engagement in Philatelic Activity	Mode of Retirement				
	Voluntary		Involuntary		
	Residential Location		Residential Location		
	Relocated	Non-Relocated	Relocated	Non-Relocated	Totals
Economically engaged	2	0	12	9	23
Not economically engaged	10	2	6	10	28
Totals	12	2	18	19	51

In Table 1, change in residential location was arbitrarily taken to mean that the subject had been relocated for two or more consecutive years in a state other than the state in which he resided prior to retirement. In 6 instances, there was relocation and also a second place of residence. In 4 of these 6 instances, the relocation included part-time residence in the pre-retirement location, but at least four months of each of two consecutive years or more had been spent in residence in the place acquired after retirement.

Only 2 of the 12 voluntarily retired were engaged, following retirement, in any economically productive way in philately. Neither was engaged in transactions in postage stamps, per se.[14]

Twenty-one of the 37 "involuntarily retired" were engaged after retirement in economically productive ways in philately. Only one of these was not buying, selling, or trading in postage stamps as a commodity: He was receiving a very small monthly salary, operating expenses, and a commission as manager of the "exchange department" of a regional stamp society. The other 20 were engaged in profit-making transactions, with postage stamps as a commodity. Only two of these were involved to the extent that

---

[14]One had become executive secretary of a national philatelic organization and was paid a substantial salary; the other had become a philatelic writer, some-time lecturer, and "expertizer" of postage stamps in his particular field of competence, and sometimes received monetary compensation for his services. There was no particular pattern in these relocations to suggest that philatelic interests were a significant factor.

they actually conceived of themselves as "stamp dealers." At the same time, however, these two also thought of themselves as "retired," although one admitted he "made more money in stamps than he had ever made in any job prior to retirement." Neither of them had residentially relocated. Both had extensive businesses which included advertising, mailed literature, and the employment of help—yet, as entrepreneurs, they insisted they were "retired," for they conceived of the extension of philatelic interest in *avocational* terms—not as a *business,* or as self-employment.

Involuntary Retirement and Relocation. Although the 51 persons in the study are not claimed as representative or typical, certain relationships seem nevertheless to be worth noticing here in summary fashion. Positive economic orientation within the framework of participation in systematized leisure activity seems to vary directly with post-retirement residential relocation.[15]

Of the 12 relocated economically actives, all except one had relocated in places which were known to be philatelic centers because of a larger than usual concentration of stamp collectors. Four relocated in the Tampa, Florida, area; 3 in the Miami, Florida, area; 2 in the metropolitan Los Angeles area, and 2 along the Seattle-Portland axis.[16] None of these eleven had pre-retirement residences in the states of relocation. Most had migrated from the eastern and eastern North Central states.

Among the 6 non-economically oriented who had relocated, there was no *philatelic* pattern. These had migrated from similar pre-retirement locations. One relocated in Arizona, 1 in Iowa, 1 in West Virginia, and the other 3 in states contiguous to the state in which they had lived prior to retirement. Five of the six indicated there were important non-philatelic reasons for relocating which were primarily expressed in terms of familial orientations; the remaining one, who moved from Pennsylvania to Arizona, expressed a "health-climate" orientation.

The 11 of the 12 economically engaged who relocated where there were high concentrations of stamp collectors had familial characteristics which were not distinguishable in any visibly significant way from the 6 who were not economically engaged, with the exception that among the latter relocation seemed to occur within the first two years following involuntary retirement (5 of the 6 cases) whereas only 2 of the 11 who were economically engaged relocated during the first two years following retirement, although all had relocated within four years. There was some indication that several of the latter might not have relocated at all had not their economic involvement in philately occurred to facilitate their relocation—an observation

---

[15]Of 21 who engaged in the economic sphere of activity in the philatelic microcosm, 12 (57 per cent) had relocated; of those who did not engage in economic activity only 6 (38 per cent) of 16 relocated.

[16]This information is based upon an analysis of the circulation of a leading philatelic newspaper, Linn's Weekly Stamp News, Sidney, Ohio, whose publishers furnished the writer with statistical information based on data required for second-class mailing, together with data concerning newsstand sales in principal metropolitan areas.

which is reinforced by the prior observation that when they did relocate they did so in places where philatelic activity was high.

Involuntary Retirement and Economic Activity. Most of the philatelists who became systematically engaged in a role activity[17] including economic activity after retirement denied: (1) that they had ever had any serious thoughts or plans to extend their avocational activity in economic directions prior to retirement; (2) that they had in any systematic way engaged in this type of economic activity prior to retirement; (3) that their present engagement constituted a refutation of their status as "retired"; (4) that their enjoyment of stamp collecting was altered or diminished by dealing.

The following interview segment[18]—selected on the basis that it includes references to all four elements common to the rationale of self-conception and economic engagement in philatelic activity—presents these points of view, and, to some extent, how they came about:

A. To me, stamp dealing never entered my mind. The way I saw it, you couldn't collect and deal at the same time, because then you had to think of your collection as so much "merchandise." I love stamps too much.

Q. You couldn't part with a stamp?

A. That's right. I remember, once, when I was collecting bureaus. I had swapped some duplicate material for a Liberty 101 [a stamp worth about $100]. That was a red-letter day for me, 'cause I knew I'd never be able to *buy* one, and this one was a beauty. It was like floating on air. I sold it because a year later, a guy offered me $125 for it. I sold it because I figured I could replace it by buying another and still have money over. But the money went for other things. I was never able to get another Liberty.

Q. That's the only time you remember *selling* a stamp?

A. Well, there *were* times when I'd run into a little lot of something—like a town nobody else had, or was on the tough list. Maybe, I'd got a sheet somewhere. I'd keep a block and a single—put that aside *first*—and swap a few for something else I'd need, or if the guy didn't have anything I needed, I might sell one for a dime or a quarter—make expenses. Sometimes I'd have to go a hundred miles out of my way to crack a town that was tough—maybe kill half a day. I never charged anybody what I might of got—like, maybe the stamp was worth five bucks? I never did that sort of thing. I just wanted to break even. I didn't rook anybody like some do when they get the chance. I was no dealer.

Q. Do you still love stamps?

A. More than ever, I guess. I spend more time, now that I got it.

Q. But now it doesn't disturb you to sell stamps . . .?

A. Well, see, I don't make a *business* out of it! I don't sell what I *collect*.

---

[17]Cf. R. K. Merton, The role set: problems in sociological theory, British Journal of Sociology, 8: 106-20, 1957; also Neal Gross, Ward Mason, and Alexander McEachern, Explorations in Role Analysis, New York: Wiley, 1958, *passim.* The encounters in the economic role sector seem to subvert an identity, e.g., "philatelist," so that denial becomes a common conscious protest. Dealing is not typical in the role playing of the philatelist. Entry into the economic role sector requires a new perception, a new situational definition, a newly situated self. Cf. Erving Goffman, Encounters, Indianapolis: Bobbs-Merrill Co., Inc. 1961, Preface; and Leon Festinger, A Theory of Cognitive Dissonance, Evanston, Ill.: Row, Peterson and Co. 1957, p. 26.

[18]Interview with involuntarily retired, relocated man who had collected thirty-one years prior to retirement. Interview was tape-recorded following two earlier "conversation sessions."

Q.   I don't understand . . .

A.   Well . . . now, I'm old. I don't know how much I got left. I sloughed off my bureaus, mostly through the sales department, and most of my general collection except the Western states. I found out that selling the bureaus the way I did was *silly*, because only the good ones sold, and then the sales books were retired and I had the common ones left. And the money came in in dribs and drabs, and I spent it. I don't know where it went.

Q.   What about the state collections you *didn't* keep?

A.   Well, I sold those off intact, at first. A state at a time. I had a pretty good Indiana, and it went for I think $1,200. My Iowa was strong, and I got $900 I think out of it. It was those two collections gave me a chance to buy the place where we're living in Florida, now.

Q.   How did you feel about selling them?

A.   Oh, I got to a point where I wasn't adding much to 'em. I needed to cut down on the collection where I could handle it. I had over 200 volumes—regular dime store notebooks, but that took a lot of space. I settled on the Western states because there you don't have a lot of bulk.

Q.   How about the other states?

A.   Well *you* bought the Maryland, remember? And a couple others I sold intact too. Oh, yes—I kept the Florida. No particular reason except there's a lot of Florida collectors, and I guess I got about as good a Florida as most. I began taking the rest of the stuff to meetings. First, Ocala. I had the stuff up in my room, and funny the way it worked out. I had in mind to build up the Westerns, so I thought I could swap out some of the stuff. Well I spent a good deal of time in the bourse, and I didn't find anybody had any good Westerns—just new stuff I bought from the dealers, but I guess I spent $40 or $50 and was getting low on money. But I always did go hog wild. I bought what I had to have. Then I bumped into B——. He was in the bourse, and we were sitting together in front of H——'s table and he said he heard I was sloughing off state collections, and he came up to the room and I sold him Georgia for $550, and he said he'd heard about I was sloughing off and why didn't I let people know? Well, it never really occurred to me, but next time in Ocala I took a table in the bourse. I felt kind of queasy, you know? I didn't know the first thing about selling stamps, and I didn't do much. I guess I was sort of embarrassed. Well, most of them that came to my table, they wanted to pick and choose, and I didn't want to break any of the collections. I think I sold West Virginia at that meeting, and I made a deal to swap Maryland, but it fell through, and you bought it later. I swapped Delaware for a Western States collection, but there was only about a dozen in it I needed. But *that's* what started it.

Q.   What do you mean? Started what?

A.   Well, I had all this Western states stuff left over—duplicates. About twelve thousand, mostly California, Oregon, and Washington, and some pretty good Colorado. It was several weeks before the next Ocala meeting and I remounted 'em on approval sheets and priced 'em individually. I really had no way of knowing what they were worth, but at the Ocala meeting I sold about $200 worth, which right there was more than I figured the Delaware was worth, and I still had 95 per cent of 'em left over.

Q.   I guess you got a kick out of that?

A.   Oh yeah! It surprised me. I was worried about the expenses, but I hated to miss a meeting. So far I always been able to make expenses and enough over to keep the Westerns up.

Q.   Must be a lot of work, getting ready for the bourse?

A.   Oh . . . it takes a little time, but I really enjoy it. It's not like *work*, I mean —I fit it into my regular messing around with stamps, and I want to keep up on the Westerns. If I didn't do it, I'd not even be able to afford the new ones that come along.

Q.   But I guess that makes you semi-retired? I mean, after all . . .?

A. No, no! Not *me!* I don't let it get to be any drudgery. When I feel like it, I mount up a couple books, and then lay 'em aside. If I don't *feel* like it, I go do something else. I take care of the garden, or maybe the wife has something planned. No, I don't pin myself down. When something stops being fun, or I don't enjoy what I'm doing I *quit.* I didn't retire to get involved in some other kind of *work.* I don't sell anything I collect. If I buy something, I buy it because there's got to be something in it for the collection. Let the dealers have the profit—all I want is to make expenses for the meetings. I couldn't go beyond that because of the social security. I'm careful about that, and I don't come close to making $100 a month over expenses. But there's nothing coming in otherwise. Both my wife and me enjoy the meetings and we both get the social security. But it gets old sitting around.

Q. Well, wouldn't you at least call yourself a "collector-dealer"?

A. Some might say it's that way, but *I* don't think so. The bourse is a handy way to work things out. It's pleasanter than being up in the room, although at first I was embarrassed. I know a lot of folks around *think* I'm a dealer, and I get put in the same category with anybody else who takes a bourse table. Like *you.* You get a bourse table, but all you do is give away literature. Some guys say you're a dealer because you got a bourse table. You and me know that as the society's business manager and as the Editor of the Forum you got to have a *table.* You sometimes bring along a lot of stuff to sell, but most don't know that it's estate stuff and that you're acting as a go-between. No sir! I'm a collector at heart, same as you. I wouldn't sell one of my Westerns for love or money. I learned my lesson with the Liberty, like I said.

Q. But it works out pretty well?

A. Very well. I think . . . and my wife and I get *around.* We make Ocala— haven't missed once in the past four years. We made LaSalle last spring, and here we are at Kansas City, and we may get to Seattle, even, and then on to Olympia for the convention. That's what I mean by *expenses.* We like to travel, we like to see the people. We go when we can, and we don't when we can't, but it would be mostly staying at home if I didn't sell a few stamps to make the *expenses.*

Goffman, discussing the concept of role distance, points out:

> . . . two different means of establishing role distance seem to be found. In one case the individual tries to isolate himself as much as possible from the contamination of the situation . . . In the other case the individual cooperatively projects a childish self, meeting the situation more than halfway, but then withdraws from this cast-off self by a little gesture signifying the joke has gone far enough. In either case the individual can slip the skin the situation would clothe him in.[19]

Whether or not they had relocated, the twenty-one stamp collectors, who had in some way or another expanded their philatelic activities to include economic roles, expressed in many ways that their sense of well-being, satisfactions, and adjustments to life after retirement were associated with the economic facet of philatelic activity. Why they had engaged in the economic sphere of this activity, and what advantages were seen to derive, is expressed in this exchange which was typical of responses focused upon this area of inquiry:[20]

---

[19]*Op. cit.,* p. 110.

[20]The informant had retired from the postal service as a railroad postoffice clerk; then, after a brief idleness, he had become a shipping clerk in order to obtain money to purchase a stamp collection, and with this goal accomplished, "retired" a second time. Both he and his wife had previous spouses, and both were stamp collectors. Tape-recorded interview segment (C.C.H.).

Q. If you had not worked two years for National Foods *after* you retired from the postal service, and hadn't bought the H—— collection . . . would you be able financially to live the winter season in Florida, and go back to G——?

A. Well, my selling the stamps allowed me to do that. The stamps bought my trailer, and a lot of things. See, when I sold my collection except the Michigan, I didn't get any . . . I got only two hundred dollars down payment from Tom. And he'd pay me two hundred dollars a month. So that gave us money so that I could have things that we wanted and also accumulate enough so that I *could* buy a collection if I wanted to. So then I bought H——'s collection on time. I paid him a hundred dollars a month out of the two hundred I was getting.

Q. This helped you financially? It makes a difference in the way you live?

A. *I* think it *has*. When I sold my main collection, why that helped. The main interest in my collecting—getting around the country and seeing . . . I've made more *friends* all over the United States through my collection than I would in any other way.

Q. So, if you think of profit at all, it would be just profit in being able to get around to do the things that you wouldn't otherwise be able to do?

A. That's right.

Q. As you travel around, do you tend to visit with people of the same age?

A. No. I don't believe so . . . that there's any particular . . . 'course, the people that I've got *real* close to have been around my age, but it's because we happened to be *thrown* together . . . like S—— . . . he was about the only other collector outside of A——, and A—— was a good deal younger.

Q. How about S——? Do you think that his life is as full as yours?

A. No, I don't. He don't get around, so his life is M—— [his wife]. That's all. There's just the two of them. 'Course their daughter comes to see them once or twice a week, but that isn't like having a friend you can drop in on and talk stamps, or they come droppin' in on *you*. He doesn't collect anymore, but he's just as interested. He give up collecting's the trouble.[21]

In the nondirective interviews, questions raised concerning the respondent's own involvement, and the satisfactions and advantages which were attributed to stamp collecting *per se* and/or to involvement in economic philatelic activities, often elicited responses providing insight into their therapeutic value. This is a partial answer to the question raised by the Midwest Council for Social Research on Aging: "How does one help to create and maintain such roles?"

The wife of a stamp collector, who had become a stamp collector of sorts herself,[22] explained her involvement in a manner typical of fully half of those cases in which wives "take up" the hobby of their husbands:

A. I began in self defense! *He* was occupied, so I had to be occupied with something in that line, too. *He* wanted to go to stamp meetings and stamp clubs and visit stamp people; and unless I had a mutual interest there was nothing for me to go for; and *he* wouldn't go unless *I* did!

Q. Do you know any women who are collectors who don't have husbands who collect?

A. Oh, yes. It was an interest they developed themselves and worked into themselves. This one that had the trains: [a topical collection of stamps the principal design of which was railroad trains] I don't know how she got started in the first place, but she was crippled—she had an artificial limb, and that may have . . .

---

[21]Tape-recorded interview segment.

[22]Spouse of the preceding quoted informant. Tape-recorded interview segment (B.H.).

she may have had to do something when she was first . . . I was the only one who had a collecting husband.

Q. But there are a lot of women at the meetings who don't collect?

A. Yes. The women of some of the other members would come; the wives of some of the members that were not collectors would just come because it was a social get-together and everybody had fun. There's Mary Jane. She's not interested in stamps as stamps; she's just interested in the *group*. Now her husband has passed on. She is a member of the group in his memory, that's all; and she *loves* the stamp people. But, as far as stamps are concerned, she has no interest in the stamp itself. That was their one social contact. They did a lot of traveling around, but they had no social . . . family or social experience.

Male collectors, who typically began collecting in childhood or early adulthood, especially when answering questions concerning their economic activities, frequently alluded to the knowledge necessary to conduct themselves adequately in the philatelic microcosm:

Collecting's one thing, dealing's another; but you got to have lots of savvy. That doesn't come overnight. You've got to study. It's the same with coins, antique glass, you got to know *value* and how to separate the junk from the good stuff. Especially you got to know value in dealing. My advice is begin *young!*[23]

A relocated, economically engaged, former school superintendent from Ohio remarked:

You know what *I* think? I'll tell you. I'm retired now thirteen years! I'm seventy-nine years old. First I thought I'd just take it easy, play with stamps, fool around the garden. But after a while, things just started closing in on me. The first three years after I left the job we tried living the same as usual, but we couldn't keep up the house, and we began to have money worries. I never figured to live this long! So we sold the house and moved to Bradenton, and I began to sell off my stamps because I figured I'd die and nobody'd know how to dispose of them. I think someday there's going to have to be something *taught*—from grade school on, showing how to get along in life after you retire besides manual training and home economics and such. A man is going to have to learn a hobby—something he can enjoy, of course—but something he can use for a rainy-day way to make a little money—not in a business way.[24]

An economically engaged New Jerseyite, relocated in Florida, said:

Almost every collecting-type hobby has catalogs showing what the things are worth, and magazines or newspapers for that particular hobby where things are advertised at a price. Take *Hobbies Magazine*. Why, out of that you can get an idea of the value of most anything that people collect: penny banks, dolls' heads, sheet music, medals, old buttons, all kinds of antiques. And there's *books*. Why, at the Collectors' Club in New York they got maybe 20,000 volumes on stamps alone! Well, now, all these are hobbies—play, pastimes—to relax with; but every one of 'em has a market. It's not drudgery to study up like it would be going to school. But in the end, you get a headful of know-how and you can make it pay off. You don't usually *intend* it that way when you're at it as a hobby, but it's a comfort to know that you've had your fun and made an investment, too. I tell my grandchildren, "take up a hobby and stick with it! Collect something—rocks, butterflies, stamps—*anything*. Learn all you can about it."[25]

[23]Reconstructed interview segment (S.G.R.).

[24]Interview segment; reconstructed.

[25]Interview segment; reconstructed.

A former United States Air Force major, relocated in Florida commented:

I'll say this: Somewhere along the line kids have got to be taught to play at something they can enjoy all their lives, and it has to be something that won't slow down with age. It could be collecting things, but somewhere in the thing there has to be a way to make a little money on the *side*. There's this retired Army Colonel. He's been all over the world, and he was a cracker-jack photographer. He's got over 20,000 color slides, pictures he took all over the world, and now he sells copies of them, *you* name the subject. And he's popular as a lecturer, although he don't push that much. He tells me he makes good money, but when he was active it was just a hobby with him.[26]

The Retired Philatelist and the Subculture of the Aged

Among the 53 persons interviewed, only 7 made statements that indicated they had identified themselves with the subculture of the aged as indicated by their having interaction patterns categorically similar. In 27 cases, there was evidence that rejection of this self-image and group reference characterized the stance of the interviewee. These individuals, responding to inquiries concerning the aged, more often than not referred to the aged categorically as "they"; this was especially true of the relocated, whether or not economically engaged in philatelic activity. The economically engaged made statements which indicated their orientation was grounded in a *philatelic* subculture and in a few cases there were overtones that the philatelic microcosm vis-à-vis the aged subculture constituted or functioned as a contraculture. For the latter, especially, the aged were seen as "in a rut," "poor souls," "dying on the vine," or as "having brought unhappiness upon themselves," or as "having only themselves to blame." Particularly insightful was a remark by a widowed philatelic philosopher eighty-one years old who had been an attorney for a New York stock-brokerage firm:

Old is *thinking* old. Some of the "kids" around sixty-five, seventy, think they're entitled to the luxury of growing old, and then to have the game they take the name. Old. So they *think* they have to *act* old. Somebody's got to fetch their pipe and slippers and stuff a pillow behind their back in their rocking chair. Well, if there's nothing wrong with them physically, and if they've got their faculties, this is nonsense. *I* can't throw in with *them*. I fetch and carry for *myself*, and the only pillow that's going to be stuffed behind *me* is going to be put there by the undertaker. I may be through with romancing the women, but I'm romancing with my stamp collection.[27]

Addressing themselves to action programs for the aged, again the disparity between the aged interviewee and those in the aged subculture group appears:

Q. Have you any idea how the older people in the trailer camp feel about Medicare?
A. Well . . . no. For *myself* I haven't talked much with anybody about it. The way I'm situated right now, I can't see that it would help *me*. Because of the hospitalization . . . the government pays part of it and then they take some of my

---

[26]Interview segment; reconstructed.
[27]Reconstructed interview segment (N.F.).

Civil Service check, and what I buy separate, why we're covered enough . . . I believe.[28]

The same respondent, referring to an aged friend:

Why, to hear them *talk,* they're ready for the poorhouse! Why, I've heard him say a good many times if [his wife] didn't work, they couldn't eat, so she's working in the library. He's always worried about their health, and it's not so they couldn't manage because he's been buying stocks for *years.* He was buying stocks before he sold out the printing business and I know he got $20,000 for that; and he had a building and printing office in A——, and he owned a house and cottage at G—— L——, and he owned property at P——. *He's* for Medicare, all right! 'Course he's a Democrat. But there's not much talk about it by the older people. I wouldn't say they talk about it any more than any place else, but that may be because I never bring it up.

Another relocated respondent, who had become the salaried executive secretary for a philatelic organization, had especially strong, but nevertheless typical, feelings regarding private projects:

Q. Did you ever give any serious thought to locating in Sun City . . .?
A. You mean that one that Webb built . . . that whole development? Houses with ramps, low counters and things? Hell *no!* We looked at one near Tampa. That was one of Webb's. We looked that place over, and my wife, she said they could just as well name it "Cemetery City." They got houses row on row like tombstones in a churchyard. For the old folks. We want to live the way we always lived, not in some damn colony where you wait to get pushed over the fence into the marble orchard.[29]

Relative to "disengagement," a remark offered by an involuntarily retired Pennsylvanian relocated in Portland, Oregon, was typical:

Nothing's changed much since we moved. I don't see any difference at all. Matter of fact, since we moved, we visit the kids more often or they visit us more than before.[30]

A non-relocated, not economically engaged Maryland former Federal Civil Service employee corroborated this feeling:

I don't feel like I been *pushed* out of *anything.* And I don't feel I'm cut off from anything or anybody. I think the ones that feel that way set themselves up for it, and it's not actually so. They're sympathy-seekers.[31]

Viewing the apparent disengagement of others, an economically engaged, involuntarily retired, former taxicab garage manager, relocated in Miami, commented:

There's this old bat lives with her husband in a trailer and she's a real gadabout, but when she hears one of her kids is coming she pretends to be all stove up with rheumatiz, and anymore she sits on her butt and complains how nobody cares whether she lives or dies and she can't get around at all, and she's just waiting to die.

---

[28]Portion of tape-recorded interview with correspondent previously quoted. See footnote 20, p. 101.
[29]Reconstructed interview segment (H.N.)
[30]Reconstructed interview segment (R.G.P.).
[31]Reconstructed interview segment (V.L.L.).

Moans she's neglected and cut off from the world. And she's not the only old fraud in the camp. They can cut up if they want to, but she just wants to be made over.[32]

This feeling that one has only one's self to blame was reiterated by an involuntarily retired accountant who had relocated in Florida following lifelong residence in Connecticut:

Some whine they got nothing to do since they retired and claim time is heavy, their friends has deserted them, and their kids don't care. It's funny, but it's the ones that retired early because they had it made—some in their fifties—they're the biggest whiners. I up and ask one of them, "So if you're crabby because you got nothing to do and got no friends and your family don't visit, why'd you *retire*?" They don't know how to answer that. I think they retired just to prove they *could* retire, but they sure bellyache.[33]

Stamp-Collecting and Life-Adjustment

Many of the characteristics of the well-adjusted older person (referred to above) were reflected in certain recurrent themes of the interviews:

"Plenty of work and a liking for it . . . " A non-relocated, involuntarily retired, economically engaged Detroiter, formerly employed as a supervisor in a paint manufacturing plant, comments:

Before I retired, I played with stamps two or three nights a week, and I attended local meetings; but it was a hobby, and sometimes I had qualms about the money I put in it, and I had the feeling that maybe it wasn't exactly fair to the wife and the kids. Now that I'm retired, I don't feel like I'm stealing time like I did, for the kids are established and far away and living their own lives. The stamps bring in a little money—enough more that I don't feel like I got to hang my head. Sometimes the wife complains when I get up at dawn and have the kitchen table all covered with stamps I'm working on to sell, but she doesn't always complain. Sometimes she'll pitch in. We been more together on stamps since I retired and we can sit for hours and talk.[34]

"Strong and varied interests . . . " An involuntarily retired, economically engaged Pittsburgher, a former print-shop pressman who had relocated, stated:

It isn't only that selling the stamps makes it possible to get around more, but we see more things we never saw before. We're on the move half the time. We get around to places. One thing we make a practice of: We never let ourselves get in a rut. Whenever we feel we're under pressure or bored we go on a trip a few days. We don't *plan* anything. We knock around, and it's surprising how many things there are. My wife she got interested in puttering around with clay and ceramic work, and she's got a little wheel now and I took some interest and we bought a little kiln. This year we got involved with a group of people, mostly a good deal younger, and we got to painting tiles. We found there's a shop in Sarasota takes on consignment. Now, with the stamp people and the clay work we're having a whale of a time.[35]

"Economic independence and security . . . " A lengthy statement, con-

---

[32]Tape-recorded interview segment (P.D.).
[33]Tape-recorded interview segment (J.E.W.).
[34]Reconstructed interview segment (J.J.McI.).
[35]Reconstructed interview segment (C.E.E.).

tributed by an economically engaged St. Louisan who had relocated, provided a wide rationale:

Now I'm Republican all my life, and I seen it coming. I came out of the service in 1918, married in 1920 and we had the three boys. The oldest is 41 now, I think. *I* never had any education: I lied about my age, and got infantry and after the war I clerked stock at the old Brown Shoe factory. My wife and I was bound and determined the boys would have a chance to go to college. When they was born we taken out insurance of $1,000 on each. It was rough as a cob keeping up the premiums. I was laid off four, five times. I got WPA a year, and the oldest he had to lay out of school, but finally finished and went to St. Louis U. night school in accounting. In 1943 we *still* had $400 borrowed on his policy, and we cashed in the other two. In 1940 I went back to Brown, and I made foreman and things was going better. The Social Security came along, but I just couldn't *see* it, 'cause I figured *then* the same would happen as to the insurance policies. When we taken out the policies, $1,000 was a pretty good lump, and would of give the kids their college, but they wouldn't buy even half way when they fell due. My wife, she never had no work. Brown broke up, and I went with Cupples and worked inventory and went on retirement in 1961. I was sixty-six, nearly, and I still had nearly $2,000 to pay out on the mortgage, but I sold it for more than double I paid and we taken the Social Security and bought the place in Clearwater. Now, the whole thing is, through thick and thin I held onto my stamps. Come hell or high water, nothing was gonna touch 'em. I had laid aside some pretty good stuff, and I got most of it from the mail room at Brown—lots of Norse, Lexington, and Walloons! Boy did I *have* 'em. Well, I never in my life sold a stamp, but we was in Clearwater maybe six months 'fore I figured we was no better off than the Depression, living hand to mouth, couldn't afford no car. That all changed when I taken the idea to go to the meetings. I could have dumped everything to Harris [world's largest wholesalers in postage stamps]. I had maybe $18,000 of used stuff, figured Gibbons' retail, but Harris offered $11,000 about, so I decided to hell with Harris and I went to meetings and nearly everybody needed the stuff from the '20's and '30's like I had. I never touched my collection though. So I began doling out from that nest-egg—I didn't push it. I reckon I taken in maybe $1,100 last year, just enough so's we can feel independent and have the little extra things we want. It makes all the difference in the world between worrying and not having to worry all the time. I reckon I could keep this up another ten years, and meantime, Gibbons goes up in the prices, so what I take in is like interest. I got my *own* social security—you get what I mean.[36]

"Many social contacts . . . " A relocated, involuntarily retired, non-economically engaged man who had been a tool-crib chief clerk, reminisced:

You move, and you leave friends behind, and worst is you leave friends behind you used to work with—but they sort of fade away or die off anyhow. Back in Toledo, my wife she says to me—first thing she turns to in the newspaper is the death notices—she says, "Well, I see in the paper where Denny Cieslak died." So, the old timers, they pass away. I used to joke with her, some day she'd read her own death notice! Always one or two a year dies or moves off. There was a bakery shop on the corner, they sold out and moved down here and we always got a letter or at least a card at Christmas, and they was having a high old time, and my wife she'd get a note from Martha (the baker's wife) and she'd say, "Why don't you all pack up and come down?" Well, I got my walking papers and was out to pasture, so to speak, and I'd pick and poke around in the backyard, play with stamps, or watch the TV or maybe we'd play cards. We'd hear a car pull up front, and my wife she's always running to the window; but nine times out of ten it was nobody to see

---

[36]Tape-recorded interview segment (J.S.).

us. Got awful dull. So awful dull! Now we been here going on three years and at first it was no better; but I got out the stamps and once I took the notion to go to a meeting. I was nearly bowled over! See, there was a nice crowd, and the first guy I see is old S—— F——! I thought he'd *died!* And then there was a fellow from Toledo I saw often at the meetings of the Central Ohio Club. I didn't recall his name but he knew me! Well, first thing you know, it was like a family reunion. Now we got so many friends through the stamps we hear a car pull up in front of the cottage and my wife—she's kidding of course—she yells, "Pull down the curtains! don't let anybody know we're home!" We don't even get a newspaper any more. My wife, she says, "I don't know any of those people that die around here." I bet we have company twice a week easy, and we go to the meetings and my wife she's got a hen party going half the time. These coffee-klatching women! They put up each other's hair, or take up hems, or tromp around. Thursdays and Saturdays is my stamp nights—either I go out, or they come here. About a dozen of us is regulars, and always five or six shows up, and we go until all hours.[37]

"Living in the present rather than in retrospect . . . " An involuntarily retired, non-relocated, not economically engaged, former leather goods buyer for a New York department store commented:

One day I was at Rotary and there was this fellow I never met before in my life somehow found out I was a stamp collector and he was in Scouting. Anyway he asked would I be interested in being merit badge examiner for the Stamp Collecting Badge. Well, I take the thing on, and the first kid that came to me—he came with his dad, and his dad was a collector sort of. We got to talking about how kids these days don't seem to have any clubs or any way to get really interested in hobbies or craft work and so on, and that the teachers didn't take no interest at the schools. Well, we talked about it some and his kid's dad, and the kid too chimed in a couple times, they wanted to know would I help start a stamp club. Well, I said I'd do it, and the kid he got permission to put up a notice on the school bulletin board about starting a club, and I had the kids over to my house to start 'er off, and eight kids— youngsters mostly teenagers—they came. Those kids were real eager and you know we talked about stamps for about three hours and I showed my collection, and I didn't know who got the biggest kick out of it, me or the kids. Couple of the kids, their father or mother came to the house to pick 'em up and the kids weren't ready to leave, so their folks came in and we got them interested right away. Well, anyway . . . that club took right off from there. We got a place to meet, regular, every Friday night, in a church community hall or whatever they call it, and in only two years, now, we have regular meetings except July and August, and naturally we got an adult group going, too. I tell you, I don't know whether the kids or me gets the biggest kick, but before we got this thing going I was getting pretty blue and grouchy with time on my hands and nothing much to do. I bet I spend half my time, now, with stamps and looking forwards to those meetings; and not only that, but the older folks—mostly the kids' parents—they drop around to the house. I kind of feel, now, that it isn't so bad being old if there's something you can do and look forward to. That visiting helps a lot. Before, I sure did a lot of feeling sorry for myself, just mooning around, thinking about the past, and how useless everything was. When you're past seventy you got a lot of time to *think,* and when you're lonely you sort of dry up inside. You know what those kids call me? "Papa Stamp." Isn't that a corker.[38]

"A desire to live life over again . . . " An involuntarily retired, economically engaged, non-relocated bachelor who had lived all his life in St. Louis summed up:

---

[37]Tape-recorded interview segment (B.D.S.).
[38]Tape-recorded interview segment (D.K.).

Once I figured, well, this is the end of the line. You work *hard* all your life and you raise your kids up, and off they go! Then you get so that at work you see all the youngsters coming up, and they're spry and cocky, and you look back and you do a lot of looking back—I put in thirty-three years with the same outfit. Once, one of these young fellas—he was my assistant and real sharp and he asked me would I go through it all over again. That was a day we got word there'd be a cut-back because we lost a big contract. I said, hell no, I wouldn't. Well, maybe I still feel that way about the *work* but not about the *stamps*. These last seven years—I'd like to live them seven years over *and* over. Lord, I'm really living! Not a worry or care. If I'd known twenty years ago how much enjoyment I'd get, I'd of retired *then,* and gone into stamps bigger. Selling is something I never done, and selling stamps I never give it a thought, seriously, but it's real nice. Yes, I think I'd do it all over again, but I think I'd have told my boss to stick it when I was maybe forty-five or fifty instead of waiting. I remember that *last* year. I'd gone to the chief draughtsman—the boss— and I told him not to give me no work I couldn't finish. The rule was you had ninety days after your sixty-fifth birthday. That ruddy bastard! What did he tell me was that I should begin easing off, and I found out he already had gave some of my assignments to the younger fellows. I didn't even realize already he'd started to jerk the rug from under me. Cold turkey. *That* part I wouldn't live over; but let me have these seven years again, and I'll take seven times those seven. My advice now is *quit*. I told that assistant of mine they'd squeezed the juice out of *me* and they'd squeeze it out of *him* and they'd toss the empty rind away. Well, I got a lot of juice left.[39]

Economic Engagement and Adjustment. Careful examination of the content of interviews comparing the 21 involuntarily retired males economically engaged with the 28 who had not engaged in economic activities in the philatelic complex, revealed that, in general, the former were: (1) more frequently inclined to attend "stamp meetings"; (2) more frequent in attendance of stamp club meetings held in distant places, where they remained two or more days; (3) more frequently visited close relatives and friends who do not reside in the same community; (4) more frequently mentioned "outside" social interests (other than philatelic) in which they were engaged and which had no age-graded qualifications; (5) less frequently made references to economic restraints as related to social activity in general; (6) less frequently referred to physical limitations as related to social activity in general; (7) less frequently referred to themselves in the future in an apprehensive manner; (8) less frequently referred to themselves retrospectively with any invidious comment in disparagement of their present situation; (9) less frequently identified themselves with groups having social, recreational, or "interest" reasons for being predicated on chronological age.

General Observations on Stamp-Collecting

Whether or not they were involuntarily retired, relocated, or economically engaged in the philatelic complex, the fifty-one stamp collectors expressed in many ways that their sense of well-being, satisfactions, and adjustments to life after retirement were in one way or another related to stamp collecting *per se*. In general, comments were couched in comparatives with

[39]Tape-recorded interview segment (J.V.R.).

the respondent comparing his own positions and roles to those of other older men whom he considered to be his economic peers but who did not have philatelic interests. In so comparing himself, he generally touched upon those attributes of others which he viewed in negative fashion—attributes he himself felt he was free of because of his philatelic activity. In their comparisons, most of the fifty-one collectors indicated that stamp-collecting activities provided relief from loneliness, provided friendly social contacts, dispelled unhappiness, gave relief to general anxiety and frustration, made life seem worthwhile and useful. A frequent theme was that time passed easily and quickly, whereas others were seen as "killing time" in boresome ways with repetitive monotony.

For those economically engaged, social contacts were expanded and there was a continuity of many contacts made prior to retirement. For those who were not economically engaged, the same was generally true, but to a somewhat lesser extent. Even so, the latter, comparing themselves with their contemporary nonphilatelic peers, felt they had a distinct advantage.

One of the most provocative insights, deserving deeper probing in future research, was the frequently expressed feeling of stamp collectors that the activity was one which "carried over" from preretirement years, and that age was no barrier to the continuity. Discussing the general "social" activities of peers who were not stamp collectors, and who enjoyed no similar activity, the fifty-one interviewed pointed out that these "others" for the most part were engaging in activities which were new to them—that is, had not been "carried over." With regard to recreational activities, it was suggested that these "others" had to engage in such group activities as shuffleboard, dart-throwing, block parties, horse-shoe pitching, and other kinds of social affairs. It was suggested by several respondents that such social affairs were "rigged" in order to provide contacts, and that the normative structures implied role calculation rather than spontaneous role playing. "Golden age" clubs, community "discussion groups" and "interest groups" seemed, from the vantage point of the fifty-one informants, to be arrangements to provide "means to ends" rather than being ends in themselves, with the manifest aims of the social arrangements only incidental to the greater need to dispel boredom, loneliness, friendlessness.

One stamp collector, an involuntarily retired, relocated, economically engaged, former public relations staff man for a Chicago promotions firm was more articulate and perceptive than others, and suspected that the appearance of organization probably cloaked considerable personal disorganization:

They got up this shuffle contest, and each one was supposed to chip in half a dollar to go to the "champ." Well, they got up thirty-four fellas and paired off seventeen teams. They drew up one of those play-off diagrams. At the end of it, the winning team was to split, and the two fellas was to play singles to decide the "champ." Well, the doggone thing got started. The wives was there, and lots of others who wasn't interested in shuffle at all. Now a few was real interested in shuffle, I grant that. But they paired up by pulling names out of a hat. That didn't suit the ones who was really interested, but it didn't make no difference to the rest—and I'd say that was about twelve of the seventeen teams. Now, some of the best individual players drew partners they didn't know, or poor players they did know, and there was a lot of grumbling. One Sunday they got started but five fellahs didn't show up at all. So, five teams defaulted. That left twelve, and they played off to leave six winners. The next Sunday, two didn't show, so the four teams played off. That left just two teams. Then there was an argument and they never did finish. Nothing serious, but a couple ladies suggested they take the $17 and buy a couple hams, some hot-dogs, and so on, and have a cook-out the following Sunday. Well, they was all prepared but it rained billy-be-damn. Most of the folks didn't go, the rest took the grub to the community house—about six, maybe seven, couples and a couple widows. Well, they eat the food and of course a lot over. There was one couple they played crib [cribbage] together, a few of the women sat around twiddling their thumbs, and in two hours they all went home. They try so hard to get something going. Just *anything*—anything to pass the time, but nothing they was ever used to. They got no organization. They invent some excuse to get a group together—any old thing. Usually somebody who's maybe interested gets it rolling, a few others who're maybe interested go along, but the majority they just go along to get out of the house; and it always falls flat. It always dribbles out. A few have fun, but then the plans change, and change again because there's no organization. They rig up one thing after another, and most of the time it leaves a bad taste in the mouth of most, and they grow apart more and more, and after a while they're back where they were—with nothing in common like they were in the first place. They only got in common their age, and no friends, and lonely and blue. And they get spiteful! Man, they just aggravate themselves to death. They kill themselves just trying to kill time. Somehow they feel they got to be together because there's nobody else to be with, and they can't stand it. That's sure hell. Nothing carries them over the hump.[40]

This recorded observation to some extent seems to exhibit an attempt to bring interaction into focus in face-to-face situations which are oriented toward some event to permit cognitive and visual attention. The attempted encounter, however, is foreign to the repertories of the individuals involved.[41]

Summary

This preliminary investigation, designed to observe some of the economic functions of the engagement of the retired aged in systematized forms of leisure activity, suggests that more thorough research in this area might be a useful addition to social gerontological investigations; it could be productive of knowledge directed ultimately toward programmatic action. There is ample evidence that latent self-conceptions pertinent to status and role performances in the systematized leisure activities of the mature adult participating in familial and economic normative roles may be nurtured and become powerful sources of satisfaction after retirement, when the larger occupational and child-rearing roles are eliminated.

Not all leisure activities include component activities in which one may intensify participation in such a way that social and economic meaning may be extracted. However, a very large number of avocational pursuits do

[40]Tape-recorded interview segment (L.J.P.).
[41]See, for example, Goffman, *op. cit.*, pp. 7-8.

have the requisite attributes to allow expansion in significant role inter-relationships, which in turn provide other avenues to social and personal satisfactions so necessary to the well-being and adjustment of older persons.

CHAPTER 7

Church Participation and Adjustment in Old Age*

DAVID O. MOBERG and MARVIN J. TAVES

Introduction

Church membership and other indicators of religious interests and values have been found to be related to personal and social adjustment in old age in a large number of studies, most of which are summarized in Gray and Moberg.[1] For example, Landis,[2] Pressey and Simcoe,[3] Pan,[4] Shanas,[5] O'Reilly,[6] and Scott,[7] among others, have found a direct relationship between church attendance and good adjustment. An analysis of persons who were poorly adjusted confirmed this pattern, for non-attendance or in-

*The authors acknowledge the assistance and suggestions of Gary D. Hansen and Ivan J. Fahs, in addition to Midwest Council Seminar members, in the preparation of this paper.

[1]Robert M. Gray and David O. Moberg, The Church and the Older Person, Grand Rapids, Mich.: Wm. B. Eerdmans Publishing Co., 1962.

[2]Judson T. Landis, Hobbies and happiness in old age, Recreation, 35 (January, 1942), p. 642.

[3]S. L. Pressey and Elizabeth Simcoe, Case study comparisons of successful and problem old people, Journal of Gerontology, 5: pp. 168-75, 1950.

[4]Ju-Shu Pan, A Comparison of Factors in the Personal Adjustment of Old People in the Protestant Church Homes for the Aged and the Old People Living Outside of Institutions. Unpublished doctoral dissertation, University of Chicago, 1950.

[5]Ethel Shanas, The Personal Adjustment of Recipients of Old Age Assistance. Unpublished doctoral dissertation, University of Chicago, 1949.

[6]Charles T. O'Reilly, Religious practice and personal adjustment, Sociology and Social Research, 42: 119-21, 1958.

[7]Frances Gillespie Scott, Factors in the personal adjustment of institutionalized and non-institutionalized aged, American Sociological Review, 20: 538-46, 1955.

frequent church attendance was one of their characteristics.[8]

Religious faith was associated with good adjustment among people residing in homes for the aged and similar institutions.[9] Other aspects of religiosity associated with good adjustment in old age are reading of the Bible or a prayer book,[10] regular listening to radio church services,[11] and belief in an afterlife.[12] A "religious activities score" representing a composite of several types of present and past religious experiences was highly correlated with personal adjustment; those who had high activities scores also tended to have high adjustment scores.[13] Since church membership tends to be correlated with religious faith, church attendance, and other religious activities, studies usually find that non-members have lower adjustment scores than members.[14] In addition, there is evidence that the lay leaders in church congregations are better adjusted in old age than other church members.[15]

The consistency of the findings of studies relating religion to adjustment in old age helps to establish their reliability. Yet most of these studies looked at religion only incidentally and were limited to small samples of persons from narrow segments of the older population. To generalize for all aging people from these studies of old age assistance recipients, residents of retirement homes, retired school teachers, and members of a large industrial company's retirement club, is at best hazardous. Although the methodological care used in applying experimental designs to the analysis of relationships between religion and adjustment by certain researchers greatly increases the significance of the findings,[16] the incontestable fact remains that the samples upon which the designs were based were in every instance limited.

[8]John F. Schmidt, Patterns of poor adjustment in old age, American Journal of Sociology, 57: 33-42, 1951.

[9]Ju-Shu Pan, A Study of the Personal and Social Adjustment of the Old People in the Homes for Aged, Unpublished master's thesis, University of Chicago, 1947; and David O. Moberg, Christian beliefs and personal adjustment in old age, Journal of the American Scientific Affiliation, 10: 8-12, 1958.

[10]Joseph H. Britton, A Study of the Adjustment of Retired School Teachers (unpublished doctoral dissertation, University of Chicago, 1949); Shanas, op. cit.; Scott, op. cit.

[11]Britton, op. cit.; Shanas, op. cit.

[12]Britton, op. cit.; Shanas, op. cit.

[13]David O. Moberg, Religious activities and personal adjustment in old age, Journal of Social Psychology, 43: 261-67, 1956.

[14]Britton, op. cit.; David O. Moberg, Church membership and personal adjustment in old age, Journal of Gerontology, 8: 207-11, 1953; Paul F. Verden and Archer L. Michael, A comparison of successfully and unsuccessfully retired groups, Geriatrics, 14: 528-34, 1959.

[15]David O. Moberg, Leadership in the church and personal adjustment in old age, Sociology and Social Research, 37: 312-16, 1953.

[16]Ibid.; Moberg, supra; David O. Moberg, Two problems of experimental designs, Midwest Sociologist, 16: 10-12, 1954; Pressey and Simcoe, op. cit.; Verden and Michael, op. cit.

The purpose of this study is to analyze data from a broad community-based sample to provide an additional test of the hypothesis that church participation during old age is correlated with good personal adjustment. The hypothesis is supported if church officers and committeemen rank highest in personal adjustment, other church members next, and non-church members lowest.

Methodology

The data upon which this analysis is based were gathered by interviews during 1959-60 with over 5,000 persons aged sixty years and over in four midwestern states.[17] The respondents in these surveys were classified on the basis of their church participation into the categories of (1) officers and committeemen in church or other religious organization, (2) other church members, and (3) non-church members.

Personal adjustment was measured in the respective surveys by modified versions of the Burgess-Cavan-Havighurst Attitudes Inventory.[18] Instead of eight separate scores which are combinable into one overall adjustment score, as is the case with the original Attitudes Inventory, only the one total adjustment score is available in each of the studies. The sections on finances, leisure time activities, and general satisfactions were dropped from the original scale. Only the most discriminating items from the other five sections were retained. Certain items which consistently appeared to respondents to overlap were eliminated. Although no formal empirical check was made to test the effects of shortening the scale for purposes of these already lengthy interviews, careful examinations of pretest data and of the results indicate that no significant biases were thus introduced. Many of the items with which interviewees have repeatedly had the greatest trouble were eliminated. Good adjustment as operationally defined by this revised instrument involves a socio-psychological combination of personal attitudes reflecting happiness, enjoyment, or satisfactions with or from one's health, friendships, employment status, religion, feeling of usefulness, family, and general orientation toward, or happiness in, the later years of life.

---

[17]Details of the sampling and other procedures are described in this volume (Chap. 19) and in "1700 elderly citizens" by Marvin J. Taves and Gary D. Hansen in Aging in Minnesota, Arnold Rose, ed., Minneapolis: University of Minnesota Press, 1963. The Iowa survey did not include computation of a personal adjustment score, so it was omitted from this study. The Minnesota Social Security recipients all had farming backgrounds; the other Minnesota survey respondents were selected from eleven non-metropolitan cities and the three metropolitan centers of the state. The latter were from city blocks chosen by an area sampling technique. Both Minnesota surveys were made to answer questions about the needs, problems, attitudes, and relations with public services of elderly citizens.

[18]Ernest W. Burgess, Ruth S. Cavan, and Robert J. Havighurst, Your Activities and Attitudes, Chicago: Science Research Associates, 1948. Construction and validation of this Chicago Inventory are described in Ruth S. Cavan, Ernest W. Burgess, Robert J. Havighurst, and Herbert Goldhamer, Personal Adjustment in Old Age, Chicago: Science Research Associates, 1949.

Minor changes made in adapting the Inventory for use in the various surveys were not uniform, so the highest and lowest possible scores differ. Direct comparisons of the actual raw adjustment scores from different states are therefore not possible. Comparisons of scores within each study, however, serve as an adequate basis for the measurement of differences in personal adjustment.

Differences in the adjustment scores for persons in each of the categories of church participation were compared and whenever possible their Chi-squares were computed to test the reliability of the observed relationships between personal adjustment and church participation.

Previously observed relationships between religion and adjustment could be a consequence primarily of the influence of non-religious factors which are correlated with religion, on the one hand, and personal adjustment, on the other. For instance, if personal adjustment and church participation are both highly correlated with educational achievement, the common relationship to education could introduce a spurious correlation between church participation and adjustment even in the absence of any direct correlation between the two variables themselves. Detailed analyses were hence made of data in the Minnesota survey. Home ownership, level of education, age, employment, organizational participation, current activity levels in organizations compared to activity levels during the respondents' fifties, and marital status were controlled through successive classification of each into subcategories within which church leaders (officers and committeemen in religious organizations), other church members, and non-church members were compared. The detailed analyses thus test the hypothesis that observed relationships between personal adjustment and church participation are independent of these intervening variables and persist even when such factors are held constant.

Table 1. Church Participation and Mean Adjustment Scores
in Five Surveys*

	Church Leaders Adjustment		Other Members Adjustment		Non-members Adjustment		Totals Adjustment	
	N	Score	N	Score	N	Score	N	Score
Minnesota:								
State survey	142	15	791	12	410	6	1343	11
Social Security recipients	16	17	226	14	46	9	288	14
Missouri	313	25	1051	19	345	13	1709	19
North Dakota	105	25	637	22	175	14	917	21
South Dakota	167	24	644	19	210	15	1021	19

*Adjustment scores of the surveys are not directly comparable; comparisons using the scores should be made within rows only, not within the columns.

Findings

Levels of Church Participation and Adjustment Scores. In the surveys in each of the four states a consistent relationship was found between the various levels of church participation and personal adjustment scores (Table 1). In every instance lay leaders in the church had the highest average adjustment scores, other church members the next, and non-church members the lowest. The differences between church officers and church committeemen in the two states in which such a comparison was possible (Missouri and North Dakota) were only one point apart; in both instances the officers' mean adjustment score was 25 and the committeemen's 24.

The adjustment differences between the membership categories were statistically significant at the .001 level when analyzed by sex in the surveys in each state except in that of North Dakota where the differences were significant at the .10 level of probability.[19]

The hypothesis that personal adjustment and church participation are positively associated is supported by these findings. Yet it is conceivable that intervening variables could account for these correlations, so more intensive analyses of the data are desirable.

The general findings of all the surveys were basically the same. Because of certain technical problems pertinent to the non-comparability of the data and the form in which they were coded for IBM tabulation, detailed analyses were made only on the larger sample of Minnesota respondents. Three inactive church members were omitted from that study, thus leaving a total of 1,340 persons in the following report.

The mean adjustment score of the 1,343 persons in the larger Minnesota Elderly Citizens Survey was 11 out of a possible "perfect score" of 24. The 11 per cent who were church leaders had an average score of 15, compared to 12 for the other active church members (59 per cent). (The three inactive church members had a score of 14.) Non-church members comprised 30 per cent of the sample and had an adjustment score of 6.

Table 2. Mean Adjustment Scores of Church Leaders, Other
Church Members and Non-church Members, by
Sex and Age

	Church Leaders		Other Church Members		Non-church Members	
	N	Adjustment	N	Adjustment	N	Adjustment
Sex:*						
Male	40	17	268	11	180	8
Female	101	14	520	12	226	8
No information	1	14	0	—	4	11
Age:**						
65-70	66	18	244	14	98	10
71-79	60	15	355	12	168	7
80 and over	10	13	173	8	139	6
No information	6	10	16	11	4	12
Total	142	15	788	12	410	6

*Chi-square $= 17.36$; p$<$ .001
**Chi-square $= 57.44$; p$<$ .001

---

[19]In only two cases were the differences between male and female mean adjustment scores within any church participation category as great as three points, so separate tabulations by sex are not presented here.

Adjustment by Age and Sex. A person has little or no control over certain of his traits, yet these may be significantly related to his adjustment either because of associated biological factors, social reactions to them, or cultural conditioning. Among the most significant of these ascribed social statuses, because they strongly influence one's roles and other life experiences, are age and sex.

Table 2 confirms the frequently observed correlation between increasing age and declining adjustment, but it fails to demonstrate any clear-cut differences in adjustment by sex, except among the church leaders. Most significant for our purposes is the pattern of declining adjustment scores within each category when progressing from church leaders to other members to non-members. (The only exception is among those few church leaders for whom "don't know" was checked on the question pertaining to age.) These differences are statistically highly significant, thus confirming the hypothesis that differences between the adjustment scores of

Mean Adjustment Scores of Church Leaders, Other Church Members and Non-members, by Schooling, Marital Status and Home Ownership

	Church Leaders		Other Church Members		Non-church Members	
	N	Adjustment	N	Adjustment	N	Adjustment
Schooling:*						
8 grades or less	45	15	418	12	238	7
9-12 grades	37	16	189	14	94	9
13 grades or more	54	14	134	11	37	10
Don't know or no information	6	16	47	11	41	11
Marital status:**						
Married, with spouse	65	15	276	15	115	12
Married, not with spouse	1	14	16	11	8	—1
Widowed	53	15	370	11	197	7
Single	21	12	102	8	70	5
Separated or divorced	0	—	16	11	16	3
Don't know or no information	1	15	8	14	4	14
Home-ownership— Residence:†						
Home-owner	99	16	394	14	131	11
Non-owner	27	13	158	11	82	9
Home for the aged or nursing home	9	14	189	6	172	4
Don't know or no information	7	14	39	14	4	4

*Chi-square =   69.58; p< .001

**Chi-square =   33.32; p< .001

†Chi-square = 100.11; p< .001

the three church participation groupings are not due simply to differences in age or sex as they are correlated with variations in participation.

Achieved Status and Adjustment. Educational attainment, marital status, and home ownership are achieved statuses to a much greater extent than age; they depend more upon an individual's ambition and efforts.[20] The data in Table 3 clearly indicate that there is a relatively consistent tendency for adjustment scores to be linked with marital status and home-ownership. A more pronounced pattern, however, is the superior adjustment of church leaders over members and of members over non-members in 10 of the 14 subcategories analyzed. The exceptions are minor; members' scores equalled those of the leaders in two instances (among married persons living with their spouses, and among persons whose residential status was not indicated), and non-members' scores equalled the members' in two (among those of unknown educational attainment, and among persons of unknown marital status).

The differences between adjustment scores of the church participation categories are highly significant. Even when marital status is analyzed for each sex separately, there are few exceptions to the pattern. Single males who are non-members have a score of 6, compared to 5 for the members, and the few persons for whom information about marital status was unavailable did not reveal a consistent pattern when analyzed by sex. In the other nine sex-marital status categories the general pattern of highest adjustment among church leaders, next among members, and lowest among non-members was confirmed. On the basis of this evidence, we can be reasonably certain that the variations in adjustment scores between the three church participation groupings are not merely a result of intercorrelations between patterns of church participation and education, marital status, and home ownership or place of residence.

Activity Patterns and Adjustment in Old Age. Activity patterns have been correlated with adjustment in old age in other studies. This general correlation is confirmed through the findings on employment, organizational participation, and changes in activity levels since the respondents were in their fifties (Table 4). Within the employment categories, the differences between church-leaders, other members, and non-members were not statistically significant, however. When these are analyzed for each sex separately, deviations from the expected pattern occur among both fully employed males and females, as well as among the partly-employed and "no information" females. Perhaps some older persons who are employed resent the necessity to continue working in a paid position, and others who are working may feel under pressure when they are expected to continue holding positions in religious organizations. An alternative possibility is

---

[20]We recognize that to attain "a ripe old age" is to *achieve* a status insofar as this is dependent upon a person's precautions in protecting, preserving, and nurturing his good health. Furthermore, marital status and home ownership, as well as education, are not a result solely of ambition and effort; they depend to some extent upon the socio-cultural forces which provide or withhold opportunities and incentives.

Table 4. Mean Adjustment Scores of Church Leaders, Other Church
Members and Non-members by Employment-Retirement
Patterns, Social Participation and Changes
In Social Participation

	Church Leaders		Other Church Members		Non-church Members	
	N	Adjustment	N	Adjustment	N	Adjustment
Employment:*						
Fully employed	7	18	32	18	16	17
Partly employed	28	16	87	16	29	13
Fully retired	58	15	362	11	221	7
Other	6	14	32	12	21	5
Don't know or no information	41	15	276	12	123	8
Participation in civic, social, or professional organizations**						
Officer or committeeman	62	15	79	16	25	12
Other member	131	16	362	13	86	10
Non-member	0	—	16	7	336	7
No information	1	4	1	9	0	—
Participation levels compared with respondents' fifties:†						
More active in religious organizations	38	16	95	13	4	9
Less active in religious organizations	40	14	370	11	107	7
More active in other organizations	40	15	102	14	21	17
Less active in other organizations	53	13	213	12	115	9
All others	82	15	331	12	238	7

  *Chi-square = 1.18, not significant
 **Chi-square = 671.86; p< .001
  †Chi-square = 145.72; p< .001

that employment contributes so significantly to adjustment that church
membership status makes no consistent observable difference among employed senior citizens.

Statistically significant relationships were observed, however, between
the three church participation categories when they were related to non-
church organizational participation and to levels of participation in organizations. Only two exceptions to the general pattern were observed. Church
leaders who also were officers or committeemen in civic, social, or professional organizations had an average adjustment score one point lower
than the other church members who also were organizational leaders, and
the 5 per cent of the non-members who are now more active in other-than-
religious organizations than they were in their fifties had a higher adjustment score (17) than church leaders (15) and church members (14).
These more active non-members ranked exceptionally high in their personal
adjustment among non-members as a whole, and so did the female non-

members of churches who were officers or committeewomen in non-religious organizations. Their adjustment score was 18, compared to 17 for church members and 15 for the church leaders who were officers and committeemen in civic, social, or professional organizations. These findings confirm the hypothesis that church participation is related to good adjustment in old age. They also lend further support to the generalization that older persons who are socially active in organizational activities of any kind have higher levels of adjustment or satisfaction than those who are inactive.

Self-Image. Underlying most activities in which people engage is some image in their own minds as to who they are and how they are related to other people and to the universe. These internalized conceptions reflect cultural values as well as those reactions of other people toward oneself which are communicated verbally and in other ways.

Two aspects of this self-image, self-rating of health and self-identification of age, are analyzed; both are related to adjustment patterns (Table 5).

Table 5. Mean Adjustment Scores of Church Leaders, Other Church Members and Non-church Members by Self-Conceptions of Health and Age

	Church Leaders		Other Church Members		Non-church Members	
	N	Adjustment	N	Adjustment	N	Adjustment
*Self-rating of health:**						
Excellent	30	17	102	14	45	13
Good	65	15	268	14	115	11
Fair	41	17	87	6	152	8
Poor	4	9	315	10	86	0
Don't know or no information	1	7	16	6	12	5
*Self-identification of age:***						
Middle-aged	77	16	276	14	115	10
Elderly	47	14	307	11	139	8
Old	9	15	134	7	115	5
Other or no information	10	15	71	9	41	5

*Chi-square $= 181.44; p < .001$
**Chi-square $= 52.82; p < .001$

Only two subcategories out of 27 (the few church leaders who considered their health to be poor and the church members who classified their health as fair) deviate from the pattern of highest adjustment among the leaders, next highest among the other church members, and lowest among the non-members. Again the hypothesis that differences in adjustment between persons of different type of church participation cannot be attributed primarily to spurious factors correlated with church participation is verified.

Summary. To summarize, in 40 comparisons of church leaders and other members in the Minnesota survey, there are only three reversals of the hypothesized pattern of higher personal adjustment among the leaders than among others. In every instance these deviations were minor with a difference of only one point between mean adjustment score for relatively small categories of persons. Similarly, reversal of the hypothesized higher adjustment scores among the other church members than among nonmembers occurred in only three instances out of 42, and only one comparison out of 41 found the non-church members to have a higher mean adjustment score than the church leaders.

The consistency of these findings from comparisons of lay leaders in churches, other church members, and non-church members gives strong support to the hypothesis that these variations are in some way directly linked with religious participation *per se* and not merely with factors that chance to be correlated with such participation.

Limitations

It would be premature, nevertheless, to state the observed relationships between church participation and adjustment in old age as an invariable relationship. Several limitations reduce the dependability of the detailed findings of the Minnesota State Survey data.

First of all, the research data used were not initially gathered for a study specifically conceived and conducted to test the relationships between church participation and adjustment in old age. Hence, certain questions about religion which could have made the analysis more precise were not included. In spite of this, the data are more adequate on the level of the categories of church participation and of the items for which cross-tabulations were made than those of most other studies which have related adjustment to religiosity.

Secondly, the adjustment scores used in this study were taken from grouped data. The mean adjustment scores were computed on the basis of mid-points of the respective categories. They, therefore, might have been slightly different had they been calculated directly from the raw data, and they may tend to minimize the extremes. This, however, is not believed to be a serious flaw except among those few persons whose adjustment was so poor that their adjustment scores were negative; all negative scores were lumped together, but positive scores were coded into one, two, or at most three specific scores (e.g., 24-22, 21-19, 18, 17-16, etc.) per coding category.

A third limitation relates to the adjustment score used in this study. Not only is it abbreviated from the original Burgess-Cavan-Havighurst Attitudes Inventory, but three of its 24 items dealt with religion. The items on religion, however, deal with *satisfactions* from and pertinent to religion, not with church participation, the independent variable of our study. The three items are: "Religion is a great comfort to me"; "Religion doesn't mean much to me"; and "Religion is the most important thing in my life." Respondents were asked simply to agree or disagree, and an "undecided" column was also provided for the interviewer's use. The scale thus reflects a subjective reaction or set of internalized evaluations of religion rather than a pattern of church participation; the latter very likely influences the former, but it is not difficult to find people with a strong subjective religious faith who are not members of any church or are only nominal members.

No effort was made to apply the tedious and costly process of analyzing the relationships by the application of multiple correlation or analysis of variance and covariance techniques. Neither did we study the data through the application of careful ex post facto experimental designs to match persons from the respective church participation categories whose backgrounds, achieved and ascribed statuses, non-religious participation patterns, and self-conceptions were similar in order to see if adjustment differences disappear when other possibly associated factors are controlled. When this was done in an earlier study of church membership and adjustment in old age, it became apparent that it was not membership *per se* but the religious factors typically associated with it that explained the relationship between membership and good personal adjustment.[21]

It can be argued validly that church leadership, and especially membership and non-membership, are not direct measures of social participation. Social participation refers to a process of social interaction; leadership and membership are merely labels for, or indicators of, certain positions or statuses within an organization. Many non-members actively attend church services and participate in religious organizations. Nevertheless, a choice to affiliate or not is reflected in one's membership status. It is common knowledge that church members as a whole participate more frequently and regularly in church activities and organizations than non-members and that few persons attain leadership roles in a church without having demonstrated their interest in it through active social participation. We do not assume that our church participation categories are direct measures of social participation in the church as such; they are merely indicators of different degrees of participation. We also recognize the complex nature and great variability of churches and their activities.

In spite of these limitations, our findings, together with the fact that more senior citizens are active in churches than in any other type of social organization, suggest that a major potential source for improving the well-being of older people is the church. Before-and-after analyses of older persons participating in various types of experimental programs established specifically to help promote their adjustment are especially desirable, for they can be used to test scientific theories pertinent to gerontology at the same time as they test the practical effects of the programs and thus provide church leaders and other social action personnel with guidelines for action. Such studies could help to indicate whether church activity contributes to good adjustment or if already well-adjusted persons are more likely than others to become active church members.

---

[21]Moberg, Church membership and personal adjustment in old age.

Conclusion

Comparisons of the personal adjustment of church leaders, other church members, and non-church members in four states have confirmed earlier research findings that church members have higher adjustment scores than non-members and that lay leaders in the church have higher scores than other members. In addition, cross-tabulations of data from the 1,340 urban respondents of the Minnesota State Survey demonstrated that the differences in adjustment between church leaders, church members, and non-church members were statistically significant at the .001 level when analyzed within categories of sex, age, education, marital status, home ownership and type of residence, participation in civic, social, and professional organizations, organizational activity levels compared to those during the respondents' fifties, self-rating of health, and self-identification of age. Only in the area of employment were the variations non-significant, but even these were in the anticipated direction. The hypothesis that church participation is related to good adjustment in old age is overwhelmingly supported by the evidence presented in this study.

CHAPTER 8

The Integration of Older Members in the Church Congregation*

DAVID O. MOBERG

Introduction

The policy statement and recommendations of the section on religion in the 1961 White House Conference on Aging included the recommendation that "every effort shall be made to see that these (special services, educational materials, and programs for the aging) do not involve an unnecessary separation from the main stream of familial or congregational life."[1] At a workshop on the role of the church in serving the aging, which was a part of the Conference on Community Resources for the Aging in Northern Virginia, "It was the unanimous opinion that the Church has a special and particular obligation to aging people to assist them in making an orderly and happy transition from middle age to elderly age. . . . The following suggestions were made: . . . 2. That older persons should be included on all committees as they have knowledge and experience; 3. That they should be integrated into the total fellowship of the Church . . . "[2] Similar statements appear repeatedly in the literature dealing with social action pertinent to the aging. Apparently it is believed by a high proportion of social workers,

*This study was made possible by a small research grant from the Hill Family Foundation and the Kansas City Association of Trusts and Foundations through the Midwest Council for Social Research on Aging. The assistance of numerous Bethel College students and especially of Ernest Beetner, my research assistant, who supervised the field work and data analysis, is deeply appreciated.

[1]Special Staff on Aging, U. S. Dept. of Health, Education, and Welfare, The Nation and Its Older People: Report of the White House Conference on Aging, Washington, D. C.: U. S. Government Printing Office, 1961, 238.

[2]Mrs. Joseph George Dunn, Conference on community resources for the aging in Northern Virginia, Aging in Virginia, 1: pp. 25-26, 1962.

family life counselors, and persons in other "helping professions" that the ideal pattern of social relationships for most senior citizens is one of integration into the mainstream of associational life rather than segregation from people of younger ages.[3]

Religious leaders are no exception to this tendency of professional people to feel that integration of all age groups is more desirable than segregation. While religious educators emphasize the need for graded instruction and curricula, they also assume that the same basic pattern of organization and the same general church services will serve all groups. They hold that, to the greatest extent possible, the aging should be integrated into existing groups, and services for them should be a normal part of the total life of the church.[4] Gray's research provides empirical evidence which supports the conclusion that, "The welcoming of all people into the church often helps to integrate older and younger persons into a common fellowship like that of an extended family which includes people of all ages. When the aging are treated as individuals who are a part of this larger fellowship, and not categorically as *old* people, the morale of the older member is greatly built up."[5]

Random observation suggests that most churches have given little attention to the peculiar interests and needs of senior citizens. Most church-leaders assume that these interests and needs are met satisfactorily through the traditional church program, and they take it for granted that the elderly are integrated into the total life of the congregation. They generally believe that the personal interests and needs of each aging individual will lead him to seek out those aspects of the church's services and program which will meet those interests and needs. As a result, they often feel that no specialized activities or services for the aging are needed. The problems of senior citizens which relate to religion and the church suggest, however, that this philosophy may be in error; even the religiously devout senior citizens who are an integral part of a church congregation experience tensions, anxieties, dissatisfactions, and frustrations in connection with the very life of the church itself, to say nothing of the additional burdens which often accompany the aging process.[6]

When the social philosophy of integration implicitly reigns over the life of a church congregation, neglect of the aging is a common result.   This

---

[3]Of interest to thousands of home builders is the increasing demand by older persons to be treated like any other citizens. "We want to live in our own homes," say the majority of oldsters, "and we want our homes to be in neighborhoods where people of all ages are living—where children are growing up, where families are enjoying life." Signs of the times: message to builders—oldsters like small homes, Adding Life to Years, 10 (January, 1963), p. 7.

[4]Charles W. Garrett, A Curriculum Structure for Older Persons in the Church Based upon a Study of the Opinions of Ministers and Older Persons (unpublished Ph.D. dissertation, New York University, 1953), p. 186, and Oscar P. Campbell, Organizing older adults in the church, International Journal of Religious Education, 30 (October, 1953) pp. 6-7.

[5]Robert M. Gray and David O. Moberg, The Church and the Older Person (Grand Rapids, Mich.: Wm. B. Eerdmans Publishing Co., 1962), p. 115.

[6]Ibid., Chap. 7, problems of the older person in the church, pp. 96-117.

neglect may be accompanied by and reflected in personal and social mal-adjustments.

On the other hand, it may be questioned, on the basis of the opinions of skilled group leaders, whether calling attention to the needs and interests of the aged through specialized programs in the church is a wise policy. To do so tends to single out and segregate the elderly, to make them more aware of their common interests, to make them interact more exclusively with one another, and thus to create a relatively isolated subculture of the aging. If statements like those quoted in the opening paragraphs of this chapter are valid, such segregation of the aging should be accompanied by more personal and social maladjustment than the policy which supports their integration into the social life of the church congregation.

The purpose of the study reported here is to explore certain facets of these problems. The research is primarily descriptive and occurred in two major stages. The first involved a description of the programs of selected churches with special reference to the place of older members in the program. The second phase consisted of interviewing individual members of the churches who were aged sixty-five years and over to test certain hypotheses related to the process of aging and the place of senior citizens in the church program.

Church Characteristics and Programs

In order to avoid theological and social differences linked with denominational variations in faith and polity, which might bias the findings, it was decided to limit the bulk of the work in the project to churches of one Protestant denomination. The denomination chosen originated as an evangelical group serving immigrants from one European nation. The European language was used in its churches until the 1920's and early 1930's. Only in 1944 did the church body decide that, instead of continuing a process of gradual assimilation into a large denomination of the same basic theological background, it should extend its ministry aggressively through significant new denominational projects. As a result, the group has grown rapidly, and informal estimates by 1960 showed that not more than one-fourth to one-third of the total membership were of the same ethnic background as the denomination. The denomination still is comparatively small, however, and it continues to hold to a conservative or evangelical theological position.

A study of this denomination's Minneapolis - St. Paul area churches in the spring of 1962 indicated that its 12 central-city congregations had an average membership of 369, while its 22 suburban churches had 154. The central-city churches had an average of 48 members aged sixty-five and over, while the suburban churches had only 9. Of these, 14 and 2, respectively, were shut-in persons unable to attend church services. There was considerable variation in the number of senior members as well as in the part they played in the life and work of the churches.[7]

---

[7]Nancy F. Erickson and Audrey Kitchell, term project for course in Methods of Social Research, Bethel College, Spring 1962. The age statistics were estimated by the pastors and hence are approximations rather than precise figures.

Four of the above congregations, all organized in the nineteenth century, had the most complete patterns of involvement on the part of their members past the age of sixty-five. Of these four churches, two were chosen for special attention in the study reported in this chapter. The chief criteria involved in their selection were basic similarities in their history, size, ecological location, denominational cooperation, and theological perspectives, together with a central difference of orientation toward the senior citizens in their membership. The one church, hereafter oversimply referred to as "Senior Club Church," has a Senior Citizens Club open to all persons past the age of fifty which meets monthly. The Club conducts a social-religious program, engages in a great deal of social fellowship, and sponsors various service projects for the church. The other church has no organized activity designed specifically for senior citizens. It assumes that their special needs are met in the usual course of the church's activities and in the programs of organized groups which are open to adults of all ages. We shall refer to it as "Conventional Church."

A summary of similarities and differences of the two congregations follows:

Similarities:	*Senior Club Church*	*Conventional Church*
Date of organization	1888	1873
Ethnic group initially served	Swedish	Swedish
Location	Inner city Minneapolis	Inner city St. Paul
Theological orientation	Evangelical Protestant	Evangelical Protestant
Denominational affiliation	A Protestant body of about 80,000	A Protestant body of about 80,000
Support of denomination	80 per cent of missions giving is through denominational channels	90 per cent of missions giving is through denominational channels
Per member contributions, 1961-62	$155	$165
Membership, 1962	666	541
Members aged 65 and over	105 (16%)	135 (25%)
Adult organizations	Women's Missionary Society with 8 sub-groups	Women's Missionary Society with 8 sub-groups
Differences:		
Membership change, 1950-1962	29-member increase	187-member decrease
Adult Education Program	Church school classes not based on age: Two special topics classes, a men's and a ladies' class	Age-graded, with highest class for all persons aged 56 and older
Other adult organizations	Men's Brotherhood meets monthly Senior Citizens Club	No separate men's organization No club for the aging
Future plans	Remain at present site	Suburban site 3 miles from present location; construction began in Spring, 1963.

In summary, both congregations attempt to integrate their senior citizens into the total church program. Until recently, Conventional Church was larger, but it has declined in membership, partly because it was influential in organizing a new suburban church. Senior Club Church has increased its membership since 1960 after a decade of no change, perhaps in part because of an aggressive program linked with a firm commitment to remain in its present neighborhood. This intention has been demonstrated tangibly and publicly through a building project and by an activity program designed to reach non-churched people in its vicinity. From the perspective of the aging, the chief difference is the Senior Citizen Club in the one church and its absence in the other. Senior Club Church hence comes closer to encouraging the development of an aging subculture, unless the senior Sunday school class in Conventional Church, which is attended by approximately half of the respondents in this study, has an equivalent latent function.

The ecological distribution of the membership of the two churches also differs. Seventeen per cent of the resident members of Senior Club Church live within one mile, compared to 36 per cent of those in Conventional Church. By comparison, 17 and 43 per cent, respectively, of the members aged sixty-five and over live within one mile.

When the area from which the churches draw their members is divided into quadrants, an imbalance of distribution is apparent. It reflects a somewhat greater concentration of industrial and warehousing facilities south of Conventional Church than there is in the vicinity of Senior Club Church:

	Per Cent Northwest	Per Cent Northeast	Per Cent Southeast	Per Cent Southwest
Senior Club Church:				
All members	22	42	18	19
Age 65+ members	21	40	17	23
Conventional Church:				
All members	24	51	13	12
Age 65+ members	24	60	6	10

The high concentration of Conventional Church's present membership in the northern quadrants and the continuing growth of population in suburbs to the north have been highly influential in its decision to relocate almost straight north of its present site. The distribution of the elderly members in terms of the direction of their residences from the church is not significantly different from that of the membership as a whole in the two churches, except for a greater proportion in Conventional Church who live in the northeast and a smaller proportion who live in the southeast.

Characteristics of Elderly Members

Of the 105 members aged sixty-five and over in the 1962 directory of members, 86 persons in Senior Club Church were active resident members. The other 19 included one who died after the directory was issued, 6 who were classified by the church as "inactive," and 12 who were non-resident (residing outside the Twin Cities metropolitan area). Of Conventional

Church's 135 elderly members, 4 had died since the directory was issued and 12 were non-resident, leaving a total of 119 who were active resident members at the time of the research. In each church 64 per cent of the active elderly resident members were interviewed (N = 55 and 76, respectively).

The resident senior members who were not interviewed are described in the following brief summary:

	Senior Club Church	Conventional Church
Innaccessible:	21	22
Out of town for extended period	0	4
Not at home, contacted once	1	0
Not at home, contacted twice	1	3
Not at home, contacted thrice or more	2	1
Moved, left no address	1	2
Sick, deaf, unable to be interviewed	9	7
Senile, incoherent, disoriented	4	3
Working, "too busy"	1	1
Sickness in the family	2	1
Refusals:	10	21
One interviewer attempt	1	2
Two interviewers	9	17
Three interviewers	0	2
Total not interviewed	31	43

Some of the refusals represent persons who began an interview but refused to complete it. The diagnosis of illness was in some instances provided by the respondent via telephone.

The age and sex of the non-interviewed resident senior members of the two churches are as follows:

	Senior Club Church	Conventional Church	Total
Men aged 65–74	6	10	16
Men aged 75 and over	2	8	10
Women aged 65–74	16	16	32
Women aged 75 and over	7	9	16
Totals	31	43	74

Comparison of these known characteristics of the non-respondents with those of the respondents (Table 1) indicates that a higher proportion of men and, especially in Senior Club Church, of the younger senior members

Table 1A. Age and Sex of Respondents (Males)

	Senior Club Church	Conventional Church	Total
Males:	15	26	41
65–69	1	8	9
70–74	3	10	13
75–79	8	6	14
80–84	2	2	4
85–89	0	0	0
90 and over	1	0	1

Table 1B. Age and Sex of Respondents (Females)

Females:	Senior Club Church	Conventional Church	Total
	40	50	90
65–69	5	17	22
70–74	13	17	30
75–79	10	12	22
80–84	6	4	10
85–89	5	0	5
90 and over	1	0	1
Totals	55	76	131

were non-respondents. This confirms the interviewers' hunch that men who were still actively employed in their professions were less likely to cooperate because of the pressures of their vocational responsibilities.

Only one man from each church was single, but 9 women from Senior Club Church and 11 from Conventional Church were unmarried. The respective figures for other marital statuses are as follows:

	Senior Club Church	Conventional Church
Married men	11	22
Widowed men	3	3
Divorced men	0	0
Married women	14	30
Widowed women	16	20
Divorced women	1	2

Conventional Church clearly has a higher proportion of married respondents than Senior Club Church. The average number of living children of the respondents was somewhat greater in Senior Club Church, perhaps because they were older than the respondents from Conventional Church. Their educational level also was lower:

	Senior Club Church	Conventional Church
Eight grades or less	36	36
Some high school	8	9
High school graduate	4	6
Business or technical school	4	6
Some college	1	7
College graduate	1	4
Post-graduate or professional school	1	8
Totals	55	76

This is closely related to their occupational status. Professional and white-collar workers were proportionately more numerous in Conventional Church, while semi-skilled, skilled, and protective and service workers were more numerous in Senior Club Church. A larger proportion of respondents in Conventional Church was still fully or partly employed. Of the 18 persons in it who were still employed, exactly one-third gave as the reason for working the need for money, one-third that they like to work, and one-third that they do not like doing nothing. A different pattern emerged for the 8 persons in Senior Club Church who still are working; only one of them said his main reason was the need for money; 4 said they like to work, and 3 do not like doing nothing.

Only four respondents from each church rated their health as below average or very poor. The majority of the remainder said it was very good or better than average. Conventional Church members rated their health somewhat higher, again perhaps because they were on the average younger in age and hence less likely to suffer from some of the more extreme physical accompaniments of the aging process.

Disengagement and Re-Engagement

Prominent among the theoretical formulations in social gerontology is the disengagement theory of Cumming and Henry.[8] They hold that, with increasing age in the later decades of life, people gradually sever their relationships with other members of society and alter the quality of those that remain. In contrast, Arnold Rose and Marvin Taves propose a re-engagement hypothesis which holds that as people lose certain social roles with the advance of old age, they assume new roles which are peculiar to older people. They thus become "re-engaged" in society in a manner different from that of their former involvement. New age-related roles replace the previous roles. For example, the new role of grandparent may replace the role of parent during and after middle age.[9] The question of the integration of older people in the church is related to various hypotheses linked with the disengagement and re-engagement theories. Some pertinent findings in this study will be summarized in relation to them, even though no crucial test of either is a product of the research.

From Table 2 it is evident that the respondents' church attendance rates show a slight tendency to decrease with advancing age. In spite of this fact, a high proportion of the respondents of all ages attend the Sunday morning service, over half of them (55 per cent) attending every Sunday. The other major church services are not attended so well. About 46 per cent do not attend the Sunday evening service, 68 per cent do not attend the midweek service and 56 per cent do not attend Sunday school. No outstanding differences appear in the attendance patterns of members of the two churches. The disengagement theory is not strongly supported by these data and they are insufficient to test the re-engagement theory. There is no direct indication as to whether the respondents who participate in these church services play different roles from those of younger church members.

Clear evidence of disengagement is evident, however, from the distribution of lay leadership positions in the church (Table 3). In both churches the highest rate of office-holding, Sunday school teaching, committee memberships, and other positions of leadership in the church was found among persons aged 25 to 44 and the next-highest among those aged 19 to 24,

---

[8]Elaine Cumming and William E. Henry, Growing Old: The Process of Disengagement, New York: Basic Books, 1961.

[9]Personal communications with Marvin J. Taves.

Table 2. Church Attendance Patterns by Age of Respondents

	Senior Club Church			Conventional Church			Both Churches		
Times Per Month	0	1–3	4+	0	1–3	4+	0	1–3	4+
Sunday morning service:									
65–69	0	2	4	2	7	16	2	9	20
70–74	2	3	11	1	11	15	3	14	26
75–79	4	3	11	2	13	3	6	16	14
80–84	2	1	5	1	0	5	3	1	10
85–89	2	2	1	—	—	—	2	2	1
90 and over	0	1	1	—	—	—	0	1	1
Total persons	10	12	33	6	31	39	16	43	72
Sunday evening service:									
65–69	2	3	1	7	1	17	9	4	18
70–74	9	6	1	10	14	3	19	20	4
75–79	10	8	0	9	5	4	19	13	4
80–84	6	0	2	4	1	1	10	1	3
85–89	3	2	0	—	—	—	3	2	0
90 and over	1	1	0	—	—	—	1	1	0
Total persons	31	20	4	30	21	25	61	41	29
Midweek service:									
65–69	5	0	1	17	7	1	22	7	2
70–74	8	5	3	19	5	3	27	10	6
75–79	13	4	1	10	4	4	23	8	5
80–84	6	1	1	5	1	0	11	2	1
85–89	5	0	0	—	—	—	5	0	0
90 and over	1	1	0	—	—	—	1	1	0
Total persons	38	11	6	51	17	8	89	28	14
Sunday school:									
65–69	4	1	1	13	4	8	17	5	9
70–74	7	4	5	16	4	7	23	8	12
75–79	9	4	5	9	2	7	18	6	12
80–84	6	0	2	3	2	1	9	2	3
85–89	4	0	1	—	—	—	4	0	1
90 and over	2	0	0	—	—	—	2	0	0
Total persons	32	9	14	41	12	23	73	21	37

Table 3. Lay Leadership Positions in the Church

Age	Senior Club Church			Conventional Church		
	No. of Positions	No. of Members	Positions per Member	No. of Positions	No. of Members	Positions per Member
Under 18	0	50	0	1	42	0.02
19–24	24	91	0.26	16	52	0.31
25–44	82	213	0.38	49	151	0.32
45–59	31	124	0.25	31	124	0.25
60–64	6	55	0.11	4	37	0.11
65–74	7	75	0.09	7	92	0.08
75 and over	1	24	0.04	1	43	0.02
Unknown	0	4	0	0	0	—
Inactive members	—	30	0	—	*	—
Totals	151	666	0.23	109	541	0.20

*Included in figures above

followed by those aged 45 to 59. Only members under the age of 18 had fewer leadership positions in proportion to their number than those aged 65 and over. As age increases among adults who have reached middle age, the number of leadership positions held decreases. The relative importance or weight of the positions does not seem to be greater among the older adults. For example, in Senior Club Church the vice chairman of the church, its treasurer, the chairman of the deacon board, and the chairmen of five other major boards and committees are aged 25 to 44; the chairman of the church, the chairmen of three major boards and committees, and the president of the men's brotherhood are aged 45 to 59. Only two outstanding positions are held by persons past the age of 60; they are the presidency of the Senior Citizens Club and the superintendency of the Sunday school.

These data are based upon analysis of the church and its organizations. When the respondents themselves were asked whether they now hold major or minor positions in the church, 4 Senior Club Church members and 3 Conventional Church members said they hold major positions, and 6 and 7, respectively, said they hold minor positions, compared to 45 and 66 who listed no positions whatever.

Patterns of church activities in the respondents' early fifties were compared to their present church activities, and these changes were in turn compared to the changes in their participation in certain other types of social activities (Table 4). The findings relative to church activities, partici-

Table 4. Changes in Church Activities in Comparison to Changes
in Other Selected Social Activities Since the Respondents' Early Fifties

Church Activities Now Compared to Early Fifties	Senior Club Church			Conventional Church		
	More Active Now	Same	Less Active Now	More Active now	Same	Less Active Now
Clubs and Organizations* outside the church:						
More active now	0	1	0	1	0	0
Same	3	7	20	0	12	18
Less active now	0	3	21	2	7	36
Associations with relatives:						
More now	0	1	27	1	3	7
Same	2	5	0	2	10	17
Less now	1	5	14	0	6	30
Associations with close friends:						
More now	0	2	4	2	2	2
Same	2	4	8	1	10	17
Less now	1	5	29	0	7	35
Number of close friends seen regularly:						
More now	0	0	5	0	2	3
Same	2	5	11	2	12	20
Less now	1	6	25	1	5	31
Time spent alone:						
More now	3	6	29	1	8	42
Same	0	3	8	2	10	8
Less now	0	2	4	0	1	4
Total number of persons	3	11	41	3	19	54

pation in clubs and organizations outside the church, associations with relatives and close friends, and time spent alone, all support the disengagement theory. Only 3 persons in each church profess to be more active in church now than in their early fifties, but 41 persons in Senior Club Church and 54 in Conventional Church said they are less active in church now than they were then. The only exception to this general pattern is among the 41 Senior Club Church members who are less active in the church now than in their early fifties; 27 of them have more associations with their relatives now than they had then, and only 14 have less association now.

Respondents were asked to name the organizations outside the church in which they were active in their early fifties but which they have now left. Fifteen per cent of the members from Senior Club Church and 39 per cent of Conventional Church members listed one or more such organizations.

Among the persons of this study, disengagement is a more common experience than re-engagement, at least when only their activity patterns are taken into consideration. Indicators of role changes and the quality of interrelationships were not analyzed, so the extent to which re-engagement outside of added activities occurred cannot be determined. The statistics given in Table 4 in the "more now" rows on participation in social organizations and on associations with relatives and friends and the figures in the "less now" row on time spent alone indicate that some persons did experience a form of re-engagement.

The Subculture of the Aging

Arnold Rose proposes elsewhere in this volume that the aging in American society are creating an emergent subculture. Distinctive factors in the status system, especially physical and mental health and social activity, help to create a separate status system for senior citizens. Wealth and education carry over from middle age as significant factors in it, but social activity and good health are not as widely distributed among the aging and take on special significance as determinants of status among them. An aging group identification or group consciousness also helps to set the aged apart as a sub-society. Many older persons have begun to think of themselves as members of a group of aging people. Recreational and other expressive associations in which they can interact primarily with persons of similar age are manifestations of this emerging subculture.

This hypothesis is closely related to the integration of the aging into society at large with its various age groups. A number of questions included in the interviewing schedule bear rather directly upon it. Foremost among these, of course, is the question of whether the respondents from Senior Club Church attend the Senior Citizens Club which is available to them there. Of the 55 respondents, 33, or 60 per cent, included it on the list of church organizations they attend. Fifty-three per cent attend women's society or men's brotherhood meetings in church, compared to 56 per cent in Conventional Church, which lacks both a brotherhood and a senior citizens club. Church business meetings are "always attended" by 24 per cent of the Senior Club Church members and by 39 per cent of the members of Conventional Church; they are never attended by 53 per cent and 24 per cent, respectively. These evidences suggest that aging members come closer to having their own subculture in Senior Club Church than in Conventional Church.

Forty-five per cent of the respondents from Senior Club Church and only 30 per cent of those from Conventional Church said they would like to "take a more active part in church." Failing health was the foremost reason given for not taking or not wanting to take a more active part in the church. It was listed by 54 per cent of the Senior Club Church members and 42 per cent of Conventional Church members. This was followed by "other people are more competent" (13 per cent and 21 per cent), "don't have enough time" (7 per cent and 9 per cent), and miscellaneous reasons, especially "old age." Only two persons, both from Conventional Church, gave "younger members won't let me" as their reason. Problems of distance and transportation were volunteered by four of its members and by five from Senior Club Church. Had the interviewing schedule specifically suggested such difficulties in this context, however, it is likely that they would have been mentioned more often. The pastor of Senior Club Church has noted that its older members do not recognize distance from the church as a factor interfering with their participation in its services and other activities, but in fact it is.

Persons who have commuted to the church for as much as half a century blame their declining participation on poor eyesight, "old age," or failing health. Driving to church, especially at night, has become an arduous task, and they do not wish to be a "bother" to or become a "burden" upon someone else by "begging" rides to all of the church's meetings. No longer attending the Sunday evening service, midweek prayer service, and church business meetings, they feel "left out" and wish that they could take a more active part in the church's program of activities. Since only 17 per cent of the older members of Senior Club Church live within one mile, compared to 43 per cent in Conventional Church, the problems associated with distance and transportation are greater in the former.

The very presence of the Senior Citizens Club might be a stimulus to some of the desire to "take a more active part in church." As the pastor stated in a letter reflecting on the findings of this study, "Perhaps our recent awakening to and emphasis upon our senior citizens has served to make our people want to feel more active than they have been." (This is another indication of the possibility that group identification on the part of the aging is increasing.) The problems of infirmity which are correlated with increasing age may also be present among a larger proportion of Senior Club Church respondents, for 60 per cent of them had passed their seventy-fifth birthday, compared to only 32 per cent of the respondents of Conventional Church.

Most of the respondents (74 per cent of those from Senior Club Church and 63 per cent from Conventional Church) named church activities in which they were active during their early fifties but in which they no longer participate. Their reasons for discontinuing such activities (in order of frequency) emphasized: inability due to illness, "I thought someone else should take their turn," desire for a rest from church work, family responsibilities, expiration of the term of office, "I thought someone else could do the work better," transfer of membership to a different church, church rules prohibiting serving consecutive terms of office, and a series of miscellaneous reasons. Only two persons, both from Conventional Church, said they were not wanted when they got old.

When asked if there ought to be more organizations and activities in their church for people of their own age group, the majority in both churches answered "no." Affirmative responses were given by only 2 per cent of Senior Club Church respondents and by 20 per cent of the respondents from Conventional Church. In addition, "don't know or uncertain" responses were given by 28 per cent of the latter but only 18 per cent of the Senior Club Church respondents. Perhaps the aging members of Conventional Church are becoming aware of special interests and needs which differentiate them from other age categories; if so, it, too, may have an emerging subculture of the aging.

Table 5. Reactions to Various Aspects of the Church Program

	Senior Club Church			Conventional Church		
	Yes	Qualified	No	Yes	Qualified	No
Are older people in good health prevented from doing things because younger people run everything?	5	13	37	10	16	50
Do younger people at church show enough respect for older people?	30	18	7	51	12	13
Are church people ignored by other members when they get sick?	4	6	45	2	7	67
Are people of all ages respected and welcomed to church services?	54	0	1	72	0	4
Do church leaders and members invite people of all ages to church?	51	4*	0	66	10*	0
Do younger members ever push senior members out of church offices?	6	0	49	12	0	64
Are people of all ages welcomed to all adult organizations?	53	0	2	70	0	6
Have you ever felt unwanted at your church?	4	0	51	1	0	75
Do you dislike any changes which have been made at church?	17	0	38	30	0	46
Have you been pushed out of any church organizations in which you once were active?	0	0	55	0	0	76
Do you think most of the older members are satisfied with the church's program?	46	0	9	51	0	25

*Don't know

It is obvious from Table 5 that most of the respondents believe that there is no significant discrimination against older people in their church. Nevertheless, a minority in each church feels that younger people hinder church action by older members, that insufficient respect is shown older people, that church members are ignored when they get sick by the other members, that younger members sometimes push senior members out of church offices, and that many older members are dissatisfied with their church's program. On the last item and on a dislike for changes that have been made at church, Conventional Church has a higher proportion of dissatisfaction among its senior members. Seventeen of its 30 respondents that disliked changes made at church referred to the new church building. (Location is perhaps the chief complaint, although architectural style, costs, and other factors were also mentioned.)

When they were asked how much influence the average older member has in their church compared to young and middle-aged members, none of the Senior Club Church respondents but 9 of the Conventional Church members answered "more." Corresponding figures for "less" were 19 and 23; "same," 14 and 25; and "don't know," 22 and 19. In Senior Club Church 2 respondents felt left out of things at church often, 39 sometimes, and 19 never, compared to 5, 10, and 61, respectively, in Conventional Church. This is additional evidence that the senior members of the latter are more fully integrated into the total church program than the senior members of Senior Club Church.

Church Integration and Personal Adjustment

As we have seen, there is some evidence that the members of Conventional Church are more fully integrated into the total church program than are the members of Senior Club Church, who more nearly have a sub-culture within the larger church fellowship. Is the pattern of a church's activities for the aging related to the personal adjustment of its members?

The interviewing schedule in this exploratory study included the modified Burgess-Cavan-Havighurst Attitudes Inventory[10] which was used in the Minnesota senior citizens surveys, described in Chapter 19. This instrument indicates the respondent's own evaluation of his adjustment in many areas of life activities. It reflects the extent to which he succeeds in reorganizing his activities and attitudes to his own satisfaction. In comparison to six other measures of adjustment in old age, it measures the activity factor especially well in men and personal relations and sociability especially well in women.[11]

The mean adjustment score of all 55 respondents in Senior Club Church was 21.3, compared to 22.7 for all 76 in Conventional Church, out of a highest possible score of 28.0. The range of the scores is almost identical:

---

[10]Ernest W. Burgess, Ruth S. Cavan, and Robert J. Havighurst, Your Activities and Attitudes, Chicago: Science Research Associates, 1948.

[11]Joseph H. Britton, Dimensions of adjustment of older adults, Journal of Gerontology, 18 (January, 1963), pp. 60-65.

from 10 to 27 in Senior Club Church and from 10 to 28 in Conventional Church. The differences in adjustment scores between the two churches largely reflect people past the age of eighty-five in Senior Club Church and their absence among the respondents of Conventional Church, for these seven persons had a mean adjustment score of only 18.1. The variations in adjustment scores between members of the two churches when age and sex are held constant are slight and insignificant (Table 6).

Table 6. Mean Personal Adjustment Scores by Age and Sex

	Senior Club Church			*Conventional Church*		
Age	Men	Women	Total	Men	Women	Total
65 – 69	26	23	24	23	24	24
70 – 74	23	21	22	21	23	22
75 – 79	20	21	21	22	20	21
80 – 84	21	21	21	23	22	23
85 – 89	—	16	16	—	—	—
90 and over	23	22	22	—	—	—
All ages	21	21	21	21	23	23

The marked decline in adjustment scores with increasing age which has been observed in other studies is not evident here. Whether this deviation is a product of the unique influence of the church upon this particular sample of respondents or a result of the selection process by which, pre-sumably, the least adjusted of the church members refused to be inter-viewed or were incapable of it remains a question for speculation.

It is clear, however, that insofar as the two churches selected for in-tensive study represent different policies of integration-segregation of their elderly members, neither policy produces better adjusted members when adjustment is measured by the modified Chicago Attitudes Inventory. Possibly the numerous similarities of the two churches were an overriding factor that eliminated other potential differences. The basic similarity of comparative figures for smaller samples of aging persons in two other churches, one a relatively new suburban congregation of the same denomi-nation and the other an independent rural church of similar theological and organizational characteristics, suggests, however, that the same generaliza-tions may apply on a much wider scale in church congregations in many types of communities and with wide variations in their programs for the aging.

Conclusions

We have seen that there are only slight differences in the attitudes of elderly church members in two similar congregations which have different programs relative to their senior members. No significant differences be-tween the churches were observed in the adjustment of the members who were interviewed. Much stronger evidence of disengagement than of re-engagement was found, although no crucial test of either hypothesis was possible. Evidences of an emerging subculture of the aging were present in both congregations; although they were not strong in either, they were somewhat more obvious in Senior Club Church.

The narrowness and exploratory nature of this study, limitations of the size and selectivity of the samples of respondents, and inconsistencies occasionally noted by interviewers between respondents' answers to different questions point to the need for caution in using these results as a basis for either accepting or rejecting any theory in social gerontology or for modifying any church program. Taken in conjunction with the findings of other investigations and the experience of skilled leaders in geriatric programs, however, they may be very helpful and enlightening. The interviewers, for instance, discovered that transportation to church is a significant problem for many senior members; that more visitation by lay or professional church leaders is desired by many of them, especially those who are shut-in; that they do not merely want activities provided for them but they do want an opportunity to feel useful and worthwhile in some activity valued for more than its simple "enjoyment"; that they do not want to be a burden to the church or its pastor but to be independent and to take care of themselves; and that they would like to be recognized for past and present services in the church. These observations of the interviewers as a result of their conversations with respondents are consistent with the conclusions of other studies. They give added weight to relevant recommendations for action made by church leaders, religious educators, social workers, and others who have a concern for the welfare of older people.

IV

Interaction in the Family

CHAPTER 9

Family Interaction Patterns
of the Aged: A Review*†

HAROLD E. SMITH

Introduction

There has been a significant accumulation of scholarly writing on the social aspects of aging in American society in the past two decades. The upsurge in research and writing on this subject in the area of the family is notable and is found in monographs, articles in professional journals, special bulletins, general reference works, and chapters in sociology and psychology textbooks. All this suggests an increased attention among sociologists to the field of social gerontology.

The bibliography for this chapter is only a sampling and no claim is made for its being exhaustive. The amount of published research, while seriously lacking in many areas, was actually greater than the author expected at the beginning. Fortunately, two excellent syntheses of the research and writing on the aged in a family context, that of Schorr (66) and that of Streib and Thompson (78), have already appeared and were of great assistance.

The outline used in preparing this chapter reflects both the author's interest and his interpretation of the nature of the subject under review. Two rather different concerns on the part of scholars have contributed to the

---

*The assistance of Catherine Bennett, Carolyn Carlson and Ingrid Erickson in the literature review is much appreciated.

†The numbers found throughout the text of this chapter refer to selected items of the bibliography, of which there are ninety-seven in all. Identification of a given reference will be facilitated if the reader will number the items in the bibliography consecutively beginning with ALBRECHT as number 1 and ending with YOUNG and WILLMOT as number 97.

development of knowledge about family interaction patterns of the aged. The first of these is an inquiry into the nature of family and kinship structure by a group of sociologists who have a strong theoretical orientation. The second is the interest of many scholars in the adjustment and morale problems of the aged; these have turned to seeking an understanding of family life and its importance in this regard.

To provide a setting for a review of the literature, there is first presented: (a) a brief conceptual framework, (b) a look at the marital status of the aged using demographic sources, and (c) some comments on the interconnections between kinship and other institutions, with attention to the influence of social change, especially a discussion of change in family and kinship institutions. Following this is the review proper arranged under five convenient subheadings.

Conceptual framework. Sociological study of the family life cycle quite generally includes a treatment of the "middle and later years" period (36). This is, for our purpose, a convenient concept to direct attention to the study of aged persons in a kinship and family context. In this paper, family and kinship is viewed primarily as a *social institution.* However, it is not considered an autonomous unit of social structure. Rather the family system is seen as having numerous ties with other aspects of society. A few examples of such interconnections may illuminate this point. Note the intrusion of the adult's working hours into his family concerns, or governmental regulation of marriage and the care of dependent children, or family adoption of religious teachings regarding character development. Thus, family-kinship structure is but one of a number of social institutions which together define the principal goals of human behavior and regulate their achievement. Common to all institutions are *cultural norms,* which are prescriptions for, or prohibitions against, certain behavior or actions, beliefs or attitudes. The existence of such rules which guide human behavior can be illustrated by reference to selected changes in family and kinship norms. The emergence of the "equalitarian family" to replace a patriarchal one, and the disappearance of chaperonage so that young people tend to be on their own in dating and courtship are cases in point. To recapitulate, the family-kinship institution may be defined as embracing those complexes of cultural norms that cohere around the values of mate selection, marriage, coitus, reproduction, the care and rearing of children, family maintenance, and the well-being of blood relatives.

Each individual from birth onward may have a mother and father, possibly one or more siblings, and other relatives. Through marriage he acquires a spouse with whom he may share the experience of reproduction and become a parent. The foregoing areas of human existence, when taken together, constitute a considerable arena for social interaction, most of which is likely to be on an intimate basis. The associations and interactions among individuals in the family are typically repeated or regularized so that, for example, a child learns what to expect from his father or sister or grandmother, and they in turn learn what to expect of him. Thus, mutual expectations arise from the interaction among family members, and are an indication of the existence of *interaction patterns,* or regularized interaction, within the family setting. A basic task in sociology is the systematic observation of such patterns with a view to the development of meaningful generalizations about them. The stable expectancies and interaction patterns that characterize family living may well approximate, but do not typically coincide with, the cultural norms of the kinship-family institution. It can be demonstrated that the recurring interactions among family members may conform to, evade, or modify the norms and values of the kinship-family institution. Specific situations calling for action seldom follow the cultural prescription perfectly. In addition, interaction may proceed where rules or guides are lacking and become patterned sufficiently to give rise to new norms and values. (The foregoing conceptual orientation is essentially that of Williams (93), albeit somewhat abbreviated.)

Interaction may also be analyzed from the viewpoint of the actor. The concepts "position" and "role" are helpful in this connection. Persons who are involved in interaction may be thought of as occupying certain *positions,* such as that of employer, teacher, mother, son, and so on. Typically, such a position is polar in that it implies a reciprocal position, e.g., husband-wife, mother-child, leader-follower. Each position generally includes sets of rights and duties. *Rights* are the privileges that the occupant of the position may enjoy, while *duties* represent his obligations or responsibilities. We shall refer to these sets of rights and duties that apply to the occupant of a given position as his *role.* As such they provide rules and expectations that guide the interaction between the occupants of specific positions. It follows that the rights associated with one position may likely constitute the obligations of another, but reciprocal position, e.g., the obligations of a husband provide the privileges that a wife may enjoy and vice versa. A fuller analysis of family member positions and roles may involve additional concepts in order to deal with such matters as role performance, role acceptance, role conflict. However, these concepts are not essential for the present study. Another limitation of the above formulation has to do with its lack of treatment of the two parts of role definition: (a) the cultural and (b) that which arises from the unique experiences of the interacting persons.

Marital Status of the Aged: Demographic Aspects. In March 1962, there were approximately 17.2 million persons in the United States aged sixty-five or over (89). The aging of the population has been documented elsewhere and needs no elaboration here. It is interesting to note, however, that at least one analyst predicts a reversal of this trend and tells us that in the last third of the present century, the United States' population will commence "younging" again. In other words, he predicts that the proportion of aged persons (fifty years and older) in the total will commence decreasing by 1970 (23).

A few observations on the family, marital, and residence status of the aged (sixty-five and over) in the United States will be presented, using a recent report of the U. S. Bureau of the Census (89). In March, 1962, approximately three out of four aged persons were *living in families*. In about two-thirds of the cases where the aged lived in families, both husband and wife were present. This includes both those older married couples living by themselves and those sharing a house or apartment with relatives. In general, the former pattern predominates. Approximately one in each five aged persons *lived alone* in a house, apartment, or room. This pattern applied to three times as many females as to males. It follows that of 10.3 million households headed by persons sixty-five and over in March 1962, almost one-third (32 per cent) were single person households. There is also a slight tendency for this pattern to increase (89). The remainder of the aged population (seven per cent) is somewhat equally divided between residence in (a) households with unrelated persons and (b) hospitals or other group settings.

Some information regarding the marital status of the aged in March, 1962 is presented in Table 1 and comparisons are made with March, 1950. Little more than half as many aged females as aged males were married in March, 1962. The extent of widowhood among aged females was two and one-half to three times that for aged males. The interpretation of these comparisons is not difficult. At least three factors have a bearing on this pattern: (a) the greater life expectancy of females compared to males, which leads to an unbalanced sex ratio; (b) the tendency for husbands to be about three years older than their wives, and (c) the differential in opportunities for marriage that favors males, due chiefly to the tradition of male initiative in courtship. It is interesting to note that "to get married" is the prevailing American pattern for both sexes, although this nominally occurs in the late teens or early twenties. Ninety-three per cent of both males and females reported having been married at one time compared to a lonely seven per cent who spent all of their lives as single persons.

Table 1. Marital Status, by Sex for Persons 65 Years and Older, for the United States, March 1962 and March 1950*

| | | 1962 | | 1950 | |
Marital Status	*Both Sexes* (*Thousands*)	*Male* (*Per Cent*)	*Female*	*Male* (*Per Cent*)	*Female*
Single	1,168	6.3	7.0	8.1	8.0
Married	9,271	73.0	38.4	65.8	36.0
Widowed	6,539	19.0	53.4	23.9	55.3
Divorced	252	1.7	1.2	2.2	0.7
Total	17,230	100.0	100.0	100.0	100.0
Ever married	—	93.7	92.8	—	—
Total number of individuals (thousands)	—	7,710	9,520	5,755	6,408
Per cent distribution by sex	—	44.7	55.3	47.3	52.7

*Source: Current Population Reports—Population Characteristics, Series P-20, No. 122, U. S. Department of Commerce, Washington, D. C., March 22, 1963.

The marital status of the aged in 1962 shows a marked similarity to that of the aged in 1950. There is some indication that a slightly higher proportion of the 1962 population was *married* and consequently a somewhat smaller proportion was *widowed*. In addition, the male-female contrasts in each of these categories were sharper in 1962 than in 1950 (Table 1).

Family and Kinship in Relation to Other Institutions: The Changing American Family

The interrelatedness of the several aspects of social structure are well indicated in a study of cultural change in its impacts on the family and on aged persons. The very great modification of American social forms and attitudes in recent decades confirms the notion of a ready acceptance of innovation in American culture. Social changes associated with the emergence of the nuclear family, the decline of the extended family, and the loss of roles for the aged in society have been indeed far reaching. This and other aspects of the family in transition are presented in the following discussion. An attempt is made to understand changes in family structures within a larger pattern of technological and institutional change. The approach is similar to that of Kirkpatrick and others (15, 42, 56).

Social change has been accelerating in the last one hundred years, generally fostered by a scientific approach to the manifold aspects of human existence. Technological advance which has accompanied scientific discoveries has greatly enriched mankind, and this has lead to an increased emphasis on science. For example, the use of mechanical power in factory production to replace manual labor has had wide repercussions. To it we can attribute expansion of the factory system, the growth of cities, and vastly improved systems of transportation and communication. It follows that family interaction patterns have been significantly altered by the frequency of movements of family members, and the ease of communication, compared with a generation ago.

For a second example, let us look at developments in human biology and health. Medical science and technology have made real strides in the prevention and control of human disease. Recently, increased interest has been shown in the control of fertility and in artificial insemination. Life expectancy has risen to the proverbial three score and ten, which has led to the aging of the United States population. With the increase in the number of the aged has come concern with improved services for the aged, such as health and medical care, pension plans, retraining, as well as fuller utilization of their abilities and skills.

The Social Consequences of Scientific Changes. Economic effects of the scientific and technological advances of the nineteenth and twentieth centuries have been numerous and dramatic. In the United States the material level of living has shown a marked rise, although evidences of personal insecurity still remain. The expansion of the American economic system has been accompanied by a huge growth of population in urban centers. In the eighty years, 1880 to 1960, the United States population increased from approximately 50 millions to 180 millions. During the same period, the proportion of the United States population that is urban increased from approximately 28 per cent to 70 per cent. Associated with urban life are such characteristics as high mobility of individuals, contrasts in wealth and poverty, and a lack of conditions favorable to the extended family. In the city, wealth and its symbols are often criteria of social status, and this reflects a pattern of life that heightens individualism. As these forces have impinged on the family, it has veered away from traditional patterns.

As a producing unit, the urban family has long since been eclipsed. Its chief remaining economic activity is that of consumption. Lost is the solidifying effect of family members sharing in a common productive enterprise. New values have appeared which reflect the competition of economic and familial institutions for the loyalty of the individual. These include a broadened choice of vocation, opportunities for a sense of achievement apart from the family, and most importantly, financial independence. Vertical mobility through occupational achievement and its possible change of status represented still another challenge to family influence and control over the individual.

Another consequence of the shift to factory production was the employment of women outside the home. Often women replaced male workers, since they were willing to work for less pay than men, or they moved into jobs for which females were more suitable. Employed wives have made a substantial contribution to the increased level of living of American families. A reduced birth rate and fewer children per family were other results of the changed economic patterns.

A revolution in parental authority appeared before the turn of the century in the urban centers and later became quite widespread. The time-honored tradition of the husband as the family patriarch gave way to the newer values of the democratic family. With the father employed away from home, the wife necessarily assumed many authority functions formerly reserved for the husband. In fact, the blurring of male and female roles in the American culture today is a product of (a) economic changes and the movement of woman into the labor force, (b) political changes in which women secured rights equal with men, (c) the tendency for females to pursue the same educational programs as males, and (d) other factors. The growth of elaborate educational, religious and governmental institutions in American society in the past hundred years is in itself evidence of the transfer of family functions away from the family. However, the family still retains important functions, especially its role as a socializer, its provision of affection, maintenance, and social class placement.

Not the least of the modifications in family interaction patterns are those relating to the older person's role in the kinship group. As society has placed more emphasis on productivity, upward social mobility, individuality, and marital happiness, it has become increasingly difficult for the aged to maintain meaningful social relationships (56). The changed situation in the extended family comes into focus when we cite the following questions and comments from Burgess (15): "(a) Should adult children offer an aging parent or parents a home? (b) What should be the *moral* and legal responsibility of children for the financial support of indigent parents? and (c) What if any should be the reciprocal roles of aging parents and their adult married sons and daughters? At present, then, there is confusion and conflict because the relationship of the older and the younger generation has not been re-defined in terms of the present situation." While social scientists have made real strides in undertaking the basic research for securing answers to questions like those raised by Burgess, more studies are urgently needed.

Kinship Structure in Nuclear and Extended Families

In this and subsequent sections, a numbered series of "propositions" or assertions are presented. These statements are intended to convey in summary form hypotheses, conclusions, and tentative generalizations drawn from the literature, or devised by the author. Admittedly there are disadvantages to this procedure. The statements vary in type, and reflect different levels of abstraction. In addition, there are included descriptive and correlational items as well as assertions which are definitional and predictive. While they are grouped loosely in five sections, no claim is made that they fit into a logical system.

The nature of American kinship-family structure has been the subject of lively discussion among sociological researchers recently. Much of the discussion centers on the validity of Parsons' contention (58, 59) that the "isolated nuclear family" is the only type of family which is functional in an industrial, bureaucratized society. The pressures of increased geographic mobility and upward social mobility operate to "nuclearize" the family, according to Parsons (58, 59). Other sociologists, notably Litwak, Sussman and Burchinal, find in their researches evidence of a viable extended family adapted to present conditions of occupational and geographic mobility. In fact, they stress the function of this extended family, especially its support for the nuclear family (53, 54, 83, 84, 85, 86). In this connection, it is important to distinguish between two forms of the extended family: (a) a vestigial one resembling the traditional extended family of nineteenth century Europe and America, and (b) one which reflects the current urban and industrial values of American society. These researchers define the extended family as consisting of two or more nuclear families which are linked together through blood and affinal ties, which have relatively equal status, and for whom family ties are an important goal. A basic argument for the foregoing view of kinship-family structure is the higher rate of interaction of family members with relatives than with other persons (41, 26, 5). Some propositions follow:

1. Understanding the family as a functioning social system which is interrelated to other systems in society is possible only by conceptualizing

an extended family as well as a nuclear family (10, 12, 53, 54, 85, 88, 65).

2. The extended family in urban areas is no more disintegrated than in rural areas and has, in fact, gained in importance since it provides companionship, affection, and other primary group relationships for its members (41). A corollary hypothesis is: For the urban extended family, relatives are an important source of companionship and support, as well as the most important type of informal group association (5, 7, 78, 96).

3. The amount of interaction that members of the extended family engage in with others in the kinship group is not related to the degree of urbanization of their place of residence. The evidence on this subject is conflicting. Some writers (3, 22, 55) hold that there is more kinship interaction in rural communities, while other researchers contend that the urban family is as strong or stronger that the rural family (5, 57, 60, 61).

4. Extended family relationships can be maintained in an industrial, bureaucratized society despite differential rates of geographic mobility. However, the type and frequency of interaction among individuals within the extended family is associated with (a) degree of kinship, and (b) distance of residence of kin (21, 53, 62, 64, 88).

5. Persons with strong ties to the extended family are more status-oriented than are persons without such ties. In other words, extended family connections are not detrimental to occupational mobility, and they may well assist upward status movement (6, 49, 52, 54, 80). Streib (78) argues that the aged not only accept the current norms regarding achievement in American society, they want their adult children to follow an upward career path, even when they (the parents) are left in a lower status position.

6. Kinship structure, while ideally symmetrical relative to the interaction of the nuclear family with both the husband's and wife's relatives, in practice reflects stronger ties with the latter (64, 97).

7. The rate of fulfillment of obligations outside the nuclear family decreases as the nuclear family increases in size, since Ego has a relatively constant amount of time and effort to devote to interaction (64).

8. The nuclear family is basically child-centered and the roles of adult family members relative to aged and retired parents are but vaguely defined (3, 43). The foregoing reflects societal change and its impact on kinship-family institutions (15, 18, 19, 43, 45).

9. It has been theorized that there is a distinction between (a) solidarity or integration in the *nuclear* family and (b) integration in the *extended* family. Hence, persons who rate high in the former do not necessarily rate high in the latter and vice versa. Rogers and Sebald have advanced these concepts—family integration and kinship orientation—not only in recognition of the foregoing distinction, but also to clarify what a number of scholars have been studying under the concept of "familism" (65).

10. Interaction patterns characteristic of kinship-family structure vary in accordance with (a) variations in economic support among family members, (b) variations in emphasis on affectional relations among members,

and (c) other factors. (This hypothesis is adapted from a research proposal of Coult and Habenstein entitled, "The functions of extended kinship in an urban milieu" [20].)

11. The extent of social isolation of the *nuclear* family is more a function of expectations in parent-offspring interaction than of changed societal and kinship-family structure (13).

12. A certain amount of conflict between generations is to be expected as a result of the operation of such factors as (a) differential rates of socialization, and (b) age differences and their associated attitudes and values (22, 25).

Husbands and Wives

The central place of the role concept in the sociological study of interaction between husbands and wives needs no justification. Presumably, role changes occur in the lives of aged persons as well as in other stages of the family life cycle. At least one sociologist contends that when marital expectations are both understood and reciprocated by both spouses, affectional relations tend to be satisfying (78). There is a noticeable scarcity of published research on the conjugal relations of the aged. However, a sampling of the literature has yielded some hypotheses and findings:

1. Both husbands and wives experience redefinition of their marital roles after the husband's retirement. One aspect of this is the husband's increased assistance to the wife with homemaking tasks (51).

2. The greater involvement of husbands, after their retirement, in homemaking and domestic activities, is associated with a growth in companionship and compatibility with the wife (51). A corollary hypothesis is: Wives find their marriages more satisfying after their husbands' retirement than before, owing chiefly to an upsurge in common interests (51).

3. Morale of the aged is in large part a function of the consistency between performance and expectations in husband-wife interaction. Since aged married spouses have each other, their morale would likely be higher than that of single or widowed persons (39).

4. Mutual understanding of one another's roles by husbands and wives is greater for the aged than for any previous stage of the family life cycle (8).

5. Coital interaction patterns of aged couples are considerably modified from earlier stages of the family life cycle, mainly as a result of (a) reduced frequency of coitus, and (b) disappearance of fears of unwanted pregnancy following the menopause. The foregoing contribute to a greater marital satisfaction of wives (33, 50).

6. The power of husbands in the marital interaction patterns of aged couples is associated with the relative scarcity of males in the aged population (8). The implication here is that the aged wife whose husband has survived shows considerable deference to him.

7. Withdrawal of the husband from the work role (retirement) does not significantly affect his power in husband-wife interaction since (a) his

reduced economic contribution to the marriage is compensated for by an increased contribution to homemaking and domestic activities (8).

8. Patriarchal control in marital interaction will be found to a larger extent in aged couples than in middle-aged and younger couples, since the aged will have been less affected by socio-familial change than the others (8).

9. Democratic and equalitarian power structures in aged couples are more likely to be associated with high marital adjustment than are patriarchal or matriarchal power structures.

The Aged and Their Adult Children

The interaction patterns of the aged with their adult children is a central concern in a study of the aged in a family context. While there has been no broad systematic study of this important area, several smaller studies are quite suggestive of the direction research may take. These deal with patterns of interaction relating to care and affection, the flow of financial support, operation of kinship-family networks in times of crisis or for ceremonies, and the living together of three or more generations. (The latter topic is handled in a separate section of this report.)

The following propositions summarize some of the findings of this research:

1. While parents and children are expected to maintain close psychological relationships through visiting, mutual aid, and in other ways, the independence of each of the conjugal family units is considered sacrosanct. However, an important proportion of the aged, a significant minority, lacks meaningful or adequate kinship ties with their offspring or other relatives (47, 78).

2. Societal pressures may operate to influence adult children to care for and support their dependent parents. When this produces a major downward adjustment in the level of living of the former, role conflicts and personal problems likely appear. This suggests that vestigial mutual aid patterns of the traditional extended family may be still operating in aged–adult children interaction. (34, 42)

3. Material assistance moves in both directions between the aged and their adult offspring, with the net flow from the older to the younger generation. However, the reverse applies where both generations live together (66, 83, 86).

4. The aged place a higher value on care and affectional support from their children than on material or financial assistance (47, 71, 78).

5. The numerous services that adult children provide for their aged relatives reflect a valid kin and filial responsibility. Examples of these services are physical care, shelter, doing household tasks and sharing leisure time pursuits (29, 40, 66, 71, 78, 88, 97, 44).

6. The sense of duty toward the support of aged and retired parents varies among adult offspring, and also varies with sex, birth order, and

experience during childhood (30, 43).

7. A "good" son or daughter is supposed to provide financial assistance to an aged parent who is in need. The extent that parents and offspring indicate attitudes favoring filial support of aged parents is a cultural phenomenon, and varies with socioeconomic status (38, 66, 76, 78).

8. Financial contributions by adult offspring to the support of parents who live separately, are more often made to non-married women, less often to non-married men, and least often to married couples. However, only a small portion of the aged receive such assistance (66).

9. A reversal of roles is likely a characteristic of the interaction patterns between the dependent aged and their adult children, i.e., children tend to become like parents to their dependent elders, and elders become like offspring of their children. This may well operate as a psychological threat leading to and intensifying role conflict and personal problems for either or both the aged and the adult children (28, 34, 37, 42, 73).

10. The aged are not isolated from the families of their children. While they live in separate residences, they prefer to be close to their children's homes or to that of other relatives with whom they interact frequently (72, 78). Physical isolation of the aged from their offspring is not significantly associated with the extent of social isolation (10, 72, 81, 82, 88).

11. Adjustment and morale are functions of the consistency between performance and expectations in the interaction among the aged and their adult offspring.

12. The extent of conflict between the aged and their adult offspring varies in time and between families and is affected by (a) differences in child rearing practices between generations, (b) the rate of social change at any particular time, and (c) divergence in beliefs and values (22, 25).

13. Interaction between the aged and their adult children is mutually satisfying when living with or away from parents is a matter of choice and not of necessity, both for the elderly and the younger couple (14).

14. The attitudes of adult offspring regarding support of aged parents varies according to the degree of hardship present in the situation that is experienced by the children. As the population becomes more urban and secular, as levels of living have risen, adult offspring have become more reluctant to support aged parents (24, 76).

15. The norms dealing with aged–adult offspring interaction patterns are often more consistent and clear in the small community than in larger population centers. For example, Britton, Mather and Lansing studied a small Pennsylvania community and inferred the following community norms from investigation of attitudes and anecdotal statements: (a) The aged should allow their grown children to lead their own lives and function without parental guidance. However, parents should be of assistance when needed or when it can be given easily. Aged persons should be responsible for themselves, enjoy their children and grandchildren, and do as they wish. They should be willing to accept help from their own children or other persons when necessary: (b) Grown children and/or siblings (of the aged)

should assume responsibility for the older person who is senile, in physical or financial distress, or without friends (11). The foregoing findings were similar to those of Shanas (69).

The Three-Generation Family

The three-generation family in the United States falls somewhere in between the conjugal and the consanguineal types of families. When aged parents share a residence with a married son or daughter and their children, there is emphasis on consanguineal relations. On the other hand, a resourceful couple may well "take in" a mother or father into their home with but slight modification in the typical nuclear family pattern. When either of the two foregoing patterns occur, there is most likely an awareness on the part of the participants that their enlarged family does not conform to the prevailing societal kinship-family structure. Generally, the aged person(s) in such an arrangement have other offspring who are not included in the shared dwelling. This situation will have at some point required a choice of who is to join forces, as well as probable decision-making about the inequity of the burden (or good fortune) in relation to other siblings.

Available reports indicate that slightly more than one-fourth of the aged in the United States occupy a shared residence with one or more of their adult offspring (35, 69, 79). From another standpoint, it has been estimated that two or three per cent of all families are three-generation families. However, the number of American families that have had this experience at some time is probably somewhat greater (35, 76). A small number of fruitful sociological studies on this topic have already appeared which point the way to further studies. The following are some of their findings and hypotheses:

1. Who is the head of a three-generation household is determined by functional considerations, such as who provides the income, who owns or rents the home and who assumes the dominant role. The special survey completed in 1952 showed the head most generally is an adult son (35, 79).

2. A separate independent residence for the nuclear family is the preferred pattern even among those who have at some time lived in a three generation family. Sharing the home with relatives is frequently a matter of necessity and may well give rise to mixed feelings among the participants. In fact, competing and conflicting interaction patterns are implicit in the attitudes and behavior of Americans relative to sharing a home as part of a three-generation family (14, 17, 45, 47, 76, 27, 46).

3. That parent-daughter family ties are stronger than parent-son family ties is reflected in the patterns of sharing a home with relatives. Note the following examples: (a) Aged parents are more likely to live with a daughter and her husband and children, than with a son, his wife and children (35, 89). (b) Newly married couples are more likely to live with the wife's parents than with the husband's parents (35, 89). (c) Aged widowed women generally live with one of their adult children, whereas aged widowed men are more likely to live alone (18, 75).

4. The three-generation family is both efficient and functional when adult children accept responsibility for aged parents. This pattern is more prominent in the working class than in other classes, and reflects a way of sharing efficiently their limited material resources. It is also a way to meet the need of the aged family members (15, 45, 66).

5. The three-generation family is functional for all the generations involved. Benefits to the aged include having a home, aid with living expenses, protection, nursing care and affection. Benefits to the adult children and their offspring include having a home, assistance with child-care and homemaking tasks, someone to turn to in a crisis, and awareness of parental interest and concern (1, 14, 48).

6. The likelihood of the occurrence of three-generation families varies with ethnic background, and is greater for Hungarian and Italian Americans than for British, German or Irish Americans (16, 31, 32, 47).

7. There is typically no essential role for the aged person in the urban three-generation family. However, the likelihood of the aged person having an active role is increased by the following factors: (a) the presence of pre-adolescent children, (b) the adult wife has no more than a high school education, (c) the aged person is a female, (d) the adult offspring's marriage has less than sixteen years' duration, (e) the aged person has resided with the married offspring less than nine years, (f) the family is small in numbers (67, 68, 76, 95).

8. Aged persons with high incomes or wealth are more likely to have an active role in the three-generation family, since this increases the power of the aged person in interaction with other family members (67, 68).

9. As growing adolescent children assume more responsibility in the three-generation family, the aged person's roles will likely move in the direction of reduced importance (67, 68).

10. The division of labor between the adult male and the adult female in the urban three-generation family differs significantly from other families. This suggests an important adaptation to the presence of aged parents (67, 68).

11. Success and family adjustment is enhanced in the three-generation family when family functions are broadened in such ways as: (a) increased activities for socializing the young, (b) increased economic activity— perhaps food preservation, making clothes, or other home production, and (c) aid to the younger generation in occupational mobility when this seems desirable. Such broadened functions provide satisfying roles for the aged family members.

12. Success in the three generation family is enhanced when the aged mother is able to yield authority to her daughter-in-law (88).

13. Conflict between the aged and their adult offspring arises most likely from the historical and cultural setting of family life, rather than from the psychological characteristics of the aged as a group, or from the struggle for status with younger age groups. Such conflict would be aggravated by sharing a residence in a three-generation family (25),

The Aged and Their Grandchildren

Since considerable research has focused on grandparent-grandchild inter-action patterns, the topic is treated in this paper also. Presumably, the study of these interaction patterns should also take into account their possible association with parent-child and parent-grandparent interaction patterns. Caution is needed to avoid equating grandparent with "aged," since grandparenthood often arrives in middle age. The subject of the aged and their grandchildren, then, is really one aspect of a broader grandparent-grandchildren study. Several hypotheses follow:

1. Contacts with grandchildren, frequently avoided during middle age, when they make for clearer recognition of the aging process are actually sought by the aged. Hence the "aged" period marks a reversal in attitudes toward grandchildren, since they are now accepted and contacts with them are a matter of satisfaction (19, 78). Ambivalence in grandparent-grand-child interaction patterns is associated, on the one hand, with satisfaction that the family line is carried on, but on the other, with a residual un-pleasant awareness of the former's chronological maturity (4, 94).

2. The grandparent role in the extended family is really a "grandmother role," irrespective of whether the holder is male or female. The role of authority and responsibility, an earlier pattern associated with the grand-father, has been swept away by social change. The actions of providing financial support and authority are guarded jealously by a child's own father, whereas baby sitting, child care, household tasks and companionship can be provided by either grandfather or grandmother (19, 91).

3. The pattern of interaction between the aged and their grandchildren is typically one of solicitation and gratification with a minimum of obliga-tion. Older people gain much from associations with grandchildren—new ideas, emotional response, and personal enrichment. Grandparental attitudes reflect personal pleasure, pride, and a sense of duty in their interaction with grandchildren (1, 90).

4. Interaction of the aged with their grandchildren is chiefly that of social participation including: (a) visits, both short and extended, (b) exchange of gifts, (c) exchange of letters and other communications, (d) following up the growth and development and adventures of the young, and (e) sharing the wisdom of the elders when it is tapped by grandchildren or by their parents (1, 57).

5. Grandmothers who are active in the care and rearing of their grand-children are: (a) predominantly maternal, i.e., they care for their daugh-ters' children, and (b) well accepted by their daughters either through a sense of need or due to their control over their daughters (9).

6. While the community expects parents to care and to provide for their dependent offspring, this responsibility may be passed to grand-parents who are capable of performing it, provided the parents are clearly absent or are incapacitated (1).

7. Grandparents may serve as "middlemen" or "arbiters" in the conflicts of parents and children, mitigating parental anger, while risking similar

anger directed toward themselves (66). It is the nature of the extended family that grandparents, above all others, can interfere in the relations between parents and children. The roles of grandmother and grandfather are frequently in conflict with the role of mother-in-law and father-in-law, and this is likely to be associated with conflict between generations (28, 92).

8. When grandparents exercise authority over parents, the relations of the grandparents to their grandchildren tend toward formality, whereas if the grandparents do not exercise such authority, they have close, indulgent, and warm relations with their grandchildren (4).

Summary and Conclusion

Obviously, this short review falls far short of a complete summary of empirical and theoretical progress on the topic with which it deals. It is encouraging, I think, to note that substantial new knowledge has emerged as well as stimulating questions for further study. The appearance of the series of books on social gerontology under the able editorship of Clark Tibbitts and Wilma Donahue are in themselves evidence that the study of the aged has already made a substantial contribution to knowledge. It is encouraging to note, also, that kinship-family structures have a prominent place in this work.

An adequate theoretical framework for the study of family interaction patterns remains to be developed. There is an observable trend toward the use of conceptual frameworks and improved research designs so that empirical findings lend themselves to the testing of hypotheses, and this is highly commendable. As our knowledge accumulates, we will have a firm basis for applications and action programs.

BIBLIOGRAPHY

ALBRECHT, RUTH: The paternal responsibilities of grandparents, Marriage and Family Living, 16: 201-5, 1954.
———Social class in old age, Social Forces, 29: 400-5, 1951.
———Social roles of old people, Journal of Gerontology, 6: 138-45, 1951.
APPLE, DORIAN: The social structure of grandparenthood, American Anthropologist, 58: 656-63, 1956.
AXELROD, MORRIS: Urban structure and social participation, American Sociological Review, 21: 13-19, 1956.
BENDIX, R. and S. M. LIPSET: Social mobility in the U. S., in R. Bendix and S. M. Lipset, eds., Class, Status, and Power, pp. 371-500, Glencoe, Ill.: Free Press, 1953.
BLAU, ZENA S.: Structural constraints on friendship in old age, American Sociological Review, 26: 429-39, 1961.
BLOOD, ROBERT O., JR., and DONALD M. WOLFE: Husbands and Wives: The Dynamics of Married Living, New York: Glencoe, Ill.: Free Press, 1960.
BORDON, B.: The role of the grandparents in children's behavior problems, Smith College Studies in Social Work, 17: 115-16, 1946.
BOTT, E.: Urban families, conjugal roles and social networks, Human Relations, 8: 345-84, 1955.

BRITTON, J. H., W. G. MATHER, and A. K. LANSING: Expectations for older persons in a rural community: living arrangements and family relationships, Journal of Gerontology, 16: 156-62, 1961.

BROWN, JAMES S.: The conjugal family and the extended family group, Amer. Sociological Review, 17: 297-306, 1952.

BROWN, R. G.: Family structure and social isolation of older persons, Journal of Gerontology, 15: 170-74, 1960.

BURGESS, ERNEST W.: Family living in the later decades, Annals of the American Academy of Political Science, 279: 106-14, 1952.

———The older generation and the family, in Wilma Donahue and Clark Tibbitts, The New Frontiers of Aging, Ann Arbor: University of Michigan Press, pp. 158-71, 1957.

CAMPISI, P. J.: Ethnic family patterns: the Italian family in the U. S., American Journal of Sociology, 53: 443-49, 1948.

CAVAN, RUTH: The American Family, New York: Thomas Y. Crowell Co., 1963.

———Family life and family substitutes in old age, American Sociological Review, 14: 71-83, 1948.

———Self and role in adjustment during old age, in Arnold M. Rose, ed., Human Behavior and Social Processes, An Interactionist Approach, Houghton Mifflin, New York: pp. 526-36, 1962.

COULT, ALLAN D., and ROBERT W. HABENSTEIN: The study of extended kinship in urban society, The Sociological Quarterly, 3: 141-45, 1962.

CUMMING, E. and E. SCHNEIDER: Sibling solidarity: a property of American kinship, American Anthropologist, 63: 498-507, 1961.

DAVIS, KINGSLEY: The sociology of parent-youth conflict, American Sociological Review, 4: 523-25, 1939.

DICKINSON, FRANK G.: Time and Man: Revolt of the Young. Unpublished manuscript, 1963.

DINKEL, R. M.: Attitudes of children toward supporting aged parents, American Sociological Review, 9: 370-79, 1944.

———Parent-child conflict in Minnesota families, American Sociological Review, 8: 412-19, 1943.

DOTSON, F.: Patterns of voluntary association among urban working-class families, American Sociological Review, 16: 687-93, 1951.

DRAKE, JOSEPH T.: The aged in America's society, New York: The Ronald Press Co., 1958.

DUVALL, EVELYN M.: In-Laws Pro and Con: An Original Study of Inter-Personal Relations, New York: Association Press, 1954.

EPLER, ELIZABETH: Old-age assistance: determining extent of children's ability to support, Social Security Bulletin, May, 1954.

———Old age assistance: plan provisions on children's responsibility for parents, Social Security Bulletin, April, 1954.

FRAZIER, E. F.: Ethnic family patterns: the Negro family in the U. S., American Journal of Sociology, 53: 435-38, 1943.

———The Negro Family in the U. S., Chicago: University of Chicago Press, 1939.

FRIED, E. G., and K. STERN: The situation of the aged within the family, American Journal of Orthopsychiatry, 18: 31-54, 1948.

GLASSER, PAUL, and LOUIS GLASSER: Role reversal and conflict between aged parents and their children, Marriage and Family Living, 24: 46-51, 1962.

GLICK, P. C.: American Families, New York: John Wiley & Sons, 1957.

———The life cycle of the family, Marriage and Family Living, 17: 3-9, 1955.

GRAVITT, ARTHUR E.: Family relations in middle and old age: a review, Journal of Gerontology, 8: 197-204, 1953.

HART, ETHEL J.: The responsibility of relatives under the state OAA laws, Social Service Review, March, 1941.

HAVIGHURST, R. J., and R. ALBRECHT: Older People, New York: Longmans, Green and Company, 1958.

KAPLAN, SAUL: Old-age assistance: children's contributions to aged parents, Social Security Bulletin, June, 1957.

KEY, WILLIAM H.: Rural urban differences and the family, Sociological Quarterly, 2: 49-56, 1961.

KIRKPATRICK, CLIFFORD: The Family As Process and Institution, New York: The Ronald Press, 1963.

———Sociological implications of retirement, Journal of Geriatrics, 14: 312-17, 1959.

KLEEMIRER, ROBERT W.: ed., Aging and Leisure, New York: Oxford University Press, 1961.

KOLLER, MARVIN: Studies of three-generational households, Marriage and Family Living, 16: 205-6, 1954.

KOSA, JOHN, L. L. RACHIELE, and C. SCHOMMER: Sharing the home with relatives, Marriage and Family Living, 22: 129-35, 1960.

KUTNER, B., D. FANSHEL, A. M. TOGO, and T. S. LANGNER: Five Hundred Over Sixty, New York: Russell Sage Foundation, 1956.

LAJEWSKI, HENRY C.: Working mothers and their arrangements for care of their children, Social Security Bulletin, August, 1959.

LEMASTERS, E. E.: Social class mobility and family integration, Marriage and Family Living, 16: 226-32, 1954.

LEMON, CLARK: Sex life of the middle aged, Marriage and Family Living, 11: 58-60, 1949.

LIPMAN, A.: Role conceptions and morale of couples in retirement, Journal of Gerontology, 16: 267-71, 1961.

LIPSET, S., and R. BENDIX: Social mobility and occupational career pattern, American Journal of Sociology, 57: 494-504, 1952.

LITWAK, EUGENE: Geographic mobility and extended family cohesion, American Sociological Review, 25: 385-94, 1960.

———Occupational mobility and extended family cohesion, American Sociological Review, 25: 9-21, 1960.

LOOMIS, CHARLES and J. A. BEEGLE: Rural Social Systems, New York: Prentice-Hall, 1951. Pp. 87-88.

NIMKOFF, MEYER F.: Changing family relationships of older people in the United States during the last forty years, The Gerontologist, 1: 92-97, 1961.

OHBACH, HAROLD L., and DAVID M. SHAW: Social participation and the role of the aging, Geriatrics, 12: 241-6, 1957.

PARSONS, TALCOTT: Age and sex in the social structure of the U. S., in Herman D. Stein and Richard A. Cleward. Social Perspectives on Behavior, 1958, Glencoe, Ill.: Free Press. P. 200.

———The social structure of the family, in Ruth S. Anshen, ed., The Family Its Function and Destiny, New York: Harper, 1959.

QUEEN, STUART and DAVID CARPENTER: The American City, New York: McGraw-Hill, 1953. Pp. 265.

RIEMER, SVEND: The Modern City, New York: McGraw-Hill. P. 258.

REISS, PAUL: The extended kinship system: correlates of and attitudes on frequency of interaction, Marriage and Family Living, 24: 333-39, 1962.

ROBINS, A. J.: Family relations of the aging in three generation households, in C. Tibbitts, and W. Donahue, eds., Aging Around the World: Social and Psychological Aspects. New York: Columbia University Press, 1962.

ROBINS, LEE: Closeness to blood relatives outside the immediate family, Marriage and Family Living, 24: 340-46, 1962.

ROGERS, EVERETT M., and HANS SEBALD: Familism, family integration and kinship orientation, Marriage and Family Living, 24: 25-30, 1962.

SCHORR, ALVIN L.: Filial Responsibility in the Modern American Family, Washington, D. C.: U. S. Department of Health, Education and Welfare, Social Security Administration, 1960.

SCOTT, FRANCES G.: Family group structure and patterns of social interaction, American Journal of Sociology, 68: 214-28, 1962.

———The Urban Three-Generation Family Role Structure and Interaction Process, Unpublished doctoral thesis, University of California, Los Angeles, 1960.

SHANAS, E.: Family responsibility and the health of older people, Journal of Gerontology, 15: 408-11, 1960.

———The Health of Older People, Cambridge: Harvard University Press, 1962.

———Some sociological research findings about older people pertinent to social work, in Toward Better Understanding of the Aged, New York: Council on Social Work Education, 1958. P. 52.

SHELDON, HENRY D.: The older population of the U. S., New York: John Wiley & Sons, 1958.

SHEPS, JACK: New developments in family diagnosis in emotional disorders of old age, Geriatrics, 14: 443-49, 1959.

SIMMONS, L. W.: The Role of the Aged in Primitive Society, New Haven: Yale University Press, 1945.

SMITH, WILLIAM JR: Family plans for later years, Marriage and Family Living, 16: 36-42, 1954.

SMITH, W. M., JR., J. H. BRITTON and J. O. BRITTON: Relationships Within Three-Generational Families, Research Publication No. 155, University Park: Pennsylvania State University, College of Home Economics, 1958.

STREIB, GORDON F.: Family patterns in retirement, Journal of Social Issues, 14: 46-60, 1958.

STREIB, GORDON F. and WAYNE E. THOMPSON: The older person in a family context, in Tibbits, Clark, ed., Handbook of Social Gerontology, Chicago: University of Chicago Press, 1960.

STEINER, PETER O., and ROBERT DORFMAN: The Economic Status of the Aged, Berkeley: University of California Press, 1957. Pp. 68-85, 109-11.

STUCKERT, ROBERT P.: Occupational mobility and family relationships, Social Forces, 41: 301-7, 1963.

SUSSMAN, MARVIN: Activity patterns of post-parental couples and their relationship to family continuity, Marriage and Family Living, 17: 338-41, 1955.

———Family continuity: selective factors which affect relationships between families at generational levels, Marriage and Family Living, 16: 112-20, 1954.

————The help pattern in the middle class family, American Sociological Review, 18: 23-25, 1953.

————Intergenerational family relationships and social role in middle age, Journal of Gerontology, 15: 71-75, 1960.

SUSSMAN, MARVIN, and LEE BURCHNAL: Kin family network: unheralded structure in current conceptualizations of family functioning, Marriage and Family Living, 24: 231-40, 1962.

————Parental aid to married children: implications for family functioning, Marriage and Family Living, 24: 320-32, 1962.

TIBBITTS, CLARK, and WILMA DONAHUE, eds., Aging Around the World: Social and Psychological Aspects of Aging, New York: Columbia University Press, 1962.

TOWNSEND, PETER: The extended family and the kinship network, in The Family Life of Old People, London: Routledge and Kegan Paul, 1957.

U. S. Department of Commerce, Washington, D. C., Current Population Reports—Population Characteristics Series. P-20, No. 122, March 22, 1963.

VOLLMER, H.: The grandmother: a problem in childrearing, American Journal of Orthopsychiatry, 7: 378-82, 1937.

VON HENTIG, HANS: The sociological function of the grandmother, Social Forces, 24: 389-92, 1946.

WALLER, WILLIAM and REUBEN HILL: The Family: A Dynamic Interpretation, New York: Holt-Dryden, 1951. Pp. 441.

WILLIAMS, ROBIN: American Society: A Sociological Interpretation, New York: Alfred A. Knopf, 1960.

WINCH, ROBERT F.: The Modern Family, New York: Holt-Rinehart-Winston, 1963 (Revised). Pp. 544-45.

WRENN, B. R.: Three Generation Families: A Study of Three Generation Family Units and Some Impacts on the Participants. Unpublished Master's Thesis, Kent State University, 1954, quoted in Smith, W., J. Britton and J. Britton, Relationships Within Three Generation Familiies, Research Publication 155, College of Home Economics, Pennsylvania State University, April, 1958.

YOUNG, M.: The role of the extended family in a disaster, Human Relations, 7: 1954.

YOUNG, MICHAEL and P. WILLMOT: Family and Kinship in East London, London: Routledge and Kegan Paul, and Glencoe, Ill.: Free Press, 1957.

CHAPTER 10

Social Factors in Grandparent Orientation of High School Youth*

C. T. Pihlblad and Robert W. Habenstein

Investigation into the social aspects of old age and aging have obviously an integral relation to the broader sociological spectrum of studies of the family in general. It follows that when perspectives, conceptualizations, and empirical findings in either area are changed or modified, a reciprocal effect is likely to occur. The relevant point to be made at this juncture is that a recent reevaluation of kinship ties in the American family has had reverberations which are now being felt in the more applied areas of gerontological, generational and marital relations studies, and even in studies of child development and youth.

Reasons for the new look at the role of kinship in the American family stem partly from the leavening effect of current anthropological concerns with American family structure and organization,[1] and partly as a con-

---

*This report was made possible through a research grant from the Graduate Research Council of the University of Missouri, with the cooperation of the staff of Community Studies, Inc. of Kansas City, Missouri. The material dealing with kin knowledge of adults derives from an NIMH sponsored study, The functions of extended kinship in an urban milieu, MH053430, Louis P. Donovan assisted with the preparation of tables and statistical analysis. Frank Caro and Edwin Christ have given the authors useful criticisms.

[1]See John Bennett and Leo Despres, Kinship and instrumental activities: A theoretical inquiry, American Anthropologist, 62: 254-67, 1960; Helen Codere, A genealogical study of kinship in the United States, Psychiatry, 18: 65-79, 1955; Elaine Cumming and David M. Schneider, Sibling solidarity: A property of American kinship, American Anthropologist, 63: 498-507, 1961; Hope J. Leichter, Kinship values and casework intervention, Casework Papers 1961, New York: Family Service Association of America, 58-78; and David M. Schneider and George C. Homans, Kinship terminology and the American kinship system, American Anthropologist, 47: 1194-1208, 1945.

sequence of controversies among sociologists as to the degree to which the American family has in fact shed its extended kinship relations to become nuclear and isolated.[2] If sociologists are unwilling any longer to accept as viable the classical image of the large, multi-generational family, living under one roof with highly centralized authority and clearly institutionalized roles for all family members to play, they are also certainly beginning to question the counter image of the completely isolated nuclear family consisting of spouses and offspring, held together by personal attachments and functioning solely as a reproductive and socializing agency. As controversy mounts over the exact amount of modification that has occurred to make up the "modified extended family," and where precisely between these two polar types such a new family form falls, research findings and relevant research projects under way are beginning to contribute a fraction of the empirical findings necessary to resolve the issue.[3]

Our intent in this chapter is to present with brief comment a set of related findings reporting one variety of youth-grandparent relations assumed to have relevancy for those searching for the existence and saliency of kinship factors in contemporary family organization. While the variable examined, *the knowledge by high school seniors of their grandparents' occupations,* is highly specific and one whose dependency-independency status must be left open, the clear-cut patterns which appear when it is related to a number of other social variables suggest some measure of significance and can perhaps serve as a springboard for more revealing investigations. Also, since the subject matter of the present research exists systemically as a relation of grandparenthood, the findings may be expected to have suggestive value to students of gerontology who are seeking information on the nature and types of bonds that in American society link the generations together.

The Occupation of Grandparents' Dimension

Sources of the Data. The basic information for this study was obtained from a recent survey of the social backgrounds, as well as occupational aspirations and expectations, of approximately 3,300 public high school seniors in the Kansas City metropolitan region living within Jackson County,

---

[2]The nuclear versus extended or "modified extended" family controversy finds Talcott Parsons lined up against Eugene Litwak and Marvin Sussman. See Parsons; The kinship system of the contemporary United States, American Anthropologist, 45: 22-38, 1943; Litwak's The use of extended family groups in the achievement of social goals: some policy implications, Social Problems, 7: 177-87, 1959-60; and Sussman's, The isolated nuclear family, fact or fiction, Social Problems, 6: 333-40, 1959. For a possible explanation of how both of these viewpoints may be correct, see: Arnold M. Rose, Reactions against the mass society, Sociological Quarterly, 3: 316-30, 1962.

[3]A review of many of these findings is found in Allan D. Coult and Robert W. Habenstein, The study of extended kinship in urban society, Sociological Quarterly, 141-45, 1962. Harold Smith, in Chapter 9 in this volume also supplies valuable bibliographical information on the subject.

Missouri. The data were secured through the use of a highly structured questionnaire which was administered by teachers in the home rooms of the respective schools. The subjects were almost evenly divided between boys and girls. Approximately one-tenth of the students were Negroes.

In addition to queries concerning the occupational backgrounds of father and mother, each subject was also asked to report the occupation and residence of each grandfather. To simplify the present analysis, only knowledge of the occupation of each grandparent has been used as a suggested measure of kinship tie. Subjects were divided into three classes: (1) those who reported the occupation of one grandfather, (2) those who knew the occupation of both grandfathers, and (3) those who knew neither. The assumption is made that vertical kinship ties are closer among those who have knowledge concerning the occupation of their grandparents than among those who do not. Such knowledge has then been related to a number of social and personal characteristics of both the students and their parents. Finally, a brief consideration of some data drawn from another, derivative, study is undertaken in order to put the present findings in a broader perspective and emphasize the limitation of generalizing from kinship relationships that center about one highly specified variable.

White and Negro Comparisons. Table 1 classifies the subjects by knowledge of grandfathers' occupation and by race.

That white students have much greater knowledge of their grandfathers' occupation is clear in the table. Half of the white students as compared with one-fifth of the Negroes reported the occupation of both grandfathers. On the other hand, half the Negroes knew nothing of the occupation of either grandfather as compared with less than one-fifth of the white sub-

Table 1. Percentage of Students with Specific Knowledge of Grandfathers' Occupations by Race

Knowledge of Grandfathers' Occupations	Total (N-3310)	Race White (N-2937)	Negro (N-373)
Know one	32	32	29
Know both	46	49	21
Know neither	22	19	50
Total	100	100	100

sig.< .001

jects. Approximately the same proportion of both groups (about 30 per cent) reported the occupation of one grandfather. It should be kept in mind that this latter similarity is reflective of the fact that although a much larger percentage of the white students could identify both grandfathers, many more Negroes than whites knew neither.

In the light of the well known closer kinship ties of the Negro child to the mother and to her kin than to the father and his family it is interesting to compare the two race groups among those who reported the occupation of one grandfather only. This comparison is shown in Table 2. In the Negro group, where knowledge is limited to one grandfather only, the occupation of the maternal grandparent is known much more frequently than is that of the paternal grandfather. Seventy per cent of the Negro students knew the occupation of the mother's father while 30 per cent reported on the paternal grandfather. Among the white students the

Table 2. Percentage of Students Knowing Occupation of Only the Paternal or Maternal Grandfather, by Race

Knowledge of Grandfathers' Occupation	Total (N-1612)	Race White (N-1390)	Negro (N-222)
Paternal	57	61	30
Maternal	43	39	70
Total	100	100	100

sig.< .001

proportions were almost exactly reversed, three-fifths knowing the paternal as compared with two-fifths reporting the maternal line. The data in Tables 1 and 2 seems to support the conclusions that (1) Negroes are much less kinship oriented than whites, (2) Negroes are more oriented toward the maternal, while whites tend to orient to the paternal, family.[4]

Differences between the sexes classified by race were also analyzed. No statistically significant differences were apparent in either race group. There is a slight tendency for white males to show greater knowledge of grandfather's occupation than for females, suggesting that males may be more occupationally oriented than females, although the differences are too small to warrant any firm conclusions.

In the light of the wide differences between Negro and white kinship orientation and family organization the analysis of the two groups would have to be made separately. Considerations of time and space make it necessary to confine the remainder of the study to white students only.

Social Class and Knowledge of Grandfathers' Occupation

A principal interest in this study has been the analysis of the relationship between knowledge of grandfathers' occupations and social class characteristics, as reflected in the socio-economic background of our subjects as well as in their educational and vocational aspirations. Significant relationships, beyond the one per cent level of significance, were found between knowledge of grandparental occupation and the following socio-economic background variables: (1) occupational status of the father, (2) occupational status of employed mothers, (3) educational achievement of both fathers and mothers. Due to space limitations we shall not present these data in detail.

In order to obtain a more clear-cut delineation of social class than is provided by either occupation or education alone, we have grouped our subjects into three class categories on the basis of a combination of educa-

---

[4]See Franklin E. Frazier, The Negro Family in the United States, Chicago; University of Chicago Press, 1939. Also, Ethnic family patterns, The American Journal of Sociology, 53: 435-38, 1948.

tional level of the father and prestige position on the North-Hatt scale of the fathers' occupations: An upper middle class includes those students whose fathers were in high prestige occupations and had at least completed high school. A middle class was made up of the subjects with fathers in medium prestige occupations (largely in skilled work and crafts) who had at least an elementary school education and no more than two years of college. The lowest class were those with fathers in low prestige occupations (largely unskilled workers) who had not completed high school. Where the father's education was inconsistent with occupational rating, or where information concerning either education or occupation was incomplete, the subject was excluded.

The relationship between social class, as defined above, and kinship ties, as reflected in knowledge of grandparents' occupations, appears quite clearly in Table 3. Knowledge of one grandparent does not differ significantly among the three classes, but the proportion of those having knowledge of both decreases steadily from the high to medium to lowest class. Well over half of the students in the high class, as compared with only two-fifths in the low group, reported the occupations of both grandfathers. Conversely, only half as many of the high group were ignorant of the occupation of both grandparents, as were those in the lowest class.

Table 3. Knowledge of Grandfathers' Occupations and Social Class, in Percentages

Knowledge of Grandfathers' Occupations	Social Class		
	High (N-431)	Medium (N-1449)	Low (N-255)
Know one	32	32	34
Know both	56	51	40
Know neither	12	17	25
Total	100	100	100

sig.< .001

The relationship between contact with grandparents and class undoubtedly reflects the interaction of a complex of factors. It seems probable that the kinds of families in which kin are known are more likely to come

from more prestigious occupational backgrounds than are those in which less knowledge of family backgrounds prevails. Our data tend to show a considerable degree of occupational transmission in the sense that subjects with grandfathers at the upper level of the occupational scale tend themselves to aspire to more prestigeful occupations than do subjects whose grandfathers ranked lower on the scale.[5] A grandfather who was a physician, lawyer, teacher, etc., is more likely to be known to the grandson than one who was a farmer or unskilled worker. It may also be that ethnicity and immigration influences knowledge of kin. Subjects whose parents were immigrants are less likely to know the occupation of grandparents than are those whose parents were native born. Also, those with three generations as

---

[5]C. T. Pihlblad, Occupational aspirations of lower middle class high school male graduates. Unpublished manuscript.

residents of the local community are likely to have closer kinship ties than those whose parents were migrants into the city.

Religious Affiliations of Parents

It has been observed by many students of social class that religious affiliation and participation in the United States is closely associated with a great many other class characteristics, and that some religious faiths and denominations tend to hold higher status and prestige than do others. There seems to be some reason to believe, also, that family and kinship ties tend to be closer in some faiths than in others. Religious ties and affiliations tend often to be a part of the traditions transmitted in the social inheritance of the family. With these hypotheses in mind, we have attempted to relate the degree of knowledge of grandparents' occupations to the religious affiliation of parents as reported by our subjects. Since most of the parents were of the same religious faith or denomination, and since the students reported the church affiliation of the mother more frequently than that of the father, the analysis has been confined to the denominational affiliation of the mother only.

In the light of the multiplicity of religious denominations reported, and to simplify our analysis, we have grouped these into four categories: (1) Catholic, (2) Jewish, (3) "high" status Protestant (Episcopalian, Congregational, Presbyterian), and (4) other Protestant denominations. The relationship between knowledge of grandfathers' occupations and religious affiliation of mothers of our subjects is shown in Table 4.

Table 4. Knowledge of Grandfathers' Occupations and Religious Affiliation of Mother in Percentages

| Knowledge of Grandfathers' Occupations | Religious Affiliation of Mother | | | |
	Jewish (N-102)	High Protestant (N-792)	Other Protestant (N-1580)	Catholic (N-228)
Know one	31	33	32	32
Know both	49	51	49	40
Know neither	20	16	19	28
Total	100	100	100	100

sig.< .01

Children from Catholic homes clearly have the least knowledge of their grandparents' occupations. About 40 per cent of those with Catholic mothers knew the work of both grandfathers as compared with about half of those in other religious classifications, but nearly 30 per cent of the Catholic group knew that of neither grandfather compared to one-fifth or less of the Jewish and Protestant groups. Subjects with mothers in the "high" Protestant category appeared to have the greatest acquaintance with grandfathers, especially as reflected in the relatively low proportion who had no knowledge of the grandfathers' occupations. Children of Jewish mothers showed about the same distribution as did those in the "other"

Protestant group. Differences in the proportion of those knowing the occupation of both grandfathers are small, although slightly higher among the "high" Protestants. Approximately the same proportion of all the religious groups knew one grandfather. Differences among the four religious groups are statistically significant.

Probably such relationship as appears between these two variables does not reflect the direct influence of religion on kinship. Religious affiliation is associated with other factors such as income, occupation, education, ethnic origin, minority group status, and length of residence in the United States, all of which are also related to kinship ties. Status distinctions between denominational and other categories are also not very clear. The same Protestant denominations contain churches in which membership consists of high income and high status occupational adherents. The same is also true of Jewish and Catholic churches. Probably a larger proportion of Catholic children had grandparents of European origin and may have had less opportunity for contact with them than did those from Protestant families.

Approximately one-tenth of the students came from homes in which father and mother were of different religious faiths. As shown in Table 5 the mixed group showed significantly less acquaintance with grandfathers than did those whose parents were of the same religious faith. This fact suggests that wherever there are family disjunctions, or opportunities for such things to happen, there is likely to be a weakening of kinship bonds.

**Table 5. Knowledge of Grandfathers' Occupations
and Common or Different Religious Affiliations of Parents, in Percentages**

Knowledge of Grandfathers' Occupations	Religious Affiliations of Parents	
	Common (N-2550)	Different (N-292)
Know one	31	35
Know both	51	41
Know neither	18	24
Total	100	100

sig.< .01

Knowledge of Grandfathers' Occupations and Student Occupational Aspirations

The central purpose of the Kansas City Youth Study, from which the data for this paper were drawn, was to throw some light on the educational and occupational aspirations and expectations of a sample of high school youth in an urban area, and to determine some of the factors with which such hopes and ambitions were associated. The students were asked to state their immediate plans after graduating from high school and then to indicate what occupations they would like to enter and what occupations they actually expected to attain by the time they were twenty-five to thirty years of age. Since family tradition and structure appear to be influences which shape youthful ambition, it is relevant to relate kinship, as reflected in knowledge of grandfathers' occupations, to educational and occupational expectations.

Plans after High School. In the Kansas City study our subjects were first asked: "What do you plan as your major activity after graduating from high school: (1) go to work, (2) attend college, (3) attend a special school, (such as music, art, commercial, business, trade school, etc.), (4) enter military service, (5) other plans, (6) undecided at this time." The student was asked to check one of these six alternatives. More than half (55 per cent) reported their intention to attend college in the fall; about one-fifth said they planned to go to work; about one-tenth planned to attend some specialized type of school; and about one-tenth had other plans or were undecided. Less than 3 per cent planned to enter the armed services. The relation between knowledge of grandparents and post-high school plans is shown in Table 6.

Table 6. Knowledge of Grandfathers' Occupations and Post–High School Plans, in Percentages

Knowledge of Grandfathers' Occupations	Post–High School Plans				
	College (N-1609)	Work (N-608)	Special School (N-343)	Military (N-80)	Other Undecided (N-286)
Know one	31	34	32	34	34
Know both	54	43	44	40	41
Know neither	15	23	24	26	25
Total	100	100	100	100	100

sig.< .001

The college-bound group was clearly differentiated with respect to kinship knowledge. Among the four other categories the differences were insignificant. Considerably more than half the college group knew the occupation of both grandfathers while about two-fifths of the others reported such knowledge. Those having no information concerning the occupation of either grandparent made up only 15 per cent of the college group, while one-fourth of those without aspirations for college were ignorant of both. The proportion knowing that of one grandparent was about the same for all classes.

This relationship is consistent with other known characteristics of those with college ambitions, as we shall show later. Those in the college-bound group have higher scholastic aptitudes, rank higher in their graduating classes, have better-educated parents and more frequently have parents in the higher prestige occupations.[6] Some of these characteristics have already been shown to be related to vertical kinship ties.

Marriage Plans. Early marriage is often a serious obstacle to the attainment of high educational and vocational aspirations. While this obstacle may be overcome to some extent by the contributions to family support of

---

[6]C. T. Pihlblad and Francis G. Caro, Factors associated with the development of academic aptitude of middle class high school students. Unpublished manuscript.

a working wife, by special provisions made by colleges and universities for the married student, by parental assistance, and by the greater social acceptance of early marriage, nevertheless, marriage does increase the problems of completing a successful educational career and the attainment of a professional objective. Table 7 shows the relation between marriage plans and knowledge of grandparental occupations.

Table 7. Knowledge of Grandfathers' Occupations
and Marriage Plans, in Percentages

Knowledge of Grandfathers' Occupations	Marriage Plans				
	Now Married (N-39)	Engaged Marry in 6–12 Mos. (N-219)	Marry in 1–2 Yrs. (N-309)	Marry in 3–7 Yrs. (N-1702)	Undecided, No Thought (N-664)
Know one	20	37	25	33	33
Know both	49	43	48	51	46
Know neither	31	20	27	16	21
Total	100	100	100	100	100

sig.< .001

There tends to be a rather consistent relation between marriage aspirations and knowledge of grandfathers' occupations. Those who would postpone marriage beyond three years were best acquainted with the work of their grandfathers. About half of this group knew the occupation of both grandfathers, while only one-sixth lacked information about either one. At the other extreme were the short-termers who planned marriage within a year. A little over two-fifths of this group had information about both grandparents while one-fifth of them knew neither. A middle category, those who planned marriage in one to two years, fell between these two groups in knowledge of grandparents. Of those few already married, a high proportion (over 30 per cent) had no knowledge of either grandparent although nearly half knew both. The small number in this group, however, makes any generalization about them doubtful. It may well be that premarital pregnancy plays some part in explaining high school marriage and that the probability of such an accident is unrelated to any social class characteristic, or to kinship ties. The undecided category shows a quite similar distribution to that of the group as a whole. This is consistent with the results of a separate analysis of the relationship between social class and marital plans which found that, among males only, those who had no plans for marriage were about evenly distributed through three class categories, while those with long- and short-term plans for marriage were clearly differentiated by class.[7] The undecided group may contain some of those with relatively high social class background as well as high aspirations who look on marriage as something for the relatively distant future and others who are undecided as between early and late marriage.

---

[7]Francis G. Caro and C. T. Pihlblad, Aspirations and expectations: a reexamination of the basis for social class differences in the occupational orientation of male high school students, Table 5. Unpublished manuscript.

Occupational Aspiration and Expectation. Since, as already shown, knowledge of the occupations of grandfathers varies directly with all indices of social class, and since occupational aspiration is also directly related to class criteria,[8] it may be expected that kinship orientation and occupational aspiration would also show the same pattern of relationship. To obtain a measure of occupational aspiration and expectation our subjects were asked to respond to two questions: (1) What occupation would you *like to have* when you are twenty-five to thirty years old? and (2) What occupation would you *really expect* to have when you are twenty-five to thirty years old? Occupations selected were then classified into three categories on the basis of a revised version of the North-Hatt occupational status scale: a high group including largely professional and business executive occupations; a high moderate group containing technical, lower-rated professional, clerical, and some skilled occupations; a low moderate class including largely operatives, semiskilled workers and some low-rated clerical and white-collar jobs. Since no subjects aspired to occupations at the bottom of the scale, and very few for the next lowest rating, the two lowest categories on the North-Hatt scale were dropped. These three occupational aspiration classes (termed "high," "high moderate," and "low moderate") were then grouped on the basis of their knowledge of grandfathers' occupations as shown in Table 8. (The classification on the basis of occupational expectation is omitted since it corresponds very closely to that based on aspiration.)

Table 8. Knowledge of Grandfathers' Occupations and Vocational Aspiration, in Percentages

Knowledge of Grandfathers' Occupations	Vocational Aspiration		
	High (N-700)	High Moderate (N-778)	Low Moderate (N-501)
Know one	31	32	33
Know both	56	51	46
Know neither	13	17	21
Total	100	100	100

sig.< .01

The relationship between occupational aspiration and knowledge of kin is quite apparent and closely parallels the relationship between kinship orientation and all other criteria of social class analyzed above. Those who aspire to occupations at the top of the rating scale have significantly greater knowledge of the occupations of their grandfathers than do those with more modest ambitions. The proportion knowing that of both grandfathers declines steadily from 56 per cent among the high aspirants to 46 per cent among the lowest group. For those who had no knowledge of either, the proportion increases from 13 per cent among the high group to 21 per cent in the lowest aspirant class. The data again support the hypothesis that kinship ties, as measured by knowledge of grandfathers' occupations, are

[8]C. T. Pihlblad, *op. cit.*

strongest in families with highest occupational orientation. As appears to be the case in all other classifications, knowledge of the occupation of one grandfather is substantially the same for all three aspiration classes.

Academic Aptitude and Achievement. It is well known that academic aptitude, as measured by psychological test scores, and achievement, as reflected in school marks, are quite closely associated with social background and class status.[9] This relationship has also been shown in an earlier analysis of the Kansas City youth material.[10] Since, as we have shown in this paper, it appears that knowledge of grandfathers' occupations is also associated with the same factors, it seemed relevant to analyze the relation between aptitude and achievement and kinship ties.

Test scores on the School and College Aptitude Tests were provided by school officials in the Kansas City schools for all subjects. Similar scores on the Ohio Psychological Examination were also furnished from the schools in the County outside Kansas City. In addition, information on the rank in the graduating class was provided from most of the schools. For the SCAT, individual scores were given a percentile ranking based on national norms. For the Ohio Psychological Examination norms for Missouri were used since national norms were unavailable. Percentile rank on the test scores and on the basis of school marks were then grouped into three categories: (1) a high class, ranking in percentiles 70 through 90, (2) a medium group, in the fourth through the sixth decile, and (3) a low group, in the three lowest deciles. On the assumption that percentile rankings on the two psychological tests were roughly comparable, the test data were combined on a percentile basis. The relationships between test scores and class rank and knowledge of grandfathers' occupations are shown in Tables 9 and 10.

**Table 9. Knowledge of Grandfathers' Occupations
and Decile Rank on Test Scores, in Percentages**

Knowledge of Grandfathers' Occupations	Test Score Decile		
	Decile 1–3 (Low) (N-528)	Decile 4–6 (Medium) (N-691)	Decile 7–9 (High) (N-1380)
Know one	34	33	30
Know both	39	46	58
Know neither	27	21	12
Total	100	100	100

sig.< .001

It is clear that the higher-ranking students, on both test scores and ranks based on school marks, have a greater knowledge of grandfathers' occupations than do those of more mediocre performance. The brighter the student the more likely he is to have such knowledge. Approximately two-

---

[9]See articles by Becker, Wolfe, Rossi and others in Education, Economy and Society, A. M. Wolfe, Jean Floud, Arnold Anderson, eds., Glencoe: Free Press, 1961.

[10]C. T. Pihlblad and Francis G. Caro, Factors associated with development of academic aptitude of middle class high school students.

**Table 10. Knowledge of Grandfathers' Occupations
and Decile Rank Based on School Marks, in Percentages**

Knowledge of Grandfathers' Occupations	Decile Rank		
	Decile 1–3 (Low) (N-979)	Decile 4–6 (Medium) (N-848)	Decile 7–9 (High) (N-941)
Know one	34	31	29
Know both	43	51	56
Know neither	23	18	15
Total	100	100	100

sig.< .001

fifths of those ranking in the lowest group in both tables knew both grand-fathers' occupations as compared with nearly three-fifths in the high group. Conversely, the proportion knowing neither declines from about one-fourth to one-eighth from the highest to the lowest classes, both on the basis of test scores as well as class rank. In both tables, the proportion of those with knowledge limited to one grandparent shows a steady decline from the highest to the lowest percentiles although the rate of decrease is not as great as among those who knew the occupations of both grandfathers.

Interpretation of the relationship between academic aptitude and achievement and kinship ties probably does not lie so much in any direct connection between ability and curiosity about or knowledge of kin. It is more likely that youth with higher academic aptitude and performance tend to come from families with closer kinship ties more frequently than do those of lesser ability. This does not necessarily imply that tighter-knit families produce brighter children than do those in which kinship ties are more tenuous. The explanation probably lies in the fact that better-educated parents, with relatively high occupational status and upper middle class orientation, tend to produce more academically oriented children than do those families ranking lower in these class characteristics. These are also the families where grandparents are more likely to be known than in those of lower educational and occupational status. This point has already been demonstrated in our earlier analysis.

Living Arrangements

Of the 2,877 white students reporting, 2,229 (77.5 per cent) were living with both natural parents. The remaining 648 (22.5 per cent) had other living arrangements. In this latter group the dominant pattern was for the subject to live with the mother rather than the father or with mother and stepfather. A small number, 97, lived with foster parents or had other arrangements which included neither natural parent, and 21 more lived with grandparents only.

An interesting set of relationships emerges from the analysis of the patterns of living arrangements of the subject as related to ability to recall the occupations of the grandfathers, As suggested in Table 11, living with both natural parents seemingly predisposes one to know more about grand-fathers' occupations and presumably more about grandfathers generally than do all other kinds of living arrangements, when combined into one category.

It follows logically, and is borne out again in Table 11, that when one does not live with both natural parents it is much more likely that he will know about the occupational circumstances of only one grandfather than will those who live in complete families. This is certainly illustrated by Table 12

Table 11. Knowledge of Grandfathers' Occupations
and by Living Arrangements, in Percentages

Knowledge of Grandfathers' Occupations	Living with Both Parents (N-2229)	Other Arrangements (N-648)
Know one	29	38
Know both	53	41
Know neither	18	21
Total	100	100

sig.< .001

which strongly indicates that when the mother is present but the father is absent from the family the subject, more than in any other relationship examined in the study, is more likely (41 per cent) to have knowledge of the occupation of only one grandfather than of both (39 per cent). To a

Table 12. Knowledge of Grandfathers' Occupations
among Those Living with Both Natural Parents
and Those with Natural Father Absent, in Percentages

Knowledge of Grandfathers' Occupations	Living Arrangements	
	Both Natural Parents (N-2229)	Mother, Mother-Stepfather, Mother-Grandparents (N-435)
Know one	29	41
Know both	53	39
Know neither	18	20
Total	100	100

sig.< .001

lesser degree this is the case when the natural mother is absent and the natural father is present, but due to the limited number of cases of this order, statistical significance is not achieved.

Perhaps the most striking reversal of relationships involving residence patterns is shown in Table 13. Those not living with both natural parents were separated into residence with "close relatives," i.e., some combination of parent and/or grandparent, and "distant or non-relatives" including foster parents. When compared, 40 per cent of the "close relatives" group, as might be expected, knew the occupation of at least one grandparent, as against about 26 per cent for the "distant" category. But for those who knew the occupations of neither grandfather, the percentage in the latter category was twice as high—37 per cent to 19 per cent.

As suggested above, the pattern of living arrangements is a crucial datum

Table 13. Knowledge of Grandfathers' Occupations
among Those Living with Close Relatives* or with Distant or Non-Relatives, in Percentages

Knowledge of Grandfathers' Occupation	Type of Living Arrangement	
	Close Relatives (N-541)	Distant or Non-relatives (N-97)
Know one	40	26
Know both	41	38
Know neither	19	37
Total	100	100

*Not both natural parents
sig.< .001

in this study. For, of all the comparisons and relationships examined, those involving living arrangements had apparently the strongest effect on knowledge of one grandfather's occupation, and the absence of either natural parent in the family was "responsible" for the highest percentage of persons who knew the occupation of only one grandparent or of neither.

Lateral and Vertical Kinship Knowledge

Data from a Derivative Study. Tables 14 and 15 depart from the format of the materials thus far reported to present data drawn from a derivative study of extended kinship among Kansas City adults.[11] The same high school senior questionnaires were used to locate samples of blue and white collar parents who were established community members and in the "prime" of their kinship life, i.e., middle aged, with the greatest possibility of a balance of living relatives in ascending, own, and descending generations.

Table 14 shows that in closely, but not completely matched samples, blue collar adults will be able to designate by name nearly 60 per cent

Table 14. Distribution of Kin Knowledge:
Recognized or Nominated* Kin, Affinals Included, by Sex and Social Class**

Social Class	Respondents	Kin Known	Total Per Cent	Per Cent Recognized	Per Cent Nominated
Both classes total;	56	8,345	100	32	68
Blue collar;	28	5,420	100	34	66
Wife	14	3,040	100	32	68
Husband	14	2,380	100	37	63
Per cent of total	—	—	65	—	—
White collar;	28	2,925	100	28	72
Wife	15	1,735	100	25	75
Husband	13	1,190	100	33	67
Per cent of total	—	—	35	—	—

*If kin are named they are listed as "nominated." Those who cannot be named but whose identity is known are listed as "recognized."

**Source: Extended kinship in urban society: a preliminary analysis, Unpublished paper by Robert Habenstein and Allan Coult, read at the annual meeting of the Society for Applied Anthropology, Kansas City, 1962.

11Allan D. Coult and Robert W. Habenstein, *op. cit.*

more relatives than will white collar adults. And for those known as relatives but whose names cannot be recalled, the blue collar adults are twice as likely to show such recognition as are their white collar counterparts.

Table 15 again makes it clear that blue collar kin knowledge, measured by number of kin recognized or nominated, is superior. All the four classes of persons—blue collar husbands and wives, and white collar husbands and wives—nominate more kin than they can only recognize, but there is a rather sharp difference between sexes as well as across class lines. Highest average kin nominated and recognized goes to the wife of the blue collar worker with 217—101 more than her white collar counterpart, and 125 more than the bottom rung white collar husband. The blue collar husband, while falling considerably short of the kin aggregate known by his wife, nevertheless leads both white collar females and males by a substantial margin. About the only saving observation to be made for the white collar group is that if a white collar female has *any* knowledge of relatives it is likely that she can name them.

Table 15. Range and Average Distribution of Kin Knowledge by Sex and
Socio-Economic Class, Affinals Included 56 Respondents*

	Range Recognized	Range Nominated	Average Recognized	Average Nominated	Composite Average
Blue collar;					
Wife	7–120	94–261	69	148	217
Husband	7–131	32–191	62	108	170
White collar;					
Wife	7–80	49–139	29	87	116
Husband	2–63	31–118	30	62	92
Both classes;					
Wives	—	—	—	—	165
Husbands	—	—	—	—	136
All	—	—	—	—	149

*Source: *ibid.*

These findings, however, do not point unequivocally to a set of propositions, and no attempt is made here to "prove" that blue collar adults have a superior kinship knowledge.[12] The problem, of course, lies in the difficulty in showing that both blue and white collar adults have the same size pool of kin from which to make recollections. Given a smaller size family for the white collar class, one inevitably has fewer collateral relatives than would be the case if family size were larger.

But it would be hard to see where a somewhat diminished kin pool could account for all the variations among the four classes of persons. When genealogies of each are analyzed, it becomes apparent that those of the white collar class do not mirror the blue collar one only on a reduced

---

[12]It is generally accepted that blue collar relatives will have a higher rate of contact and are more likely to provide non-monetary assistance than do white collar relatives. See Alvin L. Schorr, Filial responsibility in the modern American family, Washington, D.C.: U. S. Department of Health, Education, and Welfare, Social Security Administration, 1960.

scale. Rather, the composite genealogies for the white collar group show a very pronounced patrilateral emphasis, the knowledge of kin on the father's side of the family being nearly twice as great as for the mother's. A white collar wife, for example, will know almost as many relatives on her father's side as will a blue collar wife, even though her total knowledge of kin will be considerably less. But for the blue collar wife the mother's side will receive a greater emphasis. There is no reason to believe that the kin pool on the father's side is any larger than for the mother's side for those in the white collar group; consequently, it is more likely the case that nearly anyone, regardless of socio-economic class, has a sufficiently large absolute kin pool from which to draw potentially as large if not a larger number of relatives than any other class would show on the average.

The answer, if there can be an answer, seems to lie in relevancy, utility, and effectiveness of kinship relations. This seems to be brought out by the patrilateral emphasis in the white collar group, already mentioned, and also by the fact that there is a tendency on the whole for the white collar adults to have a greater kinship knowledge of ascending generations, while for the blue collar class there is a heavier emphasis on knowledge of one's own and contiguous generations, and of collateral relatives. In short, the form of the composite white collar genealogies tends to accentuate patrilaterality, height, and narrowness; for the blue collar ones the pattern is one of somewhat less height, much greater width, and an emphasis on matrilaterality.

For the white collar group, the explanation of this pattern might center on the factors of prestige, heightened awareness of the uses and sources of capital, occupational sponsorship, the accessibility to income through inheritance, and, of course, the fact that the role of the male in the creation of these is dominant.

For the blue collar group, the maximum number of contacts with relatives becomes a function of sociability—it is cheaper to visit than to go out—and to the elaboration of a mutual aid pattern characterized by the exchange of small-scale services, and in crises by immediate personal help. Additionally, the nurturance pattern with the mother at the center but extending to include her sisters and brothers—maternal aunts and uncles are quite often "favorite" relatives—seems characteristic of blue collar families.

Summary and Comments

This paper is based on the assumption that kinship ties in the contemporary family are directly related to the degree of knowledge held by grandchildren of their grandparents. As an index of such knowledge we have used the extent to which a sample of high school youth are able to report the occupations of their grandfathers. Our data point to the following conclusions:

1. *White-Negro Comparisons:* More than twice as many white as compared with Negro students were able to report the occupations of both grandfathers. Only one-fifth of the white students as compared with half the Negroes reported the occupation of neither grandfather.

2. *White Only:* Approximately one-third (31 per cent) of the white students knew the occupation of one grandfather, about one-half (49 per cent) knew the occupations of both, while one-fifth (19 per cent) reported the occupation of neither grandparent. The extent of knowledge of grandfathers' occupations was positively and significantly associated with:

a. Higher occupational status of father and employed mother
b. Higher educational achievement of both father and mother
c. Higher social class status of father
d. Homogeneity and higher denominational status of parent's religion
e. Residence with both parents
f. Higher academic aptitude and educational achievement
g. Higher occupational aspiration of the student
h. Postponement of marriage
i. Supplementary information from a related study suggests that, unlike the case for vertical kinship ties, blue collar adults are able to recognize and to name a larger number of collateral relatives than are white collar adults.

Since the data can by no means support extensive generalizations or become the bases of demonstrated propositions, only tentative conclusions are possible. We can suggest that the relationships between generations, particularly grandparents and grandchildren, may well tie into systems or partial systems of kinship. The total parameters of these relationships are, as yet, unclear. Considerably more research is necessary before the sociological significance of our findings concerning knowledge by high school seniors of grandparents' occupations can be ascertained. That no single all-encompassing factor can be adduced to explain the patterns of relationships turned up by our study is evident—both from internal evidence, such as the factor of differential residence patterns, and from the data of kinship knowledge drawn from our derivative study and presented in the last two tables.

Very little has been said or written about the social role of the grandfather in modern urban society.[14] That he can no longer demand the prerogatives of the very old man should be evident when one considers that grandparenthood today easily begins in the late forties; and that competition for an authoritative, parental, rather than grandparental, role is not an impossibility in the present era of age denial. Whatever the changes and developments, their investigation and explanation may, in the smallest measure, be facilitated by the narrow but relatively positive[14] findings of our study.

---

[13]A recent family text is notable and an exception. See Bernard Farber, Family: Organization and Interaction, San Francisco: Chandler Publishing Co., 1964, especially Part Two, The contemporary family and kinship.

[14]A similar study by Sydney H. Croog, Harvard School of Public Health, and Peter Kong-Ming New, University of Pittsburgh Graduate School of Public Health, of 1,556 newly inducted soldiers at Fort Dix, New Jersey, in general supports the findings of the present study. See their Knowledge of Grandfather's Occupation as Clues to American Kinship Structure to be published in a forthcoming issue of Journal of Marriage and the Family.

CHAPTER 11

Wish, Expectancy, and Practice in the Interaction of Generations*

WILLIAM P. HAWKINSON

Introduction

Advocates of freedom have taken pride in the "open society" as one permitting a wide variety of choices for the individual—choice of an occupation, choice of a spouse, choice of a place of residence, and a diversity of other choices which presumably permit a relatively high degree of freedom of movement. The open society also has had its critics who point out that "freedom" may bring with it a sense of isolation and a segmentation of the social order. It is within this broad context that we wish to examine certain relationships between aged parents and their children.

The severance of the social ties which bind individuals in their relationships with each other is a condition of special significance for the aged. Basically, there are two major types of social isolation relevant to the present research. One is isolation in the sense of a low degree of involvement in primary group relations—e.g., separation of the aged from their children, friends, and neighborhood associations. This type of isolation in its more extreme forms is characterized by feelings of loneliness and a subjectively evaluated "necessity" to rely entirely on one's own resources. The second type of isolation involves divergence in the cultural values, interests, and activities which are of special significance to the young and middle-aged and differ greatly from those which are crucial in the final socialization period of the aged. This divergence provides a basis for the rise of conflict among the generational levels in any society, but even more

*The assistance of Miss Bertie L. Hagberg in the field work and data analysis is fully appreciated.

so in contemporary American society with its accelerated rate of social change. Thus there may well be objective reasons for adult children's regarding their aged parents as "obsolete" and for defining the interests of the aged parents as being incompatible with their own.[1]

Conflicting notions of the adult child's obligations toward his aged parents have been increasingly discussed in the literature. Stumpf's description of the "second-story people" tersely acknowledges that ". . . the older generation may not live literally on the second floor, but the split level between the generations is one of the primary facts about the phenomenon of aging."[2]

Our democratic, affluent society contains an increased proportion of older people, which has been reflected in the structure and the function of the family institution. For example, let us consider the conflicting role expectations of the adult child. The adult child is not only subject to pity if he sacrifices for his aged parents, but also open to criticism if he neglects them. The need for further comprehension has been aptly stated by Burgess in saying that there exists ". . . confusion and conflict because the relation of the older and the younger generation has not been re-defined in terms of the present situation."[3]

In similar fashion, Talcott Parsons has stated the problem as follows:

. . . By comparison with other societies the United States assumes an extreme position in the isolation of old age from participation in the most important social structures and interests. Structurally speaking . . . the most important single distinctive feature of our family . . . is the isolation of the individual conjugal family. It is impossible to say that with us it is "natural" for any other group than husband and wife and their dependent children to maintain a common household. Hence, when the children of a couple have become independent through marriage and occupational status the parental couple is left without attachment to any continuous kinship group.[4]

The contemporary period, by implicit demand, is one of increasing interest in appraising the position of the aged within the family context. In this connection, Beard suggests how recent such interest is by pointing out the meager references to the older family member in family life textbooks of the forties.[5] She concludes that ". . . the statements about the aged which appear in books on the family seem to be based on personal observa-

---

[1]A differing position, that in modern urban society there exists an extended kin family system closely integrated within a network of social relationships and mutual assistance along bilateral kin lines and vertically over several generations, is presented by Marvin B. Sussman and Sherwood B. Slater. A reappraisal of urban kin networks: empirical evidence, American Sociological Society meeting, 1963.

[2]Samuel Enock Stumpf, The expanding new world of second-story people, In Aging—Some Social and Biological Aspects, Nathan W. Shock, ed., Baltimore: Horn-Shaffer, 1960, p. 333.

[3]Ernest W. Burgess, The older generation and the family, The New Frontiers of Aging, Wilma Donahue and Clark Tibbitts, eds., Ann Arbor: The University of Michigan Press, 1957, p. 160.

[4]Talcott Parsons, Essays in Sociological Theory, Glencoe: Free Press, 1954, p. 230.

[5]Belle B. Beard, Are the aged ex-family? Social Forces, 20: 274-79, 1949.

tion or experience. References to research studies are noticeably lacking."[6]

Those studies that have been done suggest that the aged parent and the adult child expect to maintain their affectional and interpersonal relationships. While both generations appear to want to support the traditional relationship, the emphasis on the independence of each has been considered of primary importance. On the one hand, the norms of contemporary society stress the independence of each conjugal family, on the other, society has not made it possible for the aged parent adequately to fulfill this independent role.

As a result of this difference between expected behavior and the actual resolution of the situation, the aged parent is often faced with a common dilemma. The older person's definition of the consequences inherent in the situation is crucial for his behavior and adjustment. He is forced eventually to recognize that relinquishment of the parental authoritative role carries with it a possible reversion to a dependency role, and this contributes to the lag in social continuity.

The relation of the child to the parent and of the parent to the child is a basic aspect of the family. Although many of the functions of the family are delegated to other institutional structures from birth to death, the individual retains his identity with his initial family. With the increasing relinquishment of traditional family functions in a complex society to other functioning areas in the total system, the roles to which parents and children adapt must shift to suit ever-changing social demands. Thus, the family presumptively continues to play a predominant part in the life of the aged, but the more traditional expectations and practice are undergoing modifications.[7]

In Rose's recent analysis of the subculture of the aged,[8] attention is called to some of the responses of the elderly to rejection by younger age groups, as well as to the changing values of the American culture. The emerging subculture of the aged may be a reaction to the enforced segregation, or isolation, of the aged from the community and to pressures for relationships with peer groups rather than with the family.

The present study is focused on beliefs of aged parents concerning filial responsibility. Filial responsibility describes obligations of the child to his parent(s). For purposes of this study, only the *adult* child's obligations toward his *aged* parents were considered. From the variety of filial responsibilities of the adult child, three were selected for study: (1) personal communications, (2) financial obligations, and (3) living arrangements.

These three categories were examined from the standpoint of wishes, expectancies, and practices. The wish refers to "ideals or preference," expectancy to "normative standards or obligations," and practice to "actual behavior." Our immediate concern is with providing data on these variables

---

[6]Ibid., p. 278.

[7]For a summary of research on generational interaction patterns, see Chapter 9, Harold E. Smith. Family interaction patterns of the aged.

[8]Arnold M. Rose, The subculture of the aging (Chapter 1 of this volume).

and with interpreting their significance in terms of the American kinship system in general.

Sample

The data were obtained through interviews with a sample of 73 aged parents. The sample was randomly selected from those over sixty-five years of age in Northwood, a thriving agricultural town in the Red River Valley of the North. The particular town studied was selected on the basis of information provided by the United States Census Bureau, which indicated that in 1960 one-fourth of its total population of approximately 1200 consisted of people sixty-five years of age or older. In the typically Midwestern pattern, the community was economically dependent on the large agricultural area surrounding it.[9]

Personal Communications

Three modes of personal communication were investigated: visiting, letter-writing, and phone-calling. Analysis of the data revealed that face-to-face visits between aged parents (N-73) and their adult children (N-263) typically occurred on a monthly basis. However, 17 per cent of the children were reported as visiting their parents either less than once a year or never. (See Table 1.) Letter-writing and phone-calling followed a similar

**Table 1. Frequency of Visits from Adult Children
and to Adult Children by Aged Parents, by Number and by Per Cent***

Frequency of Visits	Visits from Children		Visits to Children	
	Number	Per Cent	Number	Per Cent
Daily or weekly	60	27	28	13
At least monthly	77	35	78	30
At least annually	47	21	32	14
Less than annually	29	13	48	22
Never	10	4	38	21
Total	223	100	224	100

*N's vary as a result of omitting cases where the relevant information about the frequency was not obtained.

pattern. The modal response in letter-writing to parents is about once a month on the average. Of the adult children living beyond a radius of fifty miles, approximately 12 per cent never write to their parents. (See Table 2.)

The findings showed that a substantial proportion of the aged, within the community studied, *wish for, but do not really expect,* more personal communications from their adult children. Seventy-eight per cent of the aged parents wished for more personal communications from their children, but

[9]Northwood is more fully described by Courtney B. Cleland in Chapter 20, Mobility of older people and by Bertie L. Hagberg, expressed beliefs of aged parents regarding their children's obligations to them, unpublished master's thesis, North Dakota State University, 1963.

Table 2. Frequency of Written Letters from Adult Children
and to Adult Children by Aged Parents, by Number and by Per Cent*

Frequency of Writing	Letters from Children		Letters to Children	
	Number	Per Cent	Number	Per Cent
Daily or weekly	45	22	36	18
At least monthly	75	37	84	42
At least annually	2	1	2	2
Less than annually	3	2	1	1
Never	77	38	76	37
Total	202	100	199	100

*N's vary as a result of omitting cases where the relevant information about the frequency of writing was not obtained.

only 22 per cent expected more frequent communications from them. Correspondingly in the three areas of personal communications investigated, the rank-ordering of discrepancy between wish and expectancy shows visits from their children to be in first place. In second place is the discrepancy between the wish for and the expectancy of letters, and least of all is the discrepancy between wish and expectancy for phone calls.

Over half of the aged parents (57 per cent) wished for more face-to-face visits from their children, rather than letters or phone calls. (See Table 3.) This finding seems to indicate that aged parents desire more personalized relationships with their children than letter writing or phone calls can sustain, and appears to be symptomatic of certain structural features of the American kinship system more generally.

Table 3. Responses to "Expect More" and "Wish More" Visits from Adult Children
by Aged Parents, by Number and by Per Cent*

Responses of Parents	"Expect More Visits"		"Wish More Visits"	
	Number	Per Cent	Number	Per Cent
Yes	6	9	38	57
No	60	91	29	43
Total	66	100	67	100

*N's vary as a result of omitting cases where the relevant information about the frequency was not obtained.

The heavy emotional investment of parents in their children, which is perhaps necessary for the socialization function, appears to be an outgrowth of the extent and quality of interaction within the family group. As Parsons has pointed out, the nuclear family unit in the American kinship system is small—reduced to its bare minimum, essentially consisting exclusively of parents and their offspring. Children are positively valued, perhaps not so much for what they are as for what they may become. Concern about the potential of the child together with the achievement emphasis of American society, places the parent in a special type of instrumental and affective relationship with the child.

The wish on the part of aged parents for more personal communications from their adult children reflects a desire for a greater continuity of the intimate personal ties generated during the period of child dependency. However, becoming an adult within American society calls for asserting independence from parental control—selecting one's own spouse, choosing one's own career, and establishing one's own place of residence. These individual acts, while manifesting the values of freedom and autonomy, tend to sever (or at least weaken) the once intimate bonds which link parents with their children and to result, eventually, in the "empty nest."

Financial Assistance

The diminishing economic maintenance function of the family takes on added importance when wish-expectancy-practice aspects of financial assistance are considered. With regard to their expectancies, 88 per cent of the aged parents believed that their children would be *willing* to provide financial support. (See Table 4). These findings are comparable to the results of similar investigations, such as Bond's California study where 90 per cent of the aged parents indicated their children's willingness to support them.[10] However, only half of these same aged parents, in both the Northwood and the California studies, believed their children were *able* to provide financial care. (See Table 5.) These findings suggest a sizeable discrepancy between what parents see as the willingness and as the ability

Table 4. Responses to "Willingness of Their Children to Assume Responsibility for Care," as Expressed by the Aged Parents, by Number and by Per Cent

Willingness of Their Children to Assume Responsibility for Care, as Expressed by the Aged Parents*	Total	
	Number	Per Cent
Would be willing to assume responsibility of care	57	88
Would not be willing to assume responsibility of care	8	12
Total	65	100

*No data on this item for eight respondents.

Table 5. Beliefs of Their Children's Ability to Provide Financial Support, as Expressed by the Aged Parents, by Number and by Per Cent

Ability of Children to Provide Financial Support, as Expressed by the Aged Parents*	Total	
	Number	Per Cent
Could afford to support without hardship	16	27
Could support with some hardship	16	27
Could not support	27	46
Total	59	100

*No response on this item for fourteen respondents.

---

[10]F. A. Bond, R. E. Baber, J. A. Vieg, L. B. Perry, A. M. Scaff, L. J. Lee, Jr., *Our Needy Aged: A California Study of a National Problem,* New York: Henry Holt and Company, 1954.

of their adult children to provide financial assistance. This definition of the situation may very well reflect a way of denying the weakness of intergenerational ties.

The actual financial contributions of adult children to their parents were more nearly in line with their parents' estimation of their ability to pay, rather than with their believed willingness. (See Table 6.) Consistent

Table 6. Material Help or Gifts Received from Adult Children during Preceding Year by Aged Parents, by Number and by Per Cent*

Material Help or Gifts Received from Children	Total	
	Number	Per Cent
Received some type of material help or gifts	47	32
Never received material help or gifts	21	68
Total	68	100

*No data on this item obtained for five respondents.

with their recognition of the inability of their children to help, 72 per cent of the Northwood parents believed that other sources, especially government agencies, should provide them with general financial aid, with a corresponding 68 per cent specifying this as emergency medical aid. (See Tables 7 and 8.)

Table 7. Sources That Should Provide General Financial Support, as Expressed by Aged Parents, by Number and by Per Cent

Sources That Should Provide General Financial Support*	Total	
	Number	Per Cent
Children	17	28
Federal government	20	32
State or local government	19	31
Employer's pension plan	2	4
Other	3	5
Total	61	100

*N's vary as a result of omitting cases where the relevant information was not obtained.

Table 8. Sources That Should Provide Emergency Medical Aid, as Expressed by Aged Parents, by Number and by Per Cent

Sources That Should Provide Emergency Medical Aid*	Total	
	Number	Per Cent
Children	20	32
Federal government	13	21
State or local government	20	32
Employer's pension plan	2	4
Other	7	11
Total	62	100

*N's vary as a result of omitting cases where the relevant information was not obtained.

Thus, although the aged parents felt their children were *willing* to support them, they did not *expect* them to do so. This congruence of expectancies with the actual provision of financial assistance by children is consistent with findings in similar studies by Sussman,[11] Bond,[12] and Smith.[13] Not only might this readiness to accept financial aid from sources other than one's own children be an indicator that the economic maintenance function of the family institution has been weakened so far as adult children and their aged parents are concerned, but by the same token it serves to support and even heighten the desire of the aged parents for independent living.

Living Arrangements

The quest for independent living by the aged in Northwood was reflected in both their expressed wishes and actual practices. Of the seventy aged parents expressing their opinions concerning living arrangements "that best meet their needs," 71 per cent felt living alone was the best way. Some of them expressed their desire to live in a rest home only if it were no longer possible to live alone. Others stated that "living alone" was best for them and made no reference to future plans in the event they should lose their ability to care for themselves. A few specifically mentioned a preference not to live with their children. This expressed wish in turn was supported by their actual behavior in that only 19 per cent of the aged parents did live with their children.

Maintenance of role and status would appear to be of primary concern for satisfactory adjustments in the aging process. Independence of living arrangements and continuance of making self-decisions are two devices which possibly may help provide this self-security. These data concerning the opinions of aged parents with reference to receiving help or advice concerning their present living arrangements indicate that 71 per cent made their own decision regarding where to live. Less than one-fourth (23 per cent) received help from their children in their present living arrangement decision. (See Table 9.) Similarly, 55 per cent of the aged parents indicated that they did not rely on their children for general advice. Instead, assistance in decision-making was sought from other sources—neighbors, friends, doctors, or other relatives.

Summary and Interpretation

In brief, the basic findings of this study may be summarized as follows: (1) The isolation of the aged in Northwood is manifested in the unfulfilled wishes of aged parents for more frequent and intimate contacts with their adult children. There is a greater preference for more visits from them, rather than for more letter-writing or telephone calls. However, the accept-

---

[11]Marvin B. Sussman, The help patterns in the middle-class family, Source-Book in Marriage and the Family, Marvin B. Sussman, ed., Cambridge, Houghton Mifflin Company, 1956, p. 305.

[12]Bond, cited in Streib and Thompson, op. cit.

[13]William M. Smith, Family plans for later years, Marriage and Family Living, 16: 40, 1954.

**Table 9. Responses to Assistance in Decision Regarding Present Living
Arrangements by Aged Parents, by Number and by Per Cent**

Assistance in Decision Regarding Living Arrangements	Total Number	Per Cent
Children assisted	16*	23
No assistance, or spouse assisted	51*	71
Others assisted	4	6
Total	71	100

*No data on this item for two respondents.

ance of the present status of their relationship with their children is reflected in a low expectancy for more sustained contact. (2) The isolation of the aged is further manifested in the emphasis upon independence in decision-making. (3) By far the preference for financial support from government or some other impersonal agency took priority over reliance on one's own adult children. However, most of the aged parents felt that in times of financial crisis, their children could be depended upon, insofar as they were financially able, to help.

We interpret these empirical observations as manifestations of certain aspects of American social structure. The initial primary parent-child relationships are intimate, affectional ones, which are difficult to sustain after the maturation of the children. Part of this difficulty seems to stem from the sharp discontinuity between the families of orientation and of procreation, and from the low frequency of social interaction with adult children. The parental emphasis upon financial independence, independence in living arrangements, and independence in the crucial areas of decision-making are reflections of the more general American values of freedom and autonomy. The lack of sustained ties with adult children appears to be a consequence of this democratic emphasis. The isolation of aged parents from their adult children occurs at the very time when the accessibility of various parts of the social system is progressively reduced through their occupational retirement, through poor health, and through the death of friends and acquaintances.

Thus, we might consider the secondary family as providing an emotional substitute for the child (substitute for the primary family), whereas the aging parents are being deprived of sustained contact with their children— or claims upon them—and there may well be an absence of cultural substitutes for refilling the vacuum created through the departure of their children.

While the data collected on the aged in Northwood represent responses to a given set of conditions at a given point in time, the specific set of facts obtained can perhaps be understood best by looking upon the interaction between aged parents and their adult children as an outgrowth of identifiable sequences of on-going, developmental, processual parent-child relationships.

Why do aged parents hold unfulfilled wishes for more sustained intimate relationships with their adult children? Why do not adult children visit, write, or telephone their aged parents more frequently? Why do parents feel that their adult children *would be willing* to help financially if they were able, but do not regard financial help from them as *necessary,* and do not regard their adult children as financially able to help? To provide some answers to these questions, it would be necessary to examine sequences of involvement, emotionality, and attachment, on the one hand, and the process of disengagement, isolation, and segmentation, on the other.

The emotional investment of parents in their children may be seen as developing into unfulfilled wishes for sustained intimate relationships with them, but, at the same time, there may very well be a growing realization that wishes, expectations, and practices are neither congruent nor structurally feasible. Such increasing frustration, correlated with aging, may not stem so much from restricted opportunities for attaining status aspirations (as Meier and Bell maintain[14]) as from the kinds and degrees of estrangement from kinship ties that develop in the course of the life cycle.

It is possible that American social life has become increasingly peer group-oriented in the areas of recreation, work activity, and other forms of central life interests. If so, the monthly visit, letter, or telephone call to aging parents may come to be regarded more and more as a "duty" or as an "obligation," rather than as mutual reinforcement of an intrinsically satisfying social relationship. Within this context, one may reasonably predict that in the future the widening social gulf will be filled either by increasing isolation of the aged or the emergence of a peer-oriented subculture exclusively for the aged.

---

[14]Dorothy Meier and Wendell Bell, Anomia and differential access to the achievement of life goals, American Sociological Review, 24: 189-202, 1959.

V

The Health of the Aging

CHAPTER 12

Mental Health of Normal Older Persons[*]

ARNOLD M. ROSE

The concept of mental health in this chapter will be limited to the mental state of the psychologically normal individual. It will not include the individual who has tendencies toward psychosis throughout his life, nor the individual who degenerates physiologically into senility. This paper will deal, rather, with those hazards characteristic of role changes involved in aging in our society and with the older individual's characteristic modes of coping with them. It will be limited further to a consideration of those older people who live in a family setting—that is, with either their spouses or their adult children—or by themselves after their mates die, rather than those who face the special difficulties of life in a nursing home, hospital, institution, hotel, or on Skid Row.

The major concepts of the discussion will be those of role, expectation, and self-conception, terms which were first added to the social-psychological literature by George H. Mead.[1]

Concept of Role

Definition. Role is a set of related behaviors, patterned by the meanings and values characteristic of a culture, by which man is able to adjust himself to a given group in a society. Most human behavior is role behavior, that is, prescribed and expected by others, as a matter of tradition (even if not always old tradition) even though it allows choices within limits and allows and encourages certain kinds of deviations. There is an old man's role in every society, a husband's role in every marriage, a grandparent's

---

*Reprinted by permission from Geriatrics, 16: 459-64, 1961.
[1]Mead, G. H., Mind, Self and Society, Chicago: University of Chicago Press, 1934.

role toward all grandchildren, a co-worker's role in every enterprise, a
friend's or acquaintance's role in every relationship, and, in general, a role
for each group of which the older individual is a member. These roles are
the "expected" aspects of an individual's behavior and personality—expected both by himself and by others. Some roles are defined more or less
clearly by the general culture of a society or by the special cultures of its
subgroups. Other roles, especially those of older individuals in our society,
are less clearly defined, and behavior consequently is less consistent and
less oriented to goals. Consistency of behavior and the degree of its orientation toward attainable and culturally appropriate goals are elements in
mental health.

Self-Conception. The individual's subjective perception of all his roles,
including his evaluation of them, is called his self. Whereas an individual's
roles diversify his behavior, his self integrates it and gives it direction and
meaning. Whereas others see an individual in terms of his roles, he sees
himself also in terms of his conception of self. The self binds together an
individual's present with his past and with his expectations for the future.
An old man's concept of himself usually includes such evaluations as those
of inadequacy, decline, dependence, fulfillment, maturity, wisdom, and so
on. These elements and the individual's evaluation of them contribute to a
specification of his mental health.

There is an underlying assumption in this analysis that mental ill health
is a function of meaninglessness or goallessness, that is, rolelessness, in
behavior and of negativeness toward self in self-conception.[2] This is a
definition of the mental ill health of the normal individual, not of the
psychotic, whose social-psychological problems probably entail some chemi-
cal imbalance in his nervous system. Consistent feelings of meaninglessness
and negativism toward self are psychological pains of an individual out of
adjustment to himself and to his social world. The purpose of this paper is
to examine some characteristics of aging which are likely to contribute to
this condition.

Causes of Negative Attitudes

Decline in Physical Powers. A change that affects all aging people is the
decline in physical powers and the resulting recognition that the incapacities
of old age and the nothingness of death are the inevitable future. For some,
physical decline is so gradual and the unwillingness to face old age so
strong that the realization that one is old may come as a traumatic shock
which results in a depression of some duration. This depression takes the
form of disorganization of one's roles and of a strongly negative self-conception. For probably the majority, however, evidences of physical decline
intrude themselves in one's self-conception as early as the thirties, so that the
traumas occur in numerous small bits over a quarter of a century and leave

[2]Rose, A. M., A social psychological theory of neurosis, in Transactions of the
Fourth World Congress of Sociology, London: International Sociological Association,
1960. An expanded version appears in: A. M. Rose, ed., Human Behavior and Social
Processes, Boston: Houghton Mifflin Co., 1962, chapter 28.

no sudden, shocking realization for the individual to cope with. Still, it is probable that no individual is pleased with or is fully adjusted to the thought of himself as permanently infirm. Whatever the general level of aspirations of the individual, he probably hopes for freedom of movement, at least, and when that seems to be disappearing, he must feel that there is little left to which he can aspire.

There is some awareness of declining mental powers, and this is just as painful an experience as that of declining physical powers. However, declining mental powers usually involve less awareness, so that their total contribution to psychological ill health may be less.

Fear of Death. While death may not be so terrifying as in the days when there was an active belief in hell, and many individuals had at least private reasons for predicting that this was to be their residence in the after-life, the fear of the permanent unknown probably is still strong in most men. Generally, death is welcomed only by those who are suffering great physical or mental pain or who have reached such a condition of lassitude that one nothingness seems to be an inconsequential substitute for another. The power of the fear of death is such that individuals who have little to live for and whose life offers them little but misery still refuse the release of death. The perception of the world is nearly always a personal one, and few individuals can conceive of the world without themselves, except perhaps in an academic sense. Most older people probably reconcile themselves to the thought of death, but, once the conception has been formulated, it hangs over all a person's thoughts and shadows all expectations for the future by which men live.

Loss of Occupation. Loss of the chief life function—an occupation for a man and child-rearing for a woman—is a major role change involved in aging. On the one hand, this may be damaging to the conception of the self if all the individual's values have been concentrated on this function and if he has no other valued activities which can provide him with substitute goals and satisfying roles. On the other hand, if he has cultivated the latter and feels a strain growing between the demands of the chief life function and his physical ability or interest in doing so, retirement can be a relief and an avenue to a happier life. There is evidence that for most males in our society, particularly in the lower and middle income classes, retiring from the job is looked forward to with pleasure and anticipation.[3, 4] Still, there is a great deal of individual variation, and, from the standpoint of life satisfaction and mental health alone, forced retirement is undesirable. The difficulty arises less from the reduction of income—various pension plans now in existence prevent income from falling too low and there are fewer expenses due to children and taxes—than from forced and rapid role change. Simple substitution of leisure for work is seldom satisfactory, unless the individual is so physically deteriorated that he can work only

[3]Dubin, R., Industrial workers' worlds: a study of the "central life interests" of industrial workers, Social Problems 3: 131–142, 1956.

[4]Streib, G. F., Morale of the Retired, Social Problems 3: 270–276, 1956.

with extreme difficulty. Work is highly valued in our culture, even if the work happens to be unpleasant, and Americans do not learn how to spend leisure time in ways that they themselves and their fellows consider desirable.

Complete and sudden retirement is almost unique to industrial society; in most other societies, there is a gradual sloughing off of the primary occupation. While the role and the group participations associated with it change suddenly, the individual's conception of himself does not change so rapidly. In this sense, sudden *retirement* is socially unnatural and is the source of some mental problems.

It is difficult to predict the future of compulsory retirement, but up until the present, at least, the trend has been toward it due to decreasing flexibility in work and to the higher salary standard that makes employers less willing to retain workers when they begin to slow down.

The situation for nongainfully employed women has changed even more drastically. Today the average woman bears her last child at the age of twenty-six years,[5] and, when she has reached the early forties, she is "retired" from child rearing. She still has to maintain a household for her husband and perhaps for an adult child or two, but household care without small children is much simplified. So the physically vigorous woman of forty-five years, like the retired man at sixty-five years, has to seek a new life role.

The tradition of the past does not prescribe a new life role, since retired persons used to be so tired out that they were likely to want only to sit in one place or to be restricted to an invalid's bed. Studies suggest that successful transition to a new life role is to be found mainly in a reduced work load, which is limited to men in self-employed occupations and to women who live with or near their grandchildren, or in activity in voluntary associations or hobbies of one type or another. Successful activity in voluntary associations or hobbies generally presupposes continued activity for many years before retirement. It seems probable that, as our society becomes old-age conscious, as it has begun to do in the past decade or two, younger people will foresee the need to prepare for old age by acquiring a hobby or voluntary activity they can continue past retirement.

It also seems likely that part-time work will be increasingly made available to older people, economic conditions permitting, by some such means as those now being utilized by organizations such as Enterprise, Incorporated, which provides the part-time advisory services of retired managers to new firms, or Goodwill Industries, which offers elderly indigents part-time work rehabilitating discarded furniture. Both part-time work and voluntary associations also offer the retired person a chance to integrate into a social group, which most people have had in their regular primary occupation. An entirely different approach to this problem, but one perhaps equally satisfactory if the rest of the culture could be changed to accommo-

---

[5]Glick, P. C., Life cycle of the family, Marriage and Family Living 17: 3–9, 1955,

date it, would be to create a higher evaluation of leisure and to create permanent groups for the pursuit of leisure.

Attitudes toward Aging. The problems of retirement are intimately connected with the problem of the reduced prestige of aging. In past centuries, wisdom was associated with age, but today the pace and complexity of events restrict an attribution of wisdom only to the expert. Also, the elderly person was relatively rare in the past; today, the percentage of those over sixty-five years of age in the population has climbed to 1 in 11. This inflation in numbers may have helped to reduce the popularly evaluated worth of the elderly person. Respect and praise in our society are generally accorded for achievement, and valued achievement is mainly a product of occupation, including child-rearing for women. Loss of occupation in retirement removes the occasion for manifestations of praise and respect. The only likely possibility of upgrading the prestige of age in our society would be the development of the elderly into an effective voting bloc and pressure group. In this way the elderly would most rapidly achieve group status within the framework of our present culture, and more favorable self-conceptions would flow from enhanced group prestige.

Change in Role. Still another facet to the problem created by retirement is the relationship of the retired man to his wife. When he was employed, there was a natural division of labor and power between them. Upon retirement, he tends to intrude into her sphere. Either he wants some chores to keep himself busy or he feels he ought to "help out" when she is busy and he has nothing to do. He expects to take on these tasks as an equal (or sometimes, if he had a superordinate role in his occupation, unconsciously he expects to be a superior), but his wife has had no equal in the running of the house. Under the circumstances, either he meets rebuff, with some damage to his self-conception; or he starts a permanent conflict; or he threatens his wife's conception of herself; or they work out a new division of labor, usually gradually.

If either or both of the old couple move in with one of their married children's families, the role adjustment that is required is even more drastic. In other societies, and in our own society up to about fifty years ago, the family included the older generation, but today in our society the older person is regarded as an extra member. The older couple living with their adult children in past centuries very often were regarded as the heads of the household, whereas today they are generally the subordinates. Either of the older folks is an intruder on the functions of the younger wife, except when she needs a baby-sitter. The young couple's interests are generally different from those of the older persons, and there is always a question whether the latter should be included in the young couple's or family's activities. Entertainment of friends is often difficult in someone else's home, and if the move into the younger couple's home has entailed a movement into another community, there are often no friends nearby for the elderly persons to invite.

Under almost all circumstances, movement into the home of a married child involves some depreciation in self-conception arising from down-grading of role from independent to dependent person. Even the role of grandparent is not a satisfying one in our society if the grandparent lives in the same home, as the younger family tends to be child-centered today, while older persons regard children as subordinates or as pets. To have to accommodate to a dominating child is an annoyance to a grandparent who lives in his own home; it can be traumatic to the grandparent who lives in the child's home. The difficulties of elderly parents living with their adult offspring in our society generally have kept them from living together; today this is the atypical living arrangement rather than the typical one.

When one of an older couple dies, the remaining person is cut off from his major social contacts. Both a role change and a narrowing of the self-conception is involved. Whereas there always may have been psychological dependency of the surviving person on the spouse, awareness of this does not always exist until the spouse is dead. If there are strong group member-ships, the psychological dependency of the surviving person can be trans-ferred partly to them. But the groups to which the older person belongs—especially the informal ones—are likely to consist also of older persons who die at an increasingly rapid rate. With each friend's death, the older person loses another role, another source of prestige, another social support, and a part of himself. At least no loss of prestige is involved in the status of widowhood itself, except in the case of the woman who has depended heavily for her social contacts on persons who have been primarily friends of her deceased husband rather than her personal friends.

Changes in Health. Deteriorating health of the older person tends to create one or the other of two mental health problems. The first is hypo-chondriasis. The aging individual becomes aware of an increasing number of specific disabilities and of a general weakening of his body and some-times reacts by complaining to others of these things and by going to the doctor frequently or by taking copious quantities of patent medicines in an effort to stave off his physical decline. The opposite reaction, equally a problem, is likely when the individual has never been much bothered by poor physical health during his life. When age brings physical disabilities, he refuses to recognize them and resists any sort of medical care. This attitude is especially likely if a person spent his youth in a rural area of the country or has had a low income throughout his life, so that seeking medical advice and care is fairly foreign to his experience.

Summary

While old age brings for some the release of not having to work at a boring job and of not having to strive for scarcely attainable goals, result-ing in the mellowness that comes to some old people, for most persons it brings disturbances to one's roles and self-conceptions that tend to result in minor forms of ill health. There tends to be a movement from head of household to dependent, from lack of awareness of psychological depend-ency to poignant awareness, from rise in prestige to decline, from having a meaningful life role to having to search for a new role, and from being an active person to being a partial invalid. Opportunities for developing negative self-conceptions multiply, and mild depressions or neuroses thereby are more likely to result. It is even conceivable that the high rate of psychosis among older people is at least partly stimulated by these conditions. All of these mental states create problems for all the younger people who have to cope with older persons or who have responsibility for them in any way.

CHAPTER 13

Physical Health and Mental Outlook Among the Aging[*]

ARNOLD M. ROSE

Introduction

Probably the most salient feature of aging is declining health. While the elderly face many problems they are not likely to have faced in earlier life—loss of chief life role, decreased income, death of spouse and of some friends—perhaps the one among them to which they ultimately become more sensitive is declining health, which forbodes death. For a very few, increased age brings better health. For a larger number, there is no decline in health, which is usually a pleasant surprise. For still others, there is a gradual and expected decline in health, but no serious disability. For a final group, there is a serious decline in health, which involves disability and the expectation of approaching death. These variations may be hypothesized to be associated with differences in outlook on life and in relationships with others. The purpose of the present paper is to ascertain some of these associations among a sample of Twin Cities' older residents, by comparing those who state that their health is good with those who state that their health is poor. Earlier research—particularly the National Health Survey—has demonstrated that statements about *specific* health conditions among the elderly are far from accurate when judged by physicians. But a *general* statement about health is far more accurate, and at least indicates perception of one's health, which is important for the context of our research.

The source of the data of this study is the same as that for the author's earlier chapter in this book, Group Consciousness Among the Aging. Thus,

*The statistical analysis for this chapter has been made possible by a small grant from the Graduate School of the University of Minnesota.

it will not be necessary to describe again the sample and the manner of collection of the data. Suffice it to say that there are 202 cases in our non-representative sample of older people living in non-institutional settings in Minneapolis and St. Paul. Findings are reported only when differences between groups are large enough to meet the test of 95 per cent probability of being statistically significant. It is understood that differences in responses to our questions which do not meet this test might do so if the sample were larger, but we shall also call attention to lack of significant differences.

Perceived Health

The primary index of state of health in this study is the response to the question, "In general, how is your health?" In our nonrepresentative sample of older people, 20 per cent answered "very good," 36.2 per cent said "pretty good," 34.3 per cent said "about average for my age," 8.6 per cent said "not very good" and 0.9 per cent said "very poor." For purposes of comparing groups of older people on the basis of their perception of their health, we combined the first two of the possible answers (calling them "healthy"), kept the "average" answer separate, and combined the last two of the possible answers (calling them "unhealthy").

The first comparison will be with other indexes of perception of health. The question was asked, "Are you able to get out by yourself without much difficulty?" Over 95 per cent of the healthy answered "yes," 86 per cent of the average answered "yes," but only 54 of the unhealthy did so. Still, a majority of even the unhealthy were quite ambulatory. To the statement, "I never felt better in my life," all of the unhealthy disagreed, but so did 51 per cent of the healthy, and 59 per cent of those in average health. In response to a question about whether they felt younger or older than their years, 57 per cent of the healthy said "younger," but this was true of only 32 per cent of the average health group and 27 per cent of the unhealthy. To the statement, "When I was younger, I felt a little better than I do now," all of the unhealthy agreed, but so did 87 per cent of the healthy, and 89 per cent of the average. To the statement, "If I can't feel better soon, I would just as soon die," only 7 per cent of the healthy agreed, but so did only 18 per cent of the unhealthy and 2 per cent of the average (a few others in each category were "undecided"). To the statement, "I feel just miserable most of the time," only 4 per cent of the healthy agreed, as compared to 9 per cent of the average and 45 per cent of the unhealthy. Thus, the perception of the state of their health on the part of these older people was relative to what it had been earlier, to what they had anticipated, to the possibility of their getting out of the house by themselves, and probably to what they saw among other old people.

There are slight age differences among the categories of older people according to their perceived health, but these are not sufficiently large to account for their differences in health. The healthy sample had an average (mean) age of 74.8 years while the unhealthy had an average age of 75.7 years (the average health sample centered on 73.1 years). None of the unhealthy was under 70 years of age, but the majority of them were between 70 and 75 years. The healthy were more varied in age: 22.5 per cent were under 70 years, 31.5 per cent were between 70 and 75 years, 35.4 per cent were between 75 and 79 years, and 10.5 per cent were over 80 years.

While men constituted only 38 per cent of the sample, they were somewhat more likely to report themselves to be in good health than did the women: 59 per cent of the men and 53 per cent of the women said they were in good health. This difference could be explained by the slight average age difference between the two sexes.

There is similarly a class difference among those reporting themselves in different states of health: Whereas 24 per cent of the healthy placed themselves in the lower classes, this was true of 36 per cent of the unhealthy (and 21 per cent of those in average health). Among the healthy, 54 per cent had a grammar school education or less, while 64 per cent of the unhealthy had only this much education, and 36 per cent of those in average health. Three-fourths of the unhealthy reported themselves currently married (the rest were widowed); on the other hand, 12 per cent of the healthy said they were single and a much higher proportion of them were widowed (46 per cent). Correspondingly, a much larger proportion of the healthy were childless (27 per cent compared to none among the unhealthy and 25 per cent among those in average health). All of the unhealthy said they were fully retired from an occupation, but this was true of 89 per cent of those in average health, and 78 per cent of those in good health.

The healthy and the average were able to keep up with their social contacts; the unhealthy mostly were not. To the statement, "I have so few friends that I am lonely much of the time," 7 per cent of the healthy and 4 per cent of the average, as compared to 27 per cent of the unhealthy, agreed. To the statement, "I have more friends now than I ever had before," 52 per cent of the healthy and 54 per cent of the average health group agreed, but only 18 per cent of the unhealthy agreed. About three-fifths of the healthy and the average group agreed that they would be happier if they could see their friends more often, but this statement was agreed to by all of the unhealthy. To the statement, "My many friends make my life happy and cheerful," 85 per cent of the healthy and 79 of the average group agreed, but only 54 per cent of the unhealthy agreed. Still, there was no difference in the responses to the statement, "I have no one to talk to about personal things." Only about 15 per cent of all three groups of respondents agreed to this statement.

Interests of the Aged

A series of questions was asked concerning how the respondent spends his time as compared to how he used to spend it before retiring. Three large and highly significant differences appeared among the samples studied: The healthy were much more likely to be spending more time doing things they wanted to do than were the unhealthy (66 per cent as compared to

27 per cent, with 52 per cent among the average health group). The un-healthy group was much more likely to indicate the increase in their time was spent in "just sitting and thinking" (73 per cent among the unhealthy as compared to 22 per cent among the healthy and 16 per cent among the average group). Participation in church and other religious activities was increased mainly among the healthy; 37 per cent indicated "more time" among the healthy as compared to 25 per cent among the average group and 9 per cent among the unhealthy (the latter indicated mainly "no differ-ence in time"). This last finding is especially significant in view of the fact, the data for which will be presented later, that the unhealthy have developed a much greater dependence on religion than the healthy.

On items regarding work there was little difference among the samples (it should be remembered that very few were still fully employed). To the statement, "I am happy only when I have definite work to do," 61 per cent of the healthy and 54 per cent of the unhealthy agreed. To the statement, "I am satisfied with the work I now do," 87 per cent of the healthy and 82 per cent of the unhealthy agreed. To the statement, "I have no work to look forward to," 22 of the healthy and 27 of the unhealthy agreed. On the other hand, there was a difference in the response to the statements about leisure time: thirty per cent of the healthy, but 46 per cent of the unhealthy, agreed to the statement, "I have more free time than I know how to use." And to the statement, "I don't have enough time to do all the things I want to do," 40 per cent of the healthy, 34 per cent of the average group, and only 18 per cent of the unhealthy, agreed. These differences can probably be explained in terms of the greater number of non-work activities among the healthy, to which we shall give consideration later.

The unhealthy have a greater reliance on religion than do the healthy, possibly reflecting a greater preoccupation with death. To the statement, "Religion is a great comfort to me," all of the unhealthy agreed as compared to 82 per cent of the healthy and 91 per cent of those in average health. To the statement, "Religion is the most important thing in my life," 60 per cent of the healthy, as compared to 68 per cent of the average and 82 per cent of the unhealthy, agreed.

Happiness and General Outlook

Differences between the healthy and unhealthy are marked in response to items about happiness and general outlook. In response to the statement, "Sometimes I feel there's just no point in living," 12 per cent of the healthy, 7 per cent of the average, and 27 per cent of the unhealthy, agreed. In response to the statement, "I am just as happy as when I was younger," 81 per cent of the healthy, 68 per cent of the average, and only 36 per cent of the unhealthy agreed. In response to the statement, "My life is full of worry," only 6 per cent of the healthy and only 7 per cent of the average agreed, as compared to 36 per cent among the unhealthy. None of the un-healthy said, "These are the best years of my life," but 48 per cent of the healthy and 36 per cent of those in average health agreed. These differences seem to be attributed by the unhealthy respondents to the fact of aging: 36 per cent of the unhealthy, as compared to only 12 per cent of the healthy and 7 per cent of the average group, agreed to the statement, "Things just keep getting worse and worse for me as I get older." Similarly, in response to the question, "Has growing old brought you happiness or unhappiness?", 48 per cent of the healthy answered "happiness" and only 4 per cent "unhappiness"; while among the unhealthy, only 27 per cent answered "happiness" but 18 per cent "unhappiness" (the other possible answer was "Neither, I feel about the same as I always did").

There are similar differences on items reflecting a sense of usefulness and meaningfulness in life. To the statement, "My life is still busy and useful," 96 per cent of the healthy and 80 per cent of the average health group, as compared to only 64 per cent of the unhealthy, agreed. To the statement, "This is the most useful period of my life," 33 per cent of the healthy, but only 16 per cent of the average and only 9 per cent of the unhealthy group, agreed. Yet on somewhat similar items, there were no significant differences among the three groups. To the statement, "I am of some use to those around me," 88 per cent of the healthy, 79 per cent of the average and 82 per cent of the unhealthy, agreed. To the statement, "My life is meaningless now," only 4 per cent of the healthy, 7 per cent of the average group, and 9 per cent of the unhealthy, agreed.

It seems quite clear from the responses that the unhealthy attribute their problems to the fact of age and poor health. They distinguish, for example, between life satisfaction today in contrast to the past. When asked, "How satisfied would you say you are with your life today?" only 1.5 per cent of the healthy answer, "not very satisfied" or "not satisfied at all," whereas 36 per cent of the unhealthy give one of these two answers (2 per cent of the average group say this). On the other hand, when asked, "How satisfied have you been with your whole life?" none of the unhealthy give negative answers, and very few of the healthy or those in average health do so. In response to the question, "As you get older, would you say things seem to be better or worse than you thought they would be?", 7 per cent of the healthy, 11 per cent of the average health group, and 27 per cent of the unhealthy, answer "worse."

Another way to get at the same matter is to ask the respondents, "If you had a chance to live your life over again, would you do the same things or do it differently?" In regard to jobs, there is some difference among the three health groups—probably reflecting their class differences: 24 per cent of the healthy say they would have preferred a different job, as compared to 36 per cent of the unhealthy, and 27 per cent of the average group. The major difference among the three groups is in regard to social activities: 9 per cent of the healthy, 14 per cent of the average group, but 27 per cent of the unhealthy, would want different social activities. On the other hand, there is practically no difference in the proportions who would want different friends (6 per cent of the healthy and 9 per cent of the unhealthy); want a different family life (18 per cent of the healthy and

18 per cent of the unhealthy); or to be more religious (30 per cent of the healthy and 27 per cent of the unhealthy). Thus, in regard to jobs and social activities—probably reflecting their class differences—there are significant differences among the groups in their life satisfaction. But in regard to more personal matters, there are no differences among the three groups in their life satisfaction.

The present dissatisfactions of the unhealthy seem to have mainly to do with their lack of social contacts and activities, which probably reflects their poor health. Among the healthy, 36 per cent see some of their relatives (other than their children) at least a few times a month, as compared to only 18 per cent among the unhealthy, and among the average health group, the proportion is 39 per cent. The unhealthy do see their relatives, but mostly just once a month, in a sort of ritual visit. Much the same thing is true in regard to seeing their friends: 64 per cent of the healthy say they get together with them at least a few times a month, as compared to only 27 per cent of the unhealthy and 75 per cent of those in average health. Most of the rest of the unhealthy do get together with their friends, but only once a month or a few times a year. In visits with neighbors there is an even greater difference: 21 per cent of the healthy, 14 per cent of the average health group, but 55 per cent of the unhealthy, say "almost never." There is no difference among the three groups in answers to the question concerning the age group they tend to associate with, or to the question whether they feel they have more in common with their own age group or a younger age group.

One set of interesting differences was in response to the question, "Would you say you're more or less active in clubs and organizations now, or were you more active when you were 50?" Of the healthy, 36 per cent said "more now" as compared to 9 per cent of the unhealthy, and 40 per cent of the average group. The answer given most frequently by the unhealthy was "never active, then or now." This was checked by 46 per cent of the unhealthy as compared to only 21 per cent of the healthy and 16 per cent of the average group. This differential in part reflects the lower social class of the unhealthy (many previous studies have shown that lower income people seldom join organizations), but the differential is too large to be explained by class alone. It suggests that the ill health of the unhealthy may be a matter of long standing.

Aging Group Consciousness

Questions were asked about the desire of the respondents to be either more active or less active in organizations. There were no significant differences among the three groups in their answers to these questions. But in response to the question, "Are there any clubs or other organizations for older people that you *could* belong to?" the unhealthy are more likely to answer that there are some (percentages answering "yes, several" were 30 per cent among the healthy, 30 per cent among the average, but 46 per cent among the unhealthy). Apparently, the greater participation of the healthy in non-age graded associations makes them less aware of the existence of the organizations for the elderly. As to actual membership in such associations, this was claimed by 40 per cent of the healthy, 57 per cent of those in average health, and 36 per cent of the unhealthy. In response to a question asking whether there ought to be more clubs and other organizations for older people, 52 per cent of the healthy, and 61 per cent of the average said "yes," but only 18 per cent of the unhealthy agreed. An additional question asked why they did not participate more in organizations for older people. The most frequent answers by the healthy were that they were not interested, did not have the time, or did not know of the availability of such organizations; the unhealthy gave ill health, dislike of clubs, and low income as their most frequent answers.

A number of questions were asked to ascertain possible resentment by the elderly respondents for their deprivations as older persons. This was somewhat more likely to be found among the healthy. In response to the question, "Do you believe that older people as a group are treated badly by younger people?" 25 per cent of the healthy answered in the affirmative, but this was true of only 9 per cent of the unhealthy and 7 per cent of those in average health. Similarly, in response to the question, "Do you believe that older people who are in good health are prevented from doing things they are able to do because younger people run everything?" 30 per cent of the healthy answered "yes," as did 23 per cent of those in average health, but only 9 per cent of the unhealthy. There were slighter differences, but in the same direction, in response to the question as to whether older people ought to organize to demand their rights. In answer to the question, "Do you think older people ought to be more active in politics?" 67 per cent of the healthy, 61 per cent of the average, but only 45 per cent of the unhealthy said "yes." The healthy were also much more likely to vote in elections. Thus the healthy may be said to have more "aging group consciousness" than did the unhealthy. On the other hand, there is no difference among the three groups as to their expressed sense of pride in having reached their present advanced age. This attitude was checked by about 90 per cent of all the respondents. The greater aging group consciousness among the healthy did not mean that they had significantly more hostility against younger people: In response to the question, "Do you feel that younger people show enough respect for older people?", 32 per cent of the healthy, 29 per cent of the average, and 27 per cent of the unhealthy, answered "no."

In regard to their perception of the respect shown by their own children, there were also no differences shown among the three groups: About 72 per cent of all three groups said their children showed as much respect toward them (the elderly parents) as they ought to. On the other hand, the unhealthy were more inclined to say that their children did not help them as much as they ought to: 27 per cent of the unhealthy gave this answer, as compared to only 7 per cent of the healthy and the average. None of the unhealthy said their children helped them more than they ought to, but this answer was given by 13 per cent of the healthy and 23 per cent of the average. The latter differentials probably reflect the greater need for help among the unhealthy. There were practically no differences among the three groups in how well they got along with their respective husbands and wives: 49 per cent of the healthy and 45 per cent of the unhealthy said they got along with their spouse.

Summary

Those who perceived themselves as in poor health in this study of 202 Twin Cities' older people were clearly different in many respects from those who perceived themselves to be in good health. While differentials in the perception of the condition of one's health had many sources, they could not be attributed merely to differences in chronological age.

The healthy were somewhat more likely to be men than women, middle class rather than lower class, better educated rather than poorly educated, partly employed rather than fully retired. The healthy were much better able to keep up with their social contacts; the unhealthy were lonely as a consequence, for they saw their friends and relatives typically only on ritual monthly visits. The unhealthy spent more time on "just sitting and thinking" and less time on things they wanted to do.

There was little difference among the groups studied on attitudes toward work, but toward free time there was a difference: The healthy kept themselves much more occupied, whereas the unhealthy were more likely to say that they did not know what to do with their free time. The unhealthy relied more on religion, but there is some evidence that they had done so earlier in life. There was also evidence that their poor health had been a long-standing matter.

The unhealthy were less likely to report themselves as happy, and more likely to be worried. There is evidence that they attributed their negative outlook to the fact that they are old. While the unhealthy were less likely to think of their lives as busy and useful, they did not agree that their lives were meaningless, or useless to those around them. The unhealthy were dissatisfied with their present lives, but not dissatisfied with their lives as a whole. On matters that reflect their lower class status, such as jobs and social activities, the unhealthy wish their past lives could have been different. But on more personal matters—family, friends, and religious activity—the unhealthy were no more likely than the healthy to have wanted their lives to have been different.

One reason for dissatisfaction with their past social activities is that a disproportionately large number of the unhealthy report that they had never joined clubs or other organizations. The unhealthy were more aware that there existed organizations for older people, but they were not more likely to be members of any such organization. Reasons for not joining differed between the healthy and the unhealthy.

The healthy gave more evidence of "aging group consciousness"—they were more inclined to resent their diminished status because of their age.

But this did not reflect itself in hostility toward their own children; if anything, the unhealthy had more resentment here by being more likely to say that their children did not help them as much as they ought to. There was no difference between the healthy and unhealthy in attitudes toward their own husbands or wives.

In general, those older people who report themselves as unhealthy were more depressed and less active than those who report themselves as healthy. The perceived condition of physical health reflected itself in many aspects of mental outlook toward life.

CHAPTER 14

Social Participation
and Health of the Aged*

RODNEY M. COE and ELIZABETH BARNHILL

This is a report of a pilot study conducted at the request of officials of the Jewish Community Centers Association (JCCA) of St. Louis. The primary purpose of this study was to determine the need for and feasibility of an experiment in health education for aged members of various clubs within the JCCA organization. In addition, we wished to test a specific hypothesis formulated on the basis of casual observations of JCCA staff members. The hypothesis was that participation by the aged in clubs requiring *active* participation is associated with fewer perceived health problems and lower utilization of health resources, while membership in clubs requiring *passive* participation is related to more perceived health problems and more frequent utilization of health resources. Moreover, it was felt that this pilot study could be used to test part of the health information section of an interview schedule for a different study.

When examining the results presented below, it should be kept in mind that this is, after all, a pilot study. As such, it has many of the shortcomings of studies of this type. For example, it has a restricted and, in this case, fairly special population, representatives of which could not be randomly selected. Many arbitrary decisions had to be made, usually on the basis of available resources. Nonetheless, it is felt that as a pilot investigation the data were good enough to permit us to make decisions with respect to

*This project was supported by the Medical Care Research Center, a joint agency of Washington University and the Jewish Hospital of Saint Louis under funds granted by the National Institutes of Health, Research Grant CH-00024. A special debt is owed to officials of the Jewish Community Centers Association of St. Louis, especially William Kahn, Executive Director, and Donald L. Feldstein, Program Director, whose cooperation made the study possible.

the specific goals outlined above. Moreover, wherever possible, these data were contrasted to comparable data from already published studies.

Description of the Sample

To facilitate interpretation of the data, it may be helpful at this point to present a brief description of the JCCA which sponsors the clubs selected for study. Founded in 1880, the JCCA in its present form represents a merger of several smaller organizations designed to provide for the "social needs" of the Jewish population in St. Louis. Specifically, the objectives of the JCCA are:

(1) to provide the individual with opportunities for personal enjoyment and enrichment through . . . broadened interests in social, cultural and recreational activities,

(2) . . . to aid the individual in becoming a valuable and useful member of his total community,

(3) to help the individual . . . develop security and satisfaction in his religion and cultural background by furthering his understanding of and participation in Jewish life.[1]

Although originally designed to provide an outlet for social participation for youth and young adults, in recent years the JCCA has added a fairly extensive program to reach the "older adult," i.e., those over age sixty. In part, this development stems from the increased number of members who reach this age category. It is also felt by the JCCA staff that older people, in general, tend to become isolated from the younger population and culturally disfranchised. For the older members of the Jewish Community there is the added factor of inability to communicate and participate in groups because of the divergence of their traditional, Eastern European culture and that of the modern, urban setting.[2] To combat this trend, the Older Adult Program was instituted under the auspices of the JCCA. This program provides a variety of clubs and group sessions which attempt to match the interests, level of communication and needs of older Jewish members. For example, there are "Golden Age" Clubs; "Lounges," similar in format to Golden Age Clubs except they include some adults under age sixty; "Volunteer Service" groups which provide opportunities for members to serve the community in various ways. One volunteer activity, for example, is a telephone service in which volunteers call other aged members, especially those who live alone, to maintain social contacts, but also to insure that the member is not in need of help. If an answer is not received, another volunteer pays a visit to the home of the member to see if assistance is needed. In addition, there are separate clubs for men and women, health clubs, specific recreational and craft clubs, English classes, and day camp programs for the aged. It is estimated that about 900 of the 15,000 members of JCCA are over age sixty.[3]

---

[1]Jewish Community Centers Association of St. Louis, By-Laws, March, 1961, p. 1.

[2]Cf., Arnold M. Rose, The subculture of the aging: a framework for research in social gerontology, in this volume, Chapter 1.

[3]Ruth Fischlowitz, The "Y" Story, St. Louis: Jewish Community Centers Association, 1964.

The staff of the JCCA felt that since health is a topic of concern for their aged members, a program in health education associated with their clubs would be beneficial. Since the members vary considerably on several criteria such as level of sophistication, education, social class, etc., it was felt that a pilot project should be conducted first. The staff also indicated an interest in testing their impression that membership in groups requiring active participation resulted in a higher level of perceived health.

To accomplish both these ends, two clubs were selected for study. One was the Golden Age Club, the other a Volunteer Service Club. In the judgment of staff members, the Golden Age Club required only passive participation while the Volunteer Service Club required active participation. A total of eighteen completed interviews was obtained from members of the Golden Age Club (GAC) and seventeen from members of the Volunteer Service Club (VSC).

The average age of GAC members was 74.5 years compared to 67.4 years for VSC members and respondents in both clubs were mostly female (72.2 per cent in GAC, 53.5 per cent in VSC). Members of both groups were predominantly Eastern European in nativity, but had spent most of their lives (over fifty years) in St. Louis. The difference in average age is reflected in the fact that 22.2 per cent of the GAC members are still married, while 82.4 per cent of VSC members are still married. Conversely, 61.1 per cent of GAC members are widowed, but this is the case for only 17.6 per cent of VSC members. Other differences which should be noted include the fact that while one-third of the GAC members had no formal education, this was true of only 11.6 per cent of VSC members. Similarly, while 11.1 per cent of the former group reached high school, 41.1 per cent of the VSC members had obtained that much education. A related difference is found in social class as measured by occupation. None of the GAC members was in the professional-managerial category (or had husbands who were), 33.3 per cent were small business owners, 50 per cent were formerly in clerical, sales, or service occupations and the remainder (16.7 per cent) were laborers. For the VSC members, however, 5.8 per cent had been in professional-managerial occupations, 47.1 per cent had been small business owners and 47.1 per cent had been in clerical, sales, or service jobs. There were no laborers in this group.

To a certain extent, social participation will depend upon proximity to relatives and friends as well an an ability to get around. For this reason, we examined living arrangements of the two groups since it was thought that location of adult children close to their aged parents may improve their chances of getting out. Table 1 shows the distribution of the members of the two clubs compared with the results of a national survey. It is immediately apparent that the living arrangements of the respondents in this sample are not representative of a national sample of persons aged sixty-five or over. Comparing just the GAC with the VSC, the influence of the high number of married respondents in the latter club can be seen. The percentage of respondents living with spouse is much higher for VSC while

Table 1. Living Arrangements of Aged Respondents, in Percentages

Respondent Lives	Golden Age Club (N=18)	Volunteer Service Club (N=18)	National Sample* (N=1,734)
Alone	27.8	10.7	20.1
With spouse	27.8	72.7	52.6
With child	27.8	10.7	15.9
With others	16.7	5.9	11.2
Totals	100.0	100.0	100.0

*Source: Ethel Shanas, *The Health of Older People,* Cambridge: Harvard University Press, 1962, p. 96.

the percentage of respondents living alone (there was only one respondent who had never married) was higher for GAC members.

In addition, the data shown in Table 2 would indicate that 80 per cent

Table 2. Residential Proximity of Aged Respondents to Adult Children, in Percentages

Location	Golden Age Club (N=18)	Volunteer Service Club (N=17)	National Sample* (N=1,350)
Same building	38.9	23.5	36.1
Within short auto ride	55.6	58.8	48.7
One day auto ride or more	—	5.9	14.6
No children	5.6	11.8	—
No answer	—	—	.5
Totals	100.0	100.0	100.0

*Source: Ethel Shanas, *The Health of Older People,* Cambridge: Harvard University Press, 1962, p. 98.

of the respondents in each sample live fairly close to their adult children. Moreover, these distributions correspond roughly to that of the national sample. The somewhat smaller percentage of VSC members living in the same building with their children is probably a reflection of the greater number of still-married members of this group since it is assumed that an older couple can maintain an independent household better than a widow or a widower. Thus, despite an attempt to obtain two groups of older persons who differ only in the type of club they belong to, these two groups differ somewhat in age and social class and markedly in marital status and living arrangements. In examining the evidence on social participation and health status, these differences should be remembered.

Social Participation

One of the purposes of the Older Adult Program is to increase the social participation of club members and to a certain extent the program has been successful. About 56 per cent of the GAC members reported increased attendance in JCCA-sponsored clubs since their retirement while 64.9 per cent of the VSC members reported increased attendance. Although frequency of attendance is about the same for members of both groups, it was found that only 22.4 per cent of the GAC members belong to groups for other than aged people, but 47.2 per cent of the VSC members belong to groups not limited to older persons. Moreover, while about one-half the respondents in each group reported no change in frequency of attendance at religious functions, increased frequency of attendance was reported by 16.7 per cent of GAC members and by 29.4 per cent of VSC members.

However, it is one thing to *attend* a meeting, but it is something else to *participate* in it. Accordingly, data were collected on frequency of interaction with others. These data show a higher rate of interaction for VSC members than for GAC members (an average of 12.1 contacts per week compared with 8.1 contacts). Interestingly enough, while participation increased after retirement for 28 per cent of the GAC group and 37 per cent of the VSC members, the frequency of participation did not change for 72 per cent of the GAC members and 63 per cent of the VSC members. That is, those who participated frequently continued to do so after retirement and those who participated infrequently did not increase their participation.[4] What is notable here is the fact that in neither group was there a single case in which participation *declined* after retirement.[5] Furthermore, of those respondents who did increase their participation, the increase was confined entirely to groups for aged persons for GAC members, but only 16.7 per cent of VSC members who increased participation did so in clubs for the aged.

Interaction with others outside the setting of club meetings also produced some differences. Apparently, the VSC members are more involved with kinsmen than GAC members. Responses to questions about persons most frequently interacted with show that about three-fourths of VSC members and two-thirds of GAC members see their adult children at least once per week with the average weekly frequency being 3.4 for VSC members and 4.0 for GAC members. The major difference, however, lies in interaction with others. Seventy-one per cent of the VSC members see other relatives at least once a week compared to 22.2 per cent of the GAC members, while 44.4 per cent of the latter interact with friends at least once per week compared to only 23.5 per cent of VSC members. The higher frequency of interaction of GAC members with children is probably related to living arrangements (more GAC members live in the same building with children) while the lower rate of interaction with other relatives for GAC members may reflect the somewhat older average age of that group (i.e., more of their age group relatives have probably died).

Thus, it could be said that members of both groups are fairly active in clubs and in outside activities, with the somewhat older GAC members interacting more frequently with their adult children and age peers while VSC members interact most often with their children and other relatives.

---

[4]Richard Videbeck and Allen B. Knox, Alternative participatory responses to aging, in this volume, Chapter 3.

[5]This is contrary to the findings of several studies, for example, Elaine Cumming and William E. Henry, Growing Old, New York: Basic Books, 1961.

It is quite likely that the differences in living arrangements exert an influence on whom the GAC members interact with, that is, they live closer to their children than VSC members do, but fewer GAC members have spouses on whom they can rely for social intercourse.

Health Status

In the course of the interview, respondents were asked to estimate their level of health and to compare it with "others their age." Their responses,

Table 3. Perceived Health Status, in Percentages

Health Status	Golden Age Club (N=18)	Volunteer Service Club (N=17)	National Sample* (N=1,405)
Good	33.3	64.7	51.4
Fair	44.4	35.3	28.8
Poor	22.3	—	19.8
Totals	100.0	100.0	100.0

*Source: Ethel Shanas, *The Health of Older People,* Cambridge: Harvard University Press, 1962, p. 144.

Table 4. Respondents' Comparison of Own Health with Others of Same Age, in Percentages

Respondents' Health Is	Golden Age Club (N=18)	Volunteer Service Club (N=17)	National Sample* (N=1,405)
Better	33.3	69.6	50.1
Same	39.1	17.7	34.8
Worse	16.6	—	13.6
No answer	11.1	11.7	1.5
Totals	100.0	100.0	100.0

*Source: Ethel Shanas, *The Health of Older People,* Cambridge: Harvard University Press, 1962, p. 144.

shown in Tables 3 and 4, would suggest that these respondents think they are in reasonably good health.[6] It would appear also that members of the VSC report themselves to be in better health than either GAC members or respondents in the national survey. Similarly, a majority of members of all three groups feel their health is at least as good as others their age. It could be further noted that there is considerable consistency between estimates of their own health and comparison of their health with others the same age. The association between these factors is Gamma $= +.77$ for GAC and Gamma $= +.81$ for VSC.

The relatively healthy state of these respondents is shown again in that the GAC members reported twenty-five specific illnesses which had bothered them in the four-week period previous to the interview. Volunteer

---

[6]Cf., Eugene A. Confrey and Marcus S. Goldstein, The health status of aging people, in Clark Tibbitts, ed., Handbook of Social Gerontology, Chicago: University of Chicago Press, 1960, pp. 165-207.

Service Club members reported seventeen illnesses during this period. The averages for these groups, 1.4 for GAC and 1.0 for VSC, compare favorably with the 1.5 reported for middle class respondents in another study.[7] As would be expected, the kinds of diseases which were reported were mostly chronic illnesses including respiratory ailments, cardio-vascular renal diseases, metabolic diseases, fractures and some minor psychiatric problems.[8] The only major chronic disease not reported by either group was cancer. The most troublesome health problem for these respondents was fractures. This is not surprising since the generally high level of perceived health status would imply that major incapacitating diseases such as heart disease and diabetes were relatively stabilized, but fractures from falls and accidents would be more of a problem. We may note further that the health problems reported were relatively minor in that respondents were not restricted in their usual activities in the majority of cases. Table 5 shows

Table 5. Limitation of Activity Imposed by Illness, in Percentages

Limitation	Golden Age Club (N=28)*	Volunteer Service Club (N=28)*
Bedfast	17.9	3.6
Housebound	7.1	25.0
No restriction	75.0	71.4
Totals	100.0	100.0

*Includes illnesses of a continuing nature in which the last acute episode was more than four weeks previous to the interview.

that for all illnesses reported only a few required immobilization while most required no restriction at all. Without knowing the length of time the restriction was imposed, one cannot judge if GAC members were more restricted than VSC members although it appears so at first glance.

Response to Illness

In an attempt to get at ways in which older people respond to symptoms of illness, respondents were asked to describe what action they took for the particular illnesses they said they had. Table 6 shows the distribution of responses for each illness according to how serious the illness was. Several things are immediately apparent from these data. First, for serious illnesses (heart disease, blindness, pneumonia, bronchitis, etc.), a majority of these illnesses were treated by a physician, but more so for VSC members than GAC members. Conversely, for nearly one-fourth of their serious illnesses, GAC members did nothing compared to only 4.0 per cent of VSC members. Secondly, also for serious illnesses, the "lay referral system"[9] does not seem to operate since respondents in both groups either did nothing

---

[7]Earl L. Koos, The Health of Regionville, New York: Columbia University Press, 1954, p. 42.

[8]Cf., Albert F. Wessen, Some sociological characteristics of long-term care, in this volume, Chapter 17.

Table 6. Action Taken in Response to Illness, in Percentages*

	Serious Illness		Non-serious Illness	
	Golden	Volunteer	Golden	Volunteer
Action Taken	Age Club	Service Club	Age Club	Service Club
	(N=29)	(N=25)	(N=34)	(N=6)
Nothing, hoped it would go away	24.1	4.0	38.2	50.0
Gave self-treatment	—	—	26.5	—
Sought advice of relatives/friends	—	—	—	—
Went to a physician	75.9	96.0	35.3	50.0
Totals	100.0	100.0	100.0	100.0

*Action taken was not recorded for all illnesses reported.

or went to a physician, but at least they did not report that they had discussed the matter with friends or relatives before seeking professional treatment. Third, even for non-serious illnesses (such as headaches, stomachaches, nervousness, etc), the lay referral system does not appear although GAC members did nothing or treated themselves with patent medicines or home remedies more often. Fourth, it is also apparent that VSC respondents did not report non-serious illnesses as frequently since there is no reason to believe that this group is that different from the GAC group. It may be that the GAC group is more concerned about health matters than the more active VSC members.

Respondents were also asked what they did for illnesses for which the symptoms were not alleviated. The data shown in Table 7 reveal a change

Table 7. Action Taken for Persisting Symptoms, in Percentages*

	Serious Illness		Non-serious Illness	
	Golden	Service Club	Volunteer	Golden
Action Taken	Age Club	Age Club	Service Club	Volunteer
	(N=16)	(N=22)	(N=14)	(N=5)
Nothing, hoped it would go away	18.8	4.5	21.4	60.0
Gave self-treatment	50.0	68.3	21.4	20.0
Sought advice of relatives/friends	—	9.0	—	—
Went to a physician	25.0	18.2	57.1	20.0
Other	6.2	—	—	—
Totals	100.0	100.0	100.0	100.0

*Symptoms were alleviated for some illnesses reported in Table 6.

in action taken for illness. Apparently, once a physician had been consulted for a serious illness and symptoms persisted, members of both clubs turned to self-treatment with patent medicines or home remedies.[10] Only in two cases was it reported that advice was sought from friends or relatives. On the other hand, when symptoms persisted for illnesses for which originally

[9]Eliot Freidson, Patients' Views of Medical Practice, New York: Russell Sage Foundation, 1961.

[10]For two cases of illness in the VSC group, it is possible that they gave self-treatment as a response when they were describing self-administration of medicine prescribed by a physician.

nothing had been done, there was a tendency for members of both groups to begin self-treatment. Interestingly enough, for non-serious ailments, GAC members increased their visits to physicians when symptoms persisted, again suggesting a greater preoccupation with health among members of this group.

Other data show that when these respondents do see a physician, they most often go to the doctor's office. For 50 per cent of their illnesses, GAC members were seen in the doctor's office compared to 59 per cent for the VSC. On the other hand, about 35 per cent of the illnesses of GAC members were seen by a physician in a clinic compared to only 19 per cent for VSC members. This difference is probably a reflection of the slight difference in social class noted earlier. Moreover, the frequency with which these respondents go to a physician approximates the national average for this age group of 6.8 visits per person per year.[11] About one-half the respondents in both groups reported they had regular check-ups from four to six times a year and otherwise went to a physician when they felt the situation called for professional attention.

Finally, we wished to know what these respondents perceived to be their human resources in a time of "health crisis." By "health crisis" is meant a period during which for health reasons, the afflicted individual becomes, at least temporarily, dependent upon others. In such a case, to whom would they or could they turn for help? Since it was assumed (and has since been demonstrated) that these respondents are relatively healthy, it was decided to employ hypothetical situations based on those so effectively used by Shanas in an earlier investigation.[12] The situation posed for respondents was as follows:

Now here is a different kind of problem. A lady, let's call her Mrs. Abrams, has just had an operation. The operation was successful, but her doctor says she will have to spend several weeks in bed in order to recover. Mrs. Abrams talked it over with her son and he arranged for someone to come in and take care of Mrs. Abrams until she got well again. Now, here is my question: Suppose you had an operation and had to stay in bed a while after you got home again. Who would you turn to to help make arrangements for your care?

The responses to this question are shown in Table 8. Again, the unusually high number of still-married couples in the VSC group is shown by the high percentage of times the spouse was named as the person expected to provide care. Perhaps also, the difference between GAC and VSC members in both human and financial resources is reflected in the identification of persons in welfare and service agencies as sources of help in over a quarter of the cases for GAC members, but not even mentioned by VSC members. The point can still be made, however, that kinsmen are perceived as major sources of assistance when needed. Two-thirds of the respondents in the

---

[11]U. S. Bureau of the Census, Statistical Abstract of the United States: 1962, (83rd Edition), Washington, D.C.: Government Printing Office, 1962, p. 75.

[12]Ethel Shanas, The Health of Older People, Cambridge: Harvard University Press, 1962.

**Table 8. Responsible Persons Named as Source of Help
in a Health Crisis, in Percentages**

Persons Named	Golden Age Club (N=18)	Volunteer Service Club (N=17)	National Sample* (N=1,734)
Spouse	11.1	58.8	1.8
Children	55.6	35.3	64.7
Siblings	—	5.9	9.5
Agency (social worker, nurse)	27.7	—	.7
Other	5.6	—	23.3
Totals	100.0	100.0	100.0

*Source: Ethel Shanas, The Health of Older People, Cambridge: Harvard University Press, 1962, p. 111.

GAC group named some kinsman as did 76 per cent of the national sample and all of the VSC members.

While there is not much of particular significance in these data alone, they do serve to raise a more important issue, namely, are adult children perceived as being *obligated* to help care for their aged parents. Numerous writers have documented the historical changes in family relationships with respect to the aged members.[13] Others suggest that the structure of the urban family is such that, with respect to useful family roles, there is no room for the older person.[14] This theorizing notwithstanding, the fact that most of the respondents in the JCCA and national samples felt they could turn to kinsmen, especially their adult children, during a health crisis suggests that older persons feel their children are obliged to help them.[15]

In order to explore this further, a second hypothetical situation was posed:

Albert and Rose Cohen have four children. They live in a small, but comfortable three-bedroom house. Rose's mother is a widow with a very small pension and her health is poor. The doctor doesn't think Rose's mother should live alone, but she doesn't need special nursing care, just someone to look out for her. What do you think Rose should do?

Responses to this question are shown in Table 9. It would appear, from these data at least, that aged parents do feel their children have an obligation to help them in a time of need. One respondent in the GAC group stated that "Rose should take care of her mother, when Rose was small her mother took care of her." Another GAC respondent stated "That's what we got children for. Mother helps them, they help mother." On the other

---

[13]See, for example, Eugene A. Friedman, The impact of aging on the social structure, in Tibbitts, *op. cit.*, pp. 120-44.

[14]Talcott Parsons and Renee Fox, Illness, therapy, and the urban American family, in E. Gartly Jaco, ed., Patients, Physicians and Illness, Glencoe, Ill.: Free Press, 1958, pp. 234-45.

[15]There is also some basis in fact for this expectation. Shanas found that responsible individuals (usually adult children) named by the aged respondents in her sample stated they would care for their aged parents even though it would likely disrupt their family's usual way of life. Shanas, *op. cit.*, pp. 114-16.

Table 9. Aged Respondents' Perception of Children's
Obligation to Help, in Percentages

Decision on Care of Aged Parent	Golden Age Club (N=18)	Volunteer Service Club (N=17)	National Sample* (N=1,734)
Take mother in home	55.6	41.2	43.7
Mother should stay alone	16.7	11.8	22.2
Make other arrangements for mother	11.1	11.8	4.9
Move mother to nursing home	11.1	29.4	9.5
No answer	5.6	5.9	19.7
Totals	100.0	100.0	100.0

*Source: Ethel Shanas, The Health of Older People, Cambridge: Harvard University Press, 1962, p. 121.

hand, another GAC member felt that life had changed so much that children could no longer be held responsible for care of their parents. She said, "Old people have no right to expect children to take them in. The family situation is different now, old people shouldn't butt in their children's business." Another said, "Children should not have to take care of parents. Rose has her hands full with her children—can't care for mother unless mother helps herself."

These examples are somewhat extreme. In most cases, the respondents' perception of the obligation of their children was qualified with "if they are able" or "if the mother [old person] would not be too great a burden." In general, there was a tendency on the part of aging parents to perceive their children as obligated to help them in crisis situations if they are able to do so. If the adult children are not in an advantageous position, the older parents suggest many rationalizations why children should not have to care for their parents.

Discussion

At this point, it is appropriate to discuss the specific hypothesis we set out to test. It is recalled that the hypothesis was that membership in a group requiring active participation is associated with better perceived health status than membership in a group requiring passive participation. In this form, the hypothesis could be supported, that is, for the total sample there is a moderate positive association between degree of participation and perceived level of health (Gamma = +.59). This association is not affected by the group to which one belongs. In other words, a similar association was found for each of the two clubs. There is an implication, however, that belonging to a club requiring active participation leads to better health. This interpretation does not stand up on close examination. While it could be inferred that there is a tendency for GAC members to be more concerned with health matters, especially non-serious illnesses, this could be attributed to their slightly older average age and their lesser ability to get around, rather than the fact that their club requires only passive participation. In view of the evidence that perceived good health is associated with high participation in GAC as well as VSC, it seems more likely that instead of saying active people are more healthy, one should say that healthy people are more active. What appears to be the crucial variable is not activity or passivity of club participation, but the nature of the interaction with other members both in and out of the club setting.

The hypothesis discussed in the preceding paragraph gives rise to a more general question which is relevant here. That is, what is the relationship between the use of leisure time by the aged and participation in organized clubs? It has frequently been pointed out that aged persons have a good deal of time on their hands.[16] Moreover, it has been suggested that older people have certain "needs" such as "need to render some socially useful service," "need to enjoy normal companionships," "need for recognition as an individual," etc.[17] It is not implied that all old people have all these needs, nor are they present in the same degree. It also has been shown that voluntary associations, in this case social clubs, have become more frequently used for satisfying the needs noted above.[18] For example, in response to another hypothetical situation which described an elderly widow in good health whose adult children ignored her except on special occasions, over one-half the members of both groups thought the widow in question should join a club or otherwise seek out her own friends. The point is this: the aged citizen (and perhaps younger ones, too) seek out those clubs in which membership offers the greatest satisfaction of felt needs. While this study did not attempt to measure directly perceived needs, data on motivation for joining either the GAC or VSC tend to support this interpretation. The data in Table 10 reveal a statistically significant difference in reasons why members joined the club they did. It might be inferred that if one had a "need to avoid boredom," membership in a group requiring only passive participation may be entirely satisfactory. We might also add that if one's

Table 10. Motivation for Joining Club, in Percentages

Motive	Golden Age Club (Passive-Oriented) (N=26)*	Volunteer Service Club (Actively-Oriented) (N=29)*
Help others, keep active	11.5	59.6
Enjoy people, be with friends	27.0	17.2
Pass time, avoid boredom	61.5	23.2
Totals	100.0	100.0

$X^2_{(2)} = 13.54$, p$<$ .001

*Some respondents gave more than one reason.

[16]See, for example, various chapters in Robert W. Kleemeier, ed., Aging and Leisure, New York: Oxford University Press, 1961.

[17]Max Kaplan, The uses of leisure, in Tibbitts, op. cit., pp. 407-43.

[18]Arnold M. Rose, The impact of aging on voluntary associations, in Tibbitts, op. cit., pp. 666-97.

health places limits on ability to actively participate in group functions, a club requiring passive participation may seem even more satisfactory.

As is usually the case with pilot studies, more questions are raised than settled. This investigation has provided some data from which inferences could be made about the relationship between health and participation of the aged in a social setting. This is an area in which little empirical evidence exists, a deficiency pointing to an urgent research need. More research is also needed on motivation for joining (or not joining) certain kinds of groups. With respect to research on social participation of the aged, we have barely scratched the surface.

CHAPTER 15

Self-Conception and Institutionalization*

RODNEY M. COE

This paper reports an investigation of the social-psychological impact of institutionalization on chronically ill, aged patients. For a variety of reasons,[1] the proportion of aged persons in the United States population has been increasing, and along with it there has been an increase in the prevalence of chronic, degenerative diseases which reflect the lengthened life span of the ordinary individual. It is estimated, for example, that about 80 per cent of the population sixty-five years old and over has at least one chronic ailment, but only 58 per cent of the population between the ages of forty-five and sixty-five are similarly afflicted.[2] This increased prevalence of chronic illnesses creates an immediate practical problem of providing long-term care for the older patient because, unlike acute illness, treatment of chronic diseases requires long periods of time and frequently is not com-

*This project was supported by the Medical Care Research Center, a joint agency of Washington University and the Jewish Hospital of Saint Louis, under funds granted by the National Institutes of Health, Research Grant RG-7739. This report has also benefited from the criticisms by members of this seminar sponsored by the Midwest Council for Social Research on Aging and Community Studies, Inc., of Kansas City, Mo.

[1]Cf., Eugene A. Friedmann, The impact of aging on the social structure, in Clark Tibbitts, ed., Handbook of Social Gerontology, Chicago: University of Chicago Press, 1960, pp. 120-44; Sidney M. Greenfield, Industrialization and the family in sociological theory, American Journal of Sociology, 67: 312-22, 1961; and Talcott Parsons and Renee Fox, Illness, therapy and the urban American family, in E. Gartly Jaco, ed., Patients, Physicians and Illness, Glencoe, Ill.: Free Press, 1958, pp. 234-45.

[2]Metropolitan Life Insurance Company, Major aspects of American morbidity, Statistical Bulletin, 41, August, 1960, pp. 1-3.

pletely successful. However, failures in treatment do not always result in the death of a patient, more often they result in a residual incapacity of the patient to perform certain activities independently. One solution to this problem is institutionalized care under the supervision of a variety of organizations ranging from chronic disease hospitals to nursing homes, rather than care within the older patient's immediate family.[3]

In view of the decreased importance of the role of the aged person in industrialized societies,[4] this investigation is an attempt to study the changes in self-conception of chronically ill, aged patients who are institutionalized in different kinds of long-term care facilities.

Conception of Self

It can probably be assumed that all societies attempt to integrate their members into the social structure via the process of role socialization. During this process members become valuable in proportion to the contribution they make through the position allocated to them by the social system.[5] However, there is a point at which both the number and value of the contributions diminish and the individual is defined as less valuable. Although this point varies through time from culture to culture and from individual to individual, the process of devaluation is essentially the reverse of socialization.[6]

Socialization has another function besides establishing a value for members; it is also a process by which a new member "becomes a person." Symbolic interaction theory indicates that as the individual becomes a person, he develops a self-image or conception of self which is a regularized way of defining social situations with reference to himself. As the individual undergoes socialization, social experiences are organized in a way that permits the individual to fit his self into the scheme (albeit, not always accurately). Perhaps still the most instructive discussion of the development of self is Cooley's "looking-glass" theory.[7] A similar theoretical framework is suggested by Mead who felt that an individual can perceive himself only through the ability to take as his own the attitudes which others express toward him. Furthermore, Mead proposed that "the attitudes of others" are sources of identities by which the individual can view himself

---

[3]For an explanation of the decreased ability of the family to undertake care of a chronically ill patient, see Parsons and Fox, *op cit.* For conflicting evidence, see Ethel Shanas, Family Relationships of Older People, New York: Health Information Foundation, Research Series 20, 1961.

[4]Arnold M. Rose, Mental health of normal older persons, Geriatrics, 16: 459-64, 1961, or present volume, chapter 12.

[5]Jules Henry, Social structure and personalization. Unpublished manuscript, Washington University, St. Louis, 1959.

[6]This conceptualization forms the basis for the theory of "disengagement." See Elaine Cumming and William E. Henry, Growing Old, New York: Basic Books, 1961.

[7]Charles H. Cooley, Human Nature and the Social Order, Glencoe, Ill.: Free Press, 1956.

as an object. Thus, a person may have as many self-identities as there are social relationships in which he engages.[8]

If it can be said that as the individual becomes devalued through a lessening of his contributions to the social system, by withdrawing from positions of importance and by reducing the sheer number of social contacts, then that individual's self-conception should theoretically also undergo a depreciation. It is felt that this depreciation of self can be conceptualized as the process of *depersonalization,* literally, the loss of personal identity.

"Total" Institutions

Before relating the conception of self to the specific research problem at hand, it is necessary to discuss the present concept of institution. There are, of course, many ways of analyzing institutions, one of which is to study them in terms of the characteristics of "total institutions."[9] Briefly, these characteristics are:

. . . *first,* all aspects of life are conducted in the same place and under the same single authority. *Second,* each phase of the member's daily activity will be carried out in the immediate company of a large batch of others, all of whom are treated alike and required to do the same thing together. *Third,* all phases of the day's activities are tightly scheduled . . . being imposed from above through a system of explicit formal rulings and a body of officials. *Finally,* the contents of the various enforced activities are brought together as parts of a single overall rational plan designed to fulfill the official aims of the institution . . .[10]

Further, there is an almost caste-like split between those who are being treated, called "inmates" or "patients," and those who do the treating, the staff. In general the gulf between the two groups is wide with little cross-communication and virtually no social mobility. In addition, authority is invested almost exclusively in the staff. This authority tends to be of the "echelon" kind, i.e., any member of the staff has authority over any patient. Like all formal organizations, total institutions are designed to achieve specific, although different, goals. Unlike other formal organizations, however, total institutions have in common the immediate goal of providing "total" maintenance for their residents, e.g., food, shelter, clothing. A peculiar aspect of the residents is that they are all devalued by the managers of the institutions before they enter the institution. Consequently, justification is provided for the manipulation of large groups of patients without regard for their wishes through tight control over their behavior, for structuring activities according to the needs of the organization, for impersonal treatment of patients, and for isolation of the patient from the rest of the society. The social organization of total institutions not only permits a small

[8]George Herbert Mead, Mind, Self and Society, Chicago: University of Chicago Press, 1934.

[9]Erving Goffman, Characteristics of total institutions, in Symposium on Preventive and Social Psychiatry, Washington, D. C.: Walter Reed Army Institute of Research, Walter Reed Army Medical Center, 1957, pp. 43-84.

[10]*Ibid,* p. 45.

number of persons (staff) to provide total maintenance for a large group (patients), but in addition offers an opportunity for the former to express their devaluation of the latter. Among the consequences flowing from this combination, three are most common: (1) "stripping," (2) control of resources, and (3) restriction of mobility.[11]

The interesting feature of these consequences is that to whatever degree they are present in the institution, they all tend to "depersonalize" the inmate. Henry has recently stated that in all cultures

> . . . the nature of the attachment of the individual to the social system varies through time, and is related to the economic and symbolic contributions made by him to the culture. Everywhere deference, access to goods and services, the ability to influence social decisions, the "capacity to be missed," and the right to control the disposition of one's own person emerge as independent criteria of "attachment" and hence, of personalization . . .[12]

Consequently, when an inmate is deprived of these modes of attachment to his own social system through stripping, routinization, loss of control over resources, decreased mobility, impersonal treatment, etc., the inmate is undergoing depersonalization.[13]

If, as noted above, a person's self-conception results from an organization of accumulated social experiences, and present experiences occur in a setting characterized as a total institution, then these reflected experiences should result in a deterioration of the self image. In other words—and this is the hypothesis that is to be tested—*the degree of depersonalization varies directly with the severity of the total characteristics of the institution.*

Method

It was felt that the above hypothesis could be tested by comparative analysis of three institutions designed for care of the chronically ill aged, which represented different points on a continuum of severity of total characteristics of the institutions. The institutions finally selected for study

---

[11]Cf., *ibid*, pp. 49-50. Here stripping refers to the process of mortification of the self. Elsewhere it is variously called devaluation, alienation, dehumanization. See, respectively, Beatrice Wright, Physical Disability—A Psychological Approach, New York: Harpers, 1960; Melvin Seeman, On the meaning of alienation, American Sociological Review, 24: 783-90, 1959; Helen M. Lynd, On Shame and the Search for Identity, New York: Harcourt-Brace, 1958.

[12]Jules Henry, *op cit.*, p. 3.

[13]The case of the bedridden patient living at home or in the home of relatives is similar to that of a patient living in an institution since both are dependent upon others for initiation of social contacts as well as for provision of physical care. On the other hand, institutionalized patients do have an opportunity to participate in the informal patient social organization. However, the informal social organization of aged patients is only weakly developed compared to inmate organizations in other total institutions, such as the prison or mental hospital ward. In other words, it seems entirely possible that the fact that these patients are aged and have already undergone the rigors of devaluation of their social roles, plus the fact that they are sick (with varying degrees of acuity) and somewhat less physically mobile, not to mention restraints imposed by institutional regulations, would all tend to reduce the frequency of interaction and, therefore, inhibit the development of an effective patient social organization.

were (1) a special unit in a large, private, general hospital, (2) a municipal institution for intermediate care of the chronically ill, and (3) a large, proprietary nursing home. On the basis of observations and an instrument especially designed for this study, the Chronic Illness Ideology Scale, the special unit was found to have the least degree of totalistic features, the public institution had an intermediate degree, and the nursing home had the most severe degree of total characteristics.

For example, a comparison of some relatively objective characteristics is found in Table 1. More importantly, however, notes on observations made in each of the three institutions indicate considerable differences in characteristics relevant to the concept of "total" institutions. The physical layout of the special unit was the same as that of other medical divisions in the same hospital. Similarly, the standards of cleanliness and sanitation were the same. The public institution was hampered by the fact that the buildings were very old and they had originally been designed for other purposes. In the nursing home, little effort was made to maintain more than minimal standards of cleanliness. As one might expect, since the special unit was located in a general hospital, the provisions for privacy as well as the general demeanor of the staff toward the patient were better than in either of the other institutions, although it was considerably better in the public institution than in the nursing home.

To a certain extent, in the special unit some activities—such as meals, physical and occupational therapy sessions, and administration of medicines —were scheduled for the patients. Most of the time, however, patients could do as they pleased. In the public institution, almost all activities were scheduled, including bedtime at 3:00 p.m. for patients who could not retire without assistance. In the nursing home, the problem was not that activities were scheduled, but that there were no activities, and yet patients were not permitted to leave the chairs provided next to their beds. In all three institutions, authority was invested in the staff, and the manner in which staff decisions were related to the patient varied little. A substantial difference, however, could be seen in the control of resources. In the special unit, patients not only had access to their private property, but also were permitted to use it as they desired. In the public institution, some patients had their own clothing but little else and most patients were completely dependent upon the institution. In the nursing home there was no private property, everything was on a communal basis including allocation of clothing, bedding, magazines and even toilet articles.

Finally, but not exhaustively, one characteristic which clearly differentiated the three institutions was the use of force and physical abuse by the staff. In the special unit this type of behavior was never observed although staff members frequently talked to each other about patients in disrespectful terms. In the public institution there were few times when a staff member was observed abusing a patient, although the staff sometimes had to force patients to comply with institutional regulations regarding being in bed, going to the toilet, etc. In the nursing home there were frequent occurrences of physical restraint used on patients, of verbal abuse of

Table 1. Summary of General Characteristics of Institutions

Characteristic	Special Unit	Public Institution*	Nursing Home
Number of beds	43	45	92
Number of patients**	43	41	82
Nursing personnel:**	27	9	13
R.N.	5	3	0
Aide	22	6	13
Cost per month	$600†	$377‡	$150§
Resources	Medical director, visiting physicians, other specialized professional personnel, diagnostic and therapeutic technicians, maintenance and housekeeping crews	Resident physician, some specialized professional personnel, diagnostic and therapeutic technicians, maintenance and housekeeping crews	Visiting physician, visiting R.N., local public general hospital for acute episodes
Type rooms	Private & semi-private	Semi-private	Ward (4 or more beds)
Number of rooms	24	36	9
Toilet and bathing facilities	One per room	One per sex	One per sex

*Figures are for each of the five Intermediate Care divisions.

**At time of data collection.

†Approximate maximum rate. Costs to patients are revised downward on ability to pay. Average rate for all patients in 1961 was $233 per month.

‡Approximate maximum rate. Costs to patients are revised downward on ability to pay. Average cost to patient is $65 per month.

§Employee informant.

patients, usually in the form of teasing, and of physical punishment for violating the rules. In addition, several fights among patients were observed in which staff members merely looked on and did little to stop the fight.

These, plus many more systematic observations and the results of the Chronic Illness Ideology Scale,[14] established the location of the three institutions on the theoretical continuum of "total" characteristics. As noted above, the special unit had the fewest (or least degree) of these characteristics; the public institution was in the middle range, while the nursing home had the most (or highest degree) of total features.

Data on patients were collected by means of a semi-structured interview schedule which included not only general information from institutional records, but also several rating scales, including the principal instrument for assessment of self-conception, The Twenty Statements Test (TST). The TST was chosen because it was developed from the same theoretical background described above. That is, this assessment device assumes, first, that a person identifies himself by means of identities which others have attributed to him and to ways others have acted toward him in these identities. Second, it assumes that important parts of the self-conception are available to awareness and can be put into words. This does not deny the possibility of "unconsciously determined" behavior, but rather emphasizes the importance of conscious controls on social behavior.[15]

The respondent's task was to answer the question "Who am I?" with up to twenty different statements which would reflect his identities. These responses to the TST were then reliably placed into one of four categories. The first category (hereafter called "role responses") included *statements referring to explicitly structured social situations,* that is, to roles and statuses which imply norms for the behavior of the incumbent. Specifically, references to kinship, occupation, religious or other group membership, sex, and possessions were included. Examples would be "I am a Jew," "I am a man," "I am a coalminer."

The second category (hereafter called "affect responses") included *statements of self-distinguishing habits, moods, preferences,* etc. Although the statements are specific they are not tied as closely to structured social situations. In this category are such statements as "I like to sew," "I am a religious person," "I don't like it here."

---

[14]This scale was comprised of 74 attitudinal statements about chronically ill, aged patients in various situations. Three broad categories of items were constructed: (1) beliefs about the behavior of the chronically ill; (2) dependence of the chronically ill patient on others; and (3) statements reflecting characteristics of ideal-typical total institutions. After pretesting, these items were administered to all nursing personnel in the three institutions. Analysis of the responses indicated a statistically significant difference in the expected direction (p<.001, Kruskal-Wallis One Way Analysis of Variance). That is, personnel in the special unit were highest (least custodial) with a mean score of 211.8 (N = 21). Personnel in the public institution were next with a score of 206.9 (N = 26) and the nursing home employees were lowest with a score of 190.4 (N = 9).

[15]Manual for the Twenty Statements Problem (Revised), Department of Research, Greater Kansas City Mental Health Foundation, Kansas City, Missouri, pp. 1-2.

In the third category (hereafter called "physical responses") are *identifications of physical attributes* (except sex). Physical attributes are classified separately because they can be stated without suggesting anything about social behavior or links with the social system. For example, this category includes references to age, height, weight, color of eyes, hair, address, telephone number, and references to a state of health or illness. In addition, the patient's name was placed in this category. Although it could be argued that the name represents kinship ties (role response), the name was included here because it does not imply norms for behavior while specific kinship references do. Finally, into the fourth category (hereafter called "global responses") go *statements so comprehensive that they do not permit a meaningful differentiation* of the respondent from others. In addition, irrelevant statements and trivia are classified here. For example, included here are such statements as "I am a child of God," "I am a human being," "I am Napoleon Bonaparte."

Theoretically, the expectation would be that a person who is fully "engaged" in his social system would tend to give mostly role responses relating to kinship (especially family roles), to occupation, or to other salient features of his identification of self. Affect responses should be the second most frequent responses given. As a person undergoes the process of devaluation, however, fewer of these roles are available to him; therefore, the frequency of role responses should decline and the frequency of responses in the categories of less social relatedness should increase, e.g., physical and global responses. If depersonalization from institutionalization is severe enough, the majority of responses would be expected to fall in the global response category. It should be noted that responses of this type —for example, "I am Napoleon Bonaparte"—are often accepted as diagnostic indicators of psychoses.[16]

The procedure for this study consisted of interviewing a sample of patients stratified by the length of time they had been institutionalized, who were at least sixty years old, and had at least one classifiable chronic disease. Two months after the initial interview all the patients of the original sample who were still in the respective institutions were re-interviewed to assess the change over time in self-conception.[17]

Results

The major hypothesis of this study was that *the degree of depersonalization varies directly with the severity of the total characteristics of the institution.* To test the hypothesis, patients' statements on the TST were evaluated on the basis of frequency and content, and these data were supported

---

[16]Tamotsu Shibutani, *Society and Personality,* Englewood Cliffs, N. J.: Prentice-Hall, 1961, p. 538.

[17]In the special unit, out of the original sample of 24 patients, 7 had been discharged to their homes and one had died. In the public institution, out of the 32 original patients, 4 had been discharged to their homes, 2 had been transferred to other institutions and 2 had died. In the nursing home, out of the 27 original patients, 6 patients had died.

by the verbatim replies of patients to other questions in the interview schedule.

First TST Administration. This mode of analysis revealed some important differences among patients in the three institutions. For example, the average number of responses to the first administration of the TST was 7.3 for the special unit, 5.0 for the public institution, and 3.4 for the nursing home. On the second administration, these averages were 4.9, 3.3 and 3.0 for those institutions, respectively. When the proportion of responses in each of the four categories (summarized in Table 2), was examined, an interesting trend appeared: For the initial assessment, it can be seen that in all three institutions the percentage of responses increases as the degree of social relatedness of the category decreases, but that it was more extreme for the nursing home than for the public institution which, in turn, was more extreme than the special unit. This would seem to give initial support to the major hypothesis that self-conception is stronger in the institutions with the least custodial characteristics.

The principal responses in the role response category for patients in the special unit were kinship and ethnicity. On the first administration of the TST, 46 per cent of the patients gave at least one response in each of these classes. In fact, fully one-third of them mentioned their ethnicity as a first response, indicating the salience of ethnicity for self-conception. It should be noted, however, that in every case the patient was Jewish, the predominant ethnic group among the patients in this institution. For the other institutions kinship was also salient, but to a lesser degree. About 25 per cent of the patients in both the public institution and the nursing home gave at least one response referring to kinship. Ethnicity, however, was indicated as a source of identification by less than 5 per cent of the patients in the public institution and the nursing home. Identifications by age were made by 25 per cent, 10 per cent and 4 per cent of the patients in the special unit, public institution and nursing home, respectively. It should also be noted that although the age differences were not significant, patients in the special unit tended to be older than in the other two institutions. A similar pattern was found with regard to responses referring to illness in the institution. About 42 per cent of the patients in the special unit made this kind of response at least once, but only 13 per cent in the public institution and 15 per cent in the nursing home did so. It is further noted that the patients in the special unit were "sicker" than in the public institution and these were "sicker" than the patients in the nursing home. Consequently, these results are not unexpected. Finally, it should be reported that the personal name was the most frequently reported source of identification in all three institutions.

Second TST Administration. Two months later, on the second assessment, only kinship remained for all the patients as a salient identification, except of course, for the personal name. That is, the percentages of kinship responses were about the same as before while changes occurred in other categories. Curiously, in the special unit, only 20 per cent mentioned

Table 2. Percentage of TST Responses in Each Category

		Initial Assessment							Final Assessment				
			TST Category							TST Category			
Institution	N	Number of Responses	Role	Affect	Physical	Global	N	Number of Responses	Role	Affect	Physical	Global
Special unit	24	176	23.9	24.4	25.0	26.7	15	73	31.5	17.8	30.1	20.5
Public institution	32	161	16.1	20.5	28.0	35.4	24	79	11.4	19.0	43.0	26.6
Nursing home	27	98	7.1	14.3	28.6	50.0	21	62	11.2	17.7	46.8	24.2

ethnicity (compared to 46 per cent on the first assessment). On the other hand, in this institution 60 per cent of the patients identified themselves in terms of illness or disease. In the public institution and the nursing home, there were no extreme changes in these modes of identification although there was a slight decline in responses relating to illness and a slight increase in responses referring to aging.

Mode of Response of Short-Term versus Long-Term Patients. Further assessment was made by examining the mode of response of short-term patients (under one month) versus long-term patients (over twelve months) in each institution and for both assessment periods.

The Special Unit. For the first assessment data, a familiar pattern emerged for newly admitted patients in the special unit.[18] About 40 per cent of the responses were physical responses and a similar percentage were global responses, that is, these new admissions had an "egocentric" preoccupation with their illness. For example, all eight of one patient's responses related to illness, some of which were "I'm a cripple," "I got sick four years ago," "It's a bad sickness and they can't cure it." Another patient in this group commented:

> . . . first I was bad sick and my children took me to the hospital. Now I got no home . . . I'm just a plain nothing. Why I got to be sick? Why I can't go home? Nobody talks to me. It is better that I should die . . . .

Still another reported:

> . . . I'm a poor woman and I have diabetes . . . mine husband is dead and I'm more worse than that . . . you see if I'm not dead like my husband . . . .

Others in this group showed a similar concern for their illness and some expressed fears about what the future held for them.

In contrast, patients in the special unit who had been there over twelve months gave modal responses in the affect response category (34 per cent) and almost the same in the global response category (32 per cent). The responses reflected affect and mood, usually directed at the institution and a desire to be active again. For example, 5 of 14 responses of one patient referred to housework. Another patient remarked how unhappy she was because she felt better and wanted to get home to look after her house. A third patient commented that "to be here is like in a morgue. I want to go home." It should also be noted that in addition to a shift in modal response category, long-term patients tended to give slightly more responses than short-term patients (7.6 and 6.2, respectively).

After two months some distinct changes are noticeable in the responses of short-term patients in the special unit. First, there was a decline in the responses only tenuously associated with the self (42 per cent and 19 per cent for initial and final assessment, respectively). This decline was reflected in the increase in role responses, especially kinship (13 per cent and 33 per cent, respectively). However, these responses did not reflect bonds

18See, for example, Henry D. Lederer, How the sick view their world, in E. Gartly Jaco, ed., Patients, Physicians and Illness, Glencoe, Ill.: Free Press, 1958, pp. 247-56; also Erving Goffman, The moral career of the mental patient, Psychiatry, 22: 123-42, 1959.

with kinsmen, but on the contrary, they expressed feelings of being detached from kinsmen, especially adult children. One patient for example, said, "I've been here a long time now (less than three months) and I got no other home now. This is my home." Another reflected the same feeling. "I got no home no more. For so many months I am away from my children." In the same vein another commented:

   . . . I am not happy here. I want to go home, but I got no home to go to. When mine husband died, the house we sold. Now I got no place to go. [Patient related how she helped build the family retail wallpaper and paint business]. Mine children they all work for a living, but they don't work so hard as their father did. They start where he left off . . . .

Finally, another short-term patient expressed her feelings by saying:

   . . . I'm sick . . . I'm tired of living and I want to die. Why should I live now? My mother is dead. My father is dead. My husband is dead. My children live in California. Why should I live now? My daughter hollered at me when I told her that. She said, "Mama, don't talk like that!" She was very angry at me . . . .

In the two-month period, however, there was only a very slight change in physical responses, especially references to illness (40 per cent and 33 per cent). That is, patients did not seem to lose their "egocentric" concern for their situation in this short a time. This is not surprising in view of the nature of their illnesses, that is, chronic illnesses. Although the disabling effects of these diseases can often be mitigated in a short time through intensive medical treatment, there does remain a residual effect preventing the patient from performing at pre-illness levels, thus the patient feels he isn't getting well.

As one might expect, few changes occurred in the responses of long-term patients in the two-month period. There is a tendency, however, for their responses to fall in all four categories in approximately equal numbers. These patients seem to inject a feeling of despair into their responses related to kinship. While patients in the short-term group are concerned about their relationships with kinfolk, patients in the long-term group seem to have given up hope for re-establishing these relationships. In addition, they tended to reflect their bitterness towards their kin, especially their children. One patient complained:

   . . . my people don't want me. My husband and niece come here to see me regularly but my young people [her children] don't care. I got a brother who is a multi-millionaire. He owns ——— in New York, but he don't help me at all . . . he doesn't care . . . .

Other responses reflecting the hopelessness of their situations include:

   I'm not satisfied here, but what can I do? I got no place to go. People who are handicapped should just go to sleep. They are no good anymore.
   You can't be too satisfied here, but what can you do? . . . I don't enjoy life now, but what is the use of fighting? You can't do nothing about it.

Another patient said:

   You call this living? This is existing. But I have to take it. What can't be cured must be endured.

Finally, a note of utter despair is heard in this response:

   . . . I wish my God would come and take me. I'm tired of living and I'm a sick lady. My arm is paralyzed and I got gangrene in the foot. I'm not happy with myself. I like it here. I'm here five years already and they are treating me very nice . . . but I'm wishing I was dead . . . .

This qualitative description would seem to illustrate the impact of institutionalization on the chronically ill patient. Comparison with the other institutions, described below, also tends to support this hypothesis.

The Public Institution. The initial responses of short-term patients in the public institution did not present so clear a pattern as those of patients in the special unit. Most of the former's responses were either affect or global responses (30 per cent each) although many were physical responses (24 per cent). It should be recalled that these patients were undergoing intermediate care, that is, the acute stage of their illness had passed and they were convalescing, although many of them still received intensive medical treatment. Consequently, although new admissions to this public institution, they had been transferred there from a public general hospital. Therefore, the tendency to give fewer responses reflecting concern for illness is not surprising. Like their counterparts in the special unit, however, the new admissions to the public institution indicated concern for the future. As one patient put it:

. . . I wish I was home again, but I don't have a home no more. I wish I could go to somebody's home. There's no room for old people . . . .

Another said his nephews "don't know I'm here; they don't know I'm alive," he further commented:

. . . you don't know what it's like, day and night all are the same; pain, pain, pain. I get worse and worse. I wish I be dead now . . . .

In contrast, the long-term patients gave fewer responses than the short-term patients (2.8 and 5.4, respectively) and all of them were physical and global responses (35 per cent and 65 per cent). It is interesting to note that these patients tended to be uncommunicative (hence, the lower number of responses) and suspicious of the interviewer. Most of these patients had been there longer than the average stay for patients in this institution and they expressed a fear of being transferred to other public institutions which had bad reputations. Generally, these patients gave their names as a first response (some could give only their name), others expressed a feeling of satisfaction that they were living in the institution (probably because they feared being transferred).

On the second assessment, there was little change in the mode of response for either short- or long-term patients, except that the average number of responses declined for both groups. The short-term group expressed a dislike for the institution and some talked about their former activities, such as housework or gardening. A significant observation was that many of these patients were uncommunicative. They didn't want to talk to the interviewer, but preferred just to sit and stare at the floor or out the window. That is, these patients seemed to be approaching the point where depersonalization was so severe that the patients became almost completely withdrawn from any social relations.

Final assessment of long-term patients revealed a note of despair similar to that found in long-term patients in the special unit, but with two differences: First, some of the patients in the public institution indicated they were "happy" there. As one patient put it, "Where else could I get food and a roof for this money?"[19] Another indicated that she was satisfied because "she had to be" since she couldn't do anything about it. A second difference related more directly to self-conception. These responses are typified by "I'm getting old and soft here" and

> . . . I don't enjoy living now. I can't wait on myself anymore. You know you feel important when you wait on yourself, more independent. I can't do this anymore . . . For me there is nothing left but my name . . . .

The Nursing Home. Comparison of nursing home residents with those in the other two institutions is somewhat difficult because of the large number of nursing home patients who had been in the institution over a year and the small number of patients who had been there less than a month. There is, however, a considerable difference in the content of the responses. Patients in the nursing home less than one year stressed past activities, either housework, or manual labor and athletics. It should be noted that patients in the nursing home were generally less seriously ill than patients in either of the other two institutions. In addition the nursing home patients gave responses indicating they felt detached, neglected by their children. For example, one patient stated:

> I wish I was home to see my people more often, but my daughter don't want me. She never comes to see me here; she has forgot me.

Another said:

> . . . I feel bad that I can't live with my daughter or some friends. I done nothing to them. They don't [come to] see me when I'm sick. They don't seem to recognize me. I know I ain't done nothing to them . . . I don't know what's the trouble . . . .

In general, these two types of responses—past activities and detachment from kinsmen—dominated the responses of this patient group.

In contrast to this, two other types of responses characterize the patients resident in the home over twelve months. Most noticeable is the large number of apparently senile patients whose responses were almost incoherent, or at least their answers were unrelated to the questions asked by the investigator. Some reported hearing voices, like the patient who "talks" to his parents (deceased) everyday. Or the patient who asked the interviewer, "Don't you hear my piano player now? It's beautiful." Other patients in this group also refer to themselves in terms of long-dead parents and other kin. For example, one patient stated, "I'm no account; my father says so."

These remarks seem to indicate that patients who are undergoing the process of depersonalization and who experience painful contacts with the immediate environment, may withdraw from those contacts and construct a delusional system of their own in which they do not have painful experiences. Cameron has described this phenomenon for a paranoid schizo-

---

19This is characteristic of a process called "institutionalism." Cf., J. K. Wing, Institutionalism in mental hospitals, British Journal of Social and Clinical Psychology, 1: 38-51, 1962. See also Robert Sommer and Humphrey Osmond, Symptoms of institutional care, Social Problems, 8: 254-63, 1960-1961.

phrenic.[20] Cameron's argument was that individual differences and inability to take on certain roles because of inadequate socialization make a person unable to communicate his fears and suspicions to others. As a result, the individual constructs a "pseudo-community" in which he organizes both delusional and real events into a coherent pattern. Eventually, norms of behavior derived from the pseudo-community conflict with those from the real community and punitive sanctions from the latter then verify the paranoid delusional expectations, thus creating a vicious cycle.

It is possible that a similar chain of events occurs with chronically ill, aged patients who are placed in institutions which have severe depersonalizing characteristics. As the older person undergoes disengagement, he is no longer able to undertake certain roles. If, in addition, he is placed in an environment in which his self-conception deteriorates, he may be forced to "turn inward" for experiences which will permit a better self-conception. The more he withdraws from contact with the environment (the institution), the less able (and less concerned) he would be to comply with the rules of behavior of the "real" world, thus bringing on punitive sanctions from the staff and further depersonalization.

Some evidence of this has already been noted in the statements made by patients in all three institutions, but especially in the nursing home where isolation of the patient and other depersonalizing characteristics are most severe. Further evidence from patient responses can be seen in the following quotation from a patient in the nursing home. This patient, when asked if he had any friends or relatives, replied:

. . . only my wife's kin, you know, not blood kin of mine.

(How often did you see them?)

Oh, they talk to me all the time, you know, I'm perfect, I never make a mistake. I know you think I'm crazy, but I've got forty people who will vouch for me. They told me last night to go and sin no more . . . .

(Who told you that?)

Moses spoke to me out of the burning bush and he told me to get my American aircraft ready to go to France or Europe. My mother and father talk to me all the time. Sometimes she says, "——— what are you doing down there? I told you to get up here" and I do it . . . .

Most patients, however, were not as verbal as this one. Their responses were usually much shorter although they tended to be similar in content. In addition, these patients spent much of their time just staring at the floor or out the window. It is, of course, possible that this type of response is due to a physical disorder, such as cerebral arteriosclerosis or senility. However, these responses were obtained more often in the nursing home than in the public institution, and more often in the latter than in the special unit. The possibility that this type of response may be due to depersonalization is suggestive of further research.

---

[20]Norman Cameron, The paranoid pseudo-community, American Journal of Sociology, 49: 32-38, 1943. See also Robert E. L. Faris, Reflections of social disorganization in the behavior of the schizophrenic patient, American Journal of Sociology, 50: 134-41, 1944.

The second type of response characterizing this group was an almost desperate attempt to salvage some fragments of self-conception, although these patients didn't think of it in these terms. One patient responded by saying:

> . . . I don't do nothing here since I came to this mud hole. I used to make good money, as high as $5 or $6 a day. Now I can't make nothing. Just set around. I wouldn't work for these people [the staff]—dead beats, thieves, bums—they'll steal all your clothes you got . . . they don't treat me like I was somebody—so I got nothing to do with them . . . .

Another, in the same vein replied:

> . . . you got to watch yourself around here. They'll steal from you, lie to you . . . there is nothing to do except sit around all day. I try to keep cleaned up to be somebody, but when I get hurting, I'm done . . . .

On the second assessment, there had been considerable change in short-term patients. Almost all references to kinship had disappeared. These patients tended to give short, direct answers to specific questions, but would only shrug or say "I don't know" or "there's not much else" for open-ended questions. These changes were also reflected in fewer responses to the TST than on the first administration (3.4 to 2.5). Generally they gave their personal name first and often gave only their name. For the long-term patients, the number of responses also declined over time (3.8 to 3.1), and again many of the patients were unable to give coherent answers. Although there were no specific references to maintaining the self-concept, several patients commented that "you can't trust people around here," or "too much humbug, they tell you a bunch of lies," and "it's bad here, I'm just sliding away."

The Aging Subculture and Response to the Institution

The data from this study also provide some empirical support for Rose's statement about the development of a subculture of the aged.[21] He postulated that a subculture of aged persons is developing because of a loss of social roles, a general reduction in physical abilities and health, reduced income, and rejection by adult children. By virtue of reduced interaction with other (younger) groups, and by clinging to "old-fashioned" cultural beliefs, the aged persons in the population demarcate themselves from the contemporary flow of life, that is, they become socially isolated and out of contact with current events.

The subjects of this study, in addition to having undergone the experiences leading to a subculture of the aged, are also physically isolated in institutions. Whereas certain conditions are present among the non-institutionalized aged which mitigate the consequences of and often even prevent participation in such a subculture, these conditions do not obtain

---

[21] Arnold M. Rose, The subculture of the aging: a framework for sociological research, Chap. 1, in this volume.

for the institutionalized aged. That is, while good physical and mental health and frequent engagement in social activities tend to confer status (among aged peers), the subjects in this study were ill and physically incapable of engaging in many activities. As indicated above, depersonalization tended to further reduce motivation for participation in any type of activity.

It is further suggested that these institutionalized patients were particularly susceptible to the phenomenon of "group self-hatred."[22] That is, a chronically ill, aged person represents a stereotype of the old and now useless societal burden. Since the reflected attitudes of the "generalized other" as well as "significant others" has been shown, for this sample at least, to be largely negative and authoritarian, it would be expected that the chronically ill, aged respondent would tend to see himself (and others like him) in these devalued terms. It would also be expected that aged patients in whom group self-hatred was incorporated into the self-concept would respond to their environment in these terms. That is, anxiety over the future, fear of and anger at unfulfilled kinship expectations, increasing dependence, and attempts to salvage some positive affect toward self would be expected after admission to a total institution. The data from this study indicate that not only did these responses occur, but they were more pronounced in institutions with the more severely depersonalizing characteristics.

Conclusions

It was stated earlier that aged persons undergo a social process of devaluation (although it affects them in differing degrees) in which the nature and strength of their attachments to the social system change. That is, the bonds which link them with the social system become weakened. When an elderly person develops a chronic illness, the ability of this person to continue action patterns which "attach" him to the social system is further reduced. The onset of a chronic illness or the recurrence of a latent chronic illness often entails a reduction in activities. Reduced activity and mobility are accompanied by a decrease in interaction with others and this should be most severe for elderly persons who live alone.[23] Furthermore, the nature of chronic illnesses often limits the elderly person's ability to provide complete self-care, thus placing him in a position of dependence on others. In addition, many valued roles must be relin-

---

[22]*Ibid.*, p. 8. This phenomenon, found so frequently among the physically handicapped, is related to a poor self-conception as a reflection of prevailing societal attitudes towards members of devalued minority groups, in this case, the aged. Cf., Donald F. Garrett, Psychological Aspects of Physical Disability, Washington, D. C.; Government Printing Office, Office of Vocational Rehabilitation, Series 210, 1957.

[23]Cf., Shanas, *op. cit.* While the onset of an illness would tend to reduce the activity, mobility and thus, the amount of interaction of any age group, it would tend to be more serious for the aged, who prior to illness, had already undergone a reduction in number of contacts and amount of interaction.

quished, at least temporarily, when the individual takes on the sick role.[24] When illness becomes severe enough that kinsmen, especially adult children, are unable (or unwilling) to provide the nursing care needed to maintain the sick member, it is likely that specialized institutional care will be chosen as the solution to the problem.[25]

However, it has been shown here that the institution has a tremendous impact on the self-conception of the chronically ill, aged patient. Certainly the relative isolation, the separation from kinsmen, the degradation of having to be cared for like a child have their effect on the self-conceptions of these patients. But it seems that one of the significant findings of this investigation is the fairly large number of patients who appeared to be depersonalized to an extreme degree. Many others have described this phenomenon in the context of mental illness, such as Shibutani who remarked, " . . . if a person finds himself immersed in a hostile environment in which he cannot find satisfaction, he may create a substitute world in which his lot is better. Such a scheme may become his only guarantee of security; if so, its preservation becomes a value in itself . . . ."[26]

This explanation is consistent with the data from this investigation. That is, the highest proportion of withdrawn and uncommunicative patients was found in the nursing home, the institution with the most severely depersonalizing characteristics. Although patients in other institutions also gave some responses which were associated with things in the past, such as references to long-dead parents, most of the obviously disoriented responses came from patients in the nursing home. In addition, observations indicated that few patients in that institution did more than just sit and stare at the floor. These patients had the lowest average number of responses to the TST and their responses were most frequently in the global (least attached) category for the first assessment. To a large extent, these characteristics were also found in the public institution, but to a much lesser degree. They were found hardly at all in the special unit.

Further support for this interpretation (that is, of extreme depersonalization) can be inferred from the differences in morbidity and mortality rates in the three institutions. In this study, the patients in the special unit were judged to be more seriously ill than patients in the public institution or the nursing home. The criteria used were: first, number of chronic illnesses

---

[24]For chronic illness, of course, the relinquishment of roles may be for much longer periods of time, perhaps permanently. Cf., Talcott Parsons, The Social System, Glencoe, Ill.: Free Press, 1951, Chapter 10. See also David Mechanic and Edmond A. Volkart, Stress, illness and the sick role, American Sociological Review, 26: 51-58, 1961. Barker and associates, however, have noted that not all chronically ill persons take on the sick role. According to them, the tuberculous patient's inability to take on completely the sick role or completely give up previous roles, especially occupation, is an important source of the patient's inability to adjust to the sanitorium. Roger G. Barker, Beatrice Wright, and Mollie R. Gonick, Adjustment to Physical Handicap and Illness, New York: Social Science Research Council, Bulletin No. 55, 1946, pp. 140-42.

[25]Parsons and Fox, op. cit.

[26]Shibutani, op. cit., p. 458; also Cameron, op. cit.; also Faris, op. cit.

diagnosed (probably subject to bias of unequal diagnostic capabilities of the institutions) and, second, the number of nursing services required by the patient. Patients in the special unit were highest on both measures; patients in the public institution were next, and patients in the nursing home were lowest. This may be partly a reflection of institutional goals and of criteria for admission: the special unit is designed to provide intensive, professional medical care for long-term patients, while the public institution is designed to provide intermediate care, and the nursing home is for maintenance, that is, custodial care. Nevertheless, the fact that the percentage of deaths among patients leaving the sample during the two-month interim period was inversely related to the degree of illness for the three institutions is suggestive of extreme depersonalization.[27] This, too, could be interpreted to mean that under conditions of extreme depersonalization, the patient may be forced to withdraw to a delusional world to evade a degraded self-conception reflected in the attitude and behavior of others.[28]

In conclusion it should be noted that there are several points which indicate the need for further research. It is felt that provision of nursing care for the chronically ill aged is of sufficient importance to warrant re-studying the effects of institutionalization using a somewhat different research design. Specifically, such a study clearly calls for a longitudinal investigation over a prolonged period of time. Further, a much larger sample selected from newly admitted patients will be required because of the high attrition rate of subjects. The present investigation also suggests a comparative study should be undertaken of the self-conceptions of the institutionalized aged, on the one hand, and the chronically ill aged who remain in their homes under private care or some sort of organized home care program, on the other. Finally, a further study is needed on background variables which may have important consequences for nursing care of the chronically ill aged patient.

---

[27]The percentage of patients discharged by death during the two-month period was 11.1 (N = 9) for the special unit; 25.0 (N = 8) in the public institution; and 100.0 (N = 6) in the nursing home.

[28]It is interesting to speculate that since the death rate is highest in the nursing home where the patients are least seriously ill, it may be that death could be attributable to extreme depersonalization, similar to that reported in studies of prison camps. Cf., Bruno Bettelheim, The Informed Heart, Glencoe, Ill.: Free Press, 1960.

CHAPTER 16

Institutionalization, Interac and Self-Conception in Aging*

NANCY NEWMAN ANDERSON

The mental health and housing of older people loom up as mountainous problems from the point of view of many—the older person himself, his relatives and friends, and those professionally involved in administering to and studying him. Of particular interest to social gerontologists concerned with these problems are the atmosphere in which the older person lives, his association with others, and his attitudes toward himself. In numerous studies, however, one of these variables eludes the investigator and escapes from its close relationship with the other two. Interaction with others and self-conception—social activity and participation, on the one hand, self-image, esteem, and adjustment, on the other—usually remain related as do either the former or the latter with institutionalization, but the interrelationship of all three is neglected. Another habit of some gerontologists, and many less scientific observers, is implying or hypothesizing that institutionalization has an unfavorable effect upon the older person's mental health without specifying how or why. This paper proposes the usefulness of investigating the concepts in a three-way linkage in which institutionalization is regarded as the independent variable and self-conception as the dependent variable, with variation in interaction as the intervening variable. Theoretically, any evaluation of the effect of institutionalization must take into account changes in interaction which may accompany the change in living arrangements. Empirically, it will be demonstrated that for one

*This report is a summary of my master's thesis conducted under the direction of Professor Arnold Rose. For a more extensive discussion the reader is referred to Nancy C. Newman, Institutionalization, Interaction, and Self-Conception in Aging, unpublished Master's thesis, University of Minnesota, 1964.

245

ample of institutionalized and non-institutionalized older persons variations in social interaction were more closely associated with the degree of favorableness of self-conception than was the place of residence.

The Issue: Explanations of Modified Self-Conceptions

Of great general social-psychological significance, the self-conception has particular importance in the study of aging and mental health. Physical and social changes which accompany growing older provide the conditions for major modifications in the way the individual regards himself and hence for his mental health. The self-conception develops as the infant begins to relate to his physical self with the linguistic symbol "mine" and to his social self as the "me" which is an object to others. Gradually he comes to have a sense of "I" and to be able to take the role of himself and also the roles of those with whom he interacts.[1] He then has internalized an "I" or "self-as-subject" which integrates and ranks his "me's" or "selves-as-objects."[2] The "I" is his self-conception—a symbol which encompasses the meaning of his identities in the various social roles he plays and their value according to individual and socially shared criteria.

Having arisen in the process of relating to one's body and to one's associates, the self-conception, though never losing a unifying bond of consistency, is modified when changes occur in physical or social conditions. Such is the case in aging. That growing older means bodily change —in the acuity of the senses, agility of limbs, and slowed circulation, to mention three of many examples—is perhaps too obvious to mention. Less often recognized, however, is the effect of these transformations upon self-conception. An obvious example is the chagrin over graying hair of a woman whose self-esteem has depended on her identity as a blonde. Just as early development of the self-conception occurs in relation to the infant's identification of his own body, so do bodily changes in aging tend to modify self-attitudes. The manner in which a person regards himself is also based upon another aspect of his life which advancing years tend to alter—his social relationships. Interaction with family and friends is often greatly reduced by his physical and financial incapacities as well as by their death, and similarly the senior citizen outlives many more structured roles, such as those having to do with his occupation and voluntary associations.

Changes in the "me's"—the individual as role player from his viewpoint—precipitate changes in the "I" which integrates and ranks them. In the case of decreased interaction accompanying advancing years, this change usually creates a drearier climate because self-esteem, nurtured in the sunshine of the highly valued roles now beclouded by age, begins to wilt. Three conditions contribute to the lowering of self-evaluation. First,

---

[1]Charles H. Cooley, Robert C. Angell, and Lowell J. Carr, Introductory Sociology, Chicago: Charles Scribner's Sons, 1933, p. 117.

[2]George H. Mead, Mind, Self, and Society, Chicago: University of Chicago Press, 1934, p. 175.

there are few roles in Western society which substitute for those which are abandoned as years advance, so aging often entails not simply a role change but a role loss. The retired man, for example, is relegated to his home where his wife's role includes home management, leaving him without a daily occupation.[3] Second, adjustment to the few alternative roles is complicated by the ambiguity of the transition and role definitions —a lack especially great in a society where "rites of passage" are few, and expectations of what an older person should do, though numerous for what he shouldn't do, are fewer. Third, such roles receive little social validation. Americans highly value youthfulness and its attributes, idealizing the marriageable girl of twenty and the potentially successful thirty-year-old man rather than the physically, psychologically, and socially mature adult. Moreover, they emphasize present achieved status and deprecate the ascribed status of age and past achievements held by senior citizens. And a rapidly changing world renders those who spent their middle years in a different decade as obsolete as last year's car. For these three reasons, decreased interaction seems to mean, at best, a change in the sources of personal worth in the individual's own eyes or, more usually, a diminution in the sources themselves.

Empirical findings have demonstrated, at least in part, this relationship between age and self-conception and, more specifically, between the amount of interaction and the positiveness of self-conception. Comparing samples of younger and older subjects, Dodge, Lehner, Mason, and Sward each report that the older the respondent, the more negative the response to various measures of self-esteem. Bloom, however, did not substantiate his hypothesis that "self-acceptance decreases and self-rejection increases as individuals grow older" and concluded that it was "too simple."[4] Since growing older may not be accompanied by decreasing and less valuable social roles and relationships for all older people, findings of studies relating age and self-conception may well lack unanimity. Numerous studies have empirically confirmed the more specific relationship between interaction and self-conception or interaction and (more inclusive) adjustment. Pioneering on the frontier of gerontological research, Cavan, Burgess, Havighurst, and Goldhamer developed inventories entitled "Your Activities and Attitudes." From the data gathered they suggest that "the Attitude Inventory appears to be measuring something substantially similar to what

---

[3]Ruth S. Cavan, Self and role in adjustment during old age, in Arnold M. Rose, ed., Human Behavior and Social Processes, Boston: Houghton Mifflin Company, 1962, pp. 527-30.

[4]Joan Dodge, Changes in the self-percept with age, Perceptual and Motor Skills, 13: 88-00, 1961; Evelyn Mason, Some correlates of self-judgment of the aging, Journal of Gerontology, 9: 324-37, 1954; and Kenneth Bloom, Age and the self-concept, Geriatrics, 17: 314-19, 1962. For a review of the studies by Lehner and Sward see Raymond Kuhlen, Aging and life adjustment in James E. Birren, ed., Handbook of Aging and The Individual: Psychological and Biological Aspects, Chicago: University of Chicago Press, 1959, p. 872.

is reported in the Activity Inventory."[5] A similar relationship between level of social activity and degree of adjustment has been reported by other investigators employing the inventories.[6] The application of different measures of the variables by Kutner and his associates and by Kaplan, to mention two of many examples, has revealed an association between interaction on the one hand, and "morale" and mental health on the other.[7] Two additional investigations have attempted to measure more than contact with other persons. Havighurst and Albrecht explored the importance of social approval, or "culture-wide definitions of success or failure," and concluded that adjustment correlated positively with playing socially approved roles. Cumming and Henry suggest as additional qualifying conditions, that the value of the activity to the individual should also be considered and find that positively evaluated disengagement is also related to morale.[8] These studies would seem to suggest that, allowing for qualifications when conditions are more rigorously defined, the broad concepts of interaction and self-conception are empirically as well as theoretically related.

In addition to decrease in interaction, institutional living arrangements are sometimes blamed for lowering self-esteem for the approximately 5 per cent of those over sixty-five who no longer live independently. Those interested in the study or welfare of older persons give three general reasons for their opposition to this solution to the housing problem. The first concerns the effects of the extensive and abrupt change in daily routine on the new resident who is confronted with a way of living radically different from that upon which his self-conception depends. His entire existence is subject to one authority; he must perform habitual tasks in the company of strangers, and according to a schedule accommodating the majority; and his activities are evaluated on the basis of group or administrative goals.[9] The common good takes precedence over individual preference, and personal desires and idiosyncrasies, especially important to one who has done things his own way for many years, are ignored, as is well illustrated by the

---

[5]Ruth S. Cavan, Ernest W. Burgess, Robert J. Havighurst, and Herbert Goldhamer, Personal Adjustment in Old Age, Chicago: Science Research Associates, Inc., 1949, pp. 168-73.

[6]Ruth Albrecht, The social roles of older people, Journal of Gerontology, 6: 138-45, 1951; Ethel Shanas, The personal adjustment of recipients of old age assistance, Journal of Gerontology, 4: 249-53, 1950; and Marvin J. Taves and Gary D. Hansen, As Senior Citizens See Themselves—A Survey of Aging in the Upper Midwest, Minneapolis: Midwest Council for Social Research in Aging, 1961.

[7]Bernard Kutner, David Fanshel, Alice M. Togo, and Thomas S. Langner, Five Hundred Over Sixty, New York: Russell Sage Foundation, 1956; and Jerome Kaplan, The significance of group activity on psychogenic manifestations of old people, in Old Age in the Modern World, London: Third Congress of the International Association of Gerontology, 1955, pp. 596-97.

[8]Robert J. Havighurst, and Ruth Albrecht, Older People, New York: Longmans, Green and Co., 1953; and Elaine Cumming and William E. Henry, Growing Older: The Process of Disengagement, New York: Basic Books Inc., 1961.

[9]Irving Goffman, Asylums, New York: Doubleday and Company, 1961, p. 6.

few who are pleased by meals planned for the many. The change also involves adjustment to an apparent loss of autonomy since many decisions previously made individually are imposed by the administrative, social service, and medical staff. The second reason for opposition is the contention that institutionalization intensifies role loss and already decreasing social interaction. Those taking this view emphasize the disruption of the individual's customary social activity. Generally less mobile already, senior citizens who change their residence tend to lose contact with old friends and cease to participate in familial groups. Their new way of living also renders such roles as homemaker and neighbor obsolete. Substitute relationships are said to be less easily established in the institution because of difficulty in adjusting to the communal situation. In addition to abrupt change and disruption of social activity, the individual and cultural stigma attached to institutional living is cited as a third argument against this solution to the housing problem for older persons. The circumstances under which an older person moves to an institution often connote defeat in the struggle to maintain an independent residence or financial solvency, and rejection by family and friends. Moreover, "institution" is an anti-model for many in a society that values individualism and autonomy, and "old people's home" in addition shares the low status given old age.[10] To the extent that these criteria of evaluation are internalized by the resident of an institution and by those with whom he interacts, and to the extent that his self-esteem depended upon his previous way of living, its social relationships, and personal habits, he tends to judge himself less favorably.

What living in an institution does to an older person's self attitudes and adjustment has been formally investigated by comparing samples of institutionalized and non-institutionalized aged. (This is an approximation of the ideal, but impractical, procedure of comparing before and after measurement of the same subject.) In one of the most extensive studies, Mason compared the self-judgments of 60 residents of a municipal infirmary with 30 subjects over sixty still "able to maintain an independent existence." Her findings led her to conclude that "an aged institutionalized group views its self-worth in a more negative fashion than does an aged independent group . . ." However, the samples did not differ in regard to their attitudes toward personal happiness and ability to contribute.[11] Pollack and his associates asked 568 residents of nursing and retirement homes "What do you see?" when a 9-by-12 inch mirror was held in front of their faces. The findings indicated "a significantly lower incidence of self-abusive remarks among those living in institutions."[12] Similarly Tuckman, Lorge, and Zeman correlated intactness of drawings, assumed to represent one's self-concep-

---

10 Roy G. Francis, The anti-model as a theoretical concept, Sociological Quarterly. 4; 198-99, 1963.

11Mason, *op. cit.*

12M. Pollack, E. Kamp, R. L. Kahn, and I. Goldfarb, Perceptions of self in institutionalized aged subjects: I. Response Patterns to Mirror Reflections, Journal of Gerontology, 17: 405-08, 1962.

tion, with institutionalization. Their sample of 39 older institutionalized aged did not differ significantly from the 69 older community residents.[13] Rather than self-conception, adjustment was the problem variable in additional comparisons of institutionalized and non-institutionalized aged. Employing the "Your Activities and Attitudes" inventories, Lepkowski, Pan, and Scott each reports failure to find significant differences attributable to the fact of institutionalization.[14] And Laverty informally compared 15 women admitted to a retirement home with 15 given nonresident aid and promised entrance at such time as they became unable to care for themselves. She found the non-residents were happier, had more outside interests, did not think of themselves as old but referred to "those poor old ladies at the home," and planned for the future.[15]

While the differences found were mostly negative, the lack of significant contrasts in several of the studies causes one to question the conclusiveness of the evidence. It is necessary to specify the conditions for changes in self-conception among the institutionalized aged, and investigate more thoroughly the effect of institutionalization. Concerning the methodology of the studies, only Mason's investigation employed an operational definition of self-conception broad enough to capture its symbolic complexity, yet narrower than the more inclusive concept of adjustment. The nature of the samples lends further doubt to the differences found since they may be attributable to concomitants of the presumably greater capability of the non-institutionalized respondents to maintain an independent existence, rather than to the one most obvious, but certainly not the only, explanatory variable—institutionalization. The nature of institutionalization suggests its inadequacy as an explanatory variable. It is a short-hand way of describing many changes because the change in one's physical surroundings does not necessarily affect self-conception, but the social-psychological meaning of the change does. Hence, accounting for more than the fact of being institutionalized is necessary if a modification in self-conception is to be explained, rather than simply described. Inconsistent findings might, therefore, reflect the measurement of different effects of institutionalization, in addition to difficulties in measurement and sampling.

Change in interaction patterns is one such aspect which could offer a supplementary explanation. The relation between one's social activities and self-conception has been described above as arising in the development of self-attitudes and in the integral place of social selves or "me's" in the

[13]Jacob Tuckman, Irving Lorge, and Frederic Zeman, The self-image in aging, Journal of Genetic Psychology. 99: 317-21, 1961.

[14]J. Richard Lepkowski, The attitudes and adjustment of institutionalized and non-institutionalized catholic aged, Journal of Gerontology, 2: 185-91, 1956; Ju-Shu Pan, factors in the personal adjustment of old people in protestant homes for the aged, American Sociological Review, 12: 379-81; 1951; and Francis Scott, factors in the personal adjustment of institutionalized and non-institutionalized aged, American Sociological Review, 16: 538-46, 1955.

[15]Ruth Laverty, Nonresident aid—community versus institutional care for older people, Journal of Gerontology, 5: 370-74, 1950.

self-conception or "I" which ranks and evaluates them. Variation in type and amount of interaction does seem, therefore, to be a sufficient condition for modification of self-conception, while institutionalization does not. It may, then, be a condition which specifies the effect of institutionalization on self-conception; that is, persons who are institutionalized have a more negative self-conception if a decrease in social interaction accompanies the change in living arrangements. To relate the variables in this three-way linkage, a connection between institutionalization and interaction must be demonstrated. That one exists is suggested by three arguments advanced against institutional living arrangements for older persons, all of which are partially comprised of objections related to the effect of institutionalization upon social interaction. The first is against the interruption or modification of daily habits which, for the most part, are customary roles performed in direct or indirect interaction with others, such as the housewife's duties carried out for the approval of spouse, relatives, or friends. The second argument is an objection to the disruption of social activity brought about by the reduced accessibility to old friends and the difficulty in adjusting to new. And the third argument concerns the negative values against which the roles and relationships are measured.

Moreover, the linkage between institutionalization and interaction can be seen in the possibility of the former bringing about an increase rather than a decrease in the latter. This is a suggestion made by proponents of institutionalization as an advantageous solution for the older person, as well as for his friends and relatives, not only to the housing problem but also to that of mental health. Writers favoring communal living point first to the increased opportunity for social contact. The new living arrangements make it possible for a resident to find social companions and to play such roles as friend, cheerful visitor, and homemaker (even if the home be only one room). Institutions can "concentrate rather than diffuse the field of potential friends and support, thereby maximizing the conditions of social integration.[16] But the addition of new friends in the retirement home need not entail the subtraction of old ones. Residents able to maintain social contacts previous to admission will probably be capable of continuing these relationships, and the administration of many institutions encourages such contact by locating facilities in the geographical and interactional center of the functioning community. They seek ties with community organizations and services as well as with the families and friends of residents and encourage visits to the institution, expeditions into the community, and liaison relationships between the two.

---

[16] Irving Rosow, Retirement housing and social integration, The Gerontologist, 1: 89, 1961. See also Maurice Linden, The new philosophy of domiciliary care of non-psychotic aged, Geriatrics, 14: 777-83, 1959; Theodore Rosen, The significance of the family to the resident's adjustment in a home for the aged, Social Casework, 43: 86, 1962; Murray Wax, The changing role of the home for the aged, The Gerontologist, 2: 128-33, 1962; and Morris Zelditch, The home for the aged—a community, The Gerontologist, 2: 37-41, 1962.

Not only can the potential range of social relationships be expanded, but also communal living conditions for the aged can provide socialization into, and favorable evaluation of, age-linked roles, thereby clarifying their ambiguity and raising the low value usually associated with the roles which replace those of middle age. Residents of a retirement home may be likened to members of a subculture; they identify with the group and distinguish themselves from non-members. The increase of this phenomenon among older people in general has been noted by Rose who observes that "some people have begun to think of themselves as members of an aging *group;* in their eyes the elderly are being transformed from a category into a group." (Chapter 1, p. 13). According to Rose, manifestations of this phenomenon include joining and taking part in groups; constructive discussion of common problems and the possibility of group rather than individual solutions; and the existence of an out-group feeling against the younger generation. He suggests that the phenomenon is contributed to by social conditions which help create feelings of affinity with other members of the category and exclusion from interaction with others. For older people in general, the latter results from the negative evaluation of old age and hence of them, and the former is augmented by common interests, similar life experiences as members of the same generation, and shared role changes. Institutional living accentuates these conditions because the residents are physically as well as socially separated from others in the community, at least for much of their social lives. Proximity, but also positive interest in group concerns, helps create identification with other residents so that a group identity develops. The subculture phenomenon within the institution helps explain how expectations are clarified and evaluations made more positive. Values are shared within the subculture and therefore expectations for behavior in age-linked roles are clearer. Written rules or codes provide explicit guidance for some types of behavior, and informal norms are almost as easily learned by the new resident. In addition to norms, unique ideals are shared by members of a sub-culture. These provide standards of evaluation tailored to older persons, and members are therefore judged in terms of their own rather than younger values. For example, a slow gait and failing memory may well be symbols of belonging in a senior citizens home, even though society at large tends to devalue such attributes, and reduced activity does not contradict an ideal of energy and busyness since the latter probably is not shared in the subculture.

These arguments in favor of communal living suggest that institutionalization and interaction may be positively associated, as well as negatively linked as its opponents would suggest. The specific nature of the linkage depends on the social-psychological meaning of the living arrangements for each individual since it must become a personal condition for individual changes in interaction. Nonetheless, in the light of this relationship and that between interaction and self-conception, the three-way linkage between the variables in which interaction intervenes the effect of institutionalization upon self-conception appears to be a satisfactory explanation of changes in self-conception for those older persons living in communal housing arrangements. Thus in our search for more evidence about its effect on the older person's self-conception, we turn to an empirical investigation of the three.

The Investigation: Association of Institutionalization and Interaction with Self-Conception

In this study theoretical explanations of the effect of institutionalization upon interaction and in turn upon self-conception were translated into empirical associations between operational measures of the three variables. More specifically, the social interaction and self-conceptions of 101 residents of a church-sponsored retirement home in an upper midwestern city were compared with those of 56 applicants to the same home (now living in the community). Ideally the design would have included a longitudinal study in which changes in interaction and self-conception could have been observed and inferred from the subjects' behavior, verbal and non-verbal, before and after institutionalization. But the common difficulties of a panel study—lack of time and subject mortality (literal as well as figurative in this population)—necessitated a compromise. The technique of sampling persons related to the same institution in different ways, that is, as resident and applicant, improved the approximation of measuring the same individuals before and after institutionalization. Also the ability to maintain oneself in the community and one's attitude toward the retirement home were believed to be more equivalent than would be the case if a sample of institutionalized aged had been compared with a sample of all persons over sixty-five. The samples were also matched in regard to health (physically ambulatory and mentally lucid), sex, occupation, education, nationality, location and length of residence, and marital status. The average age of the applicants was four years younger than that of the residents, but the statistical analysis eliminated age as an explanatory condition, so the difference probably did not account for the associations revealed.

The data were collected by means of a closed-ended questionnaire which was distributed to the residents in person by the investigator and mailed to the applicants. Measures of interaction and self-conception developed by Cavan and her associates, Cumming and Henry, Mason, and Phillips were adapted for use.[17] Respondents were asked to report the frequency of contact with relatives, friends, and employees, and of participation in church, clubs, and retirement home activities. In addition they indicated agreement or disagreement with ten statements about themselves and five about older people in general and wrote three answers to the question, "Who are you?" Scores on the amount, variety, and change of interaction were arrived

---

[17]Cavan and Others, *op. cit.;* Cumming and Henry, *op. cit.;* Mason, *op. cit.;* and Bernard S. Phillips. A role theory approach to adjustment in old age. American Sociological Review, 22: 212-17, 1957, and Role change, subjective age, and adjustment; a correlational analysis, Journal of Gerontology, 16: 347-52, 1961.

at by assigning points for each daily contact, different role, and indicated maintenance of social contact. Chi-square tests of association in two by two tables constituted the statistical analysis of the data, which was performed as if random sampling techniques had been employed.

The findings were analyzed in respect to three hypotheses which flowed from a theoretical consideration of explanations of the self-conception. It was first hypothesized that there would be no significant differences in social interaction and self-conception between the institutionalized and non-institutionalized subjects. A test of this hypothesis was intended to help substantiate the proposition that the state of being institutionalized in itself could not fully explain the decreased social interaction and negative self-conception often attributed to older people in general and to residents of retirement homes in particular, and to suggest the need for specifying the conditions under which changes in living arrangements might bring about a modification of the self-conception. The data do, in fact, reveal no significant overall differences between the two samples. Scores on the amount of interaction and the self-conception scale combining attitudes toward self and old age (both measures being the most inclusive indices of the interaction and self-conception variables) showed that the differences obtained would have occurred by chance 20 per cent of the time for interaction and 70 per cent for self-conception.

Table 1. Association of Interaction and Self-Conception with Institutionalization in Percentages

Variable		Residents	Applicants	Significance	
Interaction:					
Amount:					
High		57.44	41.07	$x^2 =$	2.074
Low		42.56	58.93	$p =$	.20
Variety:					
High		71.29	30.36	$x^2 =$	22.942
Low		28.71	69.64	$p =$	.001
Change:					
Little		59.41	35.71	$x^2 =$	7.171
Great		40.59	64.29	$p =$	.01
Self-Conception:					
Mason	+	51.04	56.36	$x^2 =$	.213
	−	48.96	43.64	$p =$	.70
Phillips	+	40.21	36.36	$x^2 =$	.356
	−	59.79	63.64	$p =$	.70
Combined	+	50.00	56.36	$x^2 =$	.341
	−	50.00	43.64	$p =$	.70

Upon closer examination of the findings reported in Table 1, interesting differences in less inclusive measures of interaction are discovered. The residents have a greater variety of social role relationships while the applicants perceive less change in the amount of social interaction, both differences being statistically significant at the one per cent level. These findings are consistent with each other since a change in interaction might well result in the performance of more roles, though less intensive, than the role playing of the individuals who continued old role relationships without adopting new ones. It would be expected that the institutionalized older person would abandon entirely or in part certain pre-admission roles, such as neighbor or club member, but that he would assume new roles—eating partner or handicrafter, for example—upon moving into the retirement home. He would therefore experience more change in social interaction and interact in a greater variety of roles. When the frequency of the residents' contact with friends and participation in church and club activities in the community are compared with those of the applicants, the lesser interaction in non-institutional activities (or those which were presumably engaged in before coming to the retirement home) is clearly evident. The extensive participation by the residents in social relationships within the institution make up for the lack of interaction in the community, to the extent that there is a (not significant) trend for the residents to have a greater amount of social interaction than the applicants.

These findings suggest that the opponents of institutional housing correctly accuse the change in living arrangements of disrupting previous social relationships but that they neglect the substitute roles provided within the resident group. Moreover, they indicate that institutionalization does not seem to be unconditionally associated with self-conception.

If the interaction variable does specify the conditions under which institutionalization is related to positiveness of self-conception, it is necessary to demonstrate a relationship between it and self-conception. Findings related to this hypothesis—that interaction and self-conception are associated—are reported in Table 2. Over 30 per cent more of the respondents reporting a low amount of interaction than those with a high score also had a low (negative) score on the self-conception index, a difference which would occur by chance less than one time in a thousand. The statistical association holds when variety and change of interaction are related to self-conception at the 1 and 5 per cent levels, respectively.

Table 2. Association of Amount, Variety, and Change of Interaction with Self-Conception

Interaction	Self-Conception (Combined)			
	$+$	$-$		
Amount:				
High	47	26	$x^2 =$	14.533
Low	25	53	$p =$	.001
Variety:				
High	54	31	$x^2 =$	8.797
Low	25	41	$p =$	.01
Change:				
Low	43	33	$x^2 =$	4.164
High	29	46	$p =$	.05

In order to establish the three-way linkage between institutionalization, interaction, and self-conception, a third hypothesis was tested. It stated that only those residents whose interaction scores were low would have negative self-conceptions. When the association between interaction and self-conception was again investigated, this time with institutionalization held constant, the results were the same, as can be seen in Table 3. Seventy-one percent of the residents with low interaction scores also had low scores on the self-conception index. The chi-square test found this difference significant at the one-tenth of one per cent level.

Table 3. Trivariate Analysis of Association of Interaction and Self-Conception with Institutionalization as the Test Factor

Residents			*Applicants*		
Interaction (Amount)	*Self-Conception (Combined)*		*Interaction (Amount)*	*Self-Conception (Combined)*	
	+	−		+	−
High	36	12	High	17	14
Low	19	29	Low	6	18
$x^2 = 10.898$	$p = .001$		$x^2 = 3.798$	$p = .10$	

On the basis of the statistical analysis, the extent of interaction and the positiveness of self-conception can be said to be more closely associated with each other than is institutionalization with either explanatory variable. Moreover, the statistical association is not vitiated when the institutionalization variable is held constant. Of course, association is not explanation. One cannot infer from the statistical relationship between interaction and self-conception that changes in the former lead to modification of the latter because precedence in time was not investigated. And it is possible that unknown variables account for the association, although most probable explanatory conditions were held constant by sampling or statistical procedures. The relevance of the empirical demonstration to the theoretical discussion also depends upon the possibility of generalizing the findings. The scope of the hypothetical universe which must be constructed from the non-random sample limits inferences to residents of and applicants to institutional and semi-protected housing units such as the ones investigated. The nature of the non-institutionalized sample has special significance because the persons included had already applied for admission to an institution and therefore probably do not represent older community residents in general. If application rather than admission marks the turning point in one's identity, the similarity between the samples is an artifact of the sampling procedure. Despite this possibility (about which further research is needed), the design was intentional—only in comparing groups matched except for the experimental variable, institutionalization, can its effects be discovered.

Conclusions

The statistical findings, then, suggest, but do not necessarily prove, the proposal that interaction better explains self-conception than does institutionalization and that it specifies one condition under which institutionalization may have an effect upon self-conception.

The following conclusions are offered, though more as beginnings for study and action than as endings of anything but this paper. First, without evidence contradictory to that presented here, or more conclusive than the findings of other investigations discussed above, institutional housing as such cannot be found guilty of decreasing the older person's self-esteem and hence his mental health. The particular conditions must be specified. Moving into an institution may involve concomitant changes which may lead to a more negative self-conception, but these need not always be present. Second, a positive self-conception can be said to be related to social interaction. If this and other investigations have emphasized the quantitative aspect of interaction, it is because quality of interaction demands more attention than the necessities of operational procedures have thus far allowed, with one or two exceptions. The general relationship of the two, however, suggests the importance of interaction for mental health. Third, and finally, the effect of institutionalization upon interaction becomes a crucial consideration for the well-being of those who, by choice or necessity, move to a retirement home. The relationship between self-conception and interaction indicates that the latter is an important area in which the institution can benefit or harm the resident's mental health. It suggests that the social affiliations of the residents, especially those which promote a meaningful group identity, deserve the close attention of institutional administrators. And for gerontologists concerned with mental health and housing problems in general, these conclusions encourage the specification of explanatory conditions of institutionalization and the three-way linkage of it with interaction and self-conception.

CHAPTER 17

Some Sociological Characteristics
of Long-Term Care*

ALBERT F. WESSEN

Long term care is hardly new. For centuries, physicians have treated patients over long periods of time. Throughout their history, hospitals have kept patients for months and even years; as a matter of fact, until the beginning of the twentieth century, the average length of stay in general hospitals would, by present-day definitions, be considered long-term care, being more than thirty days. Yet it is largely within the past few years that Americans have become aware of the emergence of long-term care as a modality different in character and scope from the kinds of medical care for acute illnesses to which medicine has been primarily oriented.

The social forces which have brought about this new awareness are obvious. The proportions of patients suffering from chronic illness have dramatically increased over the past sixty years; whereas in 1900, 25 per cent of deaths were attributable to heart disease, cancer and cerebrovascular accidents, by 1965, 70 per cent were due to these chronic diseases (Bureau of the Census, 1960). As the population continues to live longer, this tendency will continue to increase disproportionately. Over the past half century, our nation has changed from a relatively stable, rural society to an urban and mobile one. The role of kinship has diminished, and a lessened sense of the values of three-generation living is apparent. Every community is peopled by an increased proportion of retired persons and of widows or widowers who have few community responsibilities or attachments. Such social changes have rendered inadequate the traditional reli-

*This paper was first presented at a conference on "Social Aspects of Health Care for Long-Term Patients" sponsored by the Home Care Training Center of the Jewish Hospital of St. Louis, the U. S. Public Health Service and the American Hospital Association, St. Louis, Mo., April 17-19, 1963, and included in the Symposium on Long-Term Care published as a supplement to The Gerontologist, 4: 7-14, 1964. Reprinted by permission of the editor.

ance on individual and family responsibility for care of the old and infirm. Improved methods of care for the chronically ill have prolonged their lives even when their condition can be little improved. The advent of Social Security and of private retirement plans is both a witness to the economic implications of these changes and is substantially increasing the purchasing power of the aged and disabled. And the discrepancy between the needs of the chronically ill and available resources for meeting them—especially when measured against the situation of acute medical care—imparts a sense of problem and of urgency to the situation.

By "long term care" is meant, of course, a *duration* of service which is greater than "normal"; the term is conventionally, if arbitrarily, defined as involving hospitalization or institutionalization of more than thirty days. Yet the temporal dimension alone actually denotes but a small part of what is implied in the phrase. It implies, first of all, the care of patients whose disease is not self-limiting in course but chronic in nature; "long-term care" and "chronic disease" are terms which are often used almost interchangeably. Although it is for some purposes important to maintain an analytical distinction between the two terms, this correlation with *chronicity* and all that it represents to the medical world is decisive for the character of long-term care. In a word, chronic illness often implies a situation in which medical management is relatively static, the opportunities for improvement or recovery are relatively limited, and in which the involvement of the physician is hence often not intense.

Second, patients subject to long-term care can often be as well described as suffering from a "handicap" or "limitation" as from a "sickness." This implies the idea of an "irreversible" situation, a permanent deficit with which the patients are afflicted. For many of these patients, the implicit assumption that sickness is a temporary state, to be followed by recovery, must be doubly qualified: their symptoms no longer constitute an out of the ordinary affliction which has been visited upon them, but a regular and lasting, even "normal" aspect of living; hence, even though episodes of special malaise may periodically occur, their cessation does not offer hope of full recovery. The nineteenth century had a very descriptive term for such patients: it called them "invalids," and many of the social connotations of this term surround long-term care today.

Third, for many long-term patients, the prognosis is unhappy. Not only may their illness be long and a residual handicap be their lot, but progressive deterioration of their condition faces many. This doom radically affects long-term patients and all who care for them. For when all is said and done, there is the lingering suspicion that long-term care is a slow, painful process that can have but one ending. And this suspicion often casts its spell over those who might hope for rehabilitation or recovery; for them, the prophecy may become self-fulfilling.

Long-term care, therefore, may seem to many like a "regimen of limited objectives." Cure is often out of the question, and the full restoration of long-term patients' faculties is often beyond the scope of medical science today. These traditional medical goals must therefore be replaced by such more limited objectives as "maximization of the patient's remaining functional potential," or "minimization of further deterioration." The patient's goal often has to be to learn to live within his limitations.

These facts have great significance for both professional and lay attitudes toward long-term care. The professional may find that it does not satisfy his motivation to be a healer, able to restore his patients to full health. He may find that his efforts do not have the same degree of "pay-off" that can be expected in "acute" medicine. And the lay public must contend, in facing long-term illness, with the reality that for some the sick role is not a way toward recovery of normal functioning, that adults do become and remain dependent and incapacitated for long periods of time, and that there are no easy answers for problems of chronic illness. As the Cummings (1957) pointed out in another context, a common mechanism for dealing with such situations is to isolate oneself from them and, if possible, to deny their existence.

But if long-term care can be characterized as a "regimen of limited objectives," it can also be seen as a challenging and strenuous, even heroic type of care. Not only is the attainment of objectives such as "maximization of remaining functional potential" often difficult, but they must be won too often in the face of apathy and non-support on the part of the community. Moreover, because the long-term patient typically is forced to live within limitations which affect *all* his activities, long-term care becomes, perforce, care of the *whole* patient. The magnitude and duration of the patient's physical handicap force attention to its psychological and social consequences in a way that the problems of acute illness often do not.

These paragraphs suggest that long-term care involves much more than simple duration and its psychological and economic consequences might imply. They suggest to me that it must be seen and dealt with as a distinctive problem of medical care, with unique characteristics and needs. What some of these are will be developed in the remainder of this discussion. They will be presented in the form of eight propositions which, it is hoped, will be descriptive of the broad picture of long-term care today.

1. *The need for long-term care will, in the foreseeable future, continue to increase both quantitatively and qualitatively.* This proposition is the corollary of two basic demographic facts already alluded to: the changing nature of morbidity, involving relative increase in the prevalence and significance of chronic diseases, and the fact that ours is an aging population.

The life expectancy of our population has, of course, been rapidly increasing, from about 45 years in 1900 to better than 70 years at the present time; experts forsee its continued increase, perhaps toward a theoretical maximum of some 125 years. The demographic consequences of this increased life expectancy are obvious, yet the statistics still seem surprising. Thus, while less than 5 per cent of the United States population in 1900 was over sixty-five, by 1959 it was 8.1 per cent; by 1960, it had increased to 9.2 per cent, and by 1970 it will be 9.4 per cent. In numbers, while there were sixteen and a half million people over sixty-five in 1960, the Census Bureau projects that there will be some 20 million by 1970, about 26 million by 1980, and around 35 million by the year 2000. Moreover, the greatest proportionate increase is to be found in the oldest segments of the population; the population 75 and over is increasing at a faster rate than the population aged 65-74 (Bureau of the Census, 1961).

Since old age is so highly correlated with the prevalence of chronic disease, our needs for long-term care are going to continue to increase. The extent of this need may be sensed by citing a few statistics from the National Health Survey (1962). It found that only 40 per cent of the population under 65 reported having a chronic condition; however, for the group aged 65-74, the percentage increases to 74 per cent, and for the population 75 and over, the proportion increases to 84 per cent. If one inquires about the existence of a major limitation on activity, the National Health Survey reports less than 2 per cent of the middle-aged population (45-54) were so afflicted. But for the group aged 65-74, almost 10 per cent reported a major limitation, and almost one-fourth (23.7 per cent) of those 75 and over have a major limitation on their activity.

Taken together, these statistics not only show the demographic source of our current problem of long-term care, but indicate that "we ain't seen nuthin' yet." Not only will our nation's need for long-term care increase, but one may predict an increased demand for action that will provide for our population the maximal benefits which medical science can provide. A political corollary of an aging population will be the emergence of "medi-care"—particularly, of provision for long-term care—as a continuing public issue.

The fact that tremendous differences exist in the quality of long-term care presently available adds to the intensity of the problem. Where good facilities are outnumbered by the inadequate facilities serving the many, the pressures for improvement of quality can be expected to mount. And it need not be pointed out that the need for upgrading facilities greatly complicates an already difficult economic problem.

2. *Long-term care has not yet emerged as a type of care which has been fully legitimated by professional values.* Stated baldly, long-term care lacks prestige and has not yet attracted its requisite share of the attention of the health professions. That this proposition is true can easily be documented, at least in an impressionistic manner.

"These patients are usually crocks." This all too common statement typifies the attitude of many professionals, who see long-term patients, whether old or young, as uninteresting—as patients whom, if they had their choice, they would prefer not to serve. Perhaps rightly, long-term care patients have been classified as inappropriate for care on the medical (or surgical) wards of the general hospital.[1] It is suggested that such patients occupy

[1]Many patients, of course, spend months on acute medical and surgical wards. However, they are the exception rather than the rule on these wards, which are not equipped to minister to the special needs which arise during long-term institutionalization. And professionals feel that a large proportion of these patients do not require the level of facilities available on a medical-surgical ward if alternative, less intensive facilities are available.

beds which ought really to be used for patients requiring more intensive therapy, and that they therefore should be transferred to other facilities. But it should be recognized that the acute wards of the general hospital are the center of professional interest and attention in modern medicine. Therefore, there is the danger that patients who are in "lesser" facilities are ipso facto beyond the center of professional interest. Certainly it is true that long-term patients have been "dumped" from the wards of general hospitals into facilities where professional care was, at best, inadequate. It is also unfortunately true that the mechanisms of professional communication and control which have developed and safeguarded the high medical standards of the general hospital are often not found in long-term care institutions such as nursing homes. These institutions tend to be beyond the professional pale.

The "dumping" phenomenon is not only to be found in general hospitals. Witness the fate of many non-active senile psychotic patients in state mental hospitals, whose staffs often have felt that they had accomplished much by discharging them to a nursing home or kindred facility. Yet in many of these institutions there are available even fewer trained personnel and even less attention is paid to the therapeutic potential of the patient than in the over-crowded state hospitals.

Certainly it is true that in most institutions—general hospitals, nursing homes, mental hospitals—chronic, long-term patients, as compared to acutely ill patients, are cared for by disproportionately larger numbers of personnel who are relatively untrained, such as aides, licensed practical nurses, and others. These patients are less frequently seen by fully trained professionals. While this may be abundantly justified in terms of the *technical* medical needs of the patient, it may not be so clearly justified in terms of patients' psychological and social needs. And it represents further evidence of the tendency for separation of professionals from problems of long-term care.

All this is not to deny the very great dedication of many physicians, nurses, social workers, and other health professionals to the problems of the chronically ill. Nor is it to argue that the problems of long-term care are the result of professional neglect; perhaps the best deployment of available professional resources has already been achieved. I merely point out that long-term care is not at the center of the interests of many clinicians, and tends to be on the periphery of the organization of medical care.

It must be noted, too, that this situation is changing. Special sections of professional societies, newer professional organizations, such as the Gerontological Society, new professional journals and professional curricula have been developing. The report of the Commission on Chronic Illness (1956) signalized a broad professional program for the development of better long-term care, and more recent action groups, such as the 1961 White House Conference on Aging, have done much to make this interest general.

Even the general hospital has begun in the past decade or so to take an interest in setting up organized programs of long-term care. A project of the Medical Care Research Center has tried to document the extent and the nature of this interest. We developed from a number of sources a listing of some 900 general hospitals which were alleged to have programs for long-term care, ranging all the way from rehabilitation wards and chronic disease wards to the operation of nursing homes, or domiciliary homes, and to affiliations of nursing homes. Of the 900 hospitals which were reported as having these units, we found that only 456 actually had operating units as of October, 1962. This is not a very large proportion of the general hospitals of the United States, actually less than 10 per cent; but it is a growing number and it is an earnest of the fact that long-term care is beginning to be legitimized as a major professional value.

One can perhaps summarize the present situation, not only for the professions, but for our culture as well, in a paragraph such as this:

It is still true for the most part that health and hospital planning, professional education, community resources and the social institutions that comprise community life, are still geared essentially to a 1900 concept of the life cycle, to the family and its organization, and to value systems, all of which fail to recognize the facts about our changing population. One of these is the fact that the proportion of aged persons—preeminently the group which requires long-term care—is increasing. The consequences of this, I think, are quite clear. Long-term care has tended not to develop an identity of its own. Either it has become assimilated in many institutions to the patterns set up for acute medical care, or long term care has been placed beyond the custodial pale, becoming simply a holding operation where minimal kinds of care have been given, but where nothing much else has been done. Only now are we beginning to overcome this cultural lag.

3. *Long-term care, thus far, has largely been unplanned on a community basis, with resultant piecemeal filling of needs, often on an opportunistic basis.* The demographic and medical revolutions discussed above have already been underway for more than a generation. During this time, communities all over the country have been faced with the need to provide new facilities for older persons and others who are no longer able to lead independent lives in the community.

Perhaps the most important fact underlying the provision of care for long-term patients was the passage of the Social Security Act of 1935. Its significance lies in both the development of general assistance and of categorical aid for those who are disabled, blind, and otherwise dependent, and in the development of old age and survivors' insurance benefits. These benefits provide economic resources for the disabled and the aged unparalleled in American history. They have relieved local communities from bearing the full burden of care for the indigent; this has made possible the abolition or transformation of the traditional poor farm. But the poor farm itself in many localities has become a chronic disease hospital as those persons who have to depend upon the welfare provided by the community become more and more a group in need of long-term care.

A more important result of the Social Security Act is that it has provided many old people with the ability to purchase their own long-term care. This ability led to the emergence of the proprietary nursing home. Very few proprietary nursing homes were in existence prior to the passage of the Social Security Act. Since that time, they have comprised one of the principal growth sectors of the medical care field, and there are now almost 600,000 nursing home beds in the nation (U. S. Public Health Service, 1963). But these nursing homes have developed, whether through the re-conditioning of old houses or the building of new facilities, almost entirely outside the influence of any overall planning.

This has meant that facilities have been provided for those who can pay, sometimes in over-abundance, while few facilities have developed for those who cannot meet the charges of the nursing homes. Moreover, the mush-rooming development of proprietary homes has taken place in a context in which there have been relatively few controls on the quality of care. All too often it has taken disasters, such as the Warrenton, Missouri, Nursing Home fire of 1957, to make licensing agencies develop even minimal regu-lations concerning the public safety of long-term patients.

It should not be thought that unplanned facilities are entirely, or even largely, proprietary institutions. Homes for the aged, whether operated by sectarian or voluntary organizations, have increasingly been ungrading their facilities to provide long-term care of patients, and as indicated above, an increasing number of general hospitals are entering the long-term care field either through providing chronic disease or rehabilitation units or through operating nursing home or domiciliary facilities. These facilities also are usually developed either to provide for a specific constituency, without regard to overall community needs, or as a non-profit organization's attempt to meet community needs on its own.

An example of the results of this lack of planning can be seen in the situation to be found currently in St. Louis (Health and Welfare Council, 1963; Bullock, 1964). In this community there are now about as many nursing home beds as there are general hospital beds, and they have been developed with almost no planning except as individuals or agencies have seen a need and have moved to meet it. The result of this lack of planning is manifest in the lack of adequate facilities for many groups in the popu-lation. Studies of long-term care beds in St. Louis show that although approximately 30 per cent of the population of the city is Negro, there are only 93 nursing home beds for this race in the city. The Negro who needs long-term care is thus forced to receive that care either in his own home setting, in a setting such as a general hospital, or at the St. Louis Chronic Hospital, upon which the burden of caring for indigent St. Louisans who need long-term care legally rests. On the other hand, for the 70 per cent of the population who are white, there are more than 6,000 available long-term beds.

Long-term care has been a late-comer to national planning as well. This is true both with respect to eligibility or chronic disease facilities for aid under the Hill-Burton Plan, and to the development of overall plans at national, state and local levels. Important strides, however, are being made, perhaps most obviously in the important work on national and state levels surrounding the White House Conference on Aging. Many communities are developing systematic planning for long-term care; one might cite Rochester and Denver as examples of this trend.

The lack of planning, coupled with the marginal position of long-term care in professional hierarchies of values, leads inevitably to one conclusion, namely, that much long-term care falls short of the standards which might reasonably be expected in view of the potentials of contemporary knowledge and resources. Everyone who has studied at all the problems of long-term care knows all too well that this is true.

4. *Because large numbers of long-term care patients are dependent, there has been a tendency to visualize this kind of care solely in terms of some form of institutionalization.* Most people think of long-term care as institutional care. Yet for the population sixty-five or over, which constitutes the larger proportion of persons receiving long-term care, the fact is that only 4 per cent are institutionalized, even though some two-thirds report a major disability. This means that most of the continuing care of patients having a chronic illness or disability is undertaken outside the walls of hospitals or other institutions. Much of it, of course, is ambulatory care. Much more involves the care of patients who are mostly confined to the home.

In this context, the development of home care programs must be cited (Littauer, Flance, and Wessen, 1961). Coordinated home care is a means of bringing the resources of team medicine, usually available only within the walls of a hospital, to the home. Perhaps because of the difficulty professionals have in visualizing how they can work effectively outside of the hospital, its development has been slow and disappointing to those who are its advocates. After almost twenty years, fewer than fifty coordinated home care programs have been identified, and these serve but a minute fraction of the population who could profit from home care. The picture is somewhat brighter when less highly developed home care resources are considered. But there is a nation-wide shortage of public health and visiting nurses, and in many areas their services are restricted to public health needs. The result is that adequate professional services to home-bound patients in need of long-term care are not available.

Until we learn to think of long-term care as involving ambulatory and home care services as well as the development of rehabilitation, nursing home, and other chronic disease facilities, our planning efforts are likely to be incomplete. This need is the more important because of the social risks of institutionalization. We are increasingly aware of the difficulties faced by patients who are dislocated from familiar environments and social contexts. Increasingly it is apparent that the patients are happier and possibly do better when they can be cared for at home rather than in an institution. This being the case, we may expect further development of alternatives to institutional care for the long-term ill.

5. *Long-term care by definition involves major role dislocations for patients and their families alike. Hence, special attention must be paid to social service supports for long-term patients, indigents and non-indigents alike.* That long-term care involves major role dislocations for patients and families should be obvious. Adults who have been independent persons, able to function in their roles as members of a family, as wage earners, home makers, or participants in community activities, become for prolonged periods of time dependent, able to play only the sick role, and accordingly exempt from many of their other social responsibilities. For their relatives the need to take up the slack left by the sick person often becomes overwhelming. And they also face the need to care for their sick member.

It seems to me that one may deduce a policy directive from all of this, namely, that special attention ought, therefore, be paid to the social needs of long-term care patients and their families, regardless of their financial status. Dr. Franz Goldmann (1961) found that only 21 per cent of patients in five hospitals who were discharged with diagnoses involving long-term care had been referred to the department of social work for attention. Moreover, while 57 per cent of the long-term patients who were ward patients and indigent had been referred to social workers, only 4 per cent of those who occupied private and semi-private rooms received social work help. One wonders if those who were able to afford private physicians could not have benefited greatly by social work service. On the other hand, one must also question whether, in its present state of development, the profession of social work is ready to take on this added task.

Goldmann also reported that most of the referrals made for long-term patients were for the purpose of discharge planning. They were, therefore, late referrals, made largely to solve an immediate problem. One must question whether the skills of social workers could not have been better used had they been made available to patients and their families during the long weeks of hospitalization.

An increasing proportion of patients receiving long-term care are in their eighties and have children who are already at or near retirement age. Thus, many "children" who already are at a point where they themselves must face some of the social consequences of aging in their own lives must bear the added burden of care for still more dependent parents. As this situation becomes more common, the needs for social support of the families of long-term care patients will become all the more demanding.

6. *Since long-term care typically involves the prolonged provision of multiple services, it ought to be team medicine par excellence.* In point of fact, however, it is often fragmented, both functionally and ecologically. It is not necessary to describe how long-term care involves the provision of multiple services. One need only name some of the important medical and paramedical specialties typically involved: physician, physiatrist, psychiatrist, nurse, social worker, physical therapist, occupational therapist. One might also point out the need for the availability of the laboratory and kindred technical services of the hospital, and of such specialists as nutritionists, or recreational therapists.

It is clear that the secret of the general hospital is in its ability to coordinate the multiple services of physicians, nurses and others so that all work closely as a team (Burling, Lentz, and Wilson, 1956). But such coordination is difficult in practice, especially outside the familiar institutional domains. Teamwork, so necessary and recognized a requisite of medical technology in settings such as the operating room, is much less obviously needed in dealing with the more intangible needs of patients. The contributions of paramedical professions toward helping patients with psychological and sociological problems are seen perhaps less clearly by the medical profession than are the contributions of paramedical personnel in biological medicine. When this care must be provided in a number of geographic settings, the problems of coordination take on additional difficulty. And when all or part of the patient's care must be provided at home by several professionals and at different times, the problems of coordination become particularly difficult. Moreover, specific services are often provided in the community by separate agencies, each of which guards its functions jealously. In this situation, when coordination takes place, it does so only when the need for it has become overwhelming. Thus, long-term care becomes often fragmented, both functionally and ecologically.

Again, change is in the wind. Team concepts are gaining ground. Coordinated home care seems to have made at least a limited place for itself. A web of affiliations is developing between nursing homes and hospitals, and between the various agencies providing special services to patients in the community—the social work agencies, the rehabilitation agencies, and others. The development of cooperating and planning is growing apace.

7. *Long-term care requires special efforts to maintain the motivation of patients if minimization of handicap and continued therapeutic progress are to occur.* The motivational problems facing the chronically ill patient in need of rehabilitation are legion. Discouragement is the order of the day, both because of the long-range outlook and because of daily difficulties in the process of regaining lost functions or preventing their further deterioration. When one is for long periods dissociated from the sources of motivation found within the normal social roles, and especially when one's ability to return to them is problematical, it is understandable that motivation may flag and apathy ensue. When one is stripped of the ability to do those things which normal adult humans expect to do—the simple activities of daily living, such as eating and attendance to matters of personal hygiene—the psychological effects can be devastating. One can understand the tendency to cling to the secondary gains that dependency brings about. Thus, maintaining the patient's morale and motivation becomes a central problem of the whole field of long-term care.

This being the case, one may question the utility of traditional concepts of the role of the patient and of traditional relationships between patients and therapeutic personnel. When a patient's motivation is weak or lacking, are traditional expectations of passive patients who will faithfully and unquestioningly follow the orders of doctor or nurse realistic? In dealing with long-term patients, therapeutic personnel must become not only the providers of care, but the partners of patients in their efforts to become independent. They become, perforce, colleagues who not only advise but actively help the patient. For professionals and their paramedical assistants to be able fully to undertake this responsibility, the traditional social distance between patients and professionals must in part be bridged or transcended. One of the great achievements of workers in the field of rehabilitation is that they have found ways of doing this. One of the outstanding developments in the field of caring for the mentally ill has been the development of the concept of the therapeutic community (Jones, 1953; Vitale, 1964). In such settings, not only are patients encouraged to play active roles in achieving their recovery, but the roles of the staff are seen to be as co-participants in achieving the community's goals of improving patients' mental health. Care is conceptualized not as specific medical or nursing interventions but as involving all of the patient's activities and environment. As mental health workers say, therapy is not a matter of the patient's therapeutic interview with his pysician alone, but something which involves all twenty-four hours in his day. The whole field of long-term care —and perhaps much of the field of acute medical care as well—has much to learn from developments in the field of rehabilitation and psychiatry. It is in these areas that most attention has been paid to the need for helping the patient through the motivational crises of long-term care.

8. *Since long-term care is disproportionately provided to an aged population, it is apt to be caught in our society's negative cultural attitudes toward this group.* Sociologists have for years contrasted the negative attitudes toward aging in our society with the often reverential attitudes toward this group in other societies (Simmons, 1945). Ours is a culture oriented toward youth. And we have made of the aged, it is said, a group which no one wishes to join. We have made for the aged a role which all too often can be best characterized as a "roleless role." We have saddled this growing group in our population with acute problems in the economic and psychological and, above all, the social sphere.

The ramifications of all of this for long-term care are obvious. All those who are involved in long-term care perforce must deal with their feelings toward the aged. But they also are limited by the willingness of society as a whole to discriminate against this group.

This points not only to the need for reorientation of professional values with respect to the validity and importance of long-term care, but to the need for change in our society at large. There can be little justification in a democratic society for invidious distinctions on the basis of age any more than on the basis of sex or race or creed. The problems of long-term care will not, in the long run, be solved until the aged and the disabled are seen not as categories to be avoided or patronized, but as persons who have the same rights as others and who deserve, therefore, the same attention and concern.

Summary

In this discussion, eight propositions have been offered which broadly characterize the present position of long-term care. They are:

1. The need for long-term care will, in the foreseeable future, continue to increase both quantitatively and qualitatively.

2. Long-term care has not yet emerged as a type of care which has been fully legitimated by professional values.

3. Long-term care, thus far, has largely been unplanned on a community basis, with resultant piecemeal filling of needs, often on an opportunistic basis.

4. Because large numbers of long-term care patients are dependent, there has been a tendency to visualize this kind of care solely in terms of some form of institutionalization.

5. Long-term care by definition involves major role dislocations for patients and their families alike. Hence, special attention must be paid to social service supports for long-term patients, indigents and non-indigents alike.

6. Since long-term care typically involves the prolonged provision of multiple services, it ought to be team medicine *par excellence*.

7. Long-term care requires special efforts to maintain the motivation of patients if minimization of handicap and continued therapeutic progress are to occur.

8. Since long-term care is disproportionately provided to an aged population, it is apt to be caught in our society's negative cultural attitudes toward this group.

REFERENCES

BULLOCK, JEAN: Equilibrium in Disengagement: A Study of Older People and the Institutions Society Provides for Them. Unpublished doctoral dissertation, University of Pittsburgh, 1964.

Bureau of the Census. Historical Statistics of the United States, Washington, 1960, p. 26.

Bureau of the Census: Current Population Reports, Series P-25, No. 246 and 251. Washington, 1961.

BURLING, TEMPLE, EDITH M. LENTZ, and R. N. WILSON: The Give and Take in Hospitals, New York; G. P. Putnam's Sons, 1956.

Commission on Chronic Illness: Chronic Illness in the United States, Cambridge; Harvard Univ. Press, 1956.

CUMMING, J. and ELAINE CUMMING: Closed Ranks, Cambridge; Harvard University Press, 1957.

GOLDMANN, FRANZ: What are social workers in general hospitals doing for long-term patients? Social Work, 5: 68-77, 1960.

Health and Welfare Council of Metropolitan St. Louis: Preface to a Counseling Service. St. Louis, 1963 (mimeographed).

JONES, M.: The Therapeutic Community, New York; Basic Books, 1953.

LITTAUER, D., I. J. FLANCE, and A. F. WESSEN: Home Care, American Hospital Association, Monograph Series No. 9, Chicago, 1961.

National Health Survey: Duration of Limitations of Activity Due to Chronic Conditions, United States, July, 1959–June, 1960, United States Public Health Service Publication No. 584-B31, Washington, 1962.

SIMMONS, L. W.: The Role of the Aged in Primitive Society. New Haven; Yale University Press, 1945.

VITALE, J.: The therapeutic community: a review article, in A. F. Wessen, ed., The Psychiatric Hospital as a Social System, Springfield, Ill.: Charles C Thomas, 1964.

United States Public Health Service: Nursing Homes and Related Facilities. Fact Book, Publication No. 930-F-4, Washington, 1963.

VI

Population Characteristics
and Community Setting

CHAPTER 18

The Demography of Aging in the Midwest

Donald O. Cowgill

The "population explosion" which in America began more than a century ago brought with it changes in the distribution and structure of the population some of which have not been fully analyzed or appreciated. We have lately become aware of the "revolution of aging" which is one concomitant of the demographic cycle which in its recent manifestations has been called the "population explosion." But while it is now well known that the older portion of the national population is increasing more rapidly than the total and thus bringing about an aging trend, it is not yet fully appreciated that there are very marked territorial or ecological variations in this pattern. The present study is devoted to a more intensive analysis of this variation than has been carried out heretofore.

The study is focused upon the Midwest because it is known that this is the region of the country where the aging trend has progressed farthest. It is rivaled in this respect only by New England.

As used in this study, the Midwest is defined to include nine states—the Corn Belt and the Wheat Belt—Iowa, Illinois, Missouri, Kansas, Minnesota, North Dakota, South Dakota, Nebraska and Wisconsin.

Table 1 shows the percentage of the population sixty-five years of age and over for each of the nine states and the rank of each state among the fifty states of the nation. Iowa, Missouri, and Nebraska rank first, second and third, respectively, among all of the states in the United States in the percentage of their populations which is sixty-five and over. Along with Kansas which ranks eighth, these states appear to form a pocket in the heart of the nation where there is the maximum concentration of old folks.

This paper undertakes to analyze in detail the distribution and com-

**Table 1. Percentage of the Population 65 and over
and Rank among All States for Nine
States of the Midwest, 1960**

	Percentage 65 and over	Rank among States
Iowa	11.9	1
Missouri	11.7	2
Nebraska	11.6	3
Kansas	11.0	8
South Dakota	10.5	12
Minnesota	10.4	13
Wisconsin	10.2	16
Illinois	9.7	19
North Dakota	9.3	25

position of the aging population within these nine states. Attention will be given to the distribution of the aged within the region both in terms of gross numbers and of percentages. Because in some respects the nonwhites in our population have special problems of adjustment, they will be treated separately. Many of the aged are widowed and live apart from family units and it appears that to some degree older men migrate in different directions than older women, with the result that at any given time their patterns of residence may be appreciably different. For this reason, the two sexes are analyzed separately and attention is given to the sex ratio in different parts of the region. There is also an effort to determine whether the aged population is relatively young or concentrated in the later years of old age, i.e., seventy-five and over. The study includes an analysis of the trends toward increase or decrease in the different areas of the region. Finally, attention is given to the proportion of the elderly males who are still in the labor force.

Each of these subjects is treated in two different ways. First, we use counties as the territorial units of analysis and study the patterns of variation within the region in terms of counties. Second, since conditions in cities are strikingly different from those in the rural areas, a separate analysis is carried out for cities only. In the latter analysis, only cities over 10,000 are considered along with all of the Standard Metropolitan Statistical Areas in the region.

The Aged Population by County

In the first section of this chapter, then, we utilize counties as the units of analysis. From the data of the United States Census of 1960, we have compiled nine different measurements relative to the aged population for each county. These are: (1) the total number of persons sixty-five and over, (2) the number of nonwhites sixty-five and over, (3) the percentage of persons sixty-five and over, (4) the percentage of males sixty-five and over, (5) the percentage of females sixty-five and over, (6) the number of males per 100 females in the aged population, (7) the aging ratio: the ratio of persons seventy-five and over to those sixty-five to seventy-four, (8) the percentage increase or decrease in the aged population, and (9) the percentage of males in the labor force.

A cartogram of the Midwest region has been prepared based upon each of these measurements and will constitute the basis of the following discussion.

Number of Persons Sixty-five and Over. Whereas the highest *proportions* of the aged are found in rural counties, the greatest *numbers* are found in urban centers, as shown in Figure 1. This merely shows that in terms of gross numbers the aged population follows the pattern of the general population and that while the proportion of the aged in metropolitan areas is relatively low, in sheer numbers these are the points of maximum concentration.

In the midwestern region, obviously the greatest number of the aged is concentrated in Cook County, Illinois, i.e., in Chicago. Other major concentrations are obvious in St. Louis City and St. Louis County, Missouri, in Milwaukee County, Wisconsin, in Hennepin County, Minnesota (Minneapolis), and in Jackson County, Missouri (Kansas City). Even the locations of the smaller cities are clearly evident; Duluth, St. Paul, Madison, Des Moines, Sioux City, Omaha, Lincoln, St. Joseph, Peoria, Kansas City (Kansas), Topeka, Wichita, and Joplin are clearly distinguishable on the map.

This chart has major significance in terms of the distribution of services and programs for the aged. The heavy proportions of the aged in some of our rural areas should not mislead us into thinking that the bulk of services should be placed in such rural areas. For the aged, as for all other age groups, the greatest volume of services must be concentrated in the cities.

Distribution of Aged Nonwhites. Most of the nonwhites in this region are Negroes and it is well-known that outside of the South Negroes are concentrated in cities. This is equally true of nonwhites sixty-five years of age and over.

Figure 2 shows the numerical distribution of aged nonwhites by county. Again, Chicago, or more accurately, Cook County, has by far the greatest number with only slightly less than fifty thousand. St. Louis and Kansas City follow in order. Since the cities farther north, such as Minneapolis and Milwaukee, have lower proportions of Negroes in their populations, they also have fewer aged nonwhites than the Missouri cities.

Missouri is the only state in this region which has appreciable numbers of Negroes in rural counties and this is reflected in the fact that there are notable concentrations of aged nonwhites in several counties in the Bootheel and in most of the counties along the Missouri River.

In the northern states, particularly in the Dakotas, small concentrations in rural counties are indicative of Indian population rather than Negroes.

Percentage of Persons Sixty-five and Over. While the greatest numbers of persons sixty-five and over are found in cities, the highest percentages relative to the total population are found in rural counties, as shown in Figure 3. While Iowa has the highest percentage of persons sixty-five and

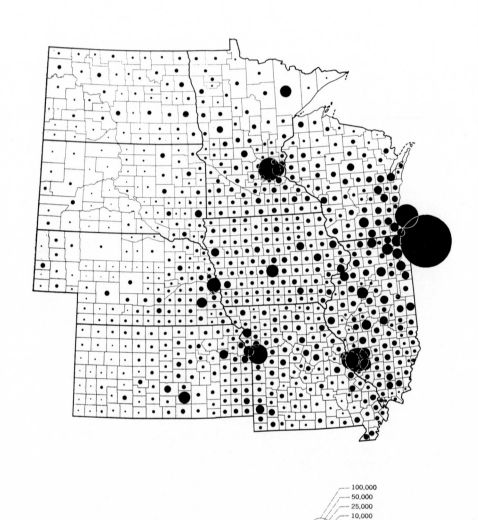

FIG. 1.   Numbers of persons sixty-five and over, by county.

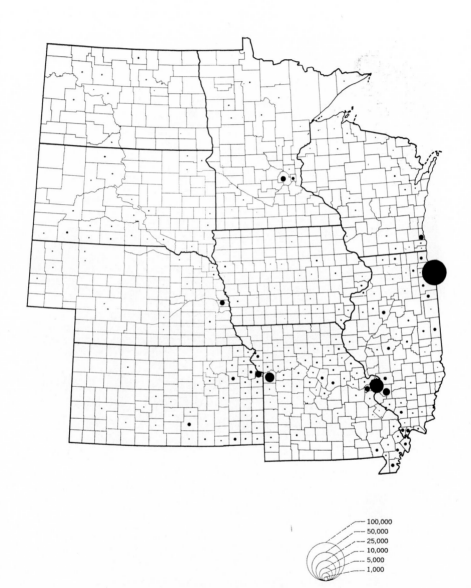

FIG. 2. Number of nonwhites sixty-five and over, by county.

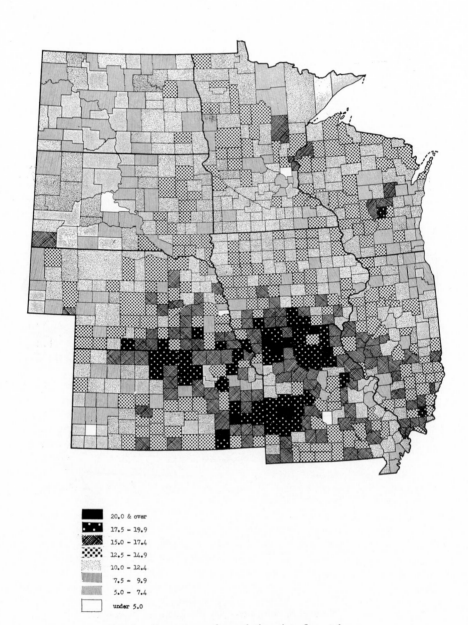

■	20.0 & over
▨	17.5 - 19.9
▧	15.0 - 17.4
▦	12.5 - 14.9
░	10.0 - 12.4
▥	7.5 - 9.9
▦	5.0 - 7.4
☐	under 5.0

FIG. 3. Percentage of population sixty-five and over.

over of all of the states, the heaviest concentrations when viewed county
by county are in Missouri and Kansas.

There are three major points of such concentrations. One is in northern
Missouri extending all the way from the Missouri River to the northern
border and including some counties in southern Iowa. Contained within
this cluster are five counties in which more than 20 per cent of the population consists of persons sixty-five and over.

A second cluster appears in southwestern Missouri and southeastern
Kansas. In this cluster one county in Missouri and two in Kansas have more
than one-fifth of their populations comprised of old folks. This is the most
compact of the three clusters and appears to center around St. Clair County
which is one of the counties with more than 20 percent of its population
sixty-five and over. This cluster includes Elk County, Kansas, which has
the highest proportion of aged of any county in the Midwest, 22.1 per cent.

The third general concentration of the aged appears to be in north
central Kansas and south central Nebraska. This is a less compact cluster
and there are scattered counties with more than 17.5 per cent over sixty-
five extending all the way east to the Missouri border and appearing almost
to link up with the cluster in northern Missouri. An oddity in this pattern
is that there is no county within the main body of this cluster with as much
as 20 per cent sixty-five and over.

The areas with high proportions of the aged appear to be predominantly
rural with much of the population living in small towns and villages. They
are areas which are some distance removed from large metropolitan
centers, but not so far removed as to be isolated or to force the inhabitants
to live under pioneer conditions. The areas with the highest proportions
of the aged are not found in the grazing and extensive farming areas of the
far west; instead, they are found in relatively intensive and diversified
farming areas in which the rural population density is fairly high. Nevertheless, they are areas of declining population and of stagnant economies
and average incomes are very low. These conditions have given rise to
extensive out-migration which is heavily selective of young migrants,
leaving the old folks behind. Only a few areas of the Midwest are affected
significantly by in-migration of the aged and in-migration is not the reason
for the heaviest concentrations of the aged.

The concentration of the aged in rural areas is not a new phenomenon;
Charles Booth noted it in England in the 1890's where he found that 7.6
per cent of the population of the most rural areas were sixty-five and over
whereas only 3.97 per cent of the most metropolitan areas consisted of
aged people. More than twenty years ago T. Lynn Smith referred to the
village as "America's Old Folks' Home."[2] Marshall has also shown that
the ratio of the aged in the rural nonfarm population of Wisconsin has

---

[1]Charles Booth, The Aged Poor in England, London and New York: Macmillan
and Co., p. 12.

[2]T. Lynn Smith, The role of the village in American rural society, Rural Sociology,
7: 10-21, 1942.

exceeded other segments since 1920.[3] Smith and Marshall have also shown that this is exclusively a characteristic of the nonfarm population; it does not apply to the farm segment of the rural population which, at least in recent years, has a lower proportion of the aged than all other categories.[4] Furthermore these same authors along with others have found that the percentage of the population sixty-five and over varies inversely with the size of the community from the largest metropolitan centers right down to the smallest hamlet. In addition, Fuguitt finds in Wisconsin that the degree of urbanization of an area strongly influences the age structure of all segments of the population, that in metropolitan counties even the rural population has low proportions of the aged, and in counties away from any large cities and in which the bulk of the population is rural even the urban population reflects the rural tendency toward a higher percentage of the aged.[6] Smith and Marshall investigated this phenomenon more systematically and found that cities as large as 25,000 manifested this rural influence.[7] In all cases, whether the largest local community is such a small city or a mere hamlet, the high proportions of the aged are attributed to the nearly universal tendency for farmers to retire into the nearest town.

Within the United States, nearly all of the ecological variation in percentages of the aged is due to selective patterns of migration. In general, the tendency for rural areas to have high proportions of old folks is due to the greater tendency for young people to leave such areas while the old folks stay behind continuing to live where they always have lived or merely retiring from the farm into the nearest town. Thus, Fuguitt reports heavy out-migration of the young from those areas which have high proportions of old folks,[8] and Smith and Marshall emphasize the proclivity of the rural older population to stay behind and to retire into the nearest town.[9] Both Dade, in Kansas,[10] and Johansen, in South Dakota,[11] had noted the same processes somewhat earlier, finding that during the depression

[3]Douglas G. Marshall, Wisconsin's Population: Changes and Prospects, Madison: University of Wisconsin, Research Bulletin No. 194, 1959, p. 13.

[4]T. Lynn Smith and Douglas G. Marshall, Our Aging Population: The United States and Wisconsin, Madison: University of Wisconsin, Department of Rural Sociology, Wisconsin's Population Series No. 5, April, 1963, p. 16.

[5]Ibid., pp. 16-19. See also Glenn V. Fuguitt, The Changing Age of Wisconsin's Population, Madison: University of Wisconsin, Department of Rural Sociology, Population Series No. 3, April, 1962, pp. 35-39; and White House Conference on Aging, Background Paper on Population Trends, Social and Economic Implications, Washington: National Advisory Committee for the White House Conference on Aging, September 1960, p. 23.

[6]Op cit., pp. 35-39.

[7]Op. cit., pp. 16-19.

[8]G. V. Fuguitt, The Changing Age Structure, p. 16.

[9]Op. cit., pp. 16-19.

[10]Emil B. Dade, Migration of Kansas Population, 1930-1945, Lawrence: University of Kansas Publications, Industrial Research Series No. 6, 1946, pp. 14-17.

[11]John P. Johansen, Population Trends in Relation to Resources Development in South Dakota, Brookings: South Dakota State College, Agricultural Experiment Station, Bulletin 440, 1954, pp. 14-15.

and the war years retirement from the farms slowed resulting in some "damming up" of old folks in rural farm areas, but with the end of World War II, Johansen found greatly increased rates of retirement of older farm operators. But, in spite of the interruption of the process during depression and war, the phenomenon appears to be an old and persistent one. Again, Booth had described it very succinctly in England in 1891. "Industrial migration is always of the same character, the young and vigorous move; the old stay behind and are reinforced by those who, as they become old, drift back."[12]

But heavy out-migration results in a declining population; hence, those areas in which there are high proportions of old folks due to the out-migration of the young are also areas of declining, or at least, slow-growing populations. This too had been remarked by Booth. " . . . decreasing populations are in every case connected with a higher proportion of old people, and except in the wholly rural districts, with a higher percentage of the old in receipt of relief."[13] Currently, Taber reports that in Iowa it is the counties which are not growing which have high proportions of the aged, [14] and Copp[15] had noted earlier that the areas of Kansas which were experiencing the greatest declines had the highest proportions of persons sixty-five and over. Similarly, Fuguitt reports that in Wisconsin, the greater the loss of population through migration and the more rural the area the higher the proportion of aged persons.[16] Furthermore, this is not merely a static condition; it is progressive. The areas of greatest loss through migration are the ones in which the proportions of the aged are increasing most rapidly.[17] Smith and Marshall refer to them as areas of "depopulation."[18]

It is a sociological axiom that migration tends to flow in the direction of economic opportunity. If this be true, we would infer that these areas of depopulation in which there is such a heavy residue of older population are areas with relatively limited economic opportunities and probably of relatively low levels of living resulting from somewhat stagnant economies. All of this appears to be true. Taber reports that in Iowa the counties with lower income levels are those in which the proportion of the aged is high,[19] and general impressions confirm the point with respect to the region as a whole.

Taber also reports that the areas with high proportions of the aged are not only rural, but they are some distance removed from any major

---

[12]Op. cit., pp. 11-12.

[13]Op. cit., p. 31.

[14]Merlin A. Taber, Socio-cultural factors in extending health services, unpublished paper, 1963, p. 5.

[15]James H. Copp, Population Trends in Kansas from 1940 to 1950, Manhattan: Kansas State College, Kansas Agricultural Experiment Station, Agricultural Economics Report No. 71, August, 1956, p. 27.

[16]The Changing Age Structure, p. 41.

[17]Ibid., p. 43.

[18]Op. cit., p. 11.

[19]Op. cit.

metropolitan center.[20] Copp made a similar observation in Kansas on the basis of the 1950 census.[21] Such a relationship also appears to be implicit in the data of Smith and Marshall on Wisconsin. However, analysis of the regional map (Figure 3) leads to the caution that there is a limitation to this generalization. It is true that the areas of maximum concentration are removed at some distance from metropolitan centers, namely St. Louis and Kansas City, but they are not the most remote rural areas; they may be from a hundred to a hundred and fifty miles from such centers, but they are not five hundred miles away; they are not out in the Great Plains of western Kansas, Nebraska and the Dakotas. Tentatively it is suggested that the aged tend to remain in villages and towns which are in reasonable proximity to urban facilities; even the aged are repelled from the more isolated communities where such facilities are completely out of commuting range. In other words, it appears probable that the ratios of the aged are not high in the Great Plains area because the aged tend to move out of these areas as rapidly as the younger population. However, more research is needed in order to test this hypothesis.

If this hypothesis is true, then here is an instance where migration of the aged as well as migration of the young is a factor in the pattern which emerges. Another instance which Smith and Marshall note for Wisconsin[22] is a limited migration of retired males into resort areas. However, this has more effect upon the sex ratio of the aged than it does upon the overall proportion of the aged, since at times the in-migration of old men is counter-balanced by out-migration of elderly females.[23]

The piling up of the aged in villages and towns of the Midwest to the degree which is reported above lends demographic support to the possibility of the development of a subculture of the aging as suggested by Rose[24] and emphasizes the importance of the type of research being conducted by Pihlblad and McNamara.[25]

Percentage of Males Sixty-five and Over. In order to explore the possibility that the pattern of distribution of elderly males might be a somewhat different one than that of the aged population in general, the percentage of males sixty-five and over was calculated separately. These figures are shown in Figure 4. In general, it appears that they do not distribute themselves completely differently and that the concentrations of males appear in the same areas as the aged population in general. Here, as in Figure 3, we note the three major clusters: northern Missouri, southwestern Missouri—eastern Kansas, and north central Kansas.

However, because the percentages for males tend to be a little lower than for females, when the same cartographic scale is used in the two

---

[20]*Op cit.,* pp. 4-5.
[21]*Op. cit.,* p. 27.
[22]*Op. cit.,* p. 37.
[23]*Ibid.*
[24]See Chapter 1.
[25]See Chapter 4.

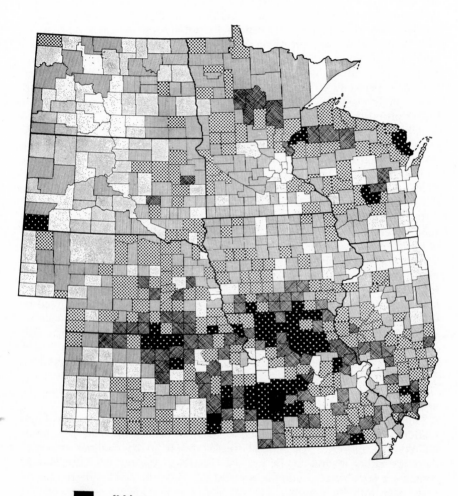

20.0 & over
17.5 – 19.9
15.0 – 17.4
12.5 – 14.9
10.0 – 12.4
7.5 – 9.9
5.0 – 7.4
under 5.0

FIG. 4.   Percentage of males sixty-five and over.

figures, the clusters for the males are not as decisive nor as extensive. There are only four counties in the whole region in which 20 per cent or more of the male population is sixty-five and over, whereas there are nine counties in which more than 20 per cent of the total population is sixty-five and over. Significantly, all four of those with the highest percentages of elderly males are in the southernmost cluster in southwest Missouri and eastern Kansas and within this cluster Elk County, Kansas, again ranks highest with 21.4 per cent. It is probable that more of the aged in this cluster are living on farms than in the more northerly areas and we may expect a higher proportion of males in a rural farm population.

All of the areas with high proportions of aged males are low income areas which are losing population through out-migration. For example, it is estimated that Elk County with a population of only about five thousand people had a net population loss through migration between 1950 and 1960 of 1,773. This out-migration, of course, accounted for the fact that during the decade the total population decreased by 24.4 per cent.

In these counties, also, natural increase has practically ceased and during some recent years the number of deaths has actually exceeded the number of births.

The median family income in Elk County in 1959 was only $3,228, or only a little more than half that of the United States as a whole. Forty-seven per cent had incomes below $3,000 and only 4 per cent had incomes in excess of $10,000. The farm operator level-of-living index computed by the Department of Agriculture for the county was only 89 on a scale on which the national average was 100. The median value of homes was only about $5,000 and only 34 per cent of the dwellings were sound, with running water and inside toilets. The median rent for rented units was $41. The buildings were old; only 5 per cent have been built since 1950.

These counties are also almost completely rural. Elk County has no urban population and 36.5 per cent of its population is rural farm.

Outside of these three main clusters in the Midwest, there are a few scattered counties in which as much as 17.5 per cent of the male population is sixty-five and over. In general, these appear to be counties in which there are either institutions or resorts. Fall River County in South Dakota contains a sizeable institutional population, while the scattered counties in Wisconsin with high proportions of elderly males appear to be areas in which fishing is a favorite activity.

Percentage of Females Sixty-five and Over. The concentrations of elderly females are even more marked than those of males. In general, the percentages sixty-five and over are higher for females than for males, hence, when the same scale is used for Figure 4 and Figure 5, higher proportions of the counties appear with the darker shades in the latter. Thus, while no county in northern Missouri had more than 20 per cent of the males sixty-five and over, no less than 13 counties had 20 per cent or more of their females sixty-five and over and there were two additional adjacent counties in Iowa which also had more than one-fifth of their females sixty-five and over.

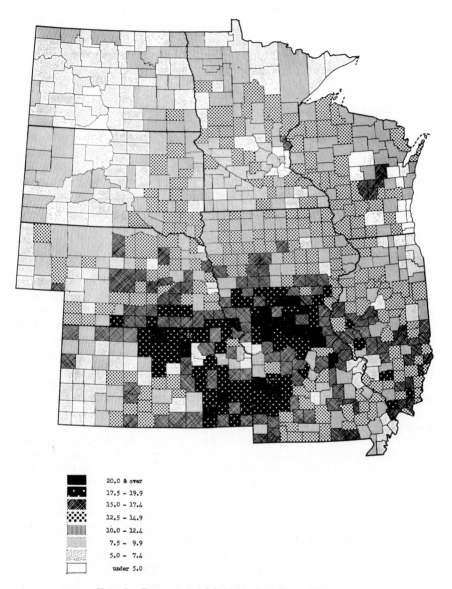

FIG. 5. Percentage of females sixty-five and over.

Elk County, Kansas, again has the highest percentage in the entire region, 22.8 per cent. Considerable detail has been given about this county elsewhere, but it may be of further interest that in the county-seat of Howard, a town of just over a thousand people, almost a third, 31.4 per cent, of the females are sixty-five and over.

Outside of the three main clusters in Figure 5 the only other counties with more than 17.5 per cent over sixty-five are five scattered counties in Illinois. One of these, Union, appears to have a sizeable institutional population, accounting for 12.8 per cent of the total population. The others appear to be merely rural counties with declining populations.

Sex Ratio in the Aged Population: Males per 100 Females. The sex ratio of the aged shows a very striking pattern in the Midwest. On the basis of Figure 6, one is tempted to say that the sex ratio is high on the periphery of the region and low in the center, but this is a relatively meaningless statement, especially when we are talking about a region which is extracted from its context in the heart of the nation. Perhaps a more meaningful way of describing the pattern is to say that the sex ratio is high in the Ozarks section of Missouri, in western Kansas and Nebraska, in much of the Dakotas, in northern Minnesota and northern Wisconsin.

Ostensibly, these areas have two characteristics which are more attractive to older males than to older females. The Ozarks and northern Minnesota and Wisconsin are resort areas which are famous for their opportunities for fishing. Some residents combine fishing with subsistence farming and thus live in semi-retirement.

By contrast, the western part of the region is an area of extensive farming, largely devoted to wheat and cattle raising. The higher sex ratio among the aged there may be merely a correlate of a higher ratio of males in the population of the area at all ages. These are generally viewed as he-man occupations and whereas an elderly widower might stay on for a time and remain active under these conditions, many widows no doubt leave the area upon the death of their husbands. In these western sections, the sex ratio is high because of selective out-migration of females, whereas in the fishing resort areas it is high because of the selective in-migration of males.

In general, the lowest sex ratios, i.e., the lowest proportions of elderly males, are found in Iowa, northern Missouri, eastern Kansas and Nebraska, central Illinois, and southern Minnesota and Wisconsin. These are the parts of the region with the highest percentages of the aged. This is the Corn Belt with moderate-sized diversified farms. It is an area with many small towns and cities to which the local aged farmers retire and live out the remaining years of their lives. But widows are more likely to remain in these towns than widowers; some of the latter are lured by the opportunities in the resort areas of the Ozarks and Minnesota and Wisconsin.

The sex ratios of the aged population vary more widely than the sex ratios of the total population and usually they vary in the same direction. Of course, in most cases the sex ratios of the aged are much lower than sex ratios for the population including all ages. For example, the sex ratio

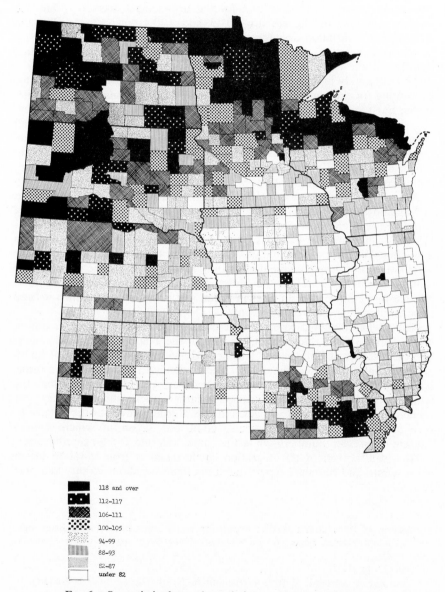

	118 and over
	112–117
	106–111
	100–105
	94–99
	88–93
	82–87
	under 82

FIG. 6.   Sex ratio in the aged population—males per 100 females.

for the population in general in the United States in 1960 was 97.1 while that for the population sixty-five and over was 82.8. For the total urban population it was 94.1 while that for the urban aged was 76.2. For the rural population, the figures are 104.3 and 100.1, respectively, but the most extreme variation apparently is for the rural farm population where the sex ratio for the aged is extremely high. For example, Smith and Marshall found that it was 130.7 in Wisconsin.[26]

This extremely high sex ratio of the aged in farm areas is the chief factor accounting for the high sex ratios in the most rural sections of the Midwest. In the most sparsely settled areas of the Great Plains where there are no large cities and where the farm population predominates over even the small village population, the sex ratios of the aged are very high. Copp had noted this for western Kansas in 1950,[27] and in 1960 in South Dakota Riley found a high average age of farm operators in the same areas which have high sex ratios in the aged population.[28]

Again, this is not a new or unexpected phenomenon; Charles Booth noted in England seventy years ago that the sex ratio of the aged was inversely correlated with the degree of urbanization.[29] At that time he sought to explain the phenomenon in terms of the shortening of men's lives in urban industries. Whether differential death rates were the sole explanation of the condition at that time may be doubted; in any case we may be sure that the same phenomenon today in the Midwestern region of the United States is not due to differential death rates in urban and rural areas, but must instead be attributed to selective migration.

Cleland has reported recently that more elderly women migrate out of North Dakota than elderly men,[30] although there is a net outward migration on the part of both sexes. This accords with the observation of Smith and Marshall that women have a greater tendency than men to leave farms and migrate to towns and villages.[31] However, Cleland suggests that the female migrants are more likely to go to larger cities, while male migrants remain in small towns and villages.[32] If this is true it reverses the pattern of rural-urban migration of the young adult population in which females migrate in greater numbers while the males migrate for longer distances.

However, not all of the migration of the aged is from rural to urban areas. Smith and Marshall report that a net figure of about 9,000 older per-

---

[26]Op. cit., p. 18.

[27]Op. cit., p. 29.

[28]Marvin P. Riley, South Dakota Population and Farm Census Facts, Brookings: South Dakota State College, Rural Sociology Department Circular 151, January, 1962, p. 28.

[29]Op. cit., pp. 12-13.

[30]Courtney B. Cleland, Shifting Population in North Dakota and its Relation to the Aged, manuscript of address at Action for the Aging Conference at University of North Dakota, Sept. 6, 1962, p. 2.

[31]Op. cit., pp. 25-28.

[32]Op. cit., p. 3.

sons appear to have moved out of Milwaukee between 1950 and 1960.[33]
They do not state whether there was any selectivity by sex in this migration,
but Taves and Hansen had reported earlier that on the basis of interviews
with older people in Minnesota more urban men than women wanted to
move to the suburbs or to a rural setting, while more urban women were
content to remain in the city.[34]

Smith and Marshall also indicate that some of the resort areas of Wisconsin were receiving aged male migrants at the same time that aged
females were migrating out of the areas.[35] It would not take a very heavy
flow of such migration to produce the high sex ratios of the aged which we
see in northern and central Wisconsin and we may surmise that it is this type
of migration pattern which is also responsible for the relatively high sex
ratios in northern Minnesota and in the Ozarks in southern Missouri.

The Aging Ratio. In the modern world, sixty-five is certainly not to be
considered extreme old age; we are now accumulating very sizeable populations eighty-five and over. But it probably makes considerable difference
in community life and the types of services in demand if most of those
sixty-five and over are in the lower ages of this range rather than in the
upper extreme.

In an effort to reveal differences in the distribution of old folks within
this broad range, I have resorted to a mathematical device which I will call
the "aging ratio." This is arrived at by dividing the number 75 and over
by the number 65 to 74, i.e., it is the ratio of those in the upper end of
the age range to those in the lower end. The higher the ratio, of course,
the older is the old population in the country; the lower the ratio the
greater is the tendency to concentrate in the younger end of the range.

Figure 7 shows the variations in these aging ratios by county. The most
obvious generalization is that the aging ratios tend to be high in the same
areas which have high proportions of the aged of all ages, i.e., sixty-five and
over. The same three areas—northern Missouri and southern Iowa, southwestern Missouri and eastern Kansas, and north central Kansas—emerge
with high aging ratios.

What this seems to indicate is that the same areas which accumulate
high proportions of persons sixty-five and over, also accumulate, or retain,
high proportions seventy-five and over. It is possible that just as the younger
working population tends to migrate out of these areas, so do some of the
younger old folks.

However, there are some differences between Figure 3 and Figure 7.
The pattern for the latter is less definitive; the areas of concentration are
somewhat less compact; and there are more scattered counties outside of
the main clusters which show markedly high ratios. For example, the

---

[33]*Op. cit.,* p. 15.

[34]Marvin J. Taves and Gary D. Hansen, Seventeen hundred elderly citizens, in
Arnold M. Rose, ed., Aging in Minnesota, Minneapolis: University of Minnesota
Press, 1963, p. 170.

[35]*Op. cit.,* p. 37.

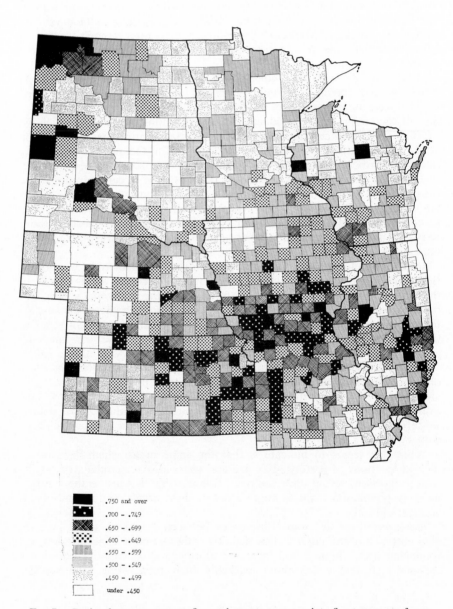

■	.750 and over
	.700 – .749
	.650 – .699
	.600 – .649
	.550 – .599
	.500 – .549
	.450 – .499
	under .450

FIG. 7. Ratio of persons seventy-five and over to persons sixty-five to seventy-four.

northwestern countries of both North Dakota and South Dakota, St. Croix and Lincoln Counties in Wisconsin, Garfield and Washington Counties in Nebraska, and Wallace and Kiowa Counties in Kansas. Notable, too, is the fact that there are several clusters in Illinois.

It is probable that these scattered cases of counties with exceedingly high aging ratios may be reflecting the location of institutions—nursing homes or hospitals. In counties with very small populations, a few extra persons in such institutions can produce considerable change in the ratio and the populations of such institutions tend to be older than a normal non-institutional population.

Increase and Decrease of Aged Population. Because the aged population increased so decisively between 1950 and 1960, it is reasonable to expect that most areas will reflect this increase. Figure 8 indicates that this expectation is borne out; most of the counties of the Midwest did experience increases of their aged populations. In general, the large increases were in areas with relatively low proportions of the aged, hence, the pattern of Figure 8 is almost the opposite of Figure 3. The points of concentration of the aged in Missouri and Kansas manifest little growth even in the aged population.

Major growth appears to have occurred in two kinds of areas. Urban areas in all states, while not having high proportions of the aged, nevertheless are areas of growth of populations of all ages including some growth of the aged population. Some rural counties with sparse populations such as the ones in western Kansas, Nebraska and South Dakota experienced increases. One of these, Shannon County, South Dakota, had the highest percentage of increase in the whole region, 175.9 per cent, but this actually represented quite small numbers; the aged population increased from 141 in 1950 to 389 in 1960.

Many of the resort areas of Wisconsin, Minnesota and Missouri appear to have higher than average rates of increase. This may reflect some tendency for older people to move into these areas for retirement as well as a tendency for those who are already there to remain and engage in various aspects of the tourist trade. Smith and Marshall found evidence of some in-migration of the aged into such tourist areas in Wisconsin.[36]

There are very few counties indeed which actually experienced losses of aged population. There are none at all in Wisconsin and Minnesota, only one in Kansas, two each in Illinois and Nebraska. However, in northern Missouri and southern Iowa in the area of maximum concentration of the aged there are seven counties which lost population, five in Missouri and two in Iowa.

However, the most marked losses occur in western North Dakota and west central South Dakota. There are eight counties in South Dakota and six counties in North Dakota in which the aged population declined. The maximum decreases are in North Dakota where two counties, Renville

[36]*Op. cit.,* p. 11.

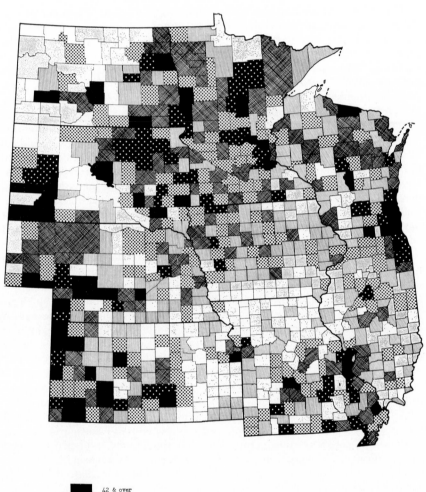

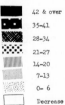

■	42 & over
	35–41
	28–34
	21–27
	14–20
	7–13
	0– 6
	Decrease

FIG. 8. Percentage increase of persons sixty-five and over, 1950-1960.

and Billings lost more than 20 per cent. However, again these losses involve relatively small numbers because of the sparse populations.

These losses in the northern Great Plains are probably only incidental to the general out-migration from this area; apparently some of the aged are moving out, too. Cleland has recently confirmed the impression that the general decrease in the rural farm population of much of this area involves some out-migration of the aged as well as the younger population.[37] Apparently this is a continuation of the trend noted by Hitt for the decade 1940-1950 during which the relative loss of the aged through migration in North Dakota was the heaviest in the nation and South Dakota was second in relative loss.[38]

There may also be some out-migration from northern Missouri, but here the movement is less dramatic and the fact that the losses coincide with the point of maximum concentration of the aged raises the question as to whether there may be a kind of saturation point. At any rate, it is evident that many of the small towns in this area are loaded with elderly people. The determination as to whether the burden of this drives some of them out or the out-migration is merely an aspect of a stagnant economy will require more research.

Percentage of Males Over Sixty-five in the Labor Force. A high proportion of males sixty-five and over are still active in the labor force in the western part of the region, as shown in Figure 9. In many counties in this area, more than half of the aged males are still in the labor force. This tendency appears to be greatest in the cattle-raising sections of Nebraska, but it is also correlated to some extent with the raising of wheat. Both of these occupations are involved with extensive farming operations and occur in semi-arid areas with the consequence that the population is quite sparse. These are areas in which the sex ratio is quite high and, as noted above, the widows tend to emigrate. It is a man's world and those who stay appear to be physically fit and tend to keep busy.

By contrast, eastern portions of the region, including more densely settled urbanized populations, have lower proportions of the elderly men in the labor force. This is especially true of the resort areas in the Ozarks and of the northern lake regions of Wisconsin and Minnesota. As noted above, these are areas to which many men migrate upon retirement, and while some of them may engage in small farming operations, raise chickens, or operate resort enterprises of one type or another, they apparently consider themselves to be retired from the labor force and the census-takers classify them accordingly.

In sum, it appears that there are high proportions of the males over sixty-five in the labor force in those areas which have heavy out-migration of both males and females with the result that high proportions of the

---

[37]*Op. cit.,* pp. 1-2. See also Cleland's discussion of mobility of the aged in Chapter 20 of this volume.

[38]Homer L. Hitt, The role of migration in population change among the aged, American Sociological Review, 19: 194-200, 1954.

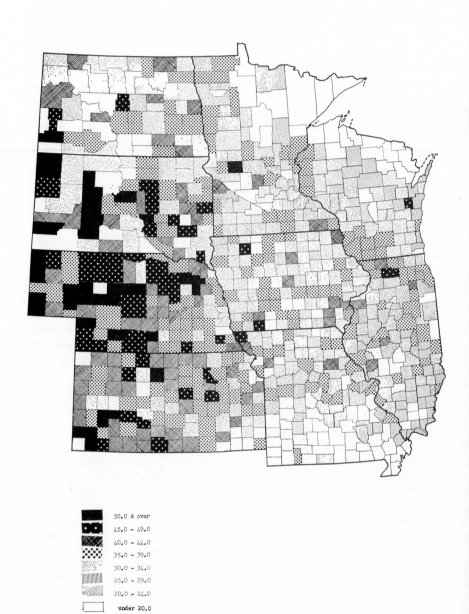

Fig. 9. Percentage of males sixty-five and over in labor force.

remaining males are still in the labor force and that, on the other hand, the areas with the lowest proportions of males in the labor force are those areas which attract males as retirement havens.

Analysis of Urban Areas

The previous section of this chapter has been devoted to an analysis of the aging population of the Midwest using counties as the units of analysis; the remainder of the chapter will concentrate upon cities. It will shortly appear that even though some rural areas have the highest percentages of the aged, the greatest numbers are still to be found in cities. Since this is true and since cities by their very nature are also the service centers for regions of varying sizes, it follows that the bulk of services for the aging must still be located in cities.

It therefore appears appropriate to analyze the cities separately from the rural areas. We shall therefore attempt to see the total size of aging populations in the various cities of the Midwest and study the nature of those populations in terms of racial composition, the relative proportions of very old to younger aged, the trends of change, the balance of the sexes, and the proportions in the labor force.

For this purpose the cities included will consist only of the larger urban places, viz., all Standard Metropolitan Statistical Areas together with all other urban places with populations of 10,000 and over.

Numbers of Aged in Cities. Figure 10 shows by relative size of circles the number of persons sixty-five and over in each of the Standard Metropolitan Statistical Areas and urban places in the region. This map is entirely about cities and is confined to those with total populations of 10,000 or more. No account is taken of smaller cities and none at all of rural populations.

This shows even more dramatically than Figure 1 the heavy concentrations of numbers in the major metropolitan areas. Of course, Chicago is without peer in the region in the number of old folks in its metropolitan area. There are more than a half million persons sixty-five and over in metropolitan Chicago alone. Its nearest rival is St. Louis which has less than half as many, under two hundred thousand. St. Louis is followed in size of aged population by Minneapolis–St. Paul, Milwaukee, Kansas City, and Omaha–Council Bluffs, in that order.

It is obvious that there are greater concentrations of the aged in highly urbanized Illinois than in the rural, sparsely settled Great Plains areas of the western part of the region.

Aged Nonwhites in Cities. Figure 2 hinted that the aged nonwhites were found largely in the urban areas in the southern and eastern part of the region. Figure 11 demonstrates this even more sharply. This cartogram shows not only the numbers of nonwhite aged in each city by the absolute size of the shaded portion of the circles, but also the proportion of the aged population of each city which is nonwhite by the ratio of the shaded portion to the entire circle.

By far the greatest numbers of aged nonwhites are found in Chicago,

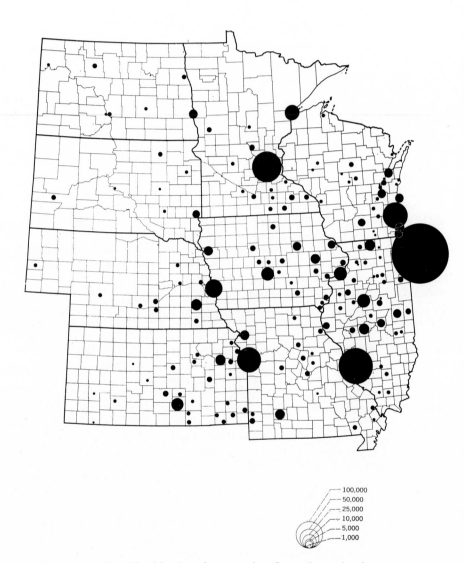

Fig. 10.   Number of persons sixty-five and over, by city.

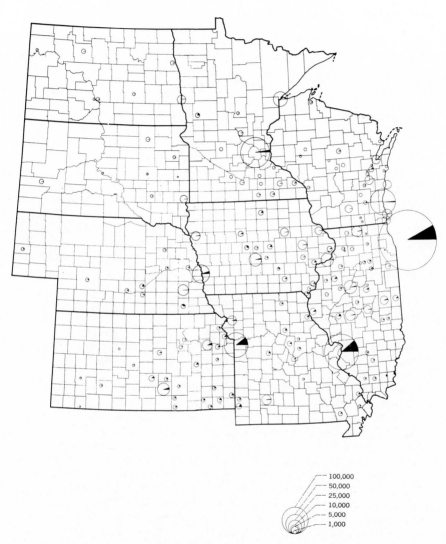

FIG. 11.   Number of nonwhite persons sixty-five and over, by city.

St. Louis, and Kansas City. Chicago has over 43,000; St. Louis has over 20,000; and Kansas City has nearly 10,000. By contrast, Minneapolis–St. Paul and Milwaukee, both larger metropolitan areas than Kansas City, have only 1,700 and 1,800, respectively. Other cities in the region have relatively small numbers of aged nonwhites.

When viewed from the standpoint of the proportions of the aged population who are nonwhite, St. Louis and Kansas City both rank ahead of Chicago; in each slightly more than 10 per cent of all of the aged are non-whites, whereas only 8 per cent of the aged are nonwhite in Chicago Metropolitan Area. In each case the percentages would be considerably higher for the central cities than for the metropolitan areas as a whole, since most of the nonwhites including the aged are concentrated in the central cities.

The aggregation of nonwhite aged in the southern and eastern cities of the region is related to the concentration of nonwhite populations as well as to the recency of migration. The nonwhite population in general is concentrated in the portions of the region closest to the South, where greater numbers of nonwhites, particularly Negroes, have migrated from the South, a migration which began essentially with World War I and has continued to the present. But, in addition, the migrations to the cities which are at greater distances from the South, such as Milwaukee and Minneapolis, are more recent, and since the migrants are practically always young people, the populations in the latter cities have not had time to reach old age, hence these northern cities not only have fewer nonwhites but, in addition, the proportion of their nonwhites who are aged is lower.

Percentage of Persons Sixty-five and Over in Cities. There is considerable variation in the proportions of the populations of the various cities that are sixty-five and over. The largest metropolitan centers have about average proportions. Chicago, St. Louis, Minneapolis–St. Paul, Milwaukee and Kansas City have from 8 to 10 per cent and fall in the same classification in Figure 12.

The smaller cities are more variable although they tend in general to have higher proportions of the aged.[39] Among the cities with 10,000 and over in the region, Moberly, Missouri, has the highest percentage, 19.3. It is significant that Moberly is adjacent to one of the centers of concentration of the aged in the region. Still more dramatic evidence of the effect of such concentration even upon urban populations is to be noted in southeastern Kansas and western Missouri. Here in the locale of another major concentration of the aged, we find a cluster of small cities with exceedingly high proportions of aged. Independence, Parsons and Pittsburg in Kansas, and Carthage, Missouri, have populations with 16 per cent or more sixty-five and over, and other small cities in the vicinity are almost as high, viz., Chanute, Winfield and Arkansas City with more than 14 per cent, and Joplin and Coffeyville with more than 12 per cent. Not far to the north is Ottawa, Kansas, with 16.3 per cent. Thus, it appears that in this particular

---

[39]In 1950 Sheldon found that the smaller the community the higher the percentage of old folks. *Op. cit.* pp. 37-38.

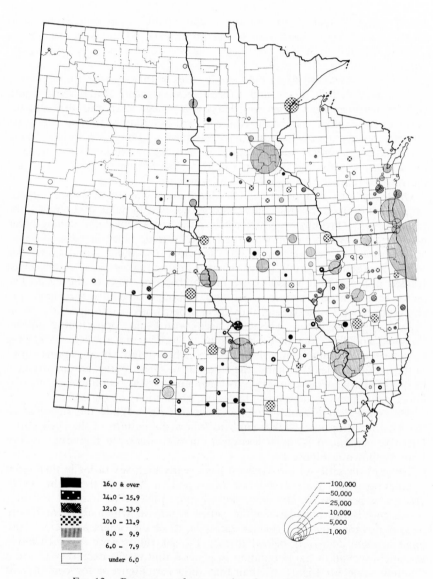

FIG. 12. Percentage of persons sixty-five and over, in cities.

area, the heavy concentration of the aged is not confined to small towns, but is reflected also in cities ranging up to a total population of 20,000.

For a city as large as 80,000, St. Joseph, Missouri, appears to have an exceptionally high proportion of the aged, with 15 per cent. It may also be noted that Duluth, Minnesota, and Springfield, Missouri, appear to be affected by the in-migration of the aged due to the adjacent resort attractions.[40]

However, there are also some small cities with low proportions of the aged. These include Hays and Liberal, Kansas, and Rapid City, South Dakota, with less than 6 per cent. Hays is a college town and no doubt the influx of students outweighs the resident aged population. Liberal is a thriving petroleum center which has also attracted a young population. Rapid City is a resort center, but its attractions as a resort are largely confined to the summer months and it does not hold out the retirement possibilities that the resort areas of Minnesota, and Missouri do.

On the whole, it appears that the large cities are about average in the proportion of aged, but that the smaller cities, with notable exceptions, tend to have higher proportions. Nevertheless the cities reflect the demographic tendencies of the regions in which they are located. Thus, in areas of heavy out-migration of younger population in which the older population tends to stay and retire to small towns, or even to small cities, as in southeastern Kansas and northern Missouri, we find high proportions of the aged. The larger centers attract people of all ages, although of course they are especially attractive to the young, thus their proportions of the aged are about average or a little below. The resort areas with fishing opportunities attract the aged and the cities in these regions as well as the rural areas receive some of the migrants, hence the cities, too, show relatively high proportions of the aged. On the other hand, the cities of the Great Plains are unattractive to the aged who tend to migrate to other areas upon retirement or widowhood, consequently these cities have low proportions of the aged.

Males per 100 Females Among Aged in Cities. While the sex ratio of the aged in cities over 10,000 tends to follow the pattern of the aged population in general, it is much less clear-cut and there are numerous exceptions as shown in Figure 13.

None of the cities of the Midwest have really high sex ratios in their aged populations. The Duluth-Superior Metropolitan Area is the highest with 102 males per 100 females, only slightly more males than females. Furthermore, this is the only city in the entire region in which there are more aged males than females; the sex ratios of all of the others are below 100, most of them decisively below. In fact, the sex ratios were so much lower in the cities than in the population in general that it was necessary to use a different scale for Figure 13 than that shown in Figure 6 for counties. In the chart relating to cities only, Figure 13, the highest classification is "90

---

[40]Smith and Marshall have noted this type of migration into northern and central Wisconsin. *Op. cit.,* p. 11.

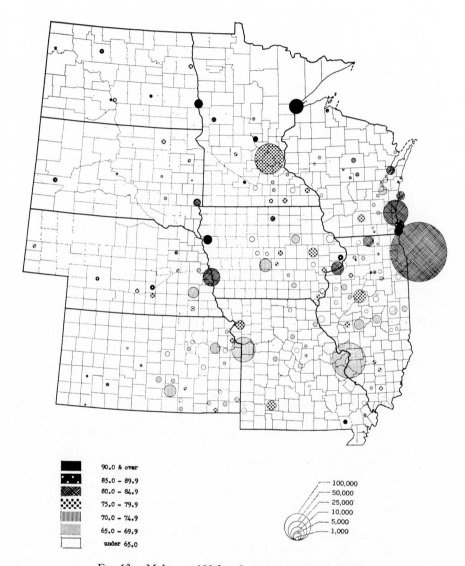

FIG. 13. Males per 100 females among aged in cities.

and over," whereas in Figure 6, relating to county populations, the top classification was "118 and over."

The fact that Duluth-Superior is the highest among these cities is due to a combination of factors. The mining and shipping industries tend to attract a male population, hence the sex ratio of the general population is high. There is a residue of an immigrant population which came to this country in the early part of the century and these people are now entering the ranks of the aged. But in addition to these factors, Duluth-Superior receives some elderly male migrants lured by the fishing opportunities in the vicinity. No doubt the relatively high ratio in St. Cloud, Minnesota, also derives from the latter type of migration. However, the relatively high ratios in Fargo-Moorhead, Jamestown, Mandan, Williston and Minot, North Dakota, probably derive from the greater out-migration of aged females than of aged males; the same tendency probably explains the high ratio in Garden City, Kansas. Poplar Bluff, Missouri, on the other hand, partakes of the retirement attractions of the Ozarks and draws in some male retirees.

Following the pattern of the aged population in general some of the small cities in the Corn Belt have very low sex ratios among their aged populations. For example, most of the smaller cities of Iowa, Illinois, northern Missouri, eastern Kansas and eastern Nebraska have sex ratios below 75. There is some evidence that college towns tend to be selective of aged females who serve as managers of rooming houses and house-mothers for dormitories and fraternities. Thus, the populations of Mankato, Minnesota; Macomb, Illinois; Columbia, Missouri, and Winfield, Kansas, appear to have exceptionally low sex ratios among their aged.[41] It is probable that somewhat similar factors are at work in the hospital center, Rochester, Minnesota, accounting for its low ratio.

Most of the larger cities have sex ratios ranging between 70 and 85, i.e., average for cities. For example, the sex ratio in Chicago is 81, in St. Louis, 73, in Kansas City, 75, in Minneapolis–St. Paul, 77, and in Milwaukee, 81. This indicates a somewhat greater in-migration on the part of aged females than of males, but the differential is not as great as it is in some of the smaller cities, particularly the college towns and health centers.

In summary, the sex ratios of the aged population in cities of the Midwest are generally quite low. While they tend to reflect the pattern of the sex ratios of the aged populations of their localities and the regional patterns of migration, there are many variations which appear to relate to the particular nature of the local community and its specialized set of institutions.

The Aging Ratio in Cities. The ratios of those seventy-five and over to those sixty-five to seventy-four appear to follow a pattern similar to that of the percentages of the aged in general. Again the high ratios, as shown in Figure 14, are found in the smaller cities of the eastern and southern

---

[41]Smith and Marshall found considerable migration of old women into Madison, no doubt for the same reason. *Op. cit.,* p. 37.

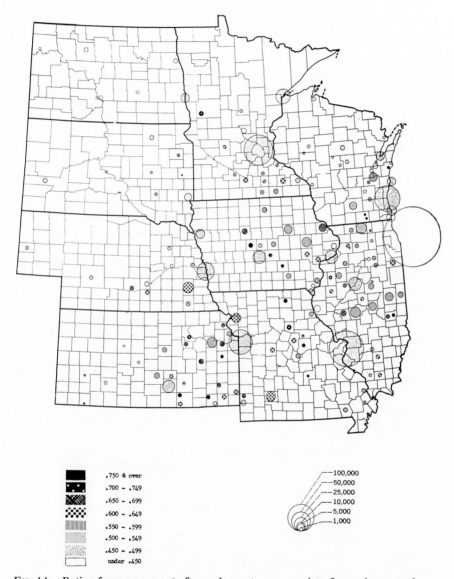

FIG. 14.   Ratio of persons seventy-five and over to persons sixty-five and seventy-four.

portions of the region. There are three cities in eastern Kansas and three in Missouri with ratios above .75. In addition there are two in Iowa, three in Wisconsin and one in Illinois with similarly high ratios. By contrast, no city over 10,000 in Minnesota, the Dakotas, or Nebraska has so high a proportion of the very elderly. Manitowoc, Wisconsin, has the highest ratio, .86, but Janesville, Wisconsin, is a close rival with .85.

In general, it appears that the larger metropolitan areas have relatively low aging ratios. Chicago has one of the lowest with only .42, but St. Louis, Milwaukee and Minneapolis–St. Paul are all below .50. The largest cities with ratios above .60 are Lincoln, St. Joseph, and Springfield, Illinois.

Most of the cities in the Dakotas, western Nebraska and western Kansas have very low aging ratios just as they have low percentages of persons sixty-five and over. Apparently the out-migration from these areas applies to all ages, even the most elderly.

The reasons for the high ratios in some of the cities mentioned above are not entirely clear. It is known that there are sizeable institutional populations in some, such as Winfield and Fulton, and these institutions may contain an inordinate number of very elderly. But it is strange that so many college towns such as Beloit, Kirksville and Rolla should have relatively heavy concentrations of persons seventy-five and over.

Increase of Aged Population in Cities. Figure 15 indicates that the numbers of aged in the populations of the western cities are increasing faster than in the populations of the eastern cities. While there are a few cities in Wisconsin, Illinois, Minnesota, Iowa and Missouri with increases over 44 per cent from 1950 to 1960, there are more in the states of North Dakota, South Dakota, Nebraska and Kansas. In fact, in the first group of states, the eastern states with many more cities, there are only ten cities which increased as much as 44 per cent, whereas the western states with many fewer cities have seventeen with increases in excess of 44 per cent. Most of these had gains well above 50 per cent and one, Jamestown, North Dakota, more than doubled its aged population. Its percentage of increase was 101.7 which was the highest among all of the cities over 10,000 in the region.

While the large metropolitan centers did not have the highest relative increases, all of them increased very substantially. Chicago increased 37 per cent, St. Louis, 31 per cent, Minneapolis–St. Paul, 40 per cent, Milwaukee, 42 per cent, and Kansas City, 35 per cent. Considering the size of the aging populations in these cities, these percentages represent massive numbers.

It is a sign of the times that no city experienced a decrease in its aged population. The smallest percentage of increase was in Fulton, Missouri, which had only a 6 per cent gain, from 1,662 in 1950 to 1,770 in 1960.

Since the communities with the lowest ratios of the aged appear to be gaining most rapidly, it would appear that at least during the recent past there is a tendency to balance out and to approach a more nearly uniform distribution of the aged relative to the total population.

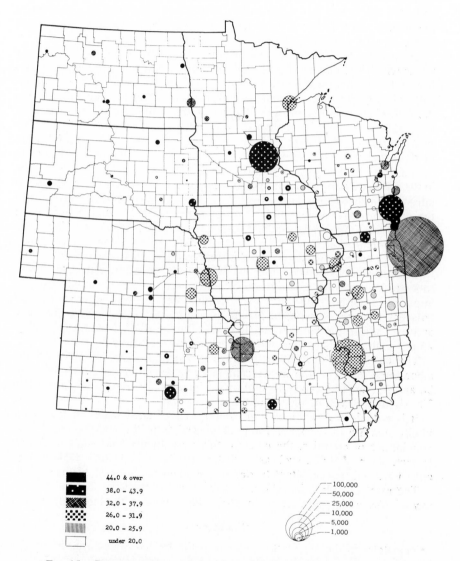

FIG. 15.   Percentage increase of persons sixty-five and over, 1950 to 1960.

Males Over Sixty-five in the Labor Force in Cities. In only one city in the Midwest are more than half of the males over sixty-five in the labor force as shown in Figure 16. This is Manhattan, Kansas, which is largely a college town. There are three other cities with more than 45 per cent of the elderly males in the labor force. Two of these, Ames, Iowa, and Emporia, Kansas, are also college towns; the other is Salina, Kansas.

These cases lead to the hypotheses that there is something about college towns which encourages the employment of males beyond the age of sixty-five. Whether this is directly related to the employment policies of educational institutions or to auxiliary industries is not clear, but the fact that the compulsory retirement age of most of the colleges and universities of the region is seventy rather than sixty-five may give part of the explanation. Another factor may be the presence of many rooming and boarding houses in these towns which aged couples can manage and thereby continue to earn a living. It does appear that college towns in general are above average in the ratio of elderly males in the labor force. All of the following additional cities in which colleges and universities comprise an important segment of the economy have higher than average percentages of aged males in the labor force: Fargo-Moorhead; Mankato, Minnesota; Madison, Wisconsin; Lincoln, Nebraska; Iowa City, Iowa; Rockford and Champaign-Urbana, Illinois; Columbia, Missouri; and Lawrence and Winfield, Kansas.

The resort areas of Wisconsin, Minnesota and Missouri generally appear to foster low ratios of employment of males over sixty-five. Thus in Duluth-Superior, Brainard and St. Cloud, Minnesota, as well as Wausau and adjacent cities in Wisconsin, less than one-fourth of the males sixty-five and over are in the labor force. Likewise Poplar Bluff, Missouri, is below 25 per cent and other cities in the Ozark region are below 30 per cent.

The large cities have about average proportions of older males in the labor force. Most of the larger centers have percentages ranging between 30 and 35, but Chicago is slightly over 35 and Milwaukee is slightly below 30. All are well within a medium range.

It is notable that whereas high proportions of aged males in the Great Plains area are in the labor force, as viewed from the standpoint of total populations of counties, the cities in this area manifest no such tendency. In fact, some of them, such as Williston and Mandan, North Dakota, are quite low, and no consistent tendency is evident in this part of the region.

The most notable thing about Figure 16 is the tendency for the college towns to have high proportions of their older males in the labor force.

Summary

The states in the Midwestern region of the United States are among the highest in the nation in the proportions of aged in their populations. Within the region, of course, the greatest numbers of old folks are concentrated in the metropolitan areas. This tendency to concentrate in the cities is even more marked for the nonwhite aged than for the aged in general.

However, several rural areas of Missouri and Kansas contain the highest

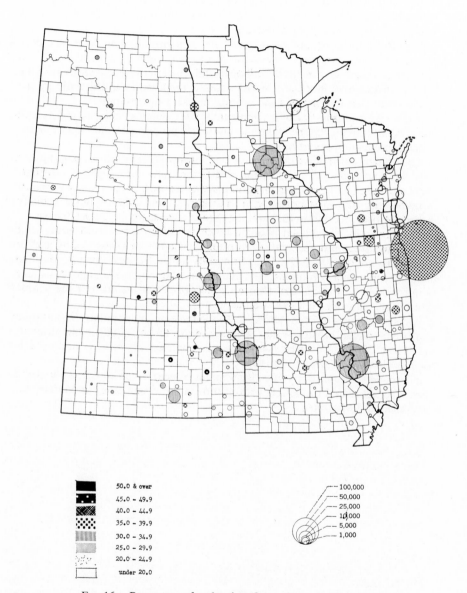

50.0 & over
45.0 - 49.9
40.0 - 44.9
35.0 - 39.9
30.0 - 34.9
25.0 - 29.9
20.0 - 24.9
under 20.0

100,000
50,000
25,000
10,000
5,000
1,000

FIG. 16. Percentage of males sixty-five and over in labor force.

proportions of aged in their populations and this generalization applies almost equally to both sexes. But the sex ratio of the aged population is highest in the Great Plains area of the West and in the resort sections of Wisconsin, Minnesota and Missouri.

Old people of very advanced years, i.e., seventy-five and over, are concentrated in the same sections as the aged population in general, i.e., with high proportions in northern Missouri and eastern Kansas. However, the aged population is increasing most rapidly in those counties with lowest proportions thus tending toward a more uniform distribution.

The highest proportions of aged males are found in the labor force in the western Great Plains and the lowest proportions in the resort areas which serve as retirement havens.

The larger cities have about average proportions of their populations sixty-five and over, but some of the small cities have very high proportions, particularly in northern Missouri and eastern Kansas. The greatest numbers of nonwhites are found not only in the metropolitan centers, but especially in those closest to the South, viz., St. Louis, Kansas City, and Chicago.

The sex ratio of the aged is much lower in cities than in rural areas, but when cities are compared with each other, those of the Great Plains and of the resort areas of Wisconsin, Minnesota and Missouri appear to have higher proportions of males. In the main, the highest aging ratios are found in the cities of eastern Kansas and northern Missouri and the lowest ratios in the cities of the Great Plains.

All of the cities of the Midwest are increasing in population sixty-five and over, but the greatest rates of increase are to be found in the cities of the Great Plains. Nevertheless, the metropolitan centers also are experiencing substantial rates of growth.

The highest proportions of elderly males appear to be in the labor force in college towns and the lowest proportions in the resort cities of Minnesota, Wisconsin and Missouri.

CHAPTER 19

Older People in the Midwest:
Conditions and Attitudes[*]

GARY D. HANSEN, SAMUEL YOSHIOKA, MARVIN J. TAVES,
and FRANCIS CARO

The later years in the human life cycle are usually characterized by important social and physical changes which may radically reshape a person's way of living. Declining health and shifting social roles lead the older person to revise both his patterns of activity and general outlook on life. Retirement, for example, has implications which reach far beyond withdrawal from a job. It is likely to affect greatly a person's income, his social life, what he does with his time, his relationships with his family and friends, and even his more general participation in the community.

Reported here are the results of surveys of older persons in five midwestern states (Iowa, Minnesota, Missouri, North Dakota, and South Dakota). The data represent a general assessment of the older person's image of himself and his environment. Specific topics dealt with include health, income, housing, work-retirement, family and friends, social participation, use of time, personal adjustment, and community services.

Six independent data collection operations are combined and summarized. In Iowa, a sample of 1,009 men and women age sixty-five and over residing in five of the state's metropolitan areas (Cedar Rapids, Davenport, Des Moines, Sioux City, and Waterloo) and eight rural coun-

*Based on Gary D. Hansen and Samuel Yoshioka, Aging in the Upper Midwest, Kansas City; Community Studies, Inc., 1962. This chapter was edited and condensed for the present volume by Marvin J. Taves and Francis Caro. The original studies were directed by Marvin J. Taves and Gary D. Hansen for Minnesota; Martin U. Martel and Merlin Taber for Iowa; Robert L. McNamara, Peter New and C. T. Pihlblad for Missouri; Courtney B. Cleland and Ernest D. Lorin for North Dakota, and Carroll M. Mickey for South Dakota.

ties were interviewed. Two studies were conducted in Minnesota. One project involved 300 Social Security beneficiaries in three counties whose eligibility was based on farming. The other included 1,400 persons sampled from eleven non-metropolitan urban communities and the state's three metropolitan areas (Duluth, Minneapolis, and St. Paul). The Missouri study included 1,700 persons drawn from the metropolitan area of Kansas City, three medium sized cities (St. Joseph, Springfield, and Joplin), nine smaller cities, and eight rural counties. In North Dakota, 917 persons from twelve counties spread throughout the state were interviewed. The South Dakota sample of 1,019 represented an effort to obtain proportional quotas from rural areas and urban communities. In all, 6,356 persons were interviewed in the five states.

Except for 400 Minnesotans, living in homes for the aged and nursing homes, the sample was restricted to persons living outside institutions for the aged. Certain biases are known to exist in the samples. On the whole they tend to somewhat over-represent women, persons with higher education and higher income, the more urban, healthy, and communicative members of the communities. All data reported were obtained by personal interviews. Highly structured interview schedules—ten to twenty pages in length—were utilized.

Where comparable questions were asked, the data generally showed only very little variability among states. Consequently only combined data are reported. Unless otherwise indicated, data represent all five states.

Health

Ability to improve and even to maintain health is a matter of major concern for the aged. Susceptibility to chronic diseases and disabilities can make health a major problem for the older person. Physiological changes which bring about senility, memory loss, and dependence are particularly threatening.

When respondents were asked if they had any *major* uncared for health conditions or health needs, slightly over one in ten answered affirmatively. Twelve per cent of those interviewed felt they were in excellent health. Forty-one per cent considered their health to be fair and the remaining 14 per cent considered themselves to be in poor health. Attitudinal items about health from Minnesota data showed that one in ten feel miserable most of the time and another one-tenth indicated that if they could not feel better soon, they would just as soon die.

In the previous year about one-half of the respondents had had contact with a doctor: 10 per cent with an eye doctor; 10 per cent with osteopaths or chiropractors; 20 per cent with dentists; 3 per cent with public health nurses; 23 per cent with a hospital; and 6 per cent with nursing homes.

For many of the older persons the cost of these medical services was considerable. Thirty-six per cent had incurred medical costs of over $200 in the previous year (see Table 1). Expenditure for medical services was related to income; those with higher incomes tended to spend more on their health. Those with hospital and surgical insurance also spent more for medical services. It is likely that lack of financial resources forced some to neglect their health needs.

Table 1. Income and Medical Expenditures, in Percentages

		Income			
Medical Costs	Total	$0–$999	$1000–$1999	$2000–$3999	$4000– and over
	(N-2899)	(N-914)	(N-887)	(N-718)	(N-380)
Below $50	25	30	26	24	14
$50–$199	42	41	44	40	40
$200–$399	20	17	18	21	27
$400 and over	14	12	12	15	19
Total	100	100	100	100	100

A source of concern for many older people was ability to handle exceptional medical expenses; many felt they had enough money to get by on only if no unexpected expenses arose. Data obtained in Iowa, Missouri, and North Dakota indicated that six in ten believe they could pay for emergency medical costs up to $1,000. Of those remaining, nine-tenths reported that they definitely could not and the others were uncertain. Only one-third indicated that they could pay emergency medical costs of $5,000.

Health insurance represents one way in which a person can protect himself against extraordinary medical expenses. Approximately half of the respondents reported owning hospital, surgical, or medical insurance. Men and women in equal proportions carried health insurance. Age, however, was strongly associated with health insurance coverage (see Table 2). Nearly three-quarters of those below seventy years of age reported

Table 2. Age and Ownership of Hospital, Surgical, or Medical Insurance, in Percentages

	Age Groups			
Insurance Ownership	65–69	70–74	75–79	80–over
	(N-2108)	(N-1382)	(N-1322)	(N-1076)
Owners	73	58	49	37
Non-owners	27	42	51	63
Total	100	100	100	100

owning medical insurance policies compared to just slightly more than a third of those over eighty years of age. In addition, those who owned health insurance were more likely than others to live in an urban area and tended to be better educated and to have higher incomes.

Income and Expenditures

Failing health, retirement, and inflation frequently combine to create serious financial problems for the elderly. All financial resources—income, investments, savings, insurance, pensions, etc.—may assume a great deal of importance. Women tended to be more limited than men in the financial resources at their disposal. Annual incomes of less than $1,000 were reported by about four women in ten; only 20 per cent of the men were in this income bracket.

The data show an inverse relationship between age and income. The proportions of both men and women with very low incomes were higher in the upper age brackets. Fourteen per cent of the men between sixty-five and seventy years of age had an income of less than $1,000; among those over eighty, 34 per cent were in this low income group. Of the women between sixty-five and seventy, 27 per cent had less than $1,000. Fifty-five per cent of the women over eighty had an annual income of less than $1,000.

Because older people vary greatly in their general situation (sex, marital status, housing, health, standard of living, etc.), income may not directly correspond to ability to meet financial commitments. Consequently, respondents were asked to judge the adequacy of their incomes to meet their needs. An overall total of 14 per cent reported that they did not have enough money on which to live. Only 17 per cent reported that they had more than enough income on which to live comfortably. Approximately forty per cent indicated that they had just enough to get by. These figures provide a basis for understanding the older person's fear of extraordinary expenses.

While there was a positive relationship between actual income and judgments of adequacy of income, the association was far from perfect (see Table 3). Some older persons with very low incomes indicated that they have more than enough money while others with relatively high incomes felt that they did not have enough money. The married and unmarried as well as the retired and employed were alike in judgments about income. Men and women did not differ in their judgments on the adequacy of income. Women have smaller incomes than men but do not as often have to support a spouse or children.

Table 3. Actual Income and Income Adequacy Judgment, in Percentages

		Actual Income			
Judgement of Adequacy of Income	Total (N-4089)	$0–$999 (N-1353)	$1000–$1999 (N-1092)	$2000–$3999 (N-1027)	$4000 and over (N-617)
More than enough	17	5	10	20	48
Just enough	32	19	35	40	39
Just enough to get by	36	48	37	33	11
Not enough	16	28	18	7	2
Total	100	100	100	100	100

Older people obtain money from a variety of sources. The most commonly occurring source listed was Social Security (56 per cent of the respondents). A combination of insurance, savings, and investments was the next most frequently cited source of funds. Pensions and current employment fell in third and fourth place, respectively. A total of 16 per cent received old age assistance and 9 per cent received income from children, friends, and relatives. Investing before reaching age sixty-five to assure an income thereafter was *not* the pattern for most older persons. Over half had not made any specific investments before reaching age sixty-five to provide an income later. One-fourth had invested in farm lands; other real estate investments were also popular.

In terms of the standards of the general population, the reported monetary needs of the elderly appear to be quite modest. Eighty per cent claimed they can live on less than $250 per month—this figure included expenses for both respondent and spouse among those married (see Table 4).

Table 4. Money Needed per Month, in Percentages

	Per cent of Total (N-4550)
$0–$99	23
$100–$249	58
$250–$349	12
$350–$499	5
$500 and over	2
Total	100

A large majority of the elderly lived in detached dwelling units, their own or a rented house. Among the non-institutionalized, 84 per cent were in detached dwelling units compared to 13 per cent residing in apartments. Over half of the respondents had been living in their present dwelling places for over ten years and only 22 per cent for less than five years. Those living in apartments tended to live in urban areas, were more residentially mobile, paid more for housing, and expressed less satisfaction with their living arrangements. There was some tendency for elderly apartment dwellers to be unmarried and female.

Over three-fourths of the respondents owned their own homes. Those living in rural areas were more likely to be home-owners than urban residents. Home-ownership tended to be associated with higher income levels (see Table 5).

Table 5. Home Ownership and Income, in Percentages

	Home Ownership	
	Home Owners (N-1628)	Non-home Owners (N-525)
$0–$999	29	46
$1000–$1999	30	31
$2000–$3999	26	17
$4000 and over	15	6
Total	100	100

Respondents were asked for their preferences in regard to location of living accommodations. Over half preferred to have them close to family and friends. The second highest proportion, 39 per cent, preferred them near shopping areas, and one out of five indicated a desire to be away from population centers. Thirteen per cent felt it would be desirable to live in a private community for the aged.

Approximately half reported an annual housing cost of over $500; 7 per cent spent more than $1,500 for housing. Urban dwellers tended to report somewhat higher housing costs than did those living in rural areas. Those with higher incomes tended to spend more for housing. Amount spent on housing was not related to satisfaction or dissatisfaction with present living accommodations.

Work and Retirement

For an adult in our society, employment is of obvious importance as a source of income. Particularly for males, work has additional significance in that it serves as one of the fundamental bases for an adult social identity. Because growing old is usually associated with departure from the labor force, and work is of such central importance in the general adult society, retirement is often one of the most serious problems facing the older person.

Of those in the present sample, 62 per cent considered themselves fully retired, 23 per cent as partly retired, and 15 per cent said they were fully employed. Employment status was related to both age and sex (see Table 6). Among those under seventy, half were fully retired while over 80 per

Table 6. Age and Employment Status by Sex, in Percentages

	Age			
Employment Status	65–69	70–74	75–79	80 and over
Men:	(N-686)	(N-563)	(N-490)	(N-427)
Fully retired	41	53	64	78
Partly retired	32	30	25	14
Fully employed	27	17	11	8
Total	100	100	100	100
Women:	(N-734)	(N-550)	(N-529)	(N-347)
Fully retired	55	63	74	89
Partly retired	27	23	18	7
Fully employed	18	14	8	4
Total	100	100	100	100

cent of those above age eighty were fully retired. At every age level, the proportion of men either partially or fully employed was greater than that for women.

Employment status was related to occupational identification (see Table 7). Those in professional and managerial areas were most likely to be fully employed. Skilled workers, craftsmen, service workers, and laborers were most likely to be fully retired.

Full employment was clearly related to high current income (see Table 8). Four in ten of the fully employed compared to only one in ten of the fully retired had annual incomes of over $4,000.

Table 7. Occupational Identification and Employment Status, in Percentages

	Occupational Identification				
Employment Status	Professional, Managerial (N-851)	Farmers (Owners or Managers) (N-757)	Clerical, Sales (N-597)	Skilled Workers, Craftsmen (N-535)	Services, Laborers (N-1238)
Fully retired	60	57	62	72	68
Partly retired	24	33	26	19	24
Fully employed	16	10	12	9	8
Total	100	100	100	100	100

An attempt was made to compare preferred with actual employment status (see Table 9). In a majority of cases, desired and actual employment status were identical: 60 per cent of the fully retired liked being

Table 8. Employment Status and Income, in Percentages

Employment Status	N	Total Per Cent	$0– $999	$1000– $1999	$2000– $3999	$4000 and over
Fully retired	2358	100	32	32	22	14
Partly retired	890	100	23	32	28	17
Fully employed	380	100	10	23	26	41

fully retired; 71 per cent of the partially retired preferred that status to either full employment or full retirement; and 76 per cent of the fully employed indicated a preference for full employment. At the same time, dissatisfaction with employment status was most common among the fully retired. Forty per cent of the fully retired would prefer partial or full employment. Only 24 per cent of the fully employed would like to work less or not at all. When the employed were asked why they worked, half indicated that they did so because they liked to work. The other half worked because they needed the money. Those who were employed out of financial necessity tended to plan to retire earlier than those who were employed because they liked to work.

Table 9. Actual and Preferred Employment Status, in Percentages

Preferred Employment Status	Actual Employment Status		
	Fully Retired (N-1798)	Partly Retired (N-560)	Fully Employed (N-199)
Fully retired	60	11	6
Partly retired	23	71	18
Fully employed	17	18	76
Total	100	100	100

Those who were no longer employed were asked to indicate what problems they had encountered in retirement. For the highest proportion, the most difficult aspect of retirement was the knowledge that it was no longer possible to work. A second major difficulty was having extra time on hand and not knowing exactly what to do with it. Feelings of social isolation expressed as "living alone," having "no friends," or having "no one to talk to" ranked as the third most difficult problem.

Social Life and Participation

Participation in community organizations represents one way in which the elderly might fill some of the social vacuum created by retirement. The present data, however, tend to show that the aged are not strongly oriented toward organized activity.

Religious organizations alone claimed widespread appeal among the elderly. Over eighty per cent of those interviewed reported membership in a religious organization. Social organizations were second to churches in membership but lagged far behind with only 17 per cent of the respondents. Fourteen per cent belonged to civic organizations.

Membership in an organization cannot be equated with active participation. Overall, one-fourth of the respondents reported that they were inactive in the organizations to which they belonged. Fifty-three per cent of those who belonged to social organizations indicated that they were inactive. Only 11 per cent of the church members admitted to being inactive.

Since the elderly appear to have more leisure time available, it is noteworthy that the proportion reducing participation was two to three times greater than the proportion becoming more active. Among those in the current sample, the likelihood of membership in any organization was inversely related to age (see Table 10).

The better educated, the employed, and those with higher incomes were more likely to be organization members. A slightly higher proportion of women than of men claimed organization memberships.

Table 10. Age and Membership in any Organization, in Percentages

Membership	Age			
	65–69 (N-1860)	70–74 (N-1420)	75–79 (N-1386)	80–over (N-1137)
Member	82	79	75	66
Non-member	18	21	25	34
Total	100	100	100	100

Family and Friendships

With their departure from the labor force and limited participation in organized activities, the elderly are likely to rely heavily on their contacts with family and friends. The elderly may look to their family and friends for anything from simple companionship to special assistance in times of crisis.

Eighty per cent of those interviewed had living children. A fifth said that their children were living in the same neighborhood. Four in ten reported children living in the same town or within twenty-five miles. Three-fourths of the respondents had living brothers and sisters. One-tenth had siblings living in the same neighborhood and a third had brothers and sisters living in the same town or within twenty-five miles. Frequent contact with these children and siblings is at least well within the realm of possibility.

Frequent or regular contact with friends or work associates was reported by nine out of ten respondents. A majority indicated that they had such contact with five or more persons.

While nearly all had at least some regular interaction with family, friends, and/or work associates it is noteworthy that respondents tended to hope for more activity of this kind. Slightly over one-half of the respondents said that they would like to have more contact with their children; 45 per cent preferred to retain contact at its current level. More contact with brothers and sisters was desired by almost one-half; a similar proportion wished for more contact with friends. At a time when older persons were leaving the labor force and withdrawing from formal associations, they were interested in developing more informal interpersonal interaction.

The highest rate of regular or frequent contact with non-family members was reported by married younger males living in rural areas.

Use of Time

Except for the very young, no group has as much available free time as the elderly. For many an older person, finding a way to pass the hours of the day in some meaningful fashion represents a serious challenge.

Apart from radio and television, commercial entertainment was of limited importance for most respondents. Movies were most popular among entertainment media for which it is necessary to leave home. But of those who went to the movies, a majority attended only once a month or less. Sports events follow films in entertainment appeal for the elderly.

Among hobby activities, most popular were domestic arts which include sewing, cooking, and interior decoration. This choice, no doubt, reflects the preponderance of women in the sample. Working outdoors, gardening, and the like were also popular. Reading ranked third among hobbies. The typical respondent claimed to spend approximately ten hours per week reading. Histories and biographies ranked first among the reading materials to which respondents were attracted; religious materials ranked second.

Respondents were asked to indicate the ways in which they might want to redirect the use of their free time. Informal interpersonal contacts dominated all other preferences. Forty per cent desired to spend more of their time with brothers and sisters, children, and former work associates. Increased religious participation was hoped for by thirty per cent of the respondents. Relatively few expressed a desire to spend more time participating in social and community organizations or "just sitting and thinking."

Community Services and Facilities

Respondents were asked to indicate the ways in which the activities and services of the community might best be extended for their benefit. The highest proportion of the elderly wished for facilities which would increase opportunities for social interaction with children, brothers and sisters, friends, and work associates. Maintenance of health through low-cost nursing and clinical services was a high priority item among the elderly. Some asked for assistance with financial problems while others were interested in the development of more diversified and specialized housing arrangements for older people.

Personal Adjustment

It is possible and sometimes meaningful to distinguish between the actual characteristics of a person's life style and his own evaluation of his way of life. Personal interpretation may be at odds with actual conditions. In a society which places high value on the happiness of the individual, subjective evaluations of situations assume great importance.

In the present context an attitude scale was developed to measure the older person's evaluative reaction to his own situation. The adjustment scale covered self-perceptions in six areas: health, family, work, friendship, religion, and morale. Good personal adjustment was defined as including feeling good about one's health, enjoying a number of close friendships, satisfactions with work, finding security or comfort in religion, feeling useful, placing high value on the later years, being relatively happy, and experiencing satisfaction with one's family.

Comparable adjustment data were available from Missouri, South Dakota, and Minnesota covering a total of 4,130 persons. From this group 938 (510 with very high and 428 with very low adjustment scores) were selected for an analysis of factors associated with adjustment. Those scoring high were assumed to be characterized by good adjustment and those scoring low to be poorly adjusted.

The data show a number of variables to be associated with adjustment to aging (see Table 11). A higher proportion of women than men were among the well-adjusted. Those who were married tended to be relatively well adjusted; the widowed, in turn, scored higher on the adjustment scale than those who had never married.

Those who owned their homes tended to be better adjusted than non-home-owners. There were no rural-urban differences in adjustment level.

Both education and income were associated with adjustment to aging. The well-educated and those with higher incomes were "over represented" among the well-adjusted. Employment status was also important for adjustment—the fully employed tended to be well adjusted while the fully retired were far more likely to be poorly adjusted.

Summary

In this chapter based on interviews with persons above sixty-five years of age in five midwestern states, some of the basic social conditions confronting the older person in our society have been described. The following is a summary of the major trends reported here:

Table 11. Personal Adjustment to Aging and Selected Variables, in Percentages

Variable	Combined Favorable and Unfavorable (N-938)	Adjustment Favorable (N-510)	Unfavorable (N-428)
Sex:			
Male	44	40	48
Female	56	60	52
Marital Status:			
Married	45	57	30
Widowed	39	32	47
Others	16	11	23
Home Ownership:			
Owners	81	84	77
Non-owners	19	16	23
Residence:			
Rural	15	15	15
Urban	85	85	85
Education:			
0–8 years	61	54	68
9–12 years	22	24	20
13 years and over	17	22	12
Income:			
$0–$1,000	35	24	48
$1,000–$2,000	27	31	23
$2,000–$4,000	20	23	17
$4,000 and over	18	22	12
Employment Status:			
Fully retired	59	43	79
Partly retired	22	30	12
Fully employed	19	27	9

1) Maintenance of health was a major problem for many respondents. Ability to pay for exceptional medical services was a source of concern for many.

2) Most tended to have only very limited financial resources at their disposal, but reported their income to be adequate at least in terms of ordinary expenses.

3) Respondents tended to be residentially stable, living primarily in their own homes.

4) Most were fully retired and a majority were satisfied with their employment status. But dissatisfaction with employment status occurred most often among the fully retired and least often among the fully employed.

5) Apart from church-related activities, relatively few reported membership, participation, or interest in social or civic organizations.

6) Relationships with family and friends were very important for most respondents. Most reported a good deal of contact with children, brothers, sisters, friends, and work associates. The predominant sentiment was in the direction of an increase in contacts of this kind.

7) In making use of free time, respondents tended to show a preference for activities of an informal nature which allowed them to remain close to home.

8) When asked how the community might best extend its services for their benefit, the greatest number asked for increased opportunities for informal social interaction with family and friends.

9) Favorable adjustment to aging was shown to occur most frequently among women, the married, home-owners, the well-educated, those with higher incomes, and the fully employed.

CHAPTER 20

Mobility of Older People*

COURTNEY B. CLELAND

From the comments of most demographers and research sociologists, one mainly gains the impression that the aged do not move much—for example, that they are much less likely to migrate than younger people. This generalization almost demands further exploration. It gives no idea of the great variation in mobility among older people, particularly as related to differences in communities. It says nothing about the attitudes and the motives of the people themselves, or about the other key factors in their movements which help to shape the varieties of the aging sub-culture in midwest America. It is unsafe to assume, for example, that a community with a top-heavy age structure is necessarily a "dying" community. Only by focusing on concrete cases, individuals, and communities does one begin to sense the actual situation.

It is the aim of the writer to review the literature on this subject, to call attention to unanswered questions, and to suggest that a typology of communities can contribute to an analysis of elderly migration. An intensive look at one North Dakota community may help the discussion. The assertions of this particular chapter will be directed mainly toward the smaller communities.

Previous Research Studies

Information about mobility among the aged seems meager. Most of the published studies are statistical works dealing solely with the demography and ecology of the aged for the nation or relatively large areas, such as states. There are few researches focused on aged migrants in specific communities dealing with questions of attitude and motivation.

*Acknowledgment is made for financial support from Community Studies Inc. of Kansas City, Missouri, North Dakota State University, and the North Dakota Institute for Regional Studies, Fargo, North Dakota.

323

Vance showed that the pattern of migration of the aged from 1910 to 1950 followed that of the entire nation, in flowing to the Pacific coast, to the industrial Northeast, and to Florida, but the stream was proportionately less than that for the younger population. In the North Central states, he noted, elders "disproportionately prefer rural-nonfarm communities."[1]

For the period 1935-1940 Thompson made a study that showed migration was less significant in accounting for the location of older people in the United States than for the total population. Fewer than 4 per cent of the migrants of that period were over sixty-five years of age, although that age group then composed almost 7 per cent of the total population.[2]

Hitt developed a method to estimate gains and losses of states between 1940 and 1950.[3] California, Florida, and Texas were the leading states to gain in elderly population through in-migration. Every one of the North Central states was a "loss" state, with Iowa, Missouri, and Minnesota among the largest losers in the nation because of out-migration. On a relative basis, however, the greatest loss of oldsters was that of North Dakota. Hitt calculated that the aged population of North Dakota in 1950 was 13.4 per cent below the "expected" number. South Dakota was the second highest loser at 8.4 per cent, and Nebraska also ranked high among the states in relative loss.

The deliberations of the White House Conference on Aging in 1961 included an observation that the mobility rate of those over sixty-five in the United States was only one-quarter that of the twenty to twenty-four age group. While a relatively low rate, it had been increasing.[4] U. S. Census data indicated that as of 1950, older people were moving almost as frequently, however, as those of middle age. "In one year between 1949 and 1950, 9.4 per cent of people over sixty-five changed homes, while 10.9 per cent of those aged forty-five to sixty-four moved, and 35 per cent of those aged twenty to twenty-four changed place of residence."[5] Almost all of the moving of older people in 1949-50 (7.2 out of 9.4 per cent) involved moves within the same county. Only one-half of one per cent of people over the age of sixty-five moved to a noncontiguous state.

The 1960 Census recorded changes of residence for the five-year period, 1955 to 1960, with movement per year apparently not quite as great as in 1949-50. Still, more than one-fourth of the people past sixty-five

---

[1]Rupert B. Vance, The ecology of our aging population, social forces, 32: 332-33, 1954.

[2]Warren S. Thompson, Our old people, in T. Lynn Smith, ed., Problems of America's Aging Population, Gainesville: University of Florida Press, 1951.

[3]Homer L. Hitt, The role of migration in population change among the aged, American Sociological Review, 19: 194-200, 1954.

[4]The Nation and Its Older People, Report of the White House Conference on Aging, Washington, D. C.: U. S. Department of Health, Education and Welfare, 1961, p. 124

[5]Robert J. Havighurst and Ruth Albrecht, Older People, New York: Longmans, Green and Co., 1953, p. 164.

changed their residences in the five-year period, and the proportion was not substantially greater in the age group, forty-five to sixty-four. The peak rate was in the twenty to twenty-nine age range (73 per cent), decreasing to a low in the age range seventy to seventy-nine years (27 per cent), with slight increase among people in their eighties.[6]

The "Prairie City" study by Havighurst and Albrecht included migration for the period 1942-48 in one Corn Belt county seat of about 7,000 population, described as "similar in size and complexity to many small cities of the Middle West."[7] Four out of ten older people made one or more moves during the six-year period of the study. Only 2 per cent of the total group aged sixty-five and over changed permanent residence to a warmer climate.[8]

Reports of demographers published in the 1950's on occasion showed somewhat differing interpretations of trends in older people's mobility. Thompson, on the basis of the 1935-40 data, concluded, "Old people are not migratory. They 'stay put' more than any other age group."[9] Vance agreed, declaring that the probability the aging will not migrate is very large. He argued that retirement has not become a definite break with the previous life and location of older people and that, in the main, "both older men and couples go on living in their familiar haunts."[10]

On the other hand, in a report published at almost the same time as Vance's, Hitt asserted that migration "is becoming an even more important force in redistributing our elderly citizens."[11] He showed that the migration of oldsters was substantially greater between 1940 and 1950 than between 1930 and 1940. He felt that the transition from an agricultural to an industrial society was tending "to free oldsters from locality moorings" and that an ever increasing number of workers would reach retirement "without having developed deep roots and firm attachments for a single locality or area."[12]

T. Lynn Smith was like Hitt in emphasizing recent increases in the amount of migration of the aged and in long-distance migration to warmer areas. He also pointed out that in 1950 there were an estimated million fewer older persons on the farms of the United States than would have been the case had there been no migration during the decade 1940-1950.[13] Bowles commented that out-migration of aged from the farms is largely dependent upon such factors as: (1) death of spouse, (2) financial ability

[6]Bureau of Census, United States Census of Population: 1960, Detailed Characteristics, United States Summary, Final Report Pc(1)-1D. Washington, D. C.: United States Government Printing Office, 1963, pp. xv-xvi.

[7]Havighurst and Albrecht, op. cit., p. 227.

[8]Ibid., p. 320.

[9]Thompson, op. cit., p. 12, and Population Problems (4th ed.), New York: McGraw-Hill, 1953, p. 304.

[10]Vance, op. cit., p. 334.

[11]Hitt, op. cit., p. 200.

[12]Ibid., p. 195.

[13]T. Lynn Smith, Fundamentals of Population Study, New York: J. B. Lippincott, 1960, pp. 483-84.

to leave the farm, and (3) customs, such as moving to town when the farm is turned over to the son.[14]

In discussing reasons for elderly migration, Vance asserted that migration is a function of economic position and that the most likely migrants will be those with retirement incomes.[15] Further, if they do lack economic resources, he said, the old people will tend to move where their children have moved, and this will be more evident for single oldsters than for couples.[16]

The Prairie City study brought this question down to the community level. On the whole. Prairie City was seen as a community where older people stayed to live out their last years.[17] The usual move was from one house to another, within the same town, undertaken for reasons of personal convenience. After age seventy-five a large number of moves were the result of ill health, with the older person moving to a nursing home, county infirmary, home for the aged, or mental hospital.[18]

Needed Research and Theory

One could wish for more studies of aged migration involving field work in a variety of communities. The 1960 surveys of aging done in five Midwest states suggested the need for more specific research on the community environments of older people, particularly those who had relocated their residences.[19] For example, the village and city samples included a substantial number of former open-country residents, but there were not sufficient data to analyze the precise patterns and motives of migration.

The literature on the movement of older people as related to community variables is slim. Smith and Marshall assert that "it is logical to infer that retired farmers, their wives, and especially their widows, have moved into the villages, towns, and small cities in the districts in which their farms are located. There are, however, few, if any data which bear directly upon this subject, and all the conclusions involved must rely solely upon inference."[20]

The effort to arrive at generalizations about differences in mobility of the aged among communities on the basis of demographic and ecological data has had an inconclusive result, at best. Even Cowgill, in his excellent study published elsewhere in this volume, is exceedingly tentative about some of his generalizations. As an example, he speaks of the counties in western

---

[14]Cited in Walter L. Slocum, Agricultural Sociology, New York: Harper, 1962, pp. 79-80.

[15]Some support for this view is found in the study by Charles R. Manley, Jr. The migration of older people, American Journal of Sociology, 59: 324-331, 1954.

[16]Vance, op. cit., p. 331.

[17]Havighurst and Albrecht, op. cit., p. 329.

[18]Ibid., p. 165.

[19]Studies done in Iowa, Minnesota, Missouri, North Dakota, and South Dakota are summarized in Marvin J. Taves and Gary D. Hansen, As Senior Citizens See Themselves—A Survey of Aging in the Upper Midwest, Midwest Council for Social Research in Aging, 1961.

[20]T. Lynn Smith and D. G. Marshall, Our Aging Population: the United States and Wisconsin, No. 5, Wisconsin's Population Series, April 1963, p. 31.

North Dakota which declined in percentage of aged population from 1950 to 1960, assuming the decline to be part of the general out-migration from this area. He believes that the cities of the Great Plains are unattractive to the aged. This is best regarded as a hypothesis, however, pending further research. At least in western North Dakota, some of the low percentages of aged in these communities may be due to their recent "pulling" characteristics for young people (largely because of oil development in the 1950's), reducing the relative importance of older in-migrants but not necessarily their absolute numbers.

As a group, previous research studies on mobility of the aged do little except to paint a few broad demographic strokes, which could even be misleading. Hitt's work showing the high net losses of older migrants from the upper Midwest is a case in point. While a good contribution, taken by itself it may de-emphasize the even more important shifting of older population *within* the states.

The net loss of aged migrants from North Dakota of 13.4 per cent in the 1940's, observed by Hitt, appeared to decline in the 1950's. According to Marshall's estimate, provided especially for this volume, it was down to 7.1 per cent. Marshall goes even further: he shows the estimated losses and gains county by county. Within North Dakota, in some of the more rural counties, losses because of net out-migration in the 1950's ranged as high as an estimated 50 per cent of the elderly males in Billings County. Conversely, some of the counties with greater urban population showed substantial gains of older people because of net in-migration.[21]

This within-state mobility, outweighing the out-of-state migration, is characteristic of the aged in all Midwest states and has implications for an aging subculture. If there are clusters of older people being attracted to particular places in such numbers that they constitute large segments of those communities, this is a fact of first-rank social and economic importance. In states like North Dakota, these communities turn out to be mainly the rural trade centers. From the 1960 U. S. Census one may note that, among the fifty states, North Dakota ranked twenty-fifth in the percentage of people sixty-five or older, but it ranked twelfth in the proportion concentrated in towns of between 1000 and 2500 in population.

There is a need, then, for more field research, and there is a need also for theory to give direction to community studies of both aged migrants and aged nonmigrants. The theoretical orientation of most behavioral scientists holds that nearly all the relationships between the individual and the community are strongly affected by age. Throughout the individual's life history, age is one of the important criteria for the assigning and changing of role and status.[22] Students of migration point out that this change

---

[21]Courtney B. Cleland, Shifting population in North Dakota and its relation to the aged, in Action for the Aging, Grand Forks: University of North Dakota Press, 1962, pp. 44-46.

[22]Samuel M. Strong, Types of adjustment to aging, Proceedings of the Minnesota Academy of Science, 25-26: 398-405, 1957-1958.

of role and status is often accompanied by change in the community of residence. However, we know more about this age-linked migration in connection with younger people than with the older groups.

The opening chapter by Arnold Rose, "The Subculture of the Aging," provides a frame of reference which suggests questions to be explored, both with the aged migrants and in their communities of residence. For example:

"To what extent is there evidence of an aging subculture in the communities studied, and what part, if any, does it play in the movement of individual aged persons? Are the aged more integrated into very small communities, more segregated in larger ones? Do older people use interaction with peers as a partial substitute for interaction with children, and is it a factor affecting their decision to migrate or not to migrate? Is the virtual lack or scarcity of even part-time employment in small towns a force making for an increased 'aging group consciousness'? When one finds numerous widows living in a small town, most in their own separate domiciles, can one assume presence of an aging subculture? How do such factors operate as 'push' or 'pull' factors in aged migration? Why do the aged of one small community exhibit greater interest in adult education and recreational activities than do those in another small community in the same region? Is this to be interpreted as an index of aging subculture or, on the contrary, better integration of aged persons into the total community? Why do some aged migrants prefer the subculture in which little is offered to, or asked of, them?"

For determining the relationship of aged migration to community structure and community attitudes, it is argued that the "subculture" frame of reference provides a fresh set of concepts, capable of raising provocative questions for research. When a researcher goes into a community, then, he should be aiming not merely to interview individual oldsters as to why they choose to live there. He should also be alert to any signs that there is a pattern of life, a subculture, that has been developed by the group of older people. Are they engaged, or disengaged, in community activities? Are they preoccupied with their own interests? How do they feel about the community, and how does the rest of the community feel about them?

Such a procedure is bound to increase our knowledge of the aging subculture at the community level. Consider the probable variation among small communities alone in the United States. One could construct a typology of such small communities from the standpoint of their function as residences for older people. Each type contains an example of an aging subculture:

1. There is the village that has a declining economic base and is virtually nothing but a retirement town by default, so to speak. It has not enough young married couples raising families to provide even potential population replacements; thus it may be known as a "dying" community. Older people stay on because they believe they have no alternative. Probably more old women than old men characterize the sex composition.

2. Another type of small community has little to offer in the way of the

usual agricultural or industrial activity but because of low living costs and favorable climate, or special recreational advantages, it becomes a "target area" for retired people of moderate or poor means who seek out such places. If it is in a fishing and hunting region, it attracts more older men than women.

3. A third type of community flourishes as a rural trade center with a sound economic base. It too is the home of a substantial number of older people, chiefly because they prefer it to other places. Since the economy has diminished manpower requirements, with out-migration reducing the number of younger and middle-aged people, and because their own average length of life has increased, those older people (including many widows) have emerged as a larger and larger segment of such communities. But these are hardly "dying" communities.

Focusing on older people, then, one notes communities in which they are stranded, or held, or to which they are attracted. There are probably other types—for example, the new suburb from which older people may feel excluded or pushed out or the "bedroom" community with a bimodal age distribution involving younger adults who commute to jobs and older people who supervise the children and handle various duties at home. Each type of community has within it the possibility that the older residents may develop a way of life which can be called an "aging subculture." There may or may not be aging group consciousness as a determinant and/or result of the aging subculture.

While it is beyond the scope of the present research to provide field studies of all these community types, it may be instructive to consider one community case, illustrating the third type described above. It will be noted that the older people in the town of Northwood are not an employed group, not an impoverished group, not "stranded" or isolated, and not greatly lured by warm climates. No claim is made that this community is atypical; in fact, it is probably somewhat representative of rural trade centers serving the more prosperous agricultural areas in the Midwest.

Aging People in an Aging Community*

Recent events have made Northwood, North Dakota, increasingly aware of the "age" factor in its community life. In 1959 this town of 1,195 people celebrated the seventy-fifth anniversary of its founding, with all the special celebrations and publications appropriate to a diamond jubilee. In 1960 the Census revealed that one-fourth of its people were sixty-five years of age or older. It was publicized that no other town or city in the state had so large a percentage of aged. (See Fig. 1.) It is said that the town attracted the attention of the medical researcher, Dr. Paul Dudley White, who collected data in the community for a coronary disease study.

*Acknowledgment is made for interviewing and other assistance to the following persons: Dr. William Hawkinson, Mrs. William Hawkinson, Miss Bertie Hagberg, John Wardwell, LeRoy Bollinger, and Tom Pagel.

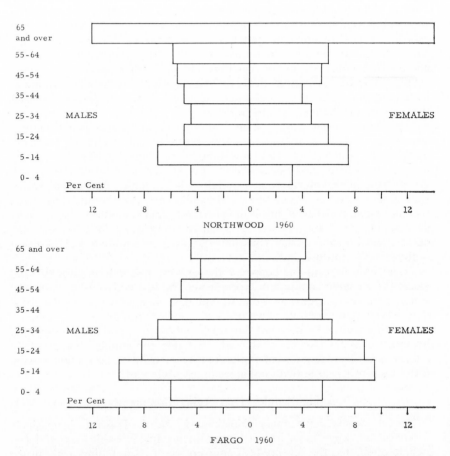

FIG. 1. Contrast in "population pyramids" showing the relative role of the aged. Northwood (upper pyramid), like many small towns, has a large percentage of people over the age of sixty-five years. Fargo, a city of 47,000 population (lower pyramid), has a much smaller proportion of aged.

Northwood is a compact village, roughly square in shape, with streets and avenues that average eight blocks in length. To the north is the paved state highway. Along the eastern edge is the railway, agribusiness, and business sections. To the south is the city park and swimming pool. Forming a logical progression along the western boundary are the medical clinic, hospital, chapel, old people's home, nursing home wing, and—the cemetery. In the approximate center of the town are found the public school and the spires of two brick Lutheran churches. These serve as focal points around which revolves the life of a community which is agricultural, politically and morally conservative, and Norwegian in ethnic background.

There is a self-contained whole to the community which impresses the observer. It is a "complete" community in that it has at least one of all the major social institutions. Yet if the town were any smaller, these facilities would hardly be adequate. It is small enough to be "primary" and almost "cumulative" in its groupways. Therein evidently lies some of its appeal for the aged group. If the town were larger, it would show more definite traits of urbanness. Since it has the asset of being comparatively rich, it can be both small and modern, with home and community improvements added frequently.

Although Northwood is aging, it is not a dying community. Its population size has been remarkably stable, hovering around the one thousand mark for forty years, but never failing to show a slight increase from decade to decade. Northwood's sizeable old people's home has operated for over fifty years. Many of the individual residences in the town are occupied by retired farm couples and elderly widows. In-migration of older people has helped to maintain population size, and servicing their needs has contributed to the town's economy.

The real basis of Northwood prosperity, however, is in the surrounding thousands of acres of flat, fertile Red River Valley farming land, devoted to such crops as potatoes, small grains, and sugar beets. The result is seen in the resources of the local bank totaling several millions of dollars, the substantial grain elevators and potato packing plant; the large local trucking line; the automobile, farm implement, hardware, and other dealers. Northwood depends upon farmer business. It appears to be gaining at the expense of other small trade centers nearby. In fact, its greatest business competition comes from larger cities like Grand Forks and Fargo, which are thirty-five to ninety miles distant.

Of particular importance for Northwood's role as a retirement town is the Deaconess Hospital and Home, basically supported by nineteen Lutheran church congregations in the area. For decades it has provided Northwood with a facility which many larger communities still only dream about—an integrated complex of residential, medical, and hospital services enabling patients to move freely back and forth between units according to their varying needs. Residents and patients are therefore drawn from a greater distance than the normal area for a trade center of this size. (See Fig. 2.)

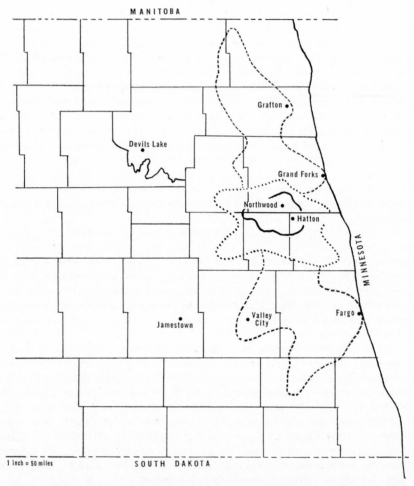

FIG. 2. The territory immediately surrounding Northwood (solid line) is its primary trade area. Beyond it is a secondary area (dotted line) which is to some extent influenced by the community or utilizes it for a particular service, such as the hospital or the weekly newspaper. The elongated area ranging up and down the North Dakota side of the Red River Valley (broken line) reflects the influence of the old people's home and is based on the origins of current residents or patients and recent applicants.

Any institution old enough and proud enough has developed its own methods of inducting new members. This the old people's home has done through its church connections and such devices as the widely circulated Northwood *Emissaeren,* an eight-page monthly newspaper of comment and news in Norwegian and English. The ninety-two-year-old chaplain of the home has served continuously as its editor since 1914.

Next to agriculture itself, the Deaconess Hospital and Home ranks as the largest industry in Northwood, providing full- or part-time employment for approximately a hundred people. Northwood also has a small hotel which functions as a kind of home for a number of unattached aged persons. But approximately two-thirds of Northwood's three hundred older citizens live in their own domiciles in the town, with the probability about four to one that they own rather than rent.

It is within this community context that one must consider the mobility of Northwood older people, which appears to be of four types:

1. Relocation of residences within the immediate community area—short moves of 15 miles or less.

2. Permanent intercommunity moves—a smaller fraction of the total movement.

3. Seasonal mobility involving winters "on the Coast" or in other warm climates—a way of life valued by some, a reality for a few.

4. Extended trips—for example, lengthy visits to an adult child in another city or state.

Out of the 109 aged residents in a 33 per cent random sample interviewed in March, 1963, only one had been a lifelong resident of the town. The largest number, 50, had moved in from farms near Northwood. Fourteen came from elsewhere in Grand Forks County. From other counties in the state, usually nearby counties, came 32 residents, and they were mostly in the old people's home. About a quarter of the other-county group came from the single community of Hatton, Traill County, twelve miles distant.

Remaining in the sample were only 11 who had migrated from another state (California, Minnesota, or Washington) and one directly from another country. Sixty out of the 109 total had moved into Northwood within the last ten years. Sixty-eight had had *two* or more changes of residence within the last ten years, and this greater mobility was noticeably more true of those in the old people's home than of those living in their own residences. Many of the latter had moved into Northwood before 1950.

The Seasonal Migrants

Practically everyone in the sample knew of residents who spend the coldest winter months in a warm climate, but it would seem the actual volume of this seasonal mobility is perhaps overestimated. There was an impression that a great amount of it existed ("half the town goes," etc.). When pinned down, the average oldster could name fewer than four persons who were seasonal migrants currently. However, there *was* a history among the more affluent elderly of wintering in a warm climate earlier in their retirement, but as they grew older, less agile (and perhaps less affluent), they tended to cease doing it.

Another clue was that only 16 in the aged sample "strongly approved" of seasonal mobility for themselves. There were 40 who approved, 21 undecided, 21 disapproved, and 7 *strongly* disapproved. Many of the disapprovals came from respondents who were of greater age, poorer health, and/or lower income than the others.

Among people who did go elsewhere for the winter, the preferred states were California, Arizona, Texas, Florida, and Washington, according to the reports of the respondents. It was their opinion that the seasonal migrants were attracted to those particular states by climate, presence of relatives there, and "curiosity." But a substantial number did not know why some winter travelers preferred certain states. These latter respondents seemed to reflect the attitude, "Why would they ever want to leave Northwood?"

Among the town's more affluent elderly and near-elderly, there is ample debate about the pro's and con's of the ideal community for retirement. Exchange of firsthand reports about Mesa, Arizona, or Sun City, California, is common coin in this group. But more such moves are planned, or at least discussed, than ever take place. Even the most assiduous of the seasonal migrants has strong reasons for returning each spring to home base. To change residence permanently would require not only painful adjustments in self-concept ("Who am I?" is in part "Where am I?") but also raises eminently practical questions such as where to vote, where to take out a driver's license, where to own property, and where to have income and pay taxes.

Seasonal mobility sometimes coincided with extended trips to visit children, but not necessarily. There were 73 parents in the sample who had a total of 263 adult children, of whom only 77 lived beyond a day's bus or train travel from Northwood. There were 20 children who lived in the same household, 91 within a one hour's automobile drive, and 46 within a day's drive. At least two-thirds of the adult children lived in North Dakota and Minnesota.

The rest of the children were scattered over twenty-two states, Canada, and overseas. Most of these states were in the West, headed by California, Washington, and Montana in that order. Only five children were in Eastern seaboard states. Fourteen parents made the long trip to visit their children every year, but a more common pattern was a trip to California or Washington every two to three years to visit several adult children who were established in the same distant state. If a parent had one child on the East coast and one on the West coast, he was likely to visit neither.

Motives for Movement

When they were asked why they had moved into Northwood, no one mentioned any of the "nine reasons why it is smart to live in a rural town" found in one of the currently popular "retirement handbooks."[23] The chief reason given by one-third of the sample members for moving into Northwood was that it was their home community; their migration was simply the change from farm to town and is sometimes better termed "relocation."

The most important motive was the desire to be near children or other relatives in Northwood. To be near property or business interests was a concern of about 20 per cent. Poor health and advancing age were mentioned next most frequently as explanations of their moves, which is another way of stating the first reason for relocation within the same community. Eleven respondents, mostly welfare recipients, said there was "no other place." Other reasons mentioned less frequently were the presence of friends in Northwood, the churches in Northwood, a desire to leave the farm, and the low living costs in Northwood.

Attitudes expressed toward the community were more favorable than adverse. When respondents were asked what things they thought were *good* about living in the town, they mentioned mainly "friendly people" or specific facilities like the hospital, the old people's home, or the churches. They used complementary words like "progressive," "clean," "moral," "civic pride," and "nice town." As a place to live, Northwood was rated as "good" by 77, "fair" by 25, "poor" by only 2. Five did not know.

In order to tap less favorable attitudes, a question was asked to determine those things which respondents thought were *not* good about living in Northwood. Half the sample offered no comment or complaint at all. Lack of recreation, or poor recreation, was cited 30 times, with a small but vocal group opposed to "booze" and "cards" and deploring the presence of beer taverns in the town. There were 26 comments which were interpreted as criticisms of local government, such as the level of taxes, the quality of town services, or activities of local officials. Ten oldsters were unhappy about poor transportation in and out of Northwood. There were 9 general complaints about people indicated by such terms as "narrow," "clannish," "hoggish," "too busy," or "too many Norwegians." Nevertheless, it should be recalled, only 2 respondents rated Northwood as a "poor" place to live.

When the respondents were asked what their *main interests* were in the community today, the replies of greatest frequency were as follows: friends, 52; church, 50; relatives, 32; children, 31; maintaining their home, 40; ownership of land or property, 19; job or business interests, 12; grandchildren, 11. Town politics and organizations such as the American Legion and the Homemakers Club were of intense interest to some.

"Sit and talk" seemed to be a primary interest and recreation for many oldsters. Yet the researchers were surprised at the number of individuals who had relatively little contact even with next-door neighbors. Perhaps after a person has spent the majority of his years in a relatively isolated occupation such as farming, he or she does not seek or expect many visitors.

---

[23]Joseph C. Buckley, The Retirement Handbook (2d ed.), New York: Harper, 1962, pp. 240-41.

On the other hand, retired businessmen and others who were in much contact with the public in their earlier years were more likely to want to "visit" with people.

It might be questioned whether the few migrants from a great distance had really changed communities much in coming to Northwood. In some cases it was simply a return to the old home town. With others it might be argued they still were circulating in a community of Norwegian Lutheranism whether it happened to be one in western Washington or one in North Dakota. On the other hand, personal factors cannot be discounted. In the old people's home there was a colony of former Hatton residents who had little interest in Northwood as such and who were hoping for the construction of a rest home in nearby Hatton, also a Norwegian Lutheran community, to which they would like to return because they "know people there."

The "Home" Subculture

If the aged of Northwood possess a subculture, then it almost might be said that the residents of the old people's home have a sub-subculture, which is characterized by distinctively less attachment to the community. In general, they have arrived in Northwood more recently and are more likely to come from outside the immediate locality. Some of them are in the home primarily because they were "shopping around" for a rest home some place, and the one in Northwood happened to have a vacancy when they needed it. They may have few acquaintances in the town and, when asked about their main interests in Northwood, may give a reply like "my room in the home" indicating little interaction with the larger community. They are not as likely as the oldsters in town to regard their incomes as adequate, and a larger proportion of them must accept at least some old age assistance. Despite their greater average age and poorer average health, the old people's home residents are potentially a more mobile group, so far as their attitudes are concerned, and are more likely to look with favor upon the possibility of moving from Northwood, as in the case of the former Hatton residents.

According to their own statements, the *only* reasons that appear capable of prying very many of the other older people out of Northwood would be in order to be closer to children, relatives, other friends. As Hawkinson points out in another chapter (Chapter 11), however, more contact with children is something wished for rather than actually expected. Seventy out of the 109 said flatly they would *never* consider moving from Northwood, and this attitude appears to be a manifestation of community loyalty rather than narrow horizons as such. Of course, there are always atypical cases—such as the oldster who was plotting how to get into another rest home which would be closer to the community in which his cemetery lot is located!

Seventy-four respondents claimed that *in the past* they had "never" considered moving from Northwood, 23 said they had "at times," and 7 had considered it "often." Those who had considered moving but chose to stay in Northwood did so for a variety of reasons. Problems of health and age, except for three individuals in the old people's home, surprisingly were not mentioned. The reasons they decided to stay were about the same ones that attracted them in the first place—presence of relatives, friends, business property, or just the fact that Northwood was familiar to them and they liked it. Only 6 reported they were now "eager to leave," 74 were "eager to stay," and 29 were classified as "probably stay but not eager to stay."

In Chapter 18, Cowgill speaks of small towns "loaded" with elderly people, perhaps leading to a kind of saturation point which drives some of them out. Another possibility he mentioned is that the out-migration of the aged is merely an aspect of a stagnant economy. Neither of these hypotheses appears to fit a community like Northwood.

At one point during the interview, sample members were asked the hypothetical question, "If you were able to choose any place in the United States in which to live after retirement, where would you choose to live?" Fifty-seven per cent still would prefer North Dakota to any other place, most of these specifying Northwood. The 48 individuals who named a location other than Northwood tended to give greater nearness to relatives as the reason for their choice, especially when naming communities in North Dakota, Minnesota, or Wisconsin. Better climate was most often given as the reason for choosing California, Arizona, and Washington.

Summary of the Sample

A few other basic characteristics of the sample should be mentioned. The mean average age of the 109 respondents was 76.1 years. Among the old people's home and hotel residents, it was higher—80.8 years. There were 49 males and 60 females. Only 39 were married and still living with their spouse. Forty-seven were widowed, 20 were single, and 3 were married but not residing with their spouse. Only 18 out of the 109 were high school graduates. Fifty-nine had been born in North Dakota, 22 in other states, and 28 in other countries. Of the latter group, 19 had been born in Norway.

Out of the 109 sample members, 74 had been farmers or farm housewives. Seventy-five had two or more sources of income, most commonly including Social Security. The latter was twice as common as the next most frequent source, which was income from a farm. Only 7 rated their present income as "not enough to live on." About half said they had "just enough to get by," and about half were living quite comfortably, according to their own estimates.

Vance had assumed that one reason why "nonmigrants" constituted so great a proportion of those over sixty-five was that they included large numbers who do not retire at sixty-five years.[24] At first glance, this point does not seem to be supported at all by the Northwood study: only 13 out of the total sample of 109 were employed part-time or full-time. On the other hand, there were 36 people who had some income from nearby farms, and it may be assumed that some of these were partly "employed" in the sense that they observed, and advised on, farm operations.

In summary, Northwood is a homogeneous, prosperous small town with which many of the aged can identify and feel comfortable. They prefer its facilities, friendliness, and familiarity. It has the basic amenities they need, particularly for medical care. For some it is literally the only community life they have known. Excursions to far-off places (including the inevitable "homecoming" to an aged relative or two in Norway) result in disillusion and reinforcement of their preference for Northwood. "I do better here," they will say. Local leaders who are now raising a half-million dollars for hospital and nursing home improvements capitalize on this feeling when they use the slogan, "People grow old in Northwood."

One limitation of the present study is that it was impracticable to search out the aged citizens, relatively few in number, who had permanently moved from Northwood, and to interview them in their new homes in other states. It is possible that they may have exhibited different attitudes toward Northwood, that they may have hated the place. A more likely hypothesis, however, is that they, too, thought highly of their former community but had moved to be closer to children and relatives or to enjoy a milder climate, or both.

It is clear that Northwood possesses many of the ingredients for one type of aging subculture. At present the aging group consciousness, however, is incipient rather than actual. The singularity of the aging subculture is simply not recognized by most of the participants. Younger and middle-aged citizens seem more aware of it than the older people themselves, who have little awareness of being considered a special group. A sizeable majority (77 out of 109) felt that Northwood residents appreciated their needs and cited as examples that "people will say 'hello'" or "they will stop and talk with you" or "in bad weather they will stop and give you rides." But older people evidently did not interpret this as special treatment. Deliberately to exclude younger people or to seek a life that would consist mainly of interaction with similar aged persons would seem to them almost a shocking idea, although that is the kind of life many of them actually have now.

In future years the effect of continued publicity, new "programs" for the aged, and their own experiences will tend to make the older people probably more conscious of their group identity. As they confirm their shared circumstances, as they come to learn from formal and informal "adult education," and as they struggle to gain or retain political power in the aging community, no doubt they will more keenly perceive and value the *new* reference group of the "senior citizen," thus providing a basis for a conscious articulation of aging subculture in Northwood.

---

[24]Vance, *op. cit.*, p. 334.

Conclusion

Some demographers have asserted that the interstate mobility of people over the age of sixty-five in the United States is relatively minor. Many (although not all) would agree that it appears to be increasing and that there is a substantial amount of seasonal mobility. All would agree that the shifting of residences by the older population within their respective states is a phenomenon of considerable magnitude.

With the limited amount of field research done in the past, it is difficult to generalize confidently about the characteristics and motives of aged migrants. There appears to be a need for more community studies focused on this particular group. The concept of aging subculture suggests the value of distinguishing among different types of communities in which older people may be variously stranded, attracted, held, or excluded.

Northwood was studied as a single case of a rural trade center with some in-migration of older people and a remarkable holding capacity for its maturing long-time residents. Apparently many oldsters feel most at home in an environment similar to that of their more youthful or productive years. Northwood has an edge over the average rural village in that it also provides services for medical care, including hospital, nursing home, and rest home. An aging subculture appears present, but not as yet an aging group consciousness.

The case of prosperous Northwood may explode some arm-chair theories which assume a rural community with top-heavy age structure is a "dying" community. It is, however, only one case. Broader generalization about the mobility of older people must await further field research, particularly in other types of communities.

CHAPTER 21

Migration and Older People in a Rural Community: The Story of Price County, Wisconsin*

DOUGLAS G. MARSHALL

Introduction

The northern counties of Wisconsin along with parts of Minnesota and Michigan form a distinctive ecological region formerly known as the "cut-over."[1] The term "Lake States Cut-Over" refers to an area defined by Forster and Beck in their research monograph of 1935, "Six Rural Problem Areas." The northern limits of this region were defined by the Great Lakes and Canadian border, and the southern boundary by growing season and soil type. The southern boundary cuts across portions of Minnesota, Wisconsin, and Michigan. In Wisconsin this area includes eighteen counties which form about the northern one-third of the state. The total area was formerly forested, but most of the area had been logged by the 1930's and hence the name "cut-over." Much of this area has been reforested or has lost its barren look. A more neutral term for the Wisconsin portion would be Northern counties or North, and when so used in this chapter refers to the original eighteen counties included in the Wisconsin cut-over, namely, Ashland, Bayfield, Burnett, Douglas, Florence, Forest, Iron, Langlade, Lincoln, Marinette, Oconto, Oneida, Price, Rusk, Sawyer, Taylor, Vilas, and Washburn. Price County is located in the heart of the Wisconsin sector of this region and, therefore, is representative of the region as a whole.

---

*An adaptation of Research Bulletin 220, University of Wisconsin Agricultural Experiment Station, June, 1960 entitled, The Story of Price County, Wisconsin, by Jon A. Doerflinger and D. G. Marshall.
[1]P. G. Beck and M. C. Forster, Six Rural Problem Areas—Relief, Resources, Rehabilitation, Washington: Federal Emergency Relief Administration, Research Monograph 1, 1935, p. 11.

Price County in Historical Context

The history of the region has been traced to show some of the major causes of the distressing situation which could be found in the county during the 1930's. The great depression accentuated the problems outlined, but the basic ingredients for a maladjustment of human to physical resources preceded the depression. The conditions which existed in the late 1930's and had their genesis in the history of settlement may be stated as follows:

1. An imbalance of human resources to the limited physical resources, actual or potential.

2. A certain degree of physical isolation caused by sparse settlement and low population density.

3. Cultural isolation caused by concentration of nationality groups within the area.

4. A sex ratio imbalance due to the in-migration of more males than females in the early settlement of the county.

5. Inefficient use of the existing agricultural land due to the prevalence of many small farms and poor farm practices.

The present data allow one to examine population trends which have occurred from 1940 to the present. Certain of these changes may be interpreted as an adjustment of the human resources to the physical resources.

Table 1. Population by Residence: Price County, Wisconsin, 1940, 1950, 1958

	1940	1950	Per cent change 1940-50	1958	Per cent change 1950-58
Urban	3,252	2,924	−10.1	2,884	− 1.4
Rural nonfarm	4,978	5,541	+11.3	6,217	+12.2
Rural farm	10,237	7,879	−23.0	5,319	−32.5
Total	18,467	16,344	−11.5	14,420	−11.8

Table 1 shows what has happened to the population of the county. One should note that the 1958 data show that the 1940-50 trends have continued in the same direction from 1950-58. Thus, total population dropped over 11 per cent from 1940 to 1950 and has continued to drop by 11 per cent between 1950 and 1958.

The most striking changes have been in the decrease of the farm population and the aging of the population. The county lost almost one-fourth of its farm population from 1940 to 1950. The 1958 statistics showed that this decrease had continued at an even greater rate. By 1958 nearly 14 per cent of the population were over sixty-five.

The rural nonfarm population is the only segment of the population that has shown a consistent increase. This increase cannot be accounted for by movement of farm people into villages, since none of the incorporated places showed an increase in population. More likely some of this gain in nonfarm population is due to a more accurate definition of what a farm is; marginal holdings classified as farm in 1940 may have been reclassified to nonfarm status in the 1950 Census and the 1958 count. It is also possible that many of the farms actually ceased farming operations between the census periods but remained as places of residence, thus swelling the non-farm population. Part of the increase can be due to the increase of in-migration to the open country, especially of older people.

A drop in the number of farms as well as in total farm population may be noted for the period. Not only has the number of farms decreased, but the trend is towards farms of larger acreage. The average size of farms has increased from 90 acres in 1940 to 155.2 acres in 1954. This change has been brought about by decreases in the proportion of farms under 140 acres and an increase in the proportion of farms over 140 acres. The per-centage of total land area in farms has not changed appreciably during the period. The figure for 1940 was 27.5 per cent, while the 1954 figure was 30.8 per cent.

The drop in the farm population, the aging of the population, the de-crease in number of farms, and the increase in size of farm, without the exploitation of much additional new land not formerly in agriculture, may be taken as signs of a basic adjustment to the problem situation. The changes in Price County have paralleled changes in the state as a whole but have occurred at a more rapid pace in Price County which has had a greater adjustment to make.

Service orientation data from the sample survey indicate that open-country people are quite mobile in meeting their trade and service needs. They are willing to travel considerable distances to exercise their pref-erences for basic services. In many of the service categories they split their patronage. A willingness to "shop around" for the best services seems to exceed the convenience of being near a center. This is especially true of health services. This evidence contradicts the image of compact, tightly organized neighborhoods and communities.

The unique nationality situation has also changed with the passage of time. Table 2 indicates that the percentage of foreign-born for the county has declined steadily since 1910. It can be seen that the proportion of foreign-born for Price County has always been higher than for the state as a whole. Quite naturally, the trend is for the proportion to decrease since the effective cutting off of immigration after 1926.

Table 2. Percentage of Population Foreign-born in Price County and in the state of Wisconsin, 1910-1950

	1910	1920	1930	1940	1950
		not			
Price County	31.2	available	21.2	16.3	12.6
Wisconsin	22.0	17.5	13.2	9.2	6.4

In the preceding section we have attempted to show that during the period from 1940 to the present the trends have been toward population and resource adjustment in Price County. Farms have become larger on the average, and there are fewer farmers than there were in the critical decade of 1930-1940. This does not mean, however, that the problems of agricultural adjustment have been solved. In 1954 the average amount of cropland per farm was only 36.7 acres as compared to an 84.6 average for the state. This indicates that probably there is still a large proportion of small farms in the county which are unable to provide a good living for their owners. Moreover, many of these operators are older people.

This is confirmed by the income data from the 1956 sample survey. In an earlier analysis of this data the basic variable was a classification of household heads by the degree of involvement in agricultural and non-agricultural activity. This classification proves to be meaningful when it is related to household income as is done in Table 3. Families of full-time farmers and of farmers with part-time nonfarm employment constitute a large proportion of the families who make less than $2,000 per year (54 per cent and 41 per cent, respectively). It is only when the head of the family has full-time nonfarm employment in addition to his farm income that the percentage of families making less than $2,000 per year drops to under 14 per cent. This does not mean farming full-time or farming with a part-time nonfarm occupation are hopeless occupational activities in the county—*some* families in both occupational categories are found in the higher income brackets. It does mean that a large proportion of Price County farmers, especially older farmers whose main pursuit is agriculture, are still economically depressed. Since farming is still the predominant occupation in the labor force and many of these farmers have low incomes, it is not unreasonable to assume that farmers contribute disproportionately to the income problem of the county as a whole.

Table 3. Total Household Income by Type of Household, Price County, Wisconsin, 1956

Household type	Under $1000	$1000-1999	$2000-2999	$3000-3999	$4000+	Total per cent
Full-time farm	26.2	27.8	18.3	10.5	17.2	100
Farm and part-time farm	15.1	26.0	27.4	19.2	12.3	100
Farm with full-time nonfarm	4.2	8.5	38.4	21.3	27.6	100
Full-time nonfarm	9.3	10.3	25.2	20.6	34.6	100
Retired	50.0	32.7	8.7	4.3	4.3	100

The population adjustments which have occurred in Price County since 1940 have in the main taken place through the mechanism of out-migration. While the trend of population reduction may be interpreted as bringing human resources into better balance with physical resources, the selective nature of migration has created an imbalance within the population which has remained in the county. The heaviest migration has occurred among the young adults (those who became twenty to thirty-four years of age at the end of the 1940 decade), both men and women. Age distributions in 1950 and 1958 reflect this loss of the youth. The 1958 population age-sex distribution (see Fig. 1) shows the deficiency of young people which one would expect in an area where large numbers of youth have emigrated.

Table 4 expresses this situation in another way. The dependent population[2] of Price County has shown a steady increase from 1940 to 1958. In 1940 the dependent population comprised 32.6 per cent of the state's population, while Price County had 35.5 per cent in this category. By 1950 over 44 per cent of the county's population was in the dependent age group, while only 36 per cent of the total state population was dependent. It is the rural nonfarm population of the county which registers the highest dependency ratio, whereas farm and nonfarm ratios were equal for the state as a whole.

Table 4. Percentage of Dependent Population, by Residence,
Price County, Wisconsin, 1940-1958

Residence	1940	1950	1958
Urban	31.0	38.0	41.9
Rural farm	36.5	39.9	42.5
Rural nonfarm	36.4	40.5	47.0
Total	35.5	39.8	44.3

Table 5 shows the number of individuals sixty-five and over as a percentage by residence of the county population. It can be seen that this figure has increased steadily from 1940 to 1958. In 1950 10.4 per cent of the county's population was sixty-five and over, whereas 9 per cent of Wisconsin's population was in this age group at that time. In 1958 nearly 14 per cent of Price County's population was over sixty-five. The non-farm element of the population has the highest proportion sixty-five and over for the county as well as for the state.

Table 5. Percentage of Total Population, Age 65 and Over, by Residence,
Price County, Wisconsin, 1940-1958

Residence	1940	1950	1958
Urban	5.2	9.0	12.3
Rural farm	7.9	9.4	10.2
Rural nonfarm	8.4	12.6	17.7
Total	7.5	10.4	13.9

The meaning of this large proportion of older citizens to the economy of the county is apparent when the income figures for the open-country families (as gathered in the sample survey) are related to the age of household heads. Among farm households, over 25 per cent of the farms with incomes less than $2,000 had heads who were sixty-five and over.

---

[2]Dependent population is defined as under fifteen years of age and sixty-five and over.

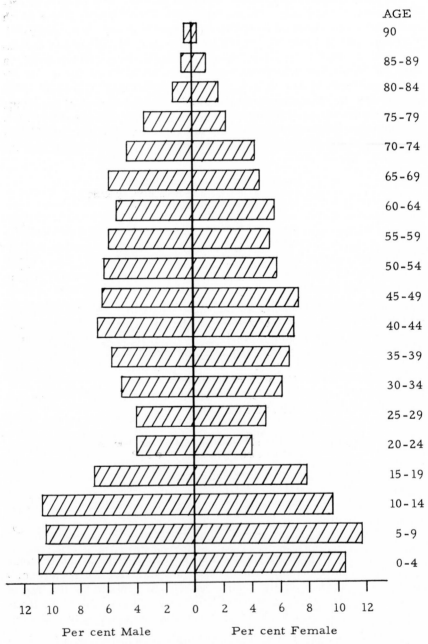

Fig. 1.   Price County, Wisconsin, age-sex pyramid, 1958.

Among those farms where income was less than $1,000 per year nearly 32 per cent of the heads were sixty-five and over. Over 82 per cent of those households classified as retired had incomes of less than $2,000 per year, and half of these households had less than $1,000 per year. The retired households were predominantly characterized by heads sixty-five and over. While low income families may be found in all age groups of heads, a disproportionate number of older people with low incomes tends to pull down the average income for the county.

An unbalanced age structure, such as that of Price County, has several disadvantages. Economically, the cost of services must be borne by a smaller proportion of the population. The high proportion of people in the older age groups also increases the welfare and health problems.

Explaining Population Change

It may be noted that in the preceding discussion of population change a comprehensive theory of population change was not employed to explain what has happened in Price County. This does not mean we have operated without a theory. Let us start with the hypothesis that an imbalance of human and physical resources leads to undesirable results. This simple statement is an abstraction of a detailed, complicated economic theory which we will have to follow in order to clarify the hypothesis. Several assumptions are inherent in this theory, and we are obliged to state these before proceeding.

First and foremost is the assumption that the individual is motivated by self-interest and that the economic self-interest of the individual coincides with the general interest. This is important, for it says in effect that any interference with the pursuit of individual self-interest will be detrimental to the economy as a whole. A "hands off" policy is recommended.

Another important assumption is that we can actually measure the effect of various combinations of human effort applied to land and capital in the process of production. This product is termed "real income," and it is the income per capita which is the relevant measure. With a given amount of capital, natural resources, and labor involved in an enterprise the addition of more labor may do one of two things: (1) It may increase per capita income because of the economics of large-scale production; or (2) it may reduce per capita income because of the operation of the law of diminishing returns.

Migration is the adjustment force in this system, for according to the assumption of self-interest, labor will drift from areas of low income to areas of high income. Theoretically, if migration is unhampered, areas which are overpopulated should lose people to underpopulated areas, and the result will be a rise in the per capita income of both places. In other words, migration has a balancing effect.

The simplest demonstration of the relation of the man-resources ratio to income level can be found in agriculture. The 1956 sample data give us a detailed picture of the farming enterprise within the county. We will not use the detailed statistics; they appear in bulletins of the Department of Agricultural Economics, University of Wisconsin. A few quotations from an earlier release will suffice:

> The sample data established the fact that average gross farm income for Price County farms ($2812) compared unfavorably with the state average ($5163). This difference cannot be accounted for in terms of poor agricultural practice because production performance per acre compares favorably to the state. It is size of cropland which accounts for much of the disparity of income. Price County farms averaged only 43 acres of cropland compared to 64 acres for the state.
>
> The importance of size of business in achieving a high level of income is demonstrated more directly by a comparison of size of business within the full-time dairy farms. (The same pattern of results is found among different sizes of business for part-time dairy farms.) In this comparison larger size (crop acres, number of milk cows, and gross sales) consistently gives higher net cash farm income.[3]

Although a large reduction in number of farms and in farm population had occurred prior to 1955, the situation we have described for that year indicates that it was still the low ratio of land and capital to manpower which accounted for the low per capita return in agriculture in Price County.

Table 6. Distribution of Households by Economic Activities of Household Head, Price County, Wisconsin, 1956

Economic Activities of Household Head	N Households	Per cent
Full-time farm	180	39.7
Farm with part-time nonfarm work	73	16.1
Farm with full-time nonfarm work	47	10.4
Full-time nonfarm work only	107	23.6
Retired	46	10.2
Total	453	100.0

Not all of Price County's income comes from agriculture. It was found convenient to divide the sample households on the basis of the involvement of the head in farm and nonfarm work. The distribution of households according to the class of economic activities of the head is indicated in Table 6.

It is apparent that only about 40 per cent of the open-country households were solely dependent upon agriculture for their livelihood. About one-fourth of these households have no connection whatsoever with agriculture. With the exception of the retired, the remainder of the families work out some sort of compromise between farm and nonfarm work. Off-farm employment does help with a critical income problem, but most nonfarm work available in the county is not sufficient to raise total income to levels which compare favorably to most other areas of the state regardless of age.

The problem is most strikingly illustrated by comparing the household income levels of Price County with their urban counterpart (see Table 7).

[3]Leo J. Moran and Sydney D. Staniforth, Rural Economic Development in Price County—The Farm Aspects, Department of Agricultural Economics, University of Wisconsin, April 1957, p. 4.

This is actually one definition of underemployment for we assume the proportion of families making less than the median figure for alternative urban employment represent the proportion underemployed. This may be an unwarranted assumption, but it certainly points up the disparity of income between Price County open-country residents and urban families in Wisconsin.

Table 7. Underemployment of Families, Price County, Wisconsin, 1955

Economic Activities of Household Head	Per cent with Income <$3,630*
Full-time farm	79.4
Farm with part-time nonfarm work	84.9
Farm with full-time nonfarm work	70.2
Full-time nonfarm work only	62.6
Retired	95.7

*Median urban income for Wisconsin, 1955.

We have already presented some data concerning emigration from Price County which were derived from the age-sex analysis of the 1940-1950 decade. It will be recalled that the heaviest emigration occurred among young adults for that period. The present evidence leads to the same conclusion: Emigration from Price County is highly selective for age, and it is the youth more than any other group who are leaving. This leaves older people.

Why does this pattern of emigration exist? It is obvious that emigration has reduced total population size, but the process has not been adjustive in the sense that real income has increased for those who have remained. It must be remembered that adjustment to optimum population size was based on the idea of productivity; therefore, we should restrict our discussion to those involved in productive enterprises. The simplest case, and the one for which we have the most data, is agriculture. Our argument can be broadened, however, if we remember that local opportunity outside of agriculture is definitely limited. The question we must answer is this: Why have not more of those persons *engaged* in low income pursuits taken advantage of higher opportunity elsewhere so as to reduce the resources-to-manpower ratio in Price County?

One of the assumptions of adjustive emigration is that people will follow their economic self-interest. But economic interest is only one of the many values people use to guide their behavior. The sum of these values constitutes the cultural heritage of a people, and cultures differ to the extent that they incorporate different values, or to the extent they differentially emphasize the same values.

It is the impression of many persons working in rural problem areas that these areas do differ in basic value orientation from the mainstreams of American life. Of course this cultural difference is more marked in the more isolated regions of our country, such as the hill and mountain regions of the Southern Appalachians. The Lake States Cut-Over has not gone through the long period of isolation which has solidified culture in these more isolated sections of our country. Some evidence indicates, however, that the value system of the northern region does differ from the more commercially oriented sections of our country. Visitors as well as natives of the North frequently remark about the slower pace of business and the high value placed on noneconomic activity. The people of Price County disclosed that they greatly valued such things as scenery, the clear air, and the availability of outdoor recreation, when asked what they liked about living in the county. They also remarked that the people—their neighbors —had the time to be friendly. These data may be interpreted as meaning that a value system exists here different from the one found in areas where commercial values predominate. For those persons who have a strong attachment to this way of life, emigration represents a sacrifice of some of their fundamental values—values which outweigh economic gain. Of course, not all residents share equally in this attitude toward their home county. By and large, *it is the older resident who has the strongest attachment to Price County.*

We do not have to rely on the idea of different value systems to explain why more adjustive out-migration has not taken place. There are reality factors about the urban job market which explain the failure of some individuals to take advantage of the lure of higher income which exists in the city or in other rural areas. Most urban employment is geared to requirements of training, education, and experience. Many of the persons who live in Price County lack minimum training and/or educational requirements to compete successfully in the urban labor market and are also older people. It is unreasonable to expect the distribution of skills found in a predominantly rural county will supply the requirements of urban demand, particularly in a time of rapidly advancing technology.

An examination of the open-country sample households reveals a level of age and education which does not favor employment on the urban market. The average age of male heads of households for the sample as a whole was 52.6 years, and the educational attainment was 7.8 years. Age and educational attainment are inversely related so that the older groups have the least amount of education. Of those engaged in both farm and nonfarm work we find that the more the involvement with agriculture the higher the age and the lower the educational attainment. Thus, full-time farmers formed the oldest group, while those who farmed and pursued full-time nonfarm work were the youngest.

Even if some of the persons in this population did possess skills which would be valuable in alternate employment, *their age and lack of formal education would be realistic factors which would count against them.* Companies may be willing to undertake training of employees, but such an investment is more likely to be undertaken in the case of younger people who will have more years of service with the company. Then, too, there are minimum requirements of formal education which might bar entry into some occupations where work is available.

Another factor which tends to inhibit adjustive emigration of the employed population is the reluctance to sacrifice equity in property. In Price County, farm ownership is among the highest in all counties of the state. Because property values are relatively low, moving in many cases means that the owner would not completely recover his investment.

The point of the foregoing discussion is that although differentials in opportunity do predict the direction of emigration, there are factors in the community which prevent emigration from achieving the ultimate economic adjustment. We know that opportunity acts as an attractive force. We have tried to show, however, that there are good and sufficient reasons why emigration will fall short of effective regional equalization. While it is true that the situation would be much worse today if emigration had not occurred, emigration of itself will not solve the problems of Price County.

The pulling out of the young people has resulted in an unbalanced age structure leaving older people. An unbalanced age structure creates an undesirable labor force potential and thus helps reduce the attractiveness of the area for new industry. Furthermore, the resultant increase in the dependent population has put additional strain on the local economy. What, then, has prevented the situation from becoming steadily worse? Why has not the cumulative chain of causation produced greater inequality than it has? Myrdal has provided an answer which is applicable to the Price County situation. He maintains that the forces of cumulative causation do not always go to extremes because in some cases we do not let them. That is to say, conscious government policy has been directed toward lessening regional inequality. A large part of the equalizing measures have taken the form of transferring financial responsibility to larger units of government. Thus, when a state takes over part of the responsibility of education by providing state aid to schools, the richer areas are in effect subsidizing the poorer. Likewise, federal categorical welfare aids are a means of combating regional inequality. We might well ask what would be the result if an area like Price County had had to provide all of its needs from its local resources? Whatever the answer, it is important to realize that we have not allowed free play to all of the forces which contribute to regional economic inequality. The policies of the past have had their effect in producing the present situation. These policies should be kept in mind when planning the future. It would be unrealistic to attribute the present situation to the free play of economic forces.

The Future

What can we expect to happen to Price County under varying conditions in the future? If we assume a general high level of national prosperity and an unchanged farm picture without an increase in local nonfarm opportunities, we can predict the established population trends will continue. Out-migration of youth will persist because the local economy does not provide for them occupationally. *Those middle-aged and older persons who choose to remain, or cannot or will not move, will swell the proportion of older persons in the remaining population.* This means that the unfavorable age structure of which we have spoken will become even worse. If, on the other hand, the general level of prosperity for the state or nation declines, we can expect a decline in the rate of out-migration for Price County. We could even look for a return of some recent emigrants, since a decline in business activities would eliminate low seniority personnel first.

Increasing local nonfarm opportunities would have the effect of re-establishing a more normal age distribution. It would also help relieve some of the farm adjustment for it is easier for most established households to shift occupationally and maintain their residence than face the double problem of a shift in residence and occupation. Increased nonfarm oppor-tunities would eventually tend to take more agricultural land out of pro-duction, since the nonfarm alternative would decrease interest in farming for those whose time is better paid in nonfarm work. The effects of change in the general business cycle would, of course, depend on the stability and permanence of the type of nonfarm economic opportunity.

Resources Use and Development. How can the goal of a smaller, but more age-sex balanced, and more prosperous, population be achieved? Fortunately, our data are of some help in plotting the course of action. We know from the past that the overemphasis on exploitation of resources for a few purposes had led to trouble. It seems clear that any plan should consider all possibilities of resource use and development. The most promis-ing seem to be in the fields of industrialization, forestry, and recreation. We will discuss these possibilities separately.

Admittedly, bringing new industry into Price County is a problem. For one thing, selective emigration has drained off some of the supply of labor needed for certain industries. This is a "chicken and egg" sort of situation: Young people leave because there is no work, and industry is reluctant to come to an area which does not have an adequate supply of young people. A second obstacle is the extreme competition now apparent in inducing new industry to come into different areas of the country.

The forest potential of Price County is very impressive if one considers the proportion of land area occupied by this important resource. Forests occupy 80 per cent of the land area of the county, with 55 per cent in private and 45 per cent in public ownership. These forests are not the virgin stands found in the 1890's or earlier. Only about 37 per cent of the stands are classified as a size above the seedling and sapling class. The greater part of commercial timber is at present in the pole size stage. Aspen is the most prevalent species comprising 36 per cent of the timber area.

The present financial contribution of forest products is an important part of the economy of the county. Estimates place the total value of rough forest products harvested at one and one-half million dollars.[4]

Woodswork is an important part of the employment picture of open-country residents. Over 13 per cent of heads of households interviewed

---

[4]Forest Management Division, Wisconsin Conservation Department, Forest re-sources of Price County, Wisconsin Forest Inventory Publication No. 32, Madison, 1958. The total value of rough forest products harvested in the county is estimated at approximately one and one-half million dollars. Over one-third of this was pulp-wood. After initial processing the value of most products was substantially increased.

derived some income from harvesting timber. These persons worked an average of nineteen weeks in the woods in 1955.

Work in developing the forest resource has concentrated on two problems: (1) increasing the proportion of higher quality timber, and (2) adding value to rough timber by secondary manufacturing of wood products within the county. Solution to these problems would increase employment opportunities for the present, and assure a more stable economy for the future.

The further development of outdoor recreation and the tourist trade is another promising field. In trying to ascertain the demand for such activities we can be sure of one thing—demand will increase because of population increases. Increased real income and more free time mean there will be more people with more time and money to spend on this kind of activity in the future. Many important questions are unanswered, however, because of lack of research. We do not know the breakdown of the particular types of facilities generally desired by the users of outdoor recreation. Nor is it known how much money tourists and vacationers bring into the local economy. Experience in other lines of merchandising would lead one to believe that people differ in the type of facilities they desire for recreational and vacation purposes. The forest and water resources are present in abundance and careful planning for recreational use can contribute to increasing local employment opportunity.

A Balanced Program. Basically, the amelioration of the problems of low income, lack of job opportunities, and other connected problems requires a balanced approach. Any plans which are developed must take cognizance of the wishes of the people and respect the rights of individuals who do not wish to become involved. It is important that individual differences be considered in the formulation of solutions. It is clear that a massive removal project would not suffice to solve the problem, but our data do indicate that some people do want to get out of agriculture but cannot do so. An agricultural program which would assist removal of these low income operators who wish to get out, while helping the more promising who wish to expand, would indeed seem preferable. Even at that, some individuals would resist because they enjoy their particular type of operation, though it may be judged inefficient by others. It represents a way of life they prefer. This is especially true of older people.

It was noted that the ultimate population of the county will probably be lower than in the past. A lower population density means that adjustments must be made in the location of services. A community organization based on a higher population cannot be supported by reduced numbers. Analysis of service orientation shows that these adjustments are being made. Open-country people are not tied to the nearest community by their needs. This means that it would be more fruitful to plan on the basis of a county level rather than on that of individual communities. Each community does not need to provide a full line of services, for what people cannot get in one community they will get in another. Such community specialization would yield a gain in efficiency and yet preserve local initiative and control.

Table 8. Percentages* of Age Groups in the Labor Force by Sex in Various Employment Statuses, Price County, Wisconsin, 1958

| | Age Groups | | | | | | | | |
	14-24	25-34	35-44	45-54	55-64	65-74	75+	Un-known	Total
Male									
Total county:									
Unemployed	21.3	6.5	2.7	2.1	3.6	0.8	1.7	...	5.0
Not fully employed	24.9	14.5	17.4	18.2	15.6	15.6	10.2	6.3	17.2
Fully employed	53.8	79.0	79.9	79.7	80.8	83.6	88.1	93.7	77.8
	(N-361)	(N-634)	(N-839)	(N-908)	(N-687)	(N-257)	(N-59)	(N-16)	(N-3,761)
Urban:									
Unemployed	10.3	3.6	2.4	1.2	3.1	2.7	14.3	...	3.4
Not fully employed	7.4	4.3	1.8	4.2	1.6	18.9	...	16.7	4.3
Fully employed	82.3	92.1	95.8	94.6	95.3	78.4	85.7	83.3	92.3
	(N-68)	(N-138)	(N-168)	(N-165)	(N-127)	(N-37)	(N-7)	(N-6)	(N-716)
Rural nonfarm:									
Unemployed	24.0	8.5	2.2	4.5	6.5	1.0	...	...	6.4
Not fully employed	20.7	10.2	13.7	16.2	15.4	18.1	20.0	...	14.8
Fully employed	55.3	81.3	84.1	79.3	78.1	80.9	80.0	100.0	78.8
	(N-121)	(N-293)	(N-322)	(N-357)	(N-279)	(N-105)	(N-25)	(N-7)	(N-1,509)
Rural farm:									
Unemployed	23.9	5.4	3.4	0.3	1.1	...	...	...	4.4
Not fully employed	34.9	27.6	28.4	25.9	22.1	12.2	3.7	...	25.5
Fully employed	41.2	67.0	68.2	73.8	76.8	87.8	96.3	100.0	70.1
	(N-172)	(N-203)	(N-349)	(N-386)	(N-281)	(N-115)	(N-27)	(N-3)	(N-1,536)
Female									
Total county:									
Unemployed	20.4	3.2	3.2	1.3	2.0	2.3	...	...	5.1
Not fully employed	6.8	19.2	21.3	19.2	15.9	15.9	16.7	16.7	17.0
Fully employed	72.8	77.6	75.5	79.5	82.1	81.8	83.3	83.3	77.9
	(N-147)	(N-125)	(N-221)	(N-234)	(N-151)	(N-44)	(N-6)	(N-12)	(N-940)
Urban:									
Unemployed	7.1	2.6	4.6	3.1	3.6	11.1	...	...	4.3
Not fully employed	4.8	7.9	10.8	20.3	21.4	11.1	...	20.0	13.2
Fully employed	88.1	89.5	84.6	76.6	75.0	77.8	100.0	80.0	82.5
	(N-42)	(N-38)	(N-65)	(N-64)	(N-28)	(N-9)	(N-2)	(N-10)	(N-258)

Male	14-24	25-34	35-44	45-54	Age Groups 55-64	65-74	75+	Un-known	Total
Rural nonfarm:									
Unemployed	15.4	1.7	2.8	....	2.1	....	....	....	3.4
Not fully employed	9.2	26.7	28.7	19.5	17.9	27.3	25.0	....	21.1
Fully employed	75.4	71.6	68.5	80.5	80.0	72.7	75.0	100.0	75.5
	(N-65)	(N-60)	(N-108)	(N-118)	(N-95)	(N-22)	(N-4)	(N-1)	(N-473)
Rural farm:									
Unemployed	42.5	7.4	2.1	1.9	....	....	....	....	10.1
Not fully employed	5.0	18.5	18.6	17.3	3.6	....	....	....	12.4
Fully employed	52.5	74.1	79.3	80.8	96.4	100.0	....	100.0	77.5
	(N-40)	(N-27)	(N-48)	(N-52)	(N-28)	(N-13)	....	(N-1)	(N-209)

*Percentages total 100.0 for each age group.

VII

Implications of Research
on the Aging

CHAPTER 22

A Current Theoretical Issue
in Social Gerontology*

ARNOLD M. ROSE

A new field of research, especially one dealing with a social problem is likely to emerge without using any explicit theory, and then gradually to adapt general theoretical formulations already in use in kindred fields. Thus, the earliest research in social gerontology was descriptive in character, but soon concepts like "adjustment," "role changes," "loss of roles," "changing self-concept" were borrowed from symbolic-interactionist theory in social psychology—a theoretical position which many of the early social gerontologists adhered to. Some authors made tentative efforts toward systematizing the adaptation of symbolic-interactionist theory for social gerontology.[1] Ernest W. Burgess, who probably can be considered to be the father of social gerontology, was also the source of the symbolic-interactionist concepts in some of the early research in the field. It was not until 1961, however, that systematic statements of symbolic-interactionist theory applied to the problems of social gerontology appeared. In the present book, we have sought to extend interactionist theory with the concepts of "the aging subculture" and "aging group consciousness." Much of the research in social gerontology today, including most of that reported in this book, is explicitly or implicitly guided by interactionist theory, broadly conceived. The utility of this theory is thus constantly being tested in empirical research work. Research in social gerontology not guided by interactionist theory has tended to be descriptive.

*A practically identical version of this paper appears in The Gerontologist, 4: 46-50, 1964. Reprinted by permission of the editor.
[1]There were two such papers written independently: (1) Arnold M. Rose, The mental health of normal older persons, Geriatrics, 16: 459-64, 1961, reprinted in this volume as chapter 12. (2) Ruth S. Cavan, Self and role in adjustment during old age, in Arnold M. Rose, ed., Human Behavior and Social Processes, Boston: Houghton Mifflin Co., 1962, pp. 526-36.

There has been one major exception, which has received considerable attention in recent years. This is the work of Elaine Cumming and her collaborators.[2] The book, "Growing Old," is a major study in the framework of functionalist theory, a theory which has guided much empirical research in anthropology but very little in sociology; hence Cumming's work is a landmark in sociological functionalism. It is the purpose of the present essay to evaluate the Cumming and Henry book as a statement of theory and as a test of a specific theory. We are not here concerned with the research method or its manner of utilization in that book. We shall also be concerned with theoretical essays written by Cumming, Henry, and Talcott Parsons after the publication of "Growing Old."[3]

There has been such widespread misinterpretation of the theory of disengagement, as expressed in the Cumming and Henry book, that it is essential to state what it is before it can be evaluated. It is *not* a hypothesis which states that, as people get older, they are gradually separated from their associations and their social functions. Such a hypothesis had been stated many times before Cumming and Henry and was generally assumed to be a fact. (After all, this is what was meant by Burgess in his discussion of the "roleless role.") Nor does the theory of disengagement state that, as people become physically feebler or chronically ill, they are thereby forced to abandon their associations and social functions. This is a matter of logic, and has also long been assumed to be a fact. Cumming and Henry wisely excluded from their sample any person who was in poor physical or mental health, and explicitly deny that their conception of disengagement rests on ill health. Finally, the theory of disengagement does *not* say that because older people tend to have a reduced income in our society, they can no longer afford to participate in many things. That also would be a matter of logic, and has long been known to be a fact. Cumming and Henry wisely excluded from their sample anyone who did not have the minimum of money needed for independence. To test *their* hypothesis, as distinguished from the popular misinterpretations of their hypothesis, Cumming and Henry had to make these exclusions.

The Cumming and Henry theory of disengagement is that the society and the individual prepare *in advance* for the ultimate "disengagement" of incurable, incapacitating disease and death by an *inevitable, gradual, and mutually satisfying process of disengagement*. Each of these terms must be understood before the theory can be understood. Disengagement is inevitable, because death is inevitable; and, according to a basic principle

---

[2] Elaine Cumming and Others, Disengagement: a tentative theory of aging, Sociometry, 23: 23-35, 1960; Elaine Cumming and William E. Henry, Growing Old, New York: Basic Books, 1961.

[3] Elaine Cumming, Further thoughts on the theory of disengagement, UNESCO International Social Science Journal, 15: 377-93, 1963. William E. Henry, The theory of intrinsic disengagement, unpublished manuscript read at the International Gerontological Research Seminar, Markaryd, Sweden, August, 1963. Talcott Parsons, Old age as consummatory phase, The Gerontologist, 3: 53-54, 1963.

of functionalism, society and the individual always accommodate themselves to the solid facts of existence. Society and the individual always seek to maintain themselves in equilibrium and avoid disruptions, according to the functionalist. Since death must soon come to an older person, both society and the older person himself prepare for it sociologically and psychologically, so that when it comes the individual has divested himself of life's functions and associations and is ready for it. In this way, the death of an older person is not disruptive to the equilibrium of a society. The death of a young person, by accident or acute disease, is disruptive, and the society has a harder time accommodating to it. Cumming and Henry compare the disengagement of an older person to the gradual and inevitable withering of a leaf or a fruit long before frost totally kills it. This total process must be gradual, in the sense that it involves a period of preparation for death, although disengagement from some *specific* association or function may come suddenly. It is mutually satisfying: Society is pleased when the death of one of its members does not disrupt its ongoing functions (such as child-rearing, carrying on economic production, or the work of one of its voluntary associations.) And the individual can face death with relative equanimity because he no longer has any social ties; he has said all his "goodbyes" and has nothing more to do, so he might as well "leave."

Because death is a universal fact, the social and psychological disengagement of the elderly must be a universal fact, according to the theory. It is thus not bound to any one culture, even though Cumming and Henry take all of their cases from Kansas City, Missouri. Of course, there are different degrees and speeds of disengagement among different societies and within any one society, some people resist disengagement while others start on its course even before they become elderly. Cumming and Henry say that the values in American culture of competitive achievement and of future orientation make this society especially negative toward aging and hence encourage disengagement. But the process itself must be understood to be inevitable and universal, according to the theory, and not limited to any one group in a society or any one society.

In an article[4] published two years after the appearance of "Growing Old," Elaine Cumming conceded the need to recognize some of the complexities of aging as modifiers of the theory, but adhered to the "main outlines" of the earlier theory. She pointed out that the original study "did not take into account such non-modal cases as widowhood before the marriage of the last child or of work protracted past the modal age of retirement."[5] She recognized that there are individual differences in disengagement, and even "typologies of withdrawal and retreat" based on deeply-rooted differences in character and in biological temperament. She went so far as to recognize that as lively oldsters were disengaged from their more important social roles, they might temporarily *increase* their recreational activities. She pointed out several other causes of disengagement

---

[4]Further thoughts on the theory of disengagement, *op. cit.*
[5]*Ibid*, p. 378.

besides the anticipation of death, such as rapid social change making obsolete some of the roles of older people, the gulf between generations in a future-oriented society, and the drastic shift in roles for men when they retire. While these latter points allow the distinctive characteristics of American society to modify the universal character of the theory, Cumming essentially has adhered quite closely to the basic outlines of the functionalist theory of disengagement.

Talcott Parsons,[6] the outstanding contemporary exponent of functional theory in sociology, accepted the Cumming theory of disengagement, while adding to it the idea that old age is the consummatory phase of life, a "period of 'harvest,' when the fruits of his [the older person's] previous instrumental commitments are primarily gathered in."

William Henry, however, in his discussion of the theory after the publication of the book,[7] deviated considerably from the theory. He started from the commonly observed *fact* of disengagement, rather than from the theoretical functional necessity of disengagement. In fact, he avoided functional theory altogether. He was interested primarily in the psychological rather than the sociological characteristics of disengagement, stating that, "engagement and disengagement become a general form of personality dynamic, and the disengagement of the aged, a special case."[8] Further, he retreated from the notion that disengagement is inevitable (although he used the word "intrinsic") and he allocated a major role to the "culture's definition of the good and the bad." He agreed with certain critics of the theory of disengagement that "several styles of aging are possible."[9] In general, one might say that Henry in 1963 was closer to certain critics of the theory of disengagement than he was to Cumming.

There have been three lines of criticism of the Cumming-Henry book. One questions the process of disengagement, holding that not only is it not inevitable but that non-engagement in the later years is simply a continuation of a *life-long* social-psychological characteristic of *some* people. One even finds this idea in Henry's 1963 paper, and it has been put upon an empirical foundation in the researches of Reichard, Livson, and Peterson,[10] of Williams and Wirths,[11] and of Videbeck and Knox.[12]

The latter authors, for example, show that 90 per cent of those non-participant after sixty-five years of age were also non-participant five years earlier, while 90 per cent of those participant after sixty-five were also participant five years earlier. Further, at each earlier period of life (since their research

[6]Old age as consummatory phase, *op. cit.*

[7]The theory of intrinsic disengagement, *op. cit.*

[8]*Ibid.*, p. 14.

[9]*Ibid.*, p. 15.

[10]Suzanne Reichard, Florence Livson and Paul G. Petersen, Aging and Personality, New York: John Wiley Company, 1962.

[11]Style of life and successful aging, unpublished manuscript read at the International Gerontological Research Seminar, Markaryd, Sweden, August, 1963.

[12]Patterns of participation among the aging (this volume, Chapter 3), and other writings not yet published.

was not limited to the elderly but traces patterns of participation for a five-year period among samples of people at all age-levels), there is a comparably high correlation between degree of participation at the beginning and end of each five-year period. For these authors, there is a type of person who throughout his life had limited or few social involvements. Thus they do not think of disengagement as a process characteristic of old age exclusively.

A second line of criticism of the Cumming-Henry book challenges their value judgment that disengagement is desirable for older people. Robert Havighurst and his associates[13] have stated this criticism most clearly and have provided empirical evidence that the engaged elderly, rather than the disengaged, are the ones who generally, although not always, are happiest and have the greatest expressed life satisfaction.

The third line of criticism of the Cumming-Henry book analyzes disengagement in the context of the social structure and social trends and finds the theory a poor interpretation of the facts. This point of view—in which I am mainly interested and to which I shall devote the remainder of this paper—acknowledges that a large proportion of the older people in the United States tend to lose many of their adult roles. But it considers this fact to be a function of American culture in this phase of its organization, not a universal for all time. American culture accords a low status to the elderly; we have a youth-centered society. Many other societies accord special prestige and power to the elderly, do not disengage them from adult roles, or create new aged-graded roles of importance for them. The situation of the elderly in the United States has been especially unfavorable in the last fifty years with the decline of the self-employed occupations and the rise of compulsory retirement. These trends have meant that the major social role for males in the society is not open to elderly persons. Forced disengagement in the occupational role has tended to cause disengagement in auxiliary roles—for example, in the occupational associations (trade union, businessmen's association, professional organization) and the "service clubs" which have a membership based on economic activity. Thus cultural values and economic structure have combined to create a condition in which a large proportion of elderly people are disengaged.

Those males who remain economically active past sixty-five years do not disengage, even in the unfavorable cultural value system of the United States. The politician, the employer, the self-employed professional, do not disengage until they become physically or mentally feeble. In fact, they often take on additional memberships and leadership roles after they pass sixty-five years.

But the great bulk of the American people are required to retire from remunerative occupations at about sixty-five years of age, and this situation

---

[13]Robert J. Havighurst, Bernice L. Neugarten, and Sheldon S. Tobin, Disengagement and patterns of aging, unpublished manuscript read at the International Gerontological Research Seminar, August, 1963.

is not likely to change. There are certain new trends, however, which are counteracting the forces making for disengagement of the elderly. Most of these trends are not "inevitable," in the functionalist's sense; some are a product of deliberate organizational effort, others emanate from conditions that have nothing to do with the elderly but their influence will touch the elderly. We have arrived at the following list of such trends by examining the major changes now occurring in American society and forecasting their effects on the aging:

1. Modern medical science and health practices are allowing an ever increasing proportion of those reaching sixty-five to remain in good health and physical vigor.[14] It is doubtful that vigorous people will be as content to disengage as are those of the present generation of the elderly who have been weakened by earlier diseases and by overly strenuous work. Loss of vigor may well be a factor in causing many old people today to disengage, and if that should be overcome, at least the motivation to disengage may diminish.

2. Social security legislation and private pension plans and annuities are slowly increasing the economic security of the retired. If older people have more money to spare from the bare necessities of life—which is true now of only a small minority—they may, like the well-to-do minority today, be more able and willing to continue their costlier participations.

3. Elsewhere in this book[15] I have shown how older people in the United States are beginning to form a social movement to raise their status and privileges, and that this movement is likely to gain an increasing number of adherents. Such a trend will influence the engagement of the elderly in several ways: (a) It will provide a new engagement especially for older people; (b) It will inform the younger generations of the plight of the elderly, and may possibly make society less insistent that older people disengage (we already see, for example, a tendency of younger people to volunteer to transport older neighbors to meetings, church services, polling places, etc.); (c) It may raise the prestige and dignity of age, reversing the negative cultural value mentioned earlier, and such a change would remove the major cause of present disengagement. If the elderly had high prestige, society would not force them to disengage, and the elderly themselves, like the few prestigious elderly today, would be less likely to want to disengage.

4. The trend toward earlier retirement from the chief life role (occupation for men and child-rearing for women), while now a factor causing disengagement, may eventually become an influence for re-engagement. Studies of the family life cycle[16] show that the average young woman today is having her *last* child at the age of twenty-six, which means that her last child is ceasing to be dependent on her at the age of forty to forty-five. Most women at this young age are just not going to be willing to disengage, even though they have lost their chief life role, and are going to

---

[14]We are not considering here any possible future increase in the span of life.
[15]Chapters 1 and 2.
[16]Paul C. Glick, Life cycle of the family, Marriage and Family Living, 17: 3-9, 1955.

have strong motivations to re-engage. The same will be true of men if the age of retirement creeps downward, as some economists tell us it will, significantly below sixty-five years. The new re-engagements have not yet emerged clearly, although for many middle-class women they seem to include voluntary associations and gainful employment. But it does seem probable that many of the new re-engagements will be continued past the age of sixty-five years, and not necessitate a second disengagement as old age is reached.

The types of engagements for which older people would be eligible have increased in number and openness. There are ever new types of voluntary activities available in American society. There are many hobbies that have recently taken on an occupational aspect—such as the stamp trading activity described by Edwin Christ—in Chapter 6—which provide satisfying and even prestigious roles for elderly males. There has also been an expansion in the cultural definition of the male role, so that males may today participate in artistic activities and hobbies that formerly were defined as feminine (including knitting, weaving, painting, etc.). Further, there has been a cultural redefinition of leisure-time activities as good in themselves, so that retired males do not necessarily feel a loss of status simply because they are no longer engaged in remunerative employment.

The disengagement theorists are completely oblivious to such trends, and assume that for any given sociocultural system—in this case, that of the United States today—the position it accords the elderly is "inevitable" and more or less universal. Their ethnocentrism is pointed up more sharply— by evidence quite different from our own—by Yonina Talmon.[17] Dr. Talmon shows how, in the different cultural system of the Israeli Kibbutz, there is little disengagement of the elderly but rather "a restructuring of roles and relationships and a shift in their relative importance rather than mere decline".[18]

I believe it is no accident that the disengagement theorists, although they are sophisticated sociologists and may be skilled researchers, are ethnocentric and ignore major social trends. I believe that it is due to the general functionalist theory which underlies Cumming's work. With this approach, one largely ignores history, with its pointing up of trends from past to present and from present to future, and even minimizes cross-cultural variations by emphasizing the universal "functional prerequisites of culture" which Cumming extends to include the necessity for society to pre-adjust to death. The approach of the functionalist is to start with a certain observation about social life—in this case disengagement—to exaggerate it so it appears to be characteristic of *all* persons in the category observed and then to seek to demonstrate why it inevitably "must be" and cannot be

---

[17]Dimensions of disengagement: aging in collective settlements, unpublished manuscript read at the International Gerontological Research Seminar, Markaryd, Sweden, August, 1963.

[18]*Ibid.*, p. 10.

changed.[19] The functionalists' assumption that "whatever is, must be" merely ruins an initially valid observation by exaggerating it and denying any possibility of countertrends by declaring its inevitability.

Two approaches have dominated research in social gerontology. One seeks to interpret the social facts of aging in a historical-cultural context; the basic facts and factual trends of American society are considered to be the matrix for the social processes of aging. The second theoretical orientation is the interactionist, which seeks to interpret the social facts of aging in terms of the interactions among the aging themselves and between the aging and others in the society. Cultural values and meanings are the most important elements in these interactions, and these are never assumed to be universal or unchanging. The neat, integrated "systems" of the functionalists may appeal to the esthetic sense of readers, but it seems to us that the facts of social life—in this case the social relations of the aging—are too complicated and varied to be encompassed in any notion of equilibrium. Cultural history and human interactions, organizing concepts which have thus far dominated research in gerontology, are better guideposts.

---

[19]A comparable sequence can be found in Talcott Parsons' taking up the observation that the nuclear family has tended to replace the extended family in American society (Age and sex in the social structure of the United States, American Sociological Review, 8: 604-16, 1942). This observation had been made earlier by Simmel and Park, but Parsons exaggerated it, ignored countertrends, and sought to show why the trend was inevitable. Since then, a spate of research articles have demonstrated factually that the trend has been reversed. See my: Reactions against the mass society, The Sociological Quarterly, 3: 316-30, 1962.

CHAPTER 23

Application of Research Findings to the Issues of Social Policy[*]

MERLIN TABER

Introduction

This volume includes a wide-ranging set of reports on aspects of the "social world" of older people. Together, the reports clearly demonstrate that the aging are a "social problem" for our society in the sense defined by Jessie Bernard.[1] Bernard points out that a social problem poses three kinds of difficulties: pain or anxiety imposed on individuals, a "social cost" or an expense to society in general, and a threat to the functioning or solidarity of the social system. The recent changes in numbers, age distribution, and morbidity patterns among old people, described by Cowgill in Chapter 2, and to some extent in other chapters, have created all three kinds of strains in Western societies. First, the widespread concern for what Bernard calls the "humanitarian-sentimental" aspect of the problem of the aging is exemplified in reports of the McNamara committee about the inhumane conditions under which many older people live, their lack of medical care, and inadequate income. Second, the "social cost" of our increased older population is also of concern. As the retirement age is pushed down to sixty-two, and as some unions plan for retirement programs at age fifty-seven, the question is raised, How will we pay for such plans? It is agreed that older people have a "right" to good medical care, but it is also known that the cost of adequate medical treatment for *all*

*Acknowledgment is made to members of the Seminar of the Midwest Council for Social Research on Aging, for clarification of ideas presented here, in discussions and correspondence. The writer is also indebted to his colleagues, Frank Itzin and William Turner, for help in developing these ideas.
[1]Jessie Bernard, Social Problems at Midcentury, New York: Henry Holt, 1957.

older people would be staggering. Third, older people as an interest group are sometimes seen as a threat to the functioning or solidarity of the social system. The passage of the Social Security Act with its two retirement programs in 1935 was clearly due in large part to the threat inherent in a group of poor and alienated old people who were taking up with the Townsend plan and other "crackpot" schemes. Thus, older people as a group are a social problem by Bernard's criteria: individual suffering, social cost, and some threat to the smooth operation of the social system.

The implications of social science facts and theories for the handling of the social problems of the aging may profitably be organized into three areas similar to Bernard's classification of criteria for social problems. Research findings have implications for *work with individual older people*— the attitudes and special skills used by professionals (social caseworkers, visiting nurses and group workers, as well as pastors and physicians) in face-to-face dealing with clients and patients. Second, application of the findings can be made to *program planning*—the assignment of priorities in a community, the identification of unmet needs, the division of responsibility among various programs, and the like. Bernard's "social cost" criterion is paramount here, along with questions of effectiveness. Third, there is the question of the *goals* and *values,* or guiding principles, for broad social policy. The tradition of laissez faire, the open market, has in this country been applied as much to health and welfare planning as to economic affairs. As a result, the question of overall goals and values, or national policy, remains implicit rather than explicit. In the third section of this paper it is suggested that confusion about goals arises, in part, from the ambiguous social position of older people in our society. As a beginning toward a better consensus about goals, several alternative rationales or guiding principles are suggested, any one of which might serve to shape a coherent social policy toward older people.

(At this point, the writer should enter a disclaimer that there is any necessary connection between the existing body of empirical knowledge about older people and the conclusions drawn in this paper. In the "ideal" world where there is a consensus about goals, and well confirmed explanatory theories about means, questions of social planning could be answered easily.[2] In the real world where there is disagreement about, and even a lack of attention to, goals, and only the beginnings of theories, social planning is hazardous at best. In other words, values of the writer affected his selection of empirical findings as well as the inferences drawn from them.)

Implications of the Findings for Medical and Social Services to Individual Older Persons

The studies reported in this volume serve to illuminate three basic and

---

[2]The conquest of communicable diseases in the United States illustrates policy formation where there is consensus about goals and theories. For the controversial policy questions about public education, public health, and public welfare there is no consensus about theory and little explicit attention to goals.

familiar concepts of the helping professions: the idea of *individualizing* the client or patient, the concept of the *motivation* for treatment, and the problem of *dependency*.

Individualization. Individualization, for the helping professional, means attention to each person's unique combination of goals, abilities and history. Paradoxically, increased attention to serving older people may encourage the categorization by age of people, as well as problems and programs.

The danger of categorizing clients or patients as "old" is dramatized by the contrast, for example, between the economically engaged stamp collectors interviewed by Christ (Chapter 6) and the deteriorated nursing home patients described by Coe (Chapter 13). For planning a community program, it may be useful to categorize all community members by age; but in dealing with individual older people any stereotype is certainly risky. Research reports in this volume would seem to indicate that many older people do not identify themselves as members of an aged group. Cleland reports that most older people in Northwood do not seem to think of themselves as members of an aged subculture, even though there are in fact some indications that such a subculture exists (Chapter 19). Pihlblad and McNamara found a strong association between self-identification as "old" and poor adjustment (Chapter 4). Christ's interview excerpts give a vivid picture of conscious and active resistance against associating with, or being identified with, "the aged."

Another aspect of "individualization" has to do with appreciating the older person's individual values and attitudes. It may well be that there is more variation among older people in values than there is between older and younger people. Marshall, for example, reports that a number of older people in Price County, Wisconsin, apparently remain there from a preference for a rural or "backwoods" way of life, and do not consider themselves deprived (Chapter 20). On the other hand, older people may be in the process of developing a special value system. Rose suggests that selective association of older people with each other may be producing a special pattern of values. More specifically, older people may adopt different criteria for social status among themselves, and may combine a generally conservative political orientation with the advocacy of such "liberal" programs as medicare (Chapter 1). Until this question is further clarified, one can only say that it behooves the professional worker to be sensitive to the individual value-orientations of older people as well as to their individual personality characteristics.

Motivation. Members of helping professions now generally recognize the importance of the motivation of the client or patient either to be helped or to get well. In social work terminology, this principle is expressed by the idea of "self-determination" and of "starting where the client is." The "well-motivated" client or patient is one who takes the role of patient or client: he is communicative; recognizes the professionals' competence while retaining a large measure of self-direction; carries out plans made with the professional. All health and welfare organizations have more or less formal mechanisms (and policies and attendant rationales) to reject the "poorly motivated" client or patient. The danger is that lack of ability, or the existence of external restraints not appreciated by the professional, may be interpreted as "poor motivation" by the professional.

The problem of older people's motivation to be helped is closely related to the question of whether older people receive a fair share of community services. The definition of a "fair share" of community services for older people would depend on their numbers; but also on an evaluation of their needs. While it is foolish to picture the aged as a submerged class, it is equally unrealistic to deny that the aged as a group have a larger proportion than other age groups of persons who are socially isolated, and who lack adequate income or medical care. The size of this "needy" group of aged is in dispute, but the existence of such a group is documented in the papers by Smith and by Peterson (Chapters 9 and 15) as well as in several of the survey reports. One would expect as a result that older people would receive, on the average, more of the services of all community programs than other age groups. Many observers have claimed the opposite to be true, and that older people receive little attention from most community programs.[3] One explanation for this discrepancy is that the reluctance of older people to ask for help, combined with the professionals' preference for the strongly motivated client (or patient or club member), combine to cut the older person off from all but the relatively impersonalized and automatic income programs. The implication for working with older people is that the worker must "reach out" to older people to engage them in group activities, social casework, or other needed services.[4]

The necessity of reaching out to older people is supported by the reports of professional workers who have served older people. Programs of recreation for older people sometimes include provision of transportation and possibly some prodding to get them there. In regard to the use of medical services by the normal older person, Rose notes that one reaction to declining health is denial of the problem and failure to seek medical aid (Chapter 16). In social casework interviews, the older person is apt to say, "You don't need to come back," or "You must have more important things to do." This kind of behavior is often interpreted as "resistance" or "lack of motivation"—even in the face of clear evidence that the older person both needs and wants medical attention, or some social experience, or a chance to discuss his personal problems.

---

[3]In a study of an Iowa community of over 100,000, it was found that people aged sixty and over, who made up over ten per cent of the population, received less than five cent of the services of local health and welfare programs (income and institutional programs excluded). Merlin Taber, Frank Itzin and William Turner, A Comprehensive Analysis of Health and Welfare Services for Older Persons in One Community, State University of Iowa, 1963.

[4]In the field of social work, the concept of "reaching out" has been developed in connection with helping "hard core" or "multi-problem" families; like older people, these disorganized family members are not likely to have esteemed and well-defined social roles.

Dependency. The third concept which is commonly used in the helping professions and is clarified by these research reports is that of "dependency." "Dependent" behavior is expecting something of others, which the professional (or other observer) believes the person could do or supply himself.

Dependency is usually thought of in terms of financial dependency, as in the demographic concept "dependent population" (Marshall, Chapter 20). Some of these studies show the older person is "dependent" in quite other ways as well. Smith finds support for the proposition that older people want more personal contact, but not more financial support, from their children. This finding is confirmed for the Northwood sample by Hawkinson (Chapter 11). Smith also notes evidence that a minority of the aged must depend on relatives (or, presumably, organized community programs) for household tasks, sharing of leisure pursuits, and physical care. Even further, Coe's study of depersonalization convincingly supports the idea that the older person is dependent on "the attitudes of others" for self-identity and personality. In the three care programs studied by Coe, the more the older person lost control of his person and belongings, and the more he was treated as a "thing," the less evidence he gave of defining himself as a person in a social system. Coe's interpretation of the process of depersonalization leads to quite different conclusions about working with older people than do the more common assumptions about the dangers of meeting needs.[5] The treatment of clients or patients in a perfunctory and impersonal manner would appear to have the effect of further disabling them, rather than stimulating them to be less dependent. This is no more than to say that clients and patients should be treated with respect, a common enough observation. This recommendation needs underlining with old people, however. Face-to-face dealings with older people require some patience. There is a "natural" tendency to avoid involvement with the older person—"involvement" meaning the older person comes to think he has a legitimate dependent relation to the professionals. The tendency is to work around the older person, do things to him rather than with him and to justify such treatment by the rationale that "we don't want to make them dependent."

Implications of the Findings for Community and Program Planning

On the community planning level, the questions of concern are quite different than on the level of individual service and care. The questions concern the optimum distribution, organization, and location of various kinds of programs. As noted above, values in this society militate against such planning. "Social planning" is considered a little immoral, or at least suspect, and the decisions go by default rather than being ad-

---

[5]Viz., that helping people makes them dependent. R. H. Tawney referred to this assumption in connection with the old English Poor Laws as, "the danger of pampering poverty."

dressed by the community. Definitions of needs, and establishment and location of services are often determined by the relative power of competing professional groups or established agencies. The division of labor among programs is not usually clear, with the result that several programs serve the same function while certain needs of older people are not met by any program. While it is true that most communities have some central control through welfare councils, it is also true that many welfare councils do not include the largest and most important programs: those under federal auspices, and the medical care and psychiatric care programs, especially if they are under state auspices.

The lack of coherence and coordination among community programs has been documented many times, and was not the subject for any of the studies in this volume. Nevertheless, many of the findings can be related to community planning, and it is important to attempt more rational and comprehensive approaches to these "inter-program" problems.

Needs and Wants for Services.   What services do older people want and need? Continued income and adequate health care are no doubt the "basics," both on a common sense basis and on the evidence of various surveys. However, another area of convergence seen in several of the research reports collected here is the matter of social participation. Cleland found almost one-third mentioning lack of recreation as a problem in Northwood—all the more striking since Northwood is evidently a homogeneous community where older people are accepted and where community services are oriented to their needs. Pihlblad and McNamara found several measures of social participation associated with adjustment, and emphasized that this finding was not merely an artifact of the adjustment-scoring procedure. It is interesting, too, that in the Missouri sample, interviewed for the Pihlblad-McNamara's study, adjustment was more highly associated with church activity than with church membership, suggesting that "doing" is more important than "belonging." A similar difference is reported by Moberg and Taves in their stiudy of church participation and adjustment (Chapter 7). Moberg also reported evidence of a low level of participation in formally organized activities by older people (Chapter 8).

In short, there is evidence for the statement that older people have a wish and need for more opportunities for social participation. Does this mean that older people are cut off from opportunities open to them earlier in life? The analysis of participation among older people by Videbeck and Knox does not support this proposition (Chapter 2). Nine-tenths of their sample reported the same level of participation they had maintained five years earlier. Further, Videbeck and Knox found almost no age differences in seven types of social participation, controlling for "change in life circumstances." Possibly some people tend to express wishes for more social experience throughout life—or possibly such an expression is simply a socially desirable answer. Another possibility is that changes in role, especially retirement, lead to a rather diffuse or vague desire for "something to do," while no social programs have been effective in meeting this felt need. Since the role change is considerably more severe for men than women, one would expect this problem to be more acute for men. Smith proposes the hypothesis that women find their marriage more satisfying after the retirement of their husbands because of greater mutuality of interests, and that men give more assistance with the housework after retirement. Pihlblad and McNamara reported that age and adjustment were negatively associated for men, and not associated for women. The idea that "something to do" may be a special problem for men certainly is supported by Miller's essay about the subjective aspects of leisure without work (Chapter 5). Loss of work may mean loss of the "right" to leisure. Miller emphasizes the meaning of the work role to the worker—both for his self-concept and for a meaningful group and a social situation. The difficulty of the older man over "what to do," then, might arise from his removal from daily contacts with co-workers, as well as from the problem of rationale, which Miller discusses. Miller suggests that one solution has been the introduction of work into leisure, and Christ describes this solution in detail. Christ's "economically engaged" collectors also make clear their contempt for planned activity that is merely time-killing. The case examples used by Christ also seem to reinforce the implication of the Knox-Videbeck report: a pattern of high participation cannot be "turned on" at retirement.

This discussion might be summarized by recommending that the problem of leisure activities and social participation for older people receive more attention from both social scientists and policymakers. There is some evidence from these studies that many older people wish more opportunities for participation. Further, several of the studies emphasize that older people desire activities that are either remunerative (Christ, Chapter 6) or socially recognized as useful (Miller, Chapter 5; Moberg, Chapter 8). On rather tenuous grounds, it was suggested that sex differences in adjustment among older people may reflect the fact that lack of opportunities for participation is an especially serious problem for older men because of the meaning of work for men and the greater role changes for men in retirement. Perhaps the leisure-time agencies should seek to devise activities for "men only," which carry either some prospect of income or some social honor, or both. Christ's and Miller's discussions would suggest that a special kind of "preparation for retirement" should be considered, that is, involvement in leisure activities which can be continued after retirement and can be both personally and economically rewarding. Volunteer services by older people is a third possible development—one which is at least foreshadowed in plans for the domestic Peace Corps. This possibility is supported by Moberg's assertion that older people "want an opportunity to feel useful and worthwhile." Even more generally, Miller sees the possibility of assigning roles important in any organization (such as "recruiter" or "keeper of the tradition") to older people.

Auspices and Location of Services. The second question for community planning which logically follows the question of needs and wants of older people, is the matter of auspices and location of needed programs. Cowgill's demographic analysis (Chapter 18) shows that the highest proportions of older people are in ". . . the small towns and villages . . . some distance removed from large metropolitan centers . . ." Marshall's case study of Price County, Wisconsin, details this pattern and seeks an explanation for it. The problem presented for program planning is that the areas with the highest proportion of aged have the least ability to provide services for them. Furthermore, specialized facilities and professionals are disproportionately concentrated in metropolitan areas. One possible solution is regional provision of selected services. Marshall suggests such a plan for Price County, and Cleland describes the "service area" of the old people's home in Northwood, which is several times as large as the business area for Northwood. The problem of the willingness and ability of local communities to supply services has in fact been skirted over the past decades due to the expansion of federal programs. There are two problems connected with this development. One problem is that the large federal programs are not included in local planning, and the other problem is that such functions as personal service, volunteer helping, leisure programs, and the like, must necessarily be organized and administered on a local basis. The nature of such services, which must be individually tailored to be effective, is incompatible with the principles of equity and impersonality which inhere in a large government program.

Perhaps what is indicated is a clarification of the best division of labor. Certain functions can best be performed by the federal government and others by state government, while still others are necessarily reserved to local and voluntary auspices. Definition of a satisfactory division of labor depends on some local body or agency being assigned an overall planning responsibility by the various government levels and bureaucracies involved.

The question of location of facilities is important for the "care" programs, ranging from acute hospital care to custodial care, and blending into residential housing. The survey samples reported in this volume are of "non-institutionalized" aged and information is not available from other sources about the location of institutionalized older people in relation to their residences. The tendency in Britain and the Scandinavian countries is apparently to move away from large, centralized and segregated facilities, toward scattered and decentralized facilities. There is some evidence in the reports of this volume that could be adduced to support such a policy. Cleland found that if local "relocations" were excluded older people selected their residence on the basis of proximity to children, and said they would move only to be nearer children. Maintenance of friendship and neighbor patterns is no doubt also important. Pihlblad and McNamara report that one-half their sample of older persons were visited daily or frequently, and that visiting with friends and neighbors was positively and highly associated with adjustment. There has been little development of home services and home health care in this country. In short, it would appear that a great deal more could be done through location of facilities and provision of home care to preserve maximum independence of older people, to preserve their ties with family, friends and community, and to reduce the incidence of the kind of depersonalization reported by Coe.

"Separate but Equal" Facilities. One policy issue already alluded to might be generalized: Should special facilities and programs be established for older people? Should separate adult education courses, casework units, housing and hospital units, etc., be established just for older people? One argument for doing so is that only in that way will older people receive the attention they should have. In the public assistance programs, for example, this argument takes the form that if assistance to the aged and to dependent children were administered as one program, the older people would suffer from the negative public attitudes toward dependent children and their parents. A second argument is that special skills or knowledge are required to work with (or "serve" or "treat") older people, hence the administrative organization should reflect professional specialty. The primary argument *against* special programs would seem to be based on the assumption of a general low valuation of the aged (see Rose, Chapter 1), which would be attached to any professional specialty or service identified with the aged. A second argument, arising from these collected research reports, might be that older people do *not* generally identify themselves as "old," and that those who do, seem not to be doing as well as others (unless they are among the few militant old people described by Rose in Chapter 2, who refuse to accept society's valuation of the aged).

In the area of church participation, Moberg's study of integration of the aged in two similar churches, one having special activities for the old, is addressed to exactly this problem of separate programs (Chapter 8). In general, Moberg finds no difference in levels of adjustment between the two groups. Those in the "Senior Club" church participated in activities of the church (other than the club) just slightly less than members of the "integrated" church.

Marshall's recommendations for Price County represent, perhaps, the other extreme from the "special provision" approach. Marshall points out that social and economic conditions in this "cut-over," declining area are not optimum for the high proportion of older people left there. His suggestions for solution, however, are addressed to the economic base rather than to the social provisions for older people. This "community development" approach may offer more promise than attempts to improve the lot of one selected group in the community. For example, the National Health Survey has shown that people in rural and small town areas have lower rates of use of medical services, even though there is no evidence that morbidity rates are lower; and it has been established (See Cowgill, Chapter 18) that these areas also have higher proportions of aged. The provision of medical care for older people in rural areas that is adequate in variety and quantity obviously depends on some solution to the general problem of distribution of medical services, and cannot be solved by some special program. Again, it has been known for some time that older people are concentrated in mental hospitals, but the creation of facilities for the "aged mentally ill" would not solve the problems of aftercare, custodial orientation, etc., which are involved.

The concept of "retirement communities," created by plan or by circumstance, seems to have some attraction and is another example of the "separate but equal" approach. One of Christ's respondents castigated such developments as "cemetery cities," and it would seem that the older persons interviewed for some of the other studies would not prefer such arrangements. Besides the desire to be near children and friends, already noted, Cleland's study also indicated a considerable tie to community. The idea that some communities would be "better" for retirement than others seems sensible, and it is interesting that this assumption was not supported by the research. The study by Pihlblad and MacNamara looked most closely at this question, including as it did samples from three communities. There were small differences in levels of adjustment between communities but the findings were interpreted as "most inconclusive." Videbeck and Knox found no significant and persistent relation between participation and size of community, when socio-economic status was controlled. Cleland suggests a typology of small communities with high proportions of aged— those where older people are "stranded," but also those which "hold" and which "attract" older people. Northwood is described as a stable community which holds the aged. As noted above, most of his respondents said they live in Northwood because it is "home" or because it is near children. As to the question of "retirement communities" one can only agree with the investigators that more research is needed about types of communities and the effects of each type on the well-being of residents. Evidence in the volume would seem to indicate that individual differences in family ties and values and style of life would be more important in a choice of residence, than the nature of the community.

Confusion about the Goals of Social Policy

Government and voluntary programs for the health and welfare of the aged are an important element in the "social world" of old people. Since these programs affect a majority of older people, the policies in these programs (and among them) have import for the subjective well-being of older people. For example, Pihlblad and McNamara found that *source* of income bore a closer relation to adjustment than *amount* of income, with Old Age Assistance recipients notably low on adjustment. Other indications that assistance recipients are disadvantaged socially, as well as economically, are found in the chapter by Cleland. Perhaps poor social functioning leads to the necessity to apply for assistance, but the reverse may be true as well. Coe's description of three different programs for similar patients even suggests that the nature of the program for care a person happens to come under may be a life or death matter.

Besides the import for the well-being of individuals, social policy decisions have consequences for social structure and social change. Rose lists eight social conditions now tending to create a subculture of the aging in this country. Three of the eight are directly or indirectly matters of social policy (costs of medical care, compulsory retirement, and socially sponsored activity programs).

If it is accepted that social policy has important consequences for individual welfare and for society as well, the next logical question to ask is: *What* consequences are desired? Do we *want* a "subculture" of the aging, with enhanced interaction among the aged, increased separation from society and the development of a special set of needs, satisfactions, and rewards within the group? Do we want older people to keep on working? To illustrate the confusion about the latter point, it is only necessary to recall that Social Security retirement benefits were passed, in part, to get the aged out of the depression labor market. More recently the policy has been established that earned income of Social Security payees above age seventy-two does not affect their entitlement to benefits. The two actions would appear to have opposite goals. The first action was based on the unemployment problem and apparently the second action was based on what Miller calls "the contemporary emphasis on action."

Some insight into the problem of goals may be gained from an analysis of the position of older people in our society, as well as from reference to specific research. Both Miller and Coe, in this volume, present interpretations of the effects of being old which emphasize the dependence of the person on his social roles. In this frame of reference, the key problem of aging is usually interpreted as the change in, or lack of, roles for the person (e.g., Rose, Chapter 12). Opportunities for interchanges with others, by which honor and power may be gained, are less open to the older person.

With respect to social policy for the aging, it is instructive to draw a parallel between the social position of older people and the position of other groups who have been "problems" to society in a similar way, such as adolescents in modern Western society, or ethnic minorities. Such analogies add nothing to knowledge, but something may be learned from the trials and errors in policy formation for other groups.

The analogy between old age and childhood is a familiar one and Miller uses this idea with respect to play activities. To develop this analogy further, there seems an interesting parallel between the social position of the "young old" (age sixty to seventy or seventy-five) and the social position of the adolescent (age fourteen to eighteen or twenty). The existence of a "youth culture" with distinctive interaction patterns and values has been well-documented. The groups are quite similar in facing ambiguity about their right to occupy the work role. Social policy for both groups has alternated between the goal of employment and the devising of strategies to remove them from the employable groups. Both groups possess the physical and mental prerequisites for participation in the usual adult roles, but meet with social constraints which work against participation. Also, in

our modern society there are no rites of passage to ease the transition between dependent childhood and adult status, or between adult status and
the relatively better defined dependent status "older old age." The popular
literature and the mental hygiene literature portray the ideal adolescent
with emphasis on dominant cultural values: He defers satisfactions while
he works hard at school (preparatory to college), has heterosexual relations of limited sorts, learns good sportsmanship and prepares for a future
useful life. In like manner, the popular press and gerontological societies
as well often present models of the ideal aged person: He is usually a
professional person who maintains some useful activity in his profession.
He is able to travel. He continues to be interested in learning, and he is
reaping certain rewards from a past useful life. While such models are
useful for inspirational purposes, it is also clear that the vast majority of
both adolescents and sixty-year-olds are effectively prevented from living
up to these models, and that many of the obstacles are inherent in the
social system and not in the individuals.

In the case of adolescents, there has recently been some realistic facing
of the fact that the social system is partly responsible. For example,
experimental programs of education are frankly designed to socialize slum
children into middle class society by teaching the necessary social skills
and inculcating the appropriate values and "needs." A major youth program in one section of New York City is designed to determine whether the
"opportunity structure" for disadvantaged youths can actually be changed
in planned ways. One may disagree with the goals of such programs, but
it seems likely their effectiveness will be enhanced because their goals—
the desired outcome in terms of "what kind of people we want"—are
clear.[6]

Programs for older people reflect more confusion about goals than
programs for adolescents. Some of the internal conflicts have been noted.
Do we want to remove older people from full participation in society for
the benefit of society?[7] Such a goal would indicate the use of congregate
institutions and the increase of legal constraints against participation by
older people. As an alternative goal, do we wish to provide *humane care
for the needy aged,* while minimizing the cost to society? Congress, in
effect, took that option in passing the Kerr-Mills Bill, an approach which
has a long history in English and American poor law. The assumption
here is that only a few older people need societal provisions, so that social
cost must be minimized by the application of a means test.

Is it our primary goal to *rehabilitate* older people, socially and
physically? The idea of rehabilitation carries a strong appeal, evocative
as it is of the American values on individualism and work. This goal

---

[6]The phrase used here was coined by Erik Erikson in raising the question of the
goals of social practice and policy in relation to children.

[7]This question is not intended to be facetious. The proposition that it is necessary
for society that older people be removed from it has been advanced in formal terms
as "the disengagement theory." For a critique of this proposition, see Rose, Chapter 22.

reflects the twin assumptions that the problem lies in the capacities of the individual, and that these capacities can be enhanced.

At present, the largest programs in sheer volume might be said to have the goal of *substitute provision*. By substitute provision is meant the provision, under organized social programs, of income, personal care and services, and opportunities for social interaction. The assumption is that most older persons are not able to receive income, services, and opportunities through the normal exchanges in the family, the economic system, etc. If this assumption is accepted, then the goal of rehabilitation may be viewed as unrealistic and the goal of minimizing cost through the means test as discriminatory.

The prime example of "substitute provision" is the Social Security retirement system under which an almost universal tax on workers and employers is used to support the provision of continued income for most older people. As already noted, the large bureaucratically organized programs are incompatible with the provision of physical care, opportunities for social activity, personal service or "home helps," and the like. Extension of the "substitute provision" philosophy into these areas may be possible through state and federal government programs to stimulate and help local communities employ specialists to organize such programs. In fact, such developments are taking place in scattered communities, and this kind of "substitute provision" would appear to be the best guess about future developments.

Several of the chapters in this volume suggest a goal which is different from disengagement, or mimimal humane care, or substitute provision. Is it practicable to design programs which enhance the *social utility* of older persons? In our society opportunities for joint activity with others, the rightful claim to esteem, and maintenance of self-identity, apparently depend on active participation in roles defined as productive or useful. The prime example is, of course, the work role, though other useful roles may be recognized and their occupants rewarded by honor and esteem. The goal of maximizing the social utility of older persons has different implications from goals which emphasize "disengagement," or the minimizing of cost, or rehabilitation, or "substitute provision." The goal of social utility would imply programs which can increase opportunities for older people with the existing social structure, rather than the stimulation of the formation of new groups made up of older people, or the establishment of new service programs.

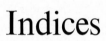

Indices

Author and Name Index

ALBRECHT, RUTH, 248, 248n; 324n, 325, 325n, 326n
Aldridge, Gordon J., 7n, 9n
Anderson, C. Arnold, 173n
Anderson, Nancy Newman, 245
Angell, Robert C., 246n
Axelrod, M., 47n

BABER, R. E., 186n
Barker, Roger G., 241n
Barnhill, Elizabeth, 211
Barron, Milton L., 14n
Beard, Belle B., 182n
Beck, P. G., 340, 340n
Becker, Howard S., 87, 87n
Bell, Wendell, 190, 190n
Bennett, John, 163n
Bernard, Jessie, 367, 367n, 368
Bettelheim, Bruno, 243n
Bloom, Kenneth, 247n
Bollinger, LeRoy, 329n
Bond, F. A., 186, 186n, 188n
Booth, Charles, 281, 281n, 283, 283n, 290, 290n
Bowles, 325, 326n
Breen, Leonard Z., 14n
Britton, Joseph H., 114n, 138n, 153
Buckley, Joseph C., 335n
Buhler, Charlotte, 82, 83n
Bullock, Jean, 265, 270n
Burchinal, Lee, 149
Burgess, Ernest W., 77n, 78n, 92n, 115, 115n, 138n, 149, 182, 182n, 247, 248n, 359, 360
Burling, Temple, 268, 270n
Bushee, Frederick A., 47n

CAMERON, NORMAN, 238n
Campbell, Angus, 14n

Caro, Francis G., 170n, 171n, 173n, 311, 311n
Carper, James W., 87, 87n
Carr, Lowell J., 246n
Cavan, Ruth Shonle, 77n, 79, 79n, 115, 115n, 138n, 247, 248n, 253, 253n, 359n
Christ, Edwin, 11n, 79n, 83, 85, 95n, 96n, 365, 369, 373, 376
Cleland, Courtney B., 184n, 290, 290n, 295, 295n, 311n, 323, 327n, 369, 372, 374, 376
Codere, Helen, 163n
Coe, Rodney M., 211, 225, 369, 371, 375, 376, 377
Confrey, Eugene A., 216n
Cooley, Charles H., 226, 226n, 246n
Copp, James H., 283, 283n, 284, 284n, 290, 290n
Coult, Allan D., 151, 164n, 176, 176n
Cowgill, Donald O., 275, 326, 337, 367, 373, 375
Croog, Sidney H., 179n
Cumming, Elaine, 12n, 26n, 64, 64n, 132, 132n, 163n, 215n, 226n, 248, 248n, 253, 253n, 261, 270n, 360, 360n. 361, 361n, 362, 363, 365
Cumming, J., 261, 270n

DADE, EMIL B., 282, 282n
Despres, Leo, 163n
Deutscher, Irwin, 77n, 93, 93n
Dodge, Joan, 247, 247n
Doerflinger, Jon A., 5n, 340n
Donahue, Wilma, 95, 95n, 157, 182n
Dubin, Robert, 195n
Dulles, Foster Rhea, 80n
Dunn, Mrs. Joseph George, 125

ERICKSON, ERIK, 378n

FANSHEL, DAVID, 248n
Farber, Bernard, 179n
Faris, Robert E. L., 238n
Festinger, Leon, 99n
Fischlowitz, Ruth, 212n
Flance, I. J., 266, 270n
Floud, Jean, 173n
Forster, M. C., 340, 340n
Foskett, John M., 43n
Fox, Renee, 220n, 225n, 242n
Francis, Roy G., 249n
Frazier, E. Franklin, 166n
Freedman, Ronald, 47n
Freidson, Eliot, 218n
Friedman, Eugene A., 220n, 225n
Fuguitt, Glen V., 282, 282n, 283, 283n

GARRETT, CHARLES W., 126n
Garrett, Donald F., 241n
Gebhard, P. H., 10n
Glick, Paul C., 46n, 196n, 364n
Goffman, Erving, 87, 87n, 88n, 90n, 99n,
  101, 111n, 227n, 235n, 248n
Goldfarb, I, 249n
Goldhamer, Herbert, 115n, 247, 248n
Goldmann, Franz, 267, 270n
Goldstein, Marcus S., 216n
Gonick, Mollie R., 241n
Gray, Robert M., 67n, 113n, 126, 126n
Greenberg, Clement, 80, 80n, 81, 81n
Greenfield, Sidney M., 225n
Greer, Scott, 81n
Gross, Edward A., 80, 80n, 82, 82n, 87,
  88n, 90n
Gross, Neal, 99n

HABENSTEIN, ROBERT W., 151, 163, 164n,
  176, 176n
Hagberg, Bertie L., 184n, 329n
Hansen, Gary, 51n, 57n, 59n, 67n, 113n,
  115n, 248n, 291, 291n, 311, 311n, 326n
Havighurst, Robert J., 77n, 115, 115n,
  138n, 247, 248, 248n, 324n, 325, 325n,
  326n, 363, 363n
Hawkinson, Mrs. William, 329n
Hawkinson, William P., 329n, 336, 371
Henry, Jules, 226n, 228, 228n
Henry, William E., 12n, 26n, 64, 64n,
  132, 132n, 215n, 226n, 248, 248n, 253,
  253n, 360, 360n, 361, 362, 362n, 363
Hitt, Homer L., 295, 295n, 324, 324n,
  325, 325n, 327
Homans, George C., 163n
Hoyt, G. C., 4n, 11n
Hughes, Everett C., 81n

ITZIN, FRANK, 370n

JACOBS, P., 14n
Johansen, John P., 282, 282n, 283
Johnson, Don E., 93n
Jones, M., 269, 270n

KAHN, R. L., 249n
Kamp, E., 249n
Kaplan, Jerome, 248, 248n
Kaplan, Max, 222n
Kinsey, A. C., 10n
Kirkpatrick, Clifford, 77n, 147
Kleemeier, Robert W., 11n, 222n
Knox, Allen B., 37, 215n, 362, 362n,
  372, 373, 376
Koos, Earl L., 217n
Kuhlen, Raymond, 247n
Kutner, Bernard, 79, 248, 248n

LANDIS, JUDSON T., 113n
Langner, Thomas S., 248n
Lansing, A. K., 153
Laverty, Ruth, 250, 250n
Lederer, Henry D., 235n
Lee, L. J., Jr., 186n
Lehner, 247, 247n
Leichter, Hope J., 163n
Lentz, Edith M., 268, 270n
Lepowski, Richard, 250, 250n
Linden, Maurice, 251n
Littauer, D., 266, 270n
Litwak, Eugene, 6n, 81n, 149, 164n
Livson, Florence, 362, 362n
Lorge, Irving, 249, 250n
Lorin, Ernest D., 311n
Lynd, Helen M., 228n

MANLEY, CHARLES R., JR., 326n
Marshall, Dougles G., 5n, 281, 282, 282n,
  283, 283n, 284, 284n, 290, 290n, 291,
  291n, 293, 293n, 302n, 304n, 326,
  326n, 327, 340, 340n, 369, 371, 374,
  375
Martel, Martin U., 311n
Martin, C. E., 10n
Mason, Evelyn, 247, 247n, 249, 249n, 250,
  253, 253n
Mason, Ward, 99n
Mather, W. G., 153
McEachern, Alexander, 99n
McNamara, Robert L., 49, 284, 284n,
  311n, 367, 368, 372, 373, 374, 376
Mead, G. H., 193, 193n, 226, 227n, 246n
Mead, Margaret, 83, 83n
Mechanic, David, 241n
Meier, Dorothy, 190, 190n
Merton, R. K., 99n

Michael, Archer L., 114n
Michelen, L. C., 11n
Mickey, Carroll M., 311n
Miller, Stephen J., 77, 89n, 373, 377
Moberg, David O., 67n, 113, 113n, 114n, 123n, 125, 126n, 372, 373, 375
Moran, Leo J., 348n
Myrdal, Gunnar, 351

NEUGARTEN, BERNICE L., 363n
New, Peter Kong-Ming, 179n, 311n

O'REILLY, CHARLES T., 113n
Osmond, Humphrey, 238n

PAGEL, TOM, 329n
Pan, Ju-Shu, 113n, 114n, 250, 250n
Park, R. E., 336n
Parsons, Talcott, 149, 164n, 182, 220n, 225n, 241n, 242n, 360, 360n, 362, 362n, 366n
Perry, L. B., 186n
Petersen, Paul G., 362, 362n, 370
Phillips, Bernard S., 253, 253n
Pihlblad, C. Terence, 49, 163, 167n, 170n, 171n, 172, 173n, 284, 284n, 311n, 369, 372, 373, 374, 376
Pinner, F. A., 14n
Pollack, M., 249, 249n
Pomeroy, W. B., 10n
Pressey, S. L., 113n, 114n

REICHARD, SUZANNE, 362, 362n
Riesman, David, 80n, 82, 82n, 96, 96n
Riley, Marvin P., 290, 290n
Rogers, Everett M., 150
Rose, Arnold M., 3, 8n, 19, 64, 64n, 71, 72, 77n, 81n, 82, 82n, 83, 88, 115n, 132, 135, 164n, 183, 183n, 193, 194n, 201, 212n, 222n, 226n, 240, 240n, 247n, 252, 284, 284n, 328, 359, 359n, 364n, 369, 370, 375, 377, 378n
Rosen, Theodore, 251n
Rosow, Irving, 12n, 251n

SCAFF, A. M., 186n
Schmidt, John F., 114n
Schneider, David M., 163n
Schock, Nathan W., 182n
Schorr, Alvin L., 143, 177n
Scott, Frances Gillespie, 113n, 250, 250n
Scott, John C., Jr., 43n
Sebald, Hans, 150
Seeman, Melvin, 228n
Selznick, P., 14n
Shanas, Ethel, 6n, 113n, 114n, 214, 220, 221n, 226n, 241n, 248n
Sheldon, Henry D., 300n

Shibutani, Tamotsu, 232n, 242, 242n
Simcoe, Elizabeth, 113n, 114n
Simmel G., 336n
Simmons, L.W., 269, 271n
Slater, Sherwood B., 182n
Slocum, Walter L., 326n
Smith, Harold E., 143, 164n
Smith, T. Lynn, 281, 281n, 282, 282n, 283, 283n, 284, 284n, 290, 290n, 291, 291n, 293, 293n, 302n, 304n, 325, 325n, 326, 326n, 370, 371
Smith, William M., 188n
Sommer, Robert, 238n
Staniforth, Sidney D., 348n
Stone, Gregory P., 79n, 87, 88n, 90n
Streib, Gordon F., 143, 195n
Strong, Samuel M., 14n, 327n
Stumpf, Samuel Enock, 182, 182n
Sussman, Marvin, 6n, 81n, 149, 164n, 182n, 188n
Sward, 247, 247n

TABER, MERLIN A., 283, 283n, 284n, 311n, 367, 370n
Talmon, Yonina, 365, 365n
Taves, Marvin J., 51n, 57n, 59n, 67n, 79n, 113, 115n, 132, 248n, 291, 291n, 311, 311n, 326n, 372
Tawney, R. H., 371n
Thompson, Warren S., 324, 324n, 325. 325n
Thompson, Wayne E., 143
Tibbitts, Clark, 14n, 157, 182n
Tobin, Sheldon S., 363n
Togo, Alice M., 248n
Tuckman, Jacob, 249, 250n
Turner, William, 370n

VANCE, RUPERT B., 324, 324n, 325, 325n, 326, 326n, 337, 337n
Verden, Paul F., 114n
Videbeck, Richard, 37, 48n, 215n, 362, 362n, 372, 373, 376
Vieg, J. A., 186n
Vitale, J., 269, 271n
Volkart, Edmond A., 241n

WARDWELL, JOHN, 329n
Wax, Murray, 251n
Wessen, Albert F., 217n, 259, 266, 270n
Wheeler, Wayne, 11n
White, Paul Dudley, 329
Williams, Richard H., 362, 362n
Williams, Robin, 145
Wilson, R. N., 268, 270n
Wing, J. K., 238n
Wirths, Claudine, 362, 362n

Wolfe, A. M., 173n
Woods, James H., 14n
Wright, Beatrice, 228n, 241n

YOSHIOKA, SAMUEL, 311, 311n

Youmans, E. Grant, 57n, 61, 62n, 65, 65n, 67, 67n

ZELDITCH, MORRIS, 251n
Zeman, Frederic, 249, 250n

Subject Index

ACTIVITY. *See also* Participation
 and aging, 43, 48, 85, 134-135, 138
 and aging group consciousness, 25
 as a factor in status, 10, 135
Adjustment
 and church leadership, 114, 115, 116-119, 120-121, 124
 and church membership, 123
 and church participation, 114-124, Chapter 7
 and community size, 56
 definition of, 115
 and education, 63-64, 116
 and family size, 155
 and friendship patterns, 66
 and income, 61-63
 and interaction, 247
 and leisure, 83
 and mental health, 194
 and mobility, 58, 59
 of old people, 50, 51, 53, 54, 57, 71, 118, 153, 320, Chapter 4
 and power-structure, 56-57
 and retirement, 79
 and sex, 118-119, 138-139
Affinity
 bases of, 3
 and formation of subcultures, 3
Age-grading. *See also* Role
 and age-graded roles, 363
 in American society, 6, 87, 126
 in church congregations, Chapter 8, 138
 definition of, 12
 ecological factors, 7
 economic factors, 363
 and family patterns, 364-365

Age-grading (*continued*)
 and responsibilities, 37
 and role, 252
Aging. *See also* Associations; Group; Group consciousness; Group formation; Medical care; Old people; Self-conception
 and behavior, 38
 church influence in, 138
 and general outlook, 204-206, 208
 and happiness, 204-206, 208
 and interests, 203-204
 and mental health, Chapter 12
 and participation, 40, 43, 44
 and prestige, 197
 and religious affiliation, 204
 and residence, 154
 role-change, 246-247
 role-model of, 378
 self-conception, 246-247
 and social adjustment, 50
 social cost of, 367-368
 as a social problem, 367-368
Association. *See also* Activity; Organizations; Participation
 with children, 32, 52, 65
 and embarrassment, 89
 with friends and neighbors, 31, 32, 65, 109, 110-111, 134-135, 318-319
Attitude
 negative, and mental health, 194-198
 and physical health, Chapter 13

BASELINE Study of Adult Participation in Nebraska, 40
Birth control, 4

387

Burgess-Cavan-Havighurst Attitudes Inventory, 115, 115n, 138, 138n

CHILDREN. *See also* Family (33, 65, 71); Parents
and assistance, to the aged, 152-153
association, with the aged, 32
and estrangement, from the aged, 32n
and family life-cycle, 47
obligations of, 182-183
residence with, 154
Chronic Illness Ideology Scale, 231, 231n
Church. *See also* Adjustment
activity in, 41, 44, 67, 133
and adjustment, 67, 68, 123, Chapter 7
and aging, 125, 126
integration in, and age-grading, 125-129, 138
and mobility, 46
Commission on Chronic Illness (1956), 263
Conflict, inter-generational, 151, 153, 155

DEPRIVATION, reaction of the aged, 19
Disengagement. *See also* Engagement; Integration
of the aged, from roles, 12
caused by illness, 13
causes of, 360-362
from cultural patterns, 15
definition of, 12n, 360-361
and functionalism, 362, 365, 366
and non-aging group consciousness, 26
from organizations, 134-135, 139-140
and role-restructuring, 365
Division of labor in the family, 155

EDUCATION
and adjustment, 63-64
and aging group consciousness, 22
and church participation, 131
interest in, of the aged, 47
and prestige, 9
Embarrassment
and identity, 88
and provision of role-identity, 91
reduction of, 90
and role incapacity, 90
and social interaction, 88, 89
Employment
and adjustment, 119, 120-121
and aging group consciousness, 24
and leisure, 49
of older people, 5
and participation, 44, 46, 47, 131
of women, 148

Engagement. *See also* Dis-engagement; Integration, Re-engagement
and aging group consciousness, 26, 27
and hobbies, 109
and non-engagement, 30
Estrangement. *See* Children
Ethnic groups
and aging group consciousness, similarity to, 24
and identification, 14

"FAMILISM" as a concept, 150
Family. *See also* Children; Kinship
extended
definition of, 81n, 148, 149
integration of, 150
interaction in, 150
and mobility, 150
"modified," 164
power structure of, 150
and social class, 155
functions of, 144-149
economic, 148, 149
interaction patterns of, Chapters 9 and 10
life-cycle of, 47
nuclearity, 146-147, 164
size of, and aging, 47
and social change, 147-149
as a social institution, 144
Finance
needs of the aging, 314-316
problems of the aging, 313-316
Forand Bill, 5
Friendship patterns of the aged, 65, 66
Functionalism and disengagement, 362

GERONTOLOGICAL Society, 263
Group consciousness
of the aged, 11, 13-15, 20, 21, 69, Chapter 2, 206-208, 328-329, 359
effects of, on self-segregation, 15
determinants of, 19
and group participation, 24
and legislation, 13
and politics, 35
and voting, 35
Group formation, of the aged, 13, 83
Group identification, of the aging, 13, 14, 20, 52, 252
Group self-hatred, 8
definition of, 8n, 241

HEALTH. *See also* Illness; Medical care
ability to pay costs, 312-313
and adjustment, 58, 66
of the aging, 9, Chapters 12 and 13, 216-221, 312-313

Health (*continued*)
  changes in, 198-199, 201, 202-203
  class differences in, 202-203, 208
  and morale, 57
  and non-participation, 29, 30
  and participation, 46, 57, 58, 59
  perception of, 202-203
  and self-rating of, 121, 124
Hobbies
  of the aged, 26, 28, 29, 82, 85, 94,
    Chapter 6
  monetary value of, 85, 98, Chapter 6
  as topic of conversation, 34

"I," THE, 246
Identity. *See also* Self-conception
  and aging, 79, 82, 90
  of aging, 121, 124, 136, 252
  development of, 87
  and functional roles, 81
  occupational, 78, 81
Illness. *See also* Long-term care
  chronic, 4
  and disengagement, 13
  irreversible, 200
  and self-identification, 235
  and treatment, of the aged, 217-221
Income, 347
  of the aged, 61, 314
  definition of, 347
  of farm population, 286
  set differences in, 314-315
Industrialization and work, 80-81
Innovation and adaptive problems, 37
Institution
  characteristics of 228-232
  and depersonalization, 228, 238-239,
    241, 243
  and motivation, 240-241
  and provision of services, for the aged,
    373-376
  and self-conception, Chapter 16, 242-
    243, 250-251, 253-254
  total, definition of, 227
Integration. *See also* Re-engagement
  in the church, Chapter 8
  and church policy, 132-140
  in the family, 150
  of older people, 125-127
  and re-engagement, 132, 133
Interaction
  with children, 152
  and embarrassment, 88
  in the family, 144-145, 151-152,
    Chapter 9
  with grandchildren, 156-157
  the "I" and the "Me," 246-247
  and self-conception, 247-250

Isolation, social
  of the aged, 183-190
  definition of, 181-182

JOB. *See* Employment; Participation

KERR-MILLS BILL, 378
Kinship
  and academic ability, 173-174
  and career plans, of children, 170-173
  class differences in, 166-168
  and hiring arrangements, 174-176
  and religious affiliation, 168-169
  structure of, 149-151, 176-178

LEADERSHIP, church, 114, 115, 116-119,
    120-121, 124, 134-135
Leadership role
  and the aged, 10, 12
  and retirement, 26
Leisure, 79
  and adjustment, 83
  and aging, 80, 89, Chapter 5
  cultural definition of, 86
  economic aspects of, 85-87
  rationale of, 87
  as a social system, 94-95, Chapter 6
  tradition of, in U.S., 80-81
Long-term care, Chapter 17
  and chronic illness, 260-261
  definition of, 260-261
  and institutionalization, 266
  and "limited objectives," 260-261
  and medical values, 262-264
  and motivating the patient, 268-269
  and team medicine, 267-268
  and trends in, 261-270

MARITAL role
  definition of, 151
  expectation of, 151
Marital status
  and adjustment, 59, 60, 119-120
  of the aged, 145-147
  and aging group consciousness, 24
  and participation, 44, 45, 46
Marriage
  of older people, 11
  patterns of, U.S., 146-147
McLain Movement, 14
"Me," the, 246
Medical care
  and aging, 371
  and aging group consciousness, 34, 105
  costs of, 32
  and dependency, 371

Medical care (continued)
  and individualization, 369
  and "involvement," with the aging, 371
Medicine, preventive, 4
Mental health
  of the aged, Chapter 12
  definition of, 193-194
  and institutionalization, Chapter 15
  and negative attitudes, 194-198
  and role-concept, 193-194
Migration, See also Price County; Mo-
    bility
  as an adjustment force, 347
  and aging, 282-283, 284, 349, 350
  and depopulation, 283
  effects of changed opportunities on,
    351-355
  and economic factors, 348-351
  motives for, 334-336
  patterns of, 324-329
  seasonal, 333-334
  and theory of, 326-329
  and types of community, 328-329
Mobility
  and adjustment, 58
  and the aging, 5, Chapter 20, 338-339
  and the extended family, 150
  and the nuclear family, 150
  and participation, 47, 48
Morale and aging, 151

NON-AGING group consciousness, 20-22
  and association with own age-group,
    33
  and disengagement, 28
  and group composition, 29
  and retirement roles, 27
Norm
  definition of, 144
  and the family, 144
  of inter-generational interaction, 153

OCCUPATION
  of the aging, 316-318
  aspirations, and kinship ties, 169-174
  and kinship relations, 164-168, 174-176
  and mental health, 195-197
  and work-role, 373
Old people
  distinctive behavior of, 6
  interests of, 203-204
  low prestige of, 15
  numbers of, 49
  political views of, 14
  programs for, 376-379

Old people (continued)
  role of, 179
    change of, 196-199
  residence of, 49, 50, 315-316
  and work, 316-318
Organization
  and aging group consciousness, 36
  and group identification, 20, 22
  and non-aging group consciousness, 29
  participation in, 42, 45
  patterns of, informal, 32
Out-group, 14

PARENTS
  communication with, 184-186
  expectations of, 184-187
  living arrangements of, 188
Participation. See also Activity; Church;
    Employment; Engagement; Organi-
    zation; Politics
  and activities, 110-111
  and adjustment, 68-69
  and aging, 38, 40, 41, 43, 44, 46, 68,
    89
  and aging group consciousness, 64
  aging, response to, 84, Chapter 3
  and community size, 42
  definition of, 37
  and health, 221-223
  measures of, 44-45
  and mobility, 48
  and retirement, 215
  in social organizations, 212-214
  and urban residents, 43
Participatory Opportunity System, of the
    aged, 40-41
Play. See also Leisure
  and aging, 103, 377
  and boredom, 110-111
  and role-play, 110
Politics
  attitudes to, 35
  participation in, 41, 42, 43-44, 47
Population. See also Price County
  and adjustment of resources, 342, 347
  of the aging, 275, 288-289
  distribution of the aging, 281-283,
    295-297
  and economic opportunity, 283-284
  explosion of, U.S., 275-276
  sex ratio of, 288-289
  theory of, 347
Price County
  change in farm holdings, 342-343
  decrease in population, 342
  income and aging, 346-349
  increase in dependent population, 345
  and under-employment, 348-349

RECREATION
and aging, 13, 78-79, 84
Re-engagement, 132-135, 139-140, 364-365. *See also* Disengagement; Engagement
Retirement
and aging, 78, 81, 316-318
communities of, 5
effects of, 11, 106, 152, 195-197
and engagement, 27
and identity, 80-81, 93
increase in compulsory, 5
and mental health, 196-197
and participation, 44, 214
Role
age-related, 132, 135
of the aging, 151, 182-183, 197-199, 226-227, 246-247
change in, 197-199
definition of, 145, 193-194
in the family, 151
and mental health, 193-194, 197-199
as "recruiter" and "socializer," 91
rehearsal of, 153
Role performance
and embarrassment, 88
and identity, 87
and role-play, 110

SATISFACTION
and aging, 31, 52, 69, 71
and church programs, 136-138
and hobbies, 109
and religion, 122-123, 126
Self, definition of, 194, 226-227
Self-conception
of the aging, 11, 12-13, 14, 55, 58, 78, 81, 109, 111, 121, 198-199, Chapters 15 and 16, 245-254, 254-255
definitions of, 121, 194, 226-227, 246-247, 250-251
of health, 121
and institutionalization, Chapter 15, 250-251
measures of, 231-232, 235-240
and mental health, 193-194, 197-199
and work, 82, 373

Sick-role, 241-242
Sociability, needs for, 21
Social change
rates of, U.S., 147-149
and urbanization, 148
Social class
and aging group consciousness, 23, 24, 36
and participation, 42
Social planning
definition of, 368, 371-372
need for, of the aged, 372-373, 376-379
and provision of services, 373-376
Social Security Act (1935), 12, 264-265, 368
Socialization, definition of, 226-227
Status
of the aging, 9, 38, 48, 135
determinants of, 134-135
and leisure, 84-85
and participation, 38
Subculture
of the aging, Chapter 1, 84, 127, 240-241, 252, 328-329, 336-337, 359, 376
class factors in, 7
conditions for, 4-8
as a contraculture, 9, 10
definition of, 3
and embarrassment, 88
Symbolic-interactionism, 359

URBANIZATION
aging, increasing proportion of, in cities, 306-308
aging, in population, 282, 290
aging ratio, in cities, 304-306

WHITE House Conference on Aging, 50, 57, 61, 125, 125n, 263, 266
Work. *See also* Leisure
as cultural values, 80-81
and identity, 82, 85